THE FEMINIST

In the early twentieth century the term 'feminist' was used by self-consciously 'modern' men and women, to distinguish their ideas from those of 'the women's movement', and even to adopt anti-suffrage positions. In the first major study of twentieth-century feminism as an Anglo-American phenomenon, Lucy Delap offers a new perspective on the politics of gender during this period, exploring the intellectual history and cultural politics of Anglo-American feminism in a way that challenges the reader to rethink the nature of both the 'avant-garde' and 'feminism'. Focusing on the development of transnational feminisms within Edwardian and inter-war print culture, feminist political argument is placed at the centre of an account of modernism, highlighting some unexpected and often uncomfortable components, including the feminist fascination with individualism and egoism; ambivalence over World War One; utopian thinking and captivation by the idea of 'the simple life', anti-Semitism; sexual radicalism; and ideas about 'the superwoman'.

LUCY DELAP is a Fellow of St Catharine's College, Cambridge, and a member of the History Faculty in the University of Cambridge. She is co-editor of *Anti-Feminism in Edwardian Literature* (with Ann Heilmann, Thoemmes-Continuum, 2005), *Anti-Feminism in the Victorian and Edwardian Debate* (with Valerie Sanders, Thoemmes-Continuum, 2008), and *Feminism and the Periodical Press 1900–1918* (with Leila Ryan and Maria DiCenzo, Routledge, 2006).

IDEAS IN CONTEXT

Edited by
Quentin Skinner and James Tully

The books in this series will discuss the emergence of intellectual traditions and of related new disciplines. The procedures, aims and vocabularies that were generated will be set in the context of the alternatives available within the contemporary frameworks of ideas and institutions. Through detailed studies of the evolution of such traditions, and their modification by different audiences, it is hoped that a new picture will form of the development of ideas in their concrete contexts. By this means, artificial distinctions between the history of philosophy, of the various sciences, of society and politics, and of literature may be seen to dissolve.

The series is published with the support of the Exxon Foundation.

A list of books in the series will be found at the end of the volume.

THE FEMINIST AVANT-GARDE: TRANSATLANTIC ENCOUNTERS OF THE EARLY TWENTIETH CENTURY

LUCY DELAP

St Catharine's College, Cambridge

CAMBRIDGE
UNIVERSITY PRESS

CAMBRIDGE UNIVERSITY PRESS
Cambridge, New York, Melbourne, Madrid, Cape Town, Singapore,
São Paulo, Delhi, Dubai, Tokyo

Cambridge University Press
The Edinburgh Building, Cambridge CB2 8RU, UK

Published in the United States of America by Cambridge University Press, New York

www.cambridge.org
Information on this title: www.cambridge.org/9780521124904

© Lucy Delap 2007

First published 2007
This digitally printed version 2009

A catalogue record for this publication is available from the British Library

ISBN 978-0-521-87651-3 Hardback
ISBN 978-0-521-12490-4 Paperback

Dedicated to my parents, Liz and Tim Delap,
for all their love and support

Contents

Illustrations

Acknowledgements

This book owes a great deal to many colleagues, readers and friends. I'm everlastingly grateful to those who so generously (and tactfully) helped me on this intellectual journey: Maria DiCenzo, Peter Mandler, Sandra Stanley Holton, Melissa Lane, Leila Ryan, Juliet Mitchell, Sigal Spigel, Andy Kuper, Mary Chapman, Sarah Tasker, AnnaLee Pauls. Colleagues and friends in Cambridge, Princeton, Sydney and Vancouver have listened and advised; Princeton University Library and the Centre for Research in Women's Studies and Gender Relations at the University of British Columbia have generously hosted me. King's College, Cambridge has provided the intellectual and material support that made the writing of this book such a pleasure. Many years ago, Jane Franklin provided the intellectual spark that started me on the path of feminist history; more recently, Christine Stansell's close reading has been invaluable and Richard Fisher has been a supportive and engaged editor. My family, Clive, Jesse and Callum, have been joyful distractions to the project, for which I thank them; Clive has been a loving support and fearless critic. Above all, Deborah Thom has been a treasured supervisor, reader and friend, whose influence has shaped my thinking on so many of these issues.

Material from this book has appeared as 'The Superwoman: Theories of Gender and Genius in Edwardian Britain', *The Historical Journal*, 47:1 (2004), pp. 101–26; '*The Freewoman*, Periodical Communities and the Feminist Reading Public", *Princeton University Library Chronicle*, 61:2 (Winter 2000), pp. 233–76; and in *Suffrage Outside Suffragism, Britain 1880–1914* (Palgrave Macmillan, 2006). I am grateful to Cambridge University Press and the editors of these journals and collections for permission to reproduce the material. I am also grateful to the Princeton University Library, the Schlesinger Library, Radcliffe Institute, The Newberry Library, Chicago, and The Women's Library, London Metropolitan University, for permission to quote from their archives and for their assistance with my research.

Abbreviations

COS	Charity Organisation Society
FW	*The Freewoman*
IJE	*The International Journal of Ethics*
ILP	Independent Labour Party
IWSA	International Woman Suffrage Alliance
NAWSA	National American Woman Suffrage Association
NFW	*The New Freewoman*
NUWSS	National Union of Women's Suffrage Societies
NWP	National Woman's Party
WILPF	Women's International League for Peace and Freedom
WLF	Women's Freedom League
WPP	Women's Peace Party
WSPU	Women's Social and Political Union

Introduction

In 1912, a leading British Catholic priest used six consecutive sermons to warn his congregation against the dangers of 'Feminism'. Respectable Catholic suffragists were incensed at the apparent slur on their character. In response, the priest explained that he was referring not to suffrage politics, but to a new grouping, those 'wicked, yea damned women who have created and written for "The Freewoman", . . . the paper whose object is to drag the souls of women down to hell'.[1] *The Freewoman*'s editor, Dora Marsden, reported the comments with delight to a friend in America, where *The Freewoman* – the first British or American journal to describe itself as 'feminist' – was held to represent 'the doctrines not of feminism but of anarchy, a philosophy particularly repugnant to the legitimate feminist'.[2] From the early years of the twentieth century, when 'feminism' was just becoming current in political argument, through the challenges of suffrage, the growing prominence of modernist politics and culture, to the 'gender quake' of the war and its aftermath, there was an intense Anglo-American struggle going on over the scope and content of 'feminism'. The group of 'ultra-feminists' associated with *The Freewoman* and the political avant-garde acted as a high-profile 'lightning rod' for the controversy.

Edwardian commentators were clear that feminism was no unified entity, but should be divided into competing groups. A survey of 'modern feminism' produced in 1914 by a British-born feminist living in the United States, Beatrice Forbes-Robertson Hale, used the metaphor of an army to delineate the main body of parliamentary suffragists, the rear of municipal suffragists, a vanguard of 'advanced feminists', and an ultra-radical group of 'skirmishers'. This study is concerned with delineating the political argument, discourse and intellectual influences drawn upon by these last two groups, whose members referred to themselves as the feminist 'vanguard', 'advanced feminists', or 'modern feminists'. I examine the languages, the conceptual resources, the political argument available to feminists, gaining a

1

sense not only of what they said, but how it was possible for them to say it, and the intellectual reception feminism had.

The term 'feminism' was relatively new to Edwardians.[3] It had been used in some late nineteenth-century British texts, but without a clear meaning or programme attached to it, and even the word was in flux. Stanley Hall's *Adolescence* (1904), for example, experimented with 'femininist', 'feministic' and 'feminist' to describe the women's movement.[4] Before 1911, 'feminism' had been generally understood to be the French term for the women's movement, and it signified a broader and less aggressive movement than the notorious British suffragists. As *The Times* put it, feminism was a more 'charmingly feminine thing' than English suffragism, though with essentially the same aims.[5] However, it quickly came to have an alternative, yet highly contested, meaning, first in Britain and subsequently in the United States. By 1908, 'feminism' was already taking on some avant-garde connotations, being used by 'advanced' women such as the writer Vernon Lee (Violet Paget) in her description of the parasitism of women. In July 1911, the London 'radical-right' periodical the *Eye-Witness* referred to 'the "feminist" movement – as it is very absurdly called'. For many British and American Edwardians, 'feminism' was used as a 'black-box' term, able to stand in for a number of meanings. In popular (and denigratory) usage it represented the 'sex war', or modern woman's new-found unwillingness to bear children. For others, it was indistinguishable from suffragism, and they greatly resented avant-garde usurpation of the term to describe other, more controversial positions. One concerned suffragist noted in the *New York Times*, 'It sometimes happens that the good repute of a word, like that of an individual, is irreparably injured through the malicious innuendo of the evil-minded. Is this to be the fate of the word "feminism"?'[6]

Over the first ten years of the twentieth century, feminism came to occupy a similar space to the idea of the 'new woman' of the 1890s, signifying a radical, subversive grouping closely associated with the avant-garde and radical movements that flourished before World War One. It connoted rupture, and was emblematic of the aggressively new century that was so widely understood as a millennial turning-point. 'Feminism is a movement born of a cubist and futurist age of extremes', declared the National Association Opposed to Woman Suffrage in the United States.[7] The reach of this movement was never great. Self-consciously elitist, the 'vanguard' of feminism never stretched beyond a few metropolitan centres in the United States. In Britain, the sense of belonging to an 'avant-garde movement' was less clearly formulated than in the United States; there were fewer physical spaces identified with avant-garde groupings, and less consciousness of this as an identity. However, Britain was perhaps more open to the establishment of provincial 'avant-gardes'.[8] Beatrice Hale was doubtful as to whether feminists could be grouped together at all; she noted that 'Individual journalists in Paris, London, and New York, too isolated to form a group, are winning a brief celebrity by exploiting their own conceptions of life under the guise of Feminism'.[9] Others noted the sympathetic relations between 'corresponding small groups' of 'extreme and radical' feminists in every country.[10] It will be my argument that the extensive, frequently transatlantic, interaction between individuals and groups did constitute an intellectual formation, a feminist network that was highly influential in defining and shaping the politics of feminism for the entire twentieth century. In this study, this group will be contrasted with other developments within feminism; the latter groupings are (reluctantly) termed 'the women's movement' or 'moderate/mainstream feminism'. But this should not indicate that they were somehow 'less radical' than the 'avant-garde feminists' – the political valency of terms such as 'radical' are so indeterminate in this context that they are simply not useful. Nor can a 'left/right' political spectrum adequately convey the complexities of affiliation within Edwardian feminism.

This book traces a conversation that occurred within and between two groups – the 'advanced' feminists of Britain and the United States, chiefly concentrated in the metropolitan centres (London, Chicago, New York).[11] Historians have tended to explore these two groups separately, and this has meant that important avenues of intellectual exchange have not received adequate attention. Recent research has begun to uncover the enormous importance of transatlantic exchange in the fields of social policy, political philosophy, and suffragism.[12] This book argues that in its turn, feminism was not only an idiosyncratic, distinctive development in each location, but also a shared conversation that spanned the Atlantic and resulted in a firmly Anglo-American intellectual tradition. This focus on interaction should not imply that the two national contexts were identical or even similar; in some instances, the conversation diverged, or faltered and broke down. Two distinct intellectual contexts situated British or American feminist political arguments, leading occasionally to conflict over, or lack of interest in, developments in each country. But in the main, 'advanced' feminists on each side of the Atlantic read each other's work, commented on it, corresponded, and understood their intellectual circle to be a transnational one.

The characterisation of Edwardian feminism as 'avant-garde' indicates the self-consciousness of this group of being 'advanced' and 'ultra-modern', as well as the sense in which these feminists formulated issues that have been turned to again and again throughout twentieth-century feminism. Their transnational conversation included an important literary and creative element; this study builds on the histories already available of what is often seen as the 'core' of avant-garde activity, within the creative arts.[13] While there may, from a literary perspective, be some apparent omissions in the people and ideas discussed in this book, the history of ideas approach which informs it, allied to its transatlantic perspective, can lead to a distinctive cast of historical actors, and some unexpected areas or investigation. This study proposes an extension of the remit of 'avant-garde' to include a more political understanding of its scope. I draw on an older, mid-nineteenth-century use of 'avant-garde' to describe a certain kind of revolutionary political radicalism.[14] 'Avant-garde', or, as Edwardians often termed it, 'vanguard', indicates a discourse or social imaginary within feminism, rather than a movement. It can be understood as a textual space, delineated by the shared discourses circulating within feminist periodicals and essays, rather than any kind of tightly drawn circle or site. Physical and social spaces – Greenwich Village restaurants and clubs, the London international suffrage shop, Clarion cycling outings, the Eustace Miles restaurant in Chandos Street, lectures in the Chandos Hall – were important, but 'advanced feminist' was an identity that could be selectively appropriated outside of these spaces. Like the 'new woman', 'feminism' was closely bound up with its representation in print – to be a feminist was very centrally a reading experience. Periodicals formed the site in which 'feminism' was most commonly enunciated and observed, and are thus a key source for this study.[15]

The history of Anglo-American feminism is, as Nancy Cott notes, littered with prefixes of 'feminism', some of which are of dubious analytic clarity.[16] 'Avant-garde feminism' is a heuristic device rather than a precise political affiliation. It loosely designates the interests of a number of thinkers who regarded themselves (in some contexts) as feminists. It certainly does not indicate that there was no disagreement within this grouping, which was marked by splenetic controversy. Without implying a coherent or conscious political grouping, 'avant-garde' usefully captures some characteristic features of feminist discourse: the idealisation of originality, rejection of forebears and sense of rupture with the past, the denial of essences and eternal truths, anti-conventionality, artistic experimentalism and so on. For the thinkers and activists included in this 'avant-garde' realm, the term 'feminist' needed no prefix to indicate these concerns. By itself, 'feminist' had come to indicate an engagement with 'modern' concerns of the psyche, individuality and sexuality.[17] The 'avant-garde' prefix offers clarity, however, since 'feminist' has become an identity unhelpfully applied across the board to more or less any woman who entered public life. Perhaps as a result, recent feminist theory has identified an urgent need to reconceptualise the categories by which the history of feminism has been understood.[18] This study contributes to this critical academic undertaking: it demonstrates the many and varied strands of political and cultural thought in (what is commonly but simplistically designated) the 'first-wave' period of feminism.

Historians have provided a number of different narratives of 'feminisms' of the twentieth century. For some, feminism represented a development from moderate social reform or equality demands to a more radical suffrage agenda, sometimes described as a move from the 'social feminism' of the moral reform movements to the 'hard-core feminism' of suffragists.[19] Others have challenged the moderate/radical division that places suffrage demands as the most radical position. Certainly, many forms of 'radicalism', including that of avant-garde feminists, are obscured by this categorisation.

Overall, the historiography of twentieth-century feminism has failed to represent all aspects of feminist affiliation. Historians have tended to read into feminism past and present a collectivist and egalitarian orientation. They have also assumed that the main focus of Edwardian feminist politics was the acquisition of the vote. My reading of avant-garde feminism upsets these assumptions, and uncovers a distinctively individualist and elitist strand within feminism. This strand of feminism was not committed to attaining the vote, nor were avant-garde feminists' ideas of emancipation focused on the state and women's inclusion within the state. The direction of avant-garde political argument strongly challenged the politics associated with more conventional aspects of the women's movement, criticising what have been assumed to be mainstays of suffrage feminism – pro-statism, theories of rights, and equality. This suggests the need for a re-evaluation of the political discourses of Edwardian feminism. Historians have rightly pointed to the radicalism and breadth of the suffrage affiliation for Edwardians. Suffragists aimed to liberate women for wider social service and to implement social, emotional and sexual transformations. Despite this, it remains anachronistic to treat suffrage as coterminous with feminism. This tense and formative period can no longer be portrayed as one of united 'liberal-suffrage' politics, and must be seen as a time of division and conflict between ideas of women's emancipation.

EDWARDIAN SUFFRAGISM

The intellectual milieu of the avant-garde feminists was surprisingly distinct from that of the suffragists, though these categories can only clumsily represent the actual fluidity of affiliations held by individuals. At first glance, it is difficult to reconcile the 'vanguard feminist' stance with the predominantly pro-state, pragmatic focus of Edwardian suffrage-feminists. Politically, the avant-garde rejected state institutions, based on the moral-individualist grounds of the corruption of personality and the individual will. The focus of political argument was therefore on the individual, and not the group. In her 1913 book *The Future of the Women's Movement*, Helena Swanwick (an active British suffragist, as well as a *Freewoman* reader and supporter) mocked the idea that 'women are one in need, capacity and character, and that this eternal feminine has been once and for all dissected, understood and catalogued, and that all variations are merely caprice … women want as many different things as there are women'.[20] In contrast, many suffragists tended to appeal to unity amongst women, arguing against the saliency of class amongst women on the basis of their shared political exclusion.[21] While feminists stressed individuality, suffragists looked for sisterhood and unity.

The historian Jonathan Rose defines the British Edwardian period as characterised by a search for harmony, synthesis and unity. He charts this 'habit of mind' in many fields – attempts to reconcile the classes, religion and science, work and leisure, childhood and adulthood. The Edwardian women's movement in some senses exemplifies this move to reconciliation; many believed that feminism, and in particular the suffrage question, united women. In contrast, the feminist avant-garde consciously opposed this trend, emphasising the divisions between women, the singularity and uniqueness of each. According to Dora Marsden, 'there is no essential virtue in unity, especially amongst women. We are becoming more convinced that women will have to move apart the better to come together in a wide understanding.'[22] Even more subversively, 'vanguard' feminists sought to distance themselves from suffrage groups. The suffragists' ideals of sisterhood and solidarity were rejected, and replaced by a new aim – the self-liberation of elites, through the cultivation of the will and personality. This was motivated by the desire to subvert the overarching category of 'woman', about whose sexual instincts or political interests so many generalisations were made. The concept of 'the feminine' was fragmented through the establishment of an 'ethnographic' hierarchy of *types* of women.[23]

The 'typology' of women functioned in terms of their psychological make-up rather than external constraints such as legal and political status. Avant-garde feminists wrote of the women of 'the cold temperament', or the sexual characteristics of 'northern women', the 'woman of large sexual appetite', 'the intellectual woman', 'the spinster'.[24] The British writer Rebecca West wrote for an American periodical of the 'failed' types of women; 'the schoolmistress' or 'the woman without fortitude'.[25] West identified as an 'advanced' feminist, socialist and literary critic, and was strongly shaped by her early experiences with the Women's Social and Political Union (WSPU) and as *The Freewoman*'s assistant editor. This interest in the internal psychological features of women represents what I term an 'introspective turn' in feminism, a desire to seek liberation not through 'externals', such as rights granted by men, but through internal transformation of one's psyche and sexual being. Edwardian feminists, investigating not 'what women may acquire, but what they may become', sought to delineate those women who might form the vanguard of feminism through their possession of 'personality', and their ability to listen to and express their inner voice.

This introspective turn was not limited to avant-garde feminists, but was a more widespread feature of the Edwardian women's movement. Even those sceptical about the feminist 'vanguard' believed that 'the mental revolution' of feminism was 'infinitely the more important' of its effects.[26] Where the 'new woman' had sought experience and knowledge of life, feminists critically gazed inward at the psychological and sexual norms within which women and men established what we might now call gender. Feminists joined a trend which, according to historians, was a broad cultural feature of American life, and which this study suggests was also prominent in British political argument, in their intense interest in personality, as against moral character, political rights or values of equality.[27] A characteristic definition comes from an American writer Ellen Glasgow, for whom feminism was 'a revolt from pretence of being – it is, at its best and worst, a struggle for the liberation of personality'.[28] Both suffragists and 'advanced feminists' shared an interest in women's psychological transformation, often expressed in terms of moral character by suffragists, and in terms of will and personality amongst avant-garde feminists. It was widely accepted that ability to achieve female emancipation depended on an *individual's* will or character, that which historian Christine Stansell has called a 'willed equality'.[29]

The avant-garde feminist shift towards individualism explored in this study must be historically located within the framework of this existing interest in character, while also influenced by the contemporary rise of egoist and Nietzschean thought. This study situates feminist affiliations to versions of individualism, and discusses why this has been particularly hard to read as compatible with feminism. I suggest that avant-garde feminists were not isolated nor 'ahead of their time' in their individualist interests. Personal 'greatness', emancipation of and through elites, and even 'superwomen' were widely debated within feminist circles, though these concerns have been largely eclipsed from the narratives of feminism in the twentieth century.

The 'introspective turn' cannot be understood without the contextualisation provided by another area of change and experimentation in 1912, the shift to a new era in the arts, an era of 'wilful modernism'. Virginia Woolf had famously considered that 'in or about December, 1910, human character changed'.[30] Yet the term 'modernism', or even 'early modernism' implies a more coherent movement than was actually the case in either Britain or the United States. The American 'modernist' commentator and journalist Floyd Dell described an ad hoc coalition of experimentalist groups, mostly in New York and Chicago. Their work spanned creative arts and lifestyle iconoclasm, and their associated politics ranged from elitist to anarchist. Historians have recently begun to understand 'modernism' as a broad range, rather than a collection of texts produced by artistic elites. It can be understood as a cultural imaginary that spanned 'high' and 'low' moderns, from Ezra Pound to H. G. Wells, using the techniques of 'mass market' print culture to construct new 'counterpublic spheres'.[31] It was only later that 'modernism' became understood as a reactive cultural formation against the development of mass media and society (though these concerns did exist in pre-war 'advanced' circles). My reading of the ideas of the feminist avant-garde contributes to this historical project of reading 'high' and 'low' modernisms as a shared discourse, speaking to a shared audience. Texts of the feminist avant-garde such as *The Freewoman*, *The Masses* and the *Little Review* subvert the distinction between high and low modernisms, in their engagement with market techniques, their free-ranging use of eclectic intellectual resources, and their attempts to bring 'modernist' political arguments to mass audiences.

A recent important book by Elizabeth Francis has traced the tense yet ongoing relationship between feminism and modernism between 1910 and 1930. Francis situates feminism as occupying an ironic, paradoxical position in relation to modernism and modernity. Femininity itself seemed to be the 'other' of modernism, associated with Victorian sentimentality.[32] And yet, the modern woman has been in some senses not a threat but a vehicle or, as Francis puts it, a symbolic substitute for modernity. Feminism has been enormously attractive to modernist writers as a means of conveying a critique of feminine characteristics; for feminists, modernists provided them with an idiom to indicate their rejection of tradition, and subversion of bourgeois respectability. Rather than adding to the already substantial literature that examines the troubled inter-relation of the two, this study examines the political argument and social thought that grew out of their interaction in the first two decades of the twentieth century. While drawing on the literature of feminist modernisms, I aim to displace 'modernism' as the prime frame in which to understand feminist political argument, and situate feminism in a far wider intellectual field.

HISTORIES AND NARRATIVES OF FEMINISM

American and British feminism has been historically located within a liberal, free thinking and radical tradition, with John Stuart Mill as a key intellectual forebear. Edwardian feminist political ideas in Britain, and to some extent in the United States, are commonly assumed to have been drawn chiefly from his work, and to have centred on claims for political rights.[33] As Brian Harrison has argued,

Edwardian suffragists ... were too preoccupied with campaigning for the vote to spend much time on sketching out the shape of the new society, or on doing more than expose particular abuses and build up a following for the programme that J. S. Mill had laid down half a century before.[34]

However, Carrie Chapman Catt, the American suffrage leader, had in 1911 described Mill's work as unfamiliar and unavailable to activist women.[35] In Britain, Dora Marsden of *The Freewoman* found Mill had little to offer: 'The position occupied by the question is wholly different from that which it occupied at the time it was championed by men like John Stuart Mill'.[36] My reading highlights some alternative political commitments found among Anglo-American Edwardian feminist thinkers, specifically an individualistic and voluntaristic belief in self-development, conveyed through the idea of 'expressing one's will' or 'developing personality'. This goal was regarded as more significant, and more radical, than the attainment of liberal rights and freedoms.

This brief crystallisation of a strand of feminism has been difficult for historians to situate within narratives of feminist history. The ideas of 'advanced feminism' have been read as part of a broader narrative of twentieth-century feminism at the expense of understanding their place within the contemporary intellectual milieu. This has meant that historians have simply labelled the 'feminist avant-garde' as 'eclectic', being unable to recognise it as formed by some distinctive elements of early twentieth-century political thought. Some commentators have focused on what seems to twenty-first-century readers to be the most explicitly controversial feature of the feminist avant-garde – their discussions of sex – and have marginalised their political argument, or read feminists as 'forebears' of 1970s feminists.[37] Others have assumed that the critical attitude towards capitalism expressed by avant-garde feminists identifies them predominantly as socialists. Many were indeed socialists, but this does not fully capture their political argument, which also included some unfamiliar or unexpected elements. Anti-Semitism, elitism, neo-medievalism, and 'the superwoman', for example, are important components of a more historically sensitive and diverse history of Anglo-American feminism.

These allegiances do not resonate with later conceptions of feminist thought; indeed, many would now be judged profoundly anti-feminist. The attention given in this study to different perspectives within feminism – particularly the individualist – serves to problematise the distinction between 'feminist' and 'anti-feminist', suggesting significant overlaps and common intellectual backgrounds between these two 'opposed' positions in the Edwardian period. A far richer, and more politically ambiguous, intellectual milieu, spanning the transnational interactions that shaped 'feminism', must be provided to narrate the origins of modern feminism.

Writing transnational history is a stimulating means of shedding new light on some old debates; some figures that appear marginal in one national context can seem very important as transmitters of ideas or practices between countries. Some voices that were derided as extremist in one country were unexpectedly listened to with great attention in another. Some figures that left few historical marks in their own country emerge as important interlocutors in another. Transnationality also offers challenges – the complexity of holding together more than one narrative of events, governments, etc. can make for a dense read. I have approached this problem of the two contexts by offering an account organised by themes rather than a chronological narrative. It is ideas that are given a history in this study – the idea of government by elites, for example, or of the individual as the key component in political argument. Each chapter explores a theme, aiming therefore to link feminism to a broad context of political argument in the late Edwardian period rather than a series of events. The late Edwardian years comprise those crucial years between the death of Edward VII in 1910, and America's entry to the First World War in 1917. This book contextualises this period through an examination of the intellectual and political trends of preceding years, and the fifteen years or so that came after. But it is at heart about the intellectual landscape of those very formative, optimistic and decisive years. A sense of their influence is gained from an examination of the impact of the war and the years of its aftermath. This study concludes with the transition beyond the late Edwardian period to the inter-war, and the difference this made for the semantic resources and transnational exchanges of feminists and the vanguard figures of political argument.

END NOTES

1. Reported by Dora Marsden to Frances Björkman, Schlesinger Library, Radcliffe Institute for Advanced Study, Harvard University, Mary Ware Dennett Papers, 001940518) (henceforth MWDP), 11 Jan. 1913.
2. Beatrice Forbes-Robertson Hale, *What Women Want: An Interpretation of the Feminist Movement* (New York, Frederick A. Stokes, 1914), pp. 214–16.
3. The origin of the term 'feminism' or 'féminisme' is commonly but mistakenly attributed to the early nineteenth-century utopian socialist, Charles Fourier. Instead, it was first used in French in 1837 as a pejorative term, to indicate 'the illness of womanly qualities appearing in men', Beatrice Wilson, 'Charles Fourier (1772–1837) and Questions of Women', Ph.D. diss. (University of Cambridge, 2002), p. 9 n. 30. Early examples in Britain date from the late 1890s, and in the United States from around 1906. 'Feminism' was included in the *Oxford English Dictionary* only in 1933, where it was defined as 'advocacy of women's rights', Nancy Cott, *The Grounding of Modern Feminism* (New Haven, Yale University Press, 1987), pp. 3–6. 'Feminism', hereafter referred to without quote marks, should remain understood as a term in transition, indicating no accepted and clearly bounded set of ideas or political agenda.
4. G. Stanley Hall, *Adolescence, its Psychology and its Relations to Physiology, Anthropology, Sociology, Sex, Crime, Religion and Education* (New York, D. Appleton, 1904), pp. xiv, 565, 564.
5. *The Times*, 3 June 1908, 14; and 17 July 1914, 11.
6. Vernon Lee, *Gospels of Anarchy and Other Contemporary Studies* (London, T. Fisher Unwin, 1908), p. 265; Jane Dale, 'The Term "Feminists"', *New York Times*, 25 May 1914, 10.
7. 'Assail the Feminists', *The Washington Post*, 18 May 1914, 4.
8. Christine Stansell's study of 'bohemian' New York acknowledges the existence of nation-wide versions of 'bohemia', but suggests that by the 1910s, New York became the dominant cultural capital of the United States.

Chicago remained a strong contender as a centre of anarchist, free love and labour politics, but the avant-garde element of these groupings slowly drifted to New York. Christine Stansell, *American Moderns: Bohemian New York and the Creation of a New Century* (New York, Henry Holt, 2000), pp. 45, 54–5. On British 'provincialism', see Tom Steele, *Alfred Orage and the Leeds Arts Club, 1893–1923* (London, Scolar Press, 1990); Jill and Norris Liddington, *One Hand Tied Behind Us: The Rise of the Women's Suffrage Movement* (London, Virago, 1978).

9. Hale, *What Women Want*, pp. 209, 216.

10. Dale, *New York Times*, 25 May 1914, 10.

11. Of course, transnational exchanges were not limited to these cities, nor even to these countries. There were well-established links between the United States, Canada and other European nations, as well as between Britain and continental Europe. For feminists, the diversity of these links is made clear in 'Feminism in Some European Countries', *American Monthly Review of Reviews*, 23 March 1906, 357–60; see also Katharine Anthony, *Feminism in Germany and Scandinavia* (London, Constable, 1916); Ellen Key, *The Woman Movement*, trans. M. B. Borthwick (London, G. P. Putnam's, 1912); Margaret H. McFadden, *Golden Cables of Sympathy: The Transatlantic Sources of Nineteenth-Century Feminism* (Kentucky, University Press of Kentucky, 1999).

12. See Sandra Stanley Holton, '"To Educate Women Into Rebellion": Elizabeth Cady Stanton and the Creation of a Transatlantic Network of Radical Suffragists', *American Historical Review*, 99 (1994); Daniel T. Rodgers, *Atlantic Crossings: Social Politics in a Progressive Age* (Cambridge, Mass., Belknap Press, 1998); James T. Kloppenberg, *Uncertain Victory: Social Democracy and Progressivism in European and American Thought, 1870–1920* (Oxford, Oxford University Press, 1986); Patricia Greenwood Harrison, *Connecting Links: The British and American Woman Suffrage Movements, 1900–1914* (Conn., Greenwood Press, 2000); Marc Stears, *Progressives, Pluralists and the Problems of the State: Ideologies of Reform in the United States and Britain, 1909–1926* (Oxford, Oxford University Press, 2002).

13. See Elizabeth Francis, *The Secret Treachery of Words: Feminism and Modernism in America* (Minneapolis, University of Minnesota Press, 2002); Sandra Gilbert and S. Gubar, *No Man's Land: The Place of the Woman Writer in the Twentieth Century* (New Haven, Yale University Press, 1988); Ann Ardis, *New Women, New Novels: Feminism and Early Modernism* (New Jersey, Rutgers University Press, 1990). The modernist avant-garde in Britain centred in the elitist and self-consciously modern circle of male and female writers, painters and cultural iconoclasts in Bloomsbury. This was a space in which feminism was debated and critically examined. But this study uncovers an alternative strand of the avant-garde, one more firmly linked to politics, more widely dispersed, less a face-to-face community than an imagined one, lived out in texts and periodicals, but nonetheless a very real one.

14. Renato Poggioli, *The Theory of the Avant-Garde* (Cambridge, Mass., Belknap Press, 1968), pp. 5–12.

15. This study is informed not only by the intellectual history literature, but also by the well-established strand of media history relating to periodicals. David Bennett, 'Periodical Fragments and Organic Culture: Modernism, the Avant-Garde, and the Little Magazine', *Contemporary Literature*, 30:4 (1989); Margaret Beetham, *A Magazine of Her Own? Domesticity and Desire in the Woman's Magazine 1800–1914* (London, Routledge, 1996); Edward Bishop, 'Re:Covering Modernism – Format and Function in the Little Magazines', in *Modernist Writers and the Marketplace*, ed. Chernaik *et al.* (Basingstoke, Macmillan, 1996); Ellen Gruber Garvey, *The Adman in the Parlour: Magazines and the Gendering of Consumer Culture, 1880s to 1910s* (Oxford, Oxford University Press, 1996).

16. Nancy F. Cott, 'What's in a Name? The Limits of "Social Feminism": or, Expanding the Vocabulary of Women's History', *The Journal of American History*, 76:3 (Dec. 1989).

17. Cott, *The Grounding of Modern Feminism*, Chapter 1; Stansell, *American Moderns*.

18. Cf. Sandra Stanley Holton, *Feminism and Democracy: Women's Suffrage and Reform Politics in Britain 1900–1918* (Cambridge, Cambridge University Press, 1986), p. 5; Olive Banks, *Faces of Feminism* (Oxford, Martin Robertson, 1981), pp. 7–8; Chilla Bulbeck, *Re-Orienting Western Feminisms* (Cambridge, Cambridge University Press, 1998), pp. 7–15.

19. Richard J. Evans, *The Feminists: Women's Emancipation Movements in Europe, America and Australasia 1840–1920* (London, Croom Helm, 1977), p. 34; W. L. O'Neill, *The Woman Movement: Feminism in the United States and England* (London, George Allen and Unwin, 1969), p. 33.

20. Helena Swanwick, *Future of the Women's Movement* (London, G. Bell, 1913), p. 14.

21. Charlotte Despard, *The Vote*, 9 Sept. 1911, 246.

22. Marsden, *The Freewoman*, 28 March 1912, 377 (hereafter *FW*).

23. Stansell, *American Moderns*, p. 17.

24. See 'A Spinster, By One', *FW*, 23 Nov. 1911, 10–11 and 'Spinsters in the Making – Type One: The College Woman', *FW* 14 Dec. 1911, 67–8.

25. West, *New Republic*, 22 Jan. and 19 Feb. 1916.

26. *The Making of Women: Oxford Essays in Feminism*, ed. Victor Gollancz (London, George Allen and Unwin, 1917), p. 16.

27. Warren Susman, ' "Personality" and the Making of Twentieth-Century Culture', in Susman, *Culture as History: The Transformation of American Society in the Twentieth Century* (New York, Pantheon Books, 1996), pp. 271–85. See also Mari Jo Buhle, *Feminism and its Discontents: A Century of Struggle with Psychoanalysis* (Cambridge, Mass., Harvard University Press, 1998), p. 24.

28. Ellen Glasgow, reported in Rose Young, 'What is Feminism?' *Good Housekeeping*, May 1914, 683.

29. Stansell, *American Moderns*, p. 227.

30. Virginia Woolf, *Virginia Woolf Reader*, ed. Mitchell A. Leaska (New York, Harcourt, 1984), p. 194.

31. Daniel Joseph Singal, 'Toward a Definition of American Modernism', *American Quarterly*, 39 (Spring 1987); Maria DiBattista and Lucy McDiarmid, *High and Low Moderns: Literature and Culture, 1889–1939* (New York, Oxford University Press, 1996), p. 6; Mark S. Morrison, *The Public Face of Modernism: Little Magazines, Audiences, and Reception, 1905–1920* (Madison, University of Wisconsin Press, 2001).

32. Elizabeth Francis, *Secret Treachery of Words: Feminism and Modernism in America* (Minneapolis, University of Minnesota Press, 2002); Andreas Huyssen, 'Mass Culture as Woman: Modernism's Other', in *After the Great Divide: Modernism, Mass Culture and Postmodernism* (Bloomington, Indiana University Press, 1986). See also Gilbert, *No Man's Land*.

33. Other concerns existed within feminism, the most prominent being purity and moral reform. But what can be termed the 'conventional' mainstream of feminism has been characterised as politically liberal, theoretically unsophisticated, and beholden to Mill for its ideas (see for example Brian Harrison, 'The Act of Militancy: Violence and the Suffragettes, 1904–1914', in *Peaceable Kingdom: Stability and Change in Modern Britain*, ed. Bentley and Stevenson (Oxford, Oxford University Press, 1982); Karen Offen, 'Defining Feminism: A Comparative Historical Approach', in *Beyond Equality and Difference: Citizenship, Feminist Politics and Female Subjectivity*, ed. Bock and James (London, Routledge, 1992)). Recent work has done much to challenge this, focusing on the political complexity and sophistication of the women's movement(s). Cf. Holton, *Feminism and Democracy*; Cott, *The Grounding of Modern Feminism*; Patricia Hollis, *Ladies Elect: Women in English Local Government 1865–1914* (Oxford, Clarendon Press, 1987); Karen Hunt, *Equivocal Feminists: The Social Democratic Federation and the Woman Question 1884–1911* (Cambridge, Cambridge University Press, 1996); Buhle, *Feminism and its Discontents*.

34. Harrison, 'The Act of Militancy'. Laura Mayhall gives a more sensitive reading of Mill's intellectual contribution to feminism, though still sees his text as 'canonical' in shaping the movement's concerns. Laura Mayhall, 'The Rhetorics of Slavery and Citizenship: Suffragist Discourse and Canonical Texts in Britain, 1880–1914', *Gender and History*, 13:3 (2001).

35. John Stuart Mill, *The Subjection of Women* (New York, Frederick A. Stokes, 1911), p. xv.

36. *Common Cause*, 23 Nov. 1911, p. 577: advertisement for *The Freewoman*.

37. See for example Sheila Jeffreys, *The Spinster and Her Enemies: Feminism and Sexuality 1880–1930* (London, Pandora Press, 1985), p. 3.

CHAPTER I

'Fastidious, difficult, different': Anglo-American feminists

It was a commonplace for American and British commentators that the two decades after the turn of the century had inaugurated a new era, one in which women were to play a central part. There was a profound sense of being at a turning-point, and that 'the great change is revealed in what is going on in the soul of woman to-day'.[1] Yet the manner in which the women's movement and feminism prompted, and became inseparable from, this sense of epochal transformation requires a historical explanation. Feminism did not simply spring fully formed from the suffrage movement, nor evolve inevitably out of the 'new woman' debates of the 1890s. An account of the coining of feminism and the intense efforts to establish its meaning in the first two decades of the twentieth century must trace the new resources provided by the intellectual milieu – ideas about personality, the turn towards 'aristocratic thinking', new ways of talking about sex, the atmosphere of experimentation in the arts and in lifestyles. This history of ideas must be complemented by some material factors that enabled participation in the intellectual realm from some previously marginalised groups – the expanding 'public sphere' available to women and to experimenters of all kinds through the flourishing and relatively inexpensive periodicals market, and the new 'conversational communities' associated with them.[2] The new ease with which ideas and people could cross the oceans, the new economic resources available to women in professions such as teaching; there were strong concentrations of suffragists and feminists in teaching and social work. Women also had vastly expanded access to the intellectual resources of higher education; all these factors made for whole new realms of political argument inhabited by new actors. This chapter situates the development of avant-garde feminism in these wider contexts – above all, in the landscape of periodical publishing and readership, public lecturing and private correspondence and discussion in Britain and the United States. It examines the political context in which 'feminism' emerged and developed, the lifestyle and cultural innovations within feminist communities, the key texts that shaped and defined what it was to be a feminist, and the conflicting visions they inspired.

This study aims to unhitch feminism from suffragism at a specific historical juncture in which they could be understood to be distinct or even opposed camps. Nonetheless, suffrage struggles provided the context in which feminism came to the fore as a deeper challenge to the status quo than suffragism. Many 'advanced' feminists continued to support suffragists, while understanding their own politics to be something quite separate.

THE POLITICAL CONTEXT

Historians have described Edwardian Britain in radically diverse terms – as a society in which originated the 'modern' urban setting and its novel anxieties, or as a final culmination of nineteenth-century Victorian trends – the intensification of 'class society', marked by a 'frivolous' aristocracy and the consolidation of empire. The period in Britain gave rise to what Jose Harris has described as a society 'in which people felt themselves to be living in many different layers of historic time'.[3] The position of women in this context cannot be easily generalised: 'women' is not a helpful category of historical analysis for this period, since their experiences were so diverse and discrepant. Edwardian women witnessed the rise of educational and professional opportunities for some women, matched by a probably more widely felt desire of others to leave the workplace and secure a comfortable home life.[4] Most women shared the belief that excessive childbirth should be limited, but the 'advanced' feminist calls to dethrone motherhood from its primary place in women's lives did not find mass resonance; Jose Harris notes that the Mother's Union, founded in 1886, was vastly more successful in terms of membership than any feminist or suffrage society.

Nonetheless, the women's movement campaigns – for the suffrage from the 1860s, against the Contagious Diseases Acts in the 1870s and 1980s, for temperance, social purity and professional opportunities throughout the period – raised women's claims to a high profile. These organised campaigns developed in parallel with a notorious and strongly Anglo-American literary development, described by its contemporaries as 'new woman literature'. The 'new woman' discourse was in part an attempt to caricature a mannish and transgressive feminine figure, labelled 'Wild' or 'Odd'. Some 'new women', however, worked to counter this image, through alternative textual or self-constructions as thoughtful, athletic, creative, yet (sometimes) still domestic and 'racially responsible'.[5] It was this combination of organisational and intellectual innovations which created the possibility for a new formation, a grouping which stressed its discontinuity with the past, and with the cultural practices of older generations. In Ellen Key's words, 'ultra' feminists in Britain and the United States came to assert 'personality in opposition to, instead of within, the race', propagating a feminism marked by the avant-garde 'keynotes' of self-concentration, and egoism.[6]

The term 'feminism' came widely into play at a moment of disruption within the British political environment. After the clear mandate given to the Liberal Party by their 1906 election victory, the general election of 1910 had returned them for a second term, with the anti-suffragist Herbert Asquith as Prime Minister. There was a diminishing political confidence, however, in the remit of 'progressive' policies. Contentious measures such as welfare provision for the unemployed and sick, taxation of land value, Irish home rule, and constitutional reform of the Lords created an atmosphere of unrest, uncertainty and anxiety in the face of radical change.[7] Historians have included women's suffrage as another factor of unrest, but in 1911, the suffrage campaign was virtually deadlocked. In 1910 and 1911, attempts to pass a 'Conciliation Bill' had initially led to a break from political violence, but legislative failure caused a further escalation of militancy and hunger-striking.[8] There was no clear (or reliable) group of advocates for suffrage within parliament, and the great weakness of the suffrage cause was its inability to attract the wholesale support of any one party. Those within the radical liberal tradition, who might have been expected to support the extension of the franchise, were split; Asquith gave high-profile leadership to the 'antis'. Irish members seeking home rule supported Asquith, who had committed himself to their cause, and therefore voted against suffrage. The Conservatives also gave no clear lead, and only the small Labour Party gave relatively consistent, if somewhat lukewarm support.

This 'late Edwardian' period was thus a moment of increasing partisanship amongst suffragists in Britain; the largest suffrage body, the National Union of Women's Suffrage Societies, abandoned its non-alignment policy of supporting any pro-suffrage candidate, and took the radical step of supporting all Labour Party candidates, through its 'election fighting fund'.[9] Suffrage was becoming a more complex political space, demanding a more wholesale commitment that might run counter to suffragists' other political affiliations. The increasingly isolated WSPU responded to this by restating their political strategy, to fight against the governing party candidates, whatever their suffrage beliefs. Other suffragists, however, became disillusioned with the entire campaign and looked for alternatives in the years directly preceding the disruption of world war.

Historians have characterised the United States in the years between the turn of the century and the First World War as a nation in transition, experiencing intense 'contrariety' and anxiety around issues of modernity and tradition, as well as a renewed interest in social and political reform.[10] While it is impossible adequately to summarise the 'temper of the times', 'progressive America' can be seen as an era of 'exuberant optimism' in the power of social reform.[11] This can be found in many spheres – in the characteristic investigative journalism of the period, the exposure of corruption and critique of the monopolies of big business, the enormous impact of novels such as Upton Sinclair's *The Jungle* (1906) or Theodore Dreiser's *Sister Carrie* (1900), with their chilling portrayal of urban poverty. The growth of the mass media in this period (cinema, periodical publishing, radio) enhanced the scope of 'muckraking' exposures and demands for change within the novel concept of a mass society.

'Progressive politics', of which the American women's movement formed a part, met a perceived need to humanise and control industry and rejuvenate democracy in the interests of 'the people'. Social and institutional reform issues had, of course, been prominent in the nineteenth century, but came to the fore more widely at the turn of the century as being of national significance.[12] In the process of shifting from grass roots to national politics, however, many seemingly radical goals were transformed into more conservative platforms, and the alleged 'progressivism' of this era was cross-cut by a sense of 'drift and doubt', and by attempts to reinstate traditional forms and to look backwards with nostalgia.[13]

In the United States, progress towards suffrage seemed to be stalled in 1910, with fourteen years of defeats in state referenda, and divisions within the main suffrage body, the National American Woman Suffrage Association (NAWSA). However, the state of Washington suffrage victory in November 1910, followed by California in 1911, gave new impetus. The formation of the Progressive Party, which contested the 1912 presidential elections, seemed to give an alternative to the less favourable Republican and Democrat parties, borne out by the 1913 women's suffrage victory in Illinois, where Progressives held the balance of power. Suffragists were, nonetheless, bitterly divided by strategic questions – whether to focus on state-level referenda or a federal constitutional amendment, whether to copy British militancy, and how to relate suffragism to the new avant-garde identity, 'feminism', which seemed to be an extreme and dangerous version of women's emancipation.

1912, the year in which *The Freewoman* became available in America and the feminist discussion circle, Heterodoxy, was founded in New York, has in particular been regarded as one of exceptional change and unrest. It was the year of the unprecedented presidential elections in which the Republican candidate, President Taft, was challenged by Roosevelt in the newly formed Progressive Party. This splitting of the Republican vote allowed a Democratic victory for Woodrow Wilson. The Socialist Party under Eugene Debs took its largest ever share of the national vote, around 6 per cent. This disruption of the usual two-party system seemed to be a moment of opportunity for changing the make-up of the polity by admitting women as voters. The feminist commentator and journalist Floyd Dell described 1912 as extraordinary for the intensity of 'woman-suffrage activity'.[14]

Yet the *ennui* that some felt with the protracted and politically convoluted suffrage struggle on both sides of the Atlantic led them to look to feminism as a promising new formation. One American suffragist acknowledged in a letter to a British counterpart that she had been feeling depressed by 'the tarnishing effects of the routine business of promoting a cause' and felt that feminism was 'a quickening force' that would help 'to indicate what all this suffrage business is really FOR'.[15] The period was also marked by utopian belief in the 'new order', and a gaze inward at the sort of 'new individual' who was to inhabit it, and this also spurred the interest of 'advanced' thinkers in feminism, as a framework which promised to turn a spotlight onto the individual sex-psyche. Influenced by the spreading currency of psychological theories (Freud lectured at Clark University in 1909, and 'sex psychology' was becoming widely discussed in both Britain and America), the period seemed to herald a vast change in how the psyche, the emotions, and sexuality could be understood and culturally represented. This promised, above all, to impact upon the relations between the sexes.[16]

One intellectual milieu in which fundamental social and psychological change was imagined, and began to be lived, was relatively narrow yet profoundly influential. The experimental, 'modern' or avant-garde circles became a vivid realm of creative and political experimentation on both sides of the Atlantic. Emancipation was located both internally, concerning self-realisation, and in society, in industrial and political reform. Women were the particular agents and subjects of such change, their status and activities epitomising the 'modern' era. Margaret Sanger coined the idea of 'a near Renaissance for women' in this period,[17] and the term 'feminism' was adopted to indicate the extension of 'women's rights' to questions of the fulfilment, creativity, sexuality and emotional relations of men and women. The introspective exploration (and transformation) of psyche and personality was a dominating Edwardian feminist concern. As one American feminist put it, 'The basic idea of feminism, with which every other idea and every material achievement must square, is the emancipation of woman as a personality. The struggle for self-consciousness is the essence of the feminist movement'. Feminism was to 'wipe out the psychological residue of subjection in the individual woman soul'.[18]

Such comments are in keeping with what Warren Susman has described as a shift in 'general social attitudes', from 'character' and its moral qualities of hard work, self-control and self-denial, to a modern phenomenon, 'personality'.[19] Citizens saw themselves governed less by duty and its moral imperatives, and more by individual self-development and fulfilment. This trend indicates an individualist core, built around anxieties about bureaucracy and collectivisation, in both British and American Edwardian society. A celebration of the individual planted against 'the machine' can be traced in many cultural spheres, from the 'frontiersman' and cowboy heroes of popular films and novels, to the resurgence of interest in anarchism. The machine, political or industrial, was a pervasive fear, responding to an increasingly bureaucratic and executive-dominated state that seemed to be working against the 'new individualism'. A. V. Dicey, the British legal scholar, had famously predicted in 1906 and 1914 that individualism was being eclipsed in Edwardian society by 'collectivism'. This was perceived by many as a wider social and cultural trend, and spoke to anxieties on both sides of the Atlantic. It was felt in the United States that the labour market was displaying anti-individualist trends, as firms merged into vast 'trusts', and unions coalesced into the national American Federation of Labor or the Industrial Workers of the World. As in Britain, this period saw competing tendencies. What was variously called organisation, co-operation or conglomeration was counterbalanced by a very persistent and growing faith in individuals as, ideally, masters of their own destinies. These conflicting tendencies formed the constitutive tensions that shaped the feminist avant-garde.

The invention of feminism

A subtle interplay between three overlapping sets of identities and practices – the 'women's movement', suffragism and feminism – characterised the politics of activist women (and small numbers of men) in this period. Nancy Cott's influential account of the development of the idea of 'feminism' in America demonstrates that it was a term only recently taken up in the 1910s, and one with avant-garde, 'modern' connotations

that made some uncomfortable. American women had broken out of the
limited realms in which they had previously been confined, and were
starting to compete with men in the labour market and the professions,
and to join men in leisure pursuits and the arts. This growing diverseness
of women's experiences made it necessary, if they were to come together in
sexual solidarity, to mobilise on a new basis. 'The Woman's Movement'
carried too many connotations of 'woman's sphere', and a bourgeois single
morality. 'Feminism' as a new formation seemed preferable, with its stress
on individualism and self-realisation within a collectivist framework. Cott
makes very clear the paradoxical, contradictory basis of feminist beliefs in
this period. She describes the twin impulses to *individualism* and the
liberty for women it was seen to bring, and *solidarity* based on sex, a
collectivism that could embrace all women (or sometimes, only white
women) just on account of being women. It is of course difficult to sustain
'individualist' movements, and Cott points out 'the self destructive
potential of a movement which makes individuation of its members a
principal goal'. She argues however that these tensions also 'vivified'
feminism.[20]

The Anglo-American *Freewoman's* explicit description of itself in
October 1911 as 'a feminist review' indicates the increasing circulation of
the term 'feminism' among those who saw themselves as 'advanced' or
'vanguard' thinkers – those whom the progressive political commentator
Walter Lippmann referred to as the 'great rag-tag of bohemianism' that he
associated with the 'woman's movement'.[21] *The Freewoman* represented,
and helped shape, the transatlantic intellectual milieu of the 'feminist
vanguard'. This journal became notorious in both Britain and the United
States during its short life, and the ideas discussed within it, and prompted
by it, came to influence a wide range of subsequent feminist thinkers.

The Freewoman was founded as a weekly threepenny journal in 1911 by
disgruntled former members of the Pankhursts' WSPU, in an atmosphere
of bitterness and rancour over the organisation of the suffrage movement.
Though it was sustained by a fervent circle of readers and contributors in
both Britain and America, it was repudiated by many within the women's
movement for its political radicalism and sexual explicitness. Olive
Schreiner, an influential South African feminist, described it to Havelock
Ellis as 'the expression of exactly that which we are going to fight against,
that we may free ourselves and the world from that brutality and selfishness
that degrades and tarnishes the divinity of sex'.[22] The journal served as a
site for debate within a section of British and American Edwardian
society – variously designated as intellectual, progressive, advanced,

modern, 'ultra', avant-garde – and achieved notoriety in this role, as a 'dark and dangerous side of the "woman movement"'.[23] Much contention stemmed from *The Freewoman*'s call for a rethinking of suffragists' tactics, and from contributors' eventual conclusions that suffrage was the wrong goal for feminists. The journal sustained high levels of public recognition, despite its low circulation, through controversies in national periodicals, suffrage journals, and other contemporary texts. An American anti-feminist described *The Freewoman* as one of two leading 'feminist journals' in the United States.[24] It played an influential role in shaping 'feminist' identity in Britain and America, at a time when 'feminism' was a newly coined and relatively fluid term.

The Freewoman fascinated its contemporaries and has continued to perplex historians, for whom it has become an iconic institution of Edwardian 'advanced' or 'modern' feminism.[25] It provided a node of stability, briefly allowing feminism to gain coherence as an avant-garde formation, before its adoption in the war years as a bland synonym for 'the women's movement'. In part, *The Freewoman* was so influential because it connected to a number of other feminist and non-feminist networks; it stimulated its readers to meet in a 'Freewoman Discussion Circle' in London and other cities; and it circulated amongst New York discussion clubs. *The Freewoman* also engaged in dialogue with non-feminist periodicals of its milieu, ranging from anarchist and socialist papers to the radical right. It shared its contributors and articles with a wide range of other titles, making it the meeting ground for a much wider range of political and cultural thought than has commonly been associated with early twentieth-century feminism.

'Freewomen'

The editor of *The Freewoman*, Dora Marsden (1882–1960), came from an impoverished single parent family in rural West Yorkshire. Joining the pupil-teacher system aged thirteen she had trained as a teacher in Owens College, Manchester, and achieved personal economic independence. Drawn to the extremely active Manchester suffrage scene, Marsden resigned her position in 1909 in order to march to the House of Commons. In doing so, she achieved immediate national notoriety through being pictured on the front page of the British *Daily Mirror*. She went on to become a paid WSPU organiser in London and Lancashire, and enjoyed the political theatre of militant suffragism, being arrested for such actions as throwing balls labelled 'bomb' through the windows of political

Figure 1: Dora Marsden, a portrait by G. Beresford, issued as a supplement to
The Freewoman in 1912. The Schlesinger Library, Radcliffe Institute, Harvard University

meetings in September 1909. Marsden was also willing to undertake such
daredevil acts of militancy as concealing herself overnight in the roof of a
hall where the Liberal politician Winston Churchill was to speak. Her
dramatic interruption of the meeting resulted in a rooftop tussle and arrest.
WSPU leaders were not, however, impressed, and their attempts to curtail
Marsden's independence led to a bitter dispute over her ability to take
autonomous decisions, and her resignation in January 1911. Her career with
the WSPU was thus marked by a frustration at the anti-democratic and

bullying leadership style, and exemplifies the frustrations which had caused other members to secede in 1907 to form the Women's Freedom League.

Mary Gawthorpe, Marsden's co-editor and former colleague within the WSPU, had similar experiences. Gawthorpe came from a Leeds working-class family, and had also become a teacher through the pupil-teacher system. She became involved in local socialist politics and the Labour Church, as well as the controversial Leeds Arts Club. Through this discussion club, she became close to A. R. Orage, who later founded the modernist *New Age*. During the very early years of the century, the WSPU still operated through these northern socialist channels, and Gawthorpe became involved in suffrage politics along with another WSPU activist Teresa Billington-Greig (1877–1964). Like Marsden and Gawthorpe, Teresa Billington used the pupil-teacher system to move from an insecure background into a new world of economic independence, though her religious rebellion made it hard for her to sustain teaching employment. She became an ILP organiser in 1904 in Manchester, but moved to London to work for the WSPU in 1907, the year she married Frederick Greig, a husband supportive of her radical politics who was also willing to adopt her name.

For such women, women's suffrage became a more vivid commitment than socialist politics; like Billington-Greig, Gawthorpe moved from the ILP to a post with the WSPU from 1906, and was a highly popular public speaker. Yet the strain caused by the autocratic leadership, as well as her ill health through overwork and imprisonment, led her to withdraw from militant activism after several years.[26] Billington-Greig had split from the WSPU in 1907 and, along with Charlotte Despard, became prominent in the Women's Freedom League (WFL), an alternative militant suffrage organisation. Despard and Billington-Greig were responsible for *The Vote*, the WFL official organ. But around 1910, Billington-Greig became increasingly critical of even the WFL approach to political activism. She hoped instead to construct an activist feminism, but sadly conceded that 'women and men who regard themselves as advanced feminists are all at sixes and sevens as to principles, theories, objects and methods ... the way is strewn with half-enunciated new ideas and half-obsolete old ones', and she proposed a feminist periodical to try to elucidate what feminism was about.[27]

Billington-Greig published a scathing attack on suffragism in 1911, at around the same time as Marsden realised that she could not publish her ideas on feminism in *The Vote*.[28] Marsden had, like Billington-Greig, been looking for a non-doctrinaire 'open' space for the expression of feminism.

Figure 2: Mary Gawthorpe, Tamiment Library, New York University, Mary Gawthorpe Photographs Collection

She began to plan a journal, hoping first to publish it as a supplement to *The Vote*. Her desire for independence and inability to restrict her voice, however, led her to sever the connection and set up an entirely independent journal. Backed initially by radical publisher Charles Granville, and later by the patron of modern literature, Harriet Shaw Weaver (who also became an editor in 1914), Marsden edited three successive titles between 1911 and 1919, *The Freewoman*, *The New Freewoman* and *The Egoist*. None was self-supporting; all attained high levels of notoriety and publicity, but not a large readership.[29]

The significance of *Freewoman* contributions to the development of an 'avant-garde' form of feminism lies in the combination of two very different, even opposed, political 'spaces' or discourses. Marsden espoused an aggressive form of anti-statist individualism that provoked rich debates among the readership of 'advanced' women about the way in which feminism might be both a collective entity and a realm of individual self-development. She held a strongly individualist view of the 'unencumbered self', whose being was determined by the freedom of the will, for those 'elite' individuals who possessed the capacity. Such a subject was coherent and singular; it was motivated by self-love, ambition and strength, and had no need for institutional support, a state to guarantee its rights, or a model of citizenship to define its public roles and duties. Yet this individualist vision was combined in *The Freewoman* with an overt feminist identity, a collective grouping based around the 'freewoman' identity that encumbered, embodied and situated the 'egoist' self.

This idea of 'the freewoman' appealed very strongly to the periodical community surrounding the journal. While intended by Dora Marsden to harness feminism to an individualist position, the idea of a 'freewoman' paradoxically engendered a strong collective identification. The constant references to the term in the journal's correspondence and articles is striking. Readers quickly incorporated it into their vocabulary and apparently identified with it. 'Freewoman' implied a personification of feminist ideals that was clearly attractive and memorable. It became a form of group identity which Dora Marsden could not control; it was not in her power to 'police' the construction of 'the freewoman', despite her editorial prerogatives. It may have been her recognition of the power of the motif, and its ability to subvert the radical individualism she proposed, that motivated the final name change of the journal in 1914, from *The New Freewoman* to *The Egoist*. Initially, however, a 'freewoman' was radically undefined.[30] There was no strong normative basis to what the term might mean, and this allowed for an inclusive, though contested identity. This ran against the grain of Dora Marsden's exclusivist definition, that 'only one woman in four' had the potential to become a freewoman. The debates prompted by the ambiguities of 'the freewoman' were never resolved, and in this study the politics of the feminist avant-garde are not read as presenting any one final position. Unlike the suffrage journals that dominated the journalism of the women's movement, *The Freewoman* and its surrounding intellectual field of 'little magazines' and radical papers were genuinely controversial, and represented sites where ideas could be worked through and evaluated.

'Masculism'

The new term 'feminism' allowed, in a way that 'women's movement' did not, for men to be included in this new identity. Male involvement within early twentieth century suffrage organisations was extensive, as indicated by the prominence of male suffragists such as Henry Blackwell, Robert LaFollette, Henry Harben, Keir Hardie, George Lansbury and Fred Pethick Lawrence, and by the existence of groups such as the Men's League for Women's Suffrage.[31] The relationships of male suffragists were extensive and transnational. Men's societies supporting women's suffrage were sufficiently well developed to sustain an International League, and the Men's Political Union for Women's Enfranchisement (essentially a British-based WSPU support group) had an American branch. Its journal, the *Men's League Monthly Paper*, circulated in both countries. But many men felt that their women's suffrage activism was precarious, and sometimes unwanted, particularly as the suffrage struggle took on more violence in Britain after 1911.[32] In 'advanced' circles, the replacement of 'woman movement' by 'feminist' (understood to be open equally to both men and women) marked a new openness to the activism of men. An initial advertisement for *The Freewoman* had noted:

Literary contributions will be sought from men equally with women, and it is hoped that the paper will find male readers as readily as women. It is considered that any theory of feminism which regards itself as the private province of women's interests is an absurdity ...[33]

Following accusations from Olive Schreiner and others that *The Freewoman* was male dominated, and propagated 'the tone of the brutal self-indulgent selfish male',[34] Dora Marsden announced that around half of the contributors were male. Many regarded the male readership as at best an

oddity for a feminist paper. One female correspondent wrote to Dora
Marsden:

I had a letter this morning from a man I have sent a circular to. He has got the first
number and is charmed – but why? Because of its condemnation of what he calls
'the disgraceful window-smashing affair'! It's odd to think that *The Freewoman*
pleases men on those grounds ... How infinitely I do prefer women to men! I
hope we shall please women too.[35]

When male readers described their feelings with regard to feminism, they
were often ambivalent, or deployed clumsy strategies to legitimate their
interest. As Bruce Clarke notes, male feminists sought to distance themselves from sexual or sentimental motives for their intervention in feminist
debates, and to attribute their interest to concern for what could be perceived as 'non-gendered' abstractions such as 'the race'.[36] The intimacy and
comfortableness of the relationship between feminism and men is supported however by their numerous contributions to *The Freewoman*. Male
readers formed a committed and articulate core of *The Freewoman*'s
supporters, and one even suggested that the second manifestation of
The Freewoman be titled *Freeman*.[37]

   Similarly in the United States, Heterodoxy members referred to their
husbands as 'fellow-feminists', and welcomed the 'new man': 'Every son
born to a feminist, and every man married to one, has the opportunity to
develop into the new type', suggested Beatrice Hale in her 1914 book, *What
Women Want: An Interpretation of the Feminist Movement*. During her
New York Cooper Union lectures in 1914, Charlotte Perkins Gilman
coined the term 'masculism' as a counterpart to 'feminism', to indicate the
centrality of masculinity to the new construction of 'the larger feminism'.[38]
The feminist anthropologist Elsie Clews Parsons claimed that the organisation in March 1914 of a 'Women's Forum' in Columbia University was
a mistake, as it failed to indicate the 'identity of interests' of the sexes. She
later welcomed the swift inclusion of men and change in name to a
'Feminist Forum'. Hutchins Hapgood, a 'free love' journalist wrote: 'I am
interested more in what feminism is doing for men', he said, 'than in what
it is doing for women'.[39] Even more bullish, Floyd Dell claimed his right to
comment upon feminism, since he viewed it ultimately as a rebellion of
men against the vacuities of conventional femininity:

Men are tired of subservient women ... Why, then, have men appeared hostile to
the woman's rebellion? Because what men desire are real individuals who have

achieved their own freedom. It will not do to pluck freedom like a flower and give it to the lady with a polite bow. She must fight for it.[40]

Although Dell's account was highly patronising, it did reflect a very common belief of 'advanced' feminists – that women and not men were to blame if women had not achieved emancipation.

'Vanguard feminism'

Despite the varied forums in which it was avidly discussed in the progressive era, feminism was certainly not a mainstream doctrine in America, and was still associated with 'ultra modern' rebellion.[41] In both countries, feminism gained cultural capital through its association with the idea of 'the new' and 'the modern'. The title of Floyd Dell's 1913 book, *Women as World Builders: Studies in Modern Feminism*, was characteristic of this stress on modernity. Dell, a working-class mid-Westerner, came to Chicago as a young journalist in 1908 and became an editor of the *Friday Literary Review*, a subsection of the *Chicago Evening Post* and an important space for literary modernism.[42] That Dell, who later moved to New York and helped edit *The Masses*, should so quickly and confidently become a commentator on feminism indicates the openness to men amongst the feminist avant-garde, and the centrality of feminism to what it was to be a 'modern'.

Nancy Cott notes the shock value of feminism, and its association with continental European ideas, and describes feminism as 'a semantic claim to female modernism'.[43] Dora Marsden, who was one of Dell's 'world builders', claimed for example, that 'the articulate consciousness of mind in women, which, in its different forms of expression is called feminism, is one of the most unmistakable features of modern times'.[44] The 1914 'Feminist Manifesto' of the poet Mina Loy illustrated the introspective conflict and challenge to complacency that characterised avant-garde feminism. Loy was born in Britain, but mainly lived in continental Europe and the United States. Engaged in a transatlantic conversation between her futurist peers in Italy and feminists such as Mabel Dodge in New York, Loy wrote her manifesto in response to the strong hostility to women from the leading futurist, Filippo Marinetti. In typical avant-garde tones, Loy derided 'the pathetic clap-trap warcry, "Woman is the equal of man". She is *not*. ... Leave off looking to men to find out what you are *not*. Seek within yourselves to find out what you *are*'.[45]

Floyd Dell

67

Figure 3: Floyd Dell, by William Gropper, reproduced with permission of the
William Gropper Estate

This 'vanguard' form of feminism was not, however, wholly divorced
from the wider women's movement in Britain and the United States; many
feminists remained indebted to and closely allied with the older concerns
of suffrage and the 'woman's movement'. Indeed, before 1920, suffrage
remained the goal which could unite the largest constituencies of women.
Feminists could still be portrayed as a subset of suffragists.[46] It is a mistake,
however, to understand suffrage as providing a nurturing environment for
its more 'radical' offspring, feminism, as this gives too gradualist a picture
of a shift from suffragism to feminism in the twentieth century, and tends
to obscure the distinctiveness of feminist political argument. There were
continued attempts by suffragists to wrest 'feminism' from its 'arbitrary'

application to 'extreme and radical' women, and reinstate its 'proper' usage compatible with a respectable suffragism of 'racial advance' or 'the family'.[47]

As late as 1907, 'feminisme' was still being spelt in its French form, but it quickly came to be absorbed as an Anglo-American term, and French feminists were forced to invent a new term, *éclairistes*, to distinguish themselves from Anglo-Saxon versions.[48] The British socialist and anti-feminist Belfort Bax used 'feminism' to identify women's rights in a broad sense in 1906.[49] By 1911, it had come to be associated with a narrower group of 'extreme radicals' or 'vanguard workers'. The launch of *The Freewoman* periodical in that year gave more weight to this usage of feminism, though it remained contested in meaning. The formation of the New York women's luncheon club, Heterodoxy, in 1912 marked the first American group that overtly identified itself as feminist.[50] Its members, the 'Heterodites', held fortnightly meetings from 1912 to the early 1940s, and used the space to discuss topics as diverse as pacifism, birth control, the Russian Revolution, black civil rights, and Irish independence, as well as providing 'background talks' on the childhoods of its members. Possibly inspired by the feminist debates of the London Freewoman Discussion Circle, it functioned in a similar manner, providing a space for riotous, frank and profound discussions.[51] Heterodoxy differed from the Freewoman Discussion Circle in its women-only basis, its lack of formality, and its policy of 'off the record' discussion. It recruited an elite group of leaders and activists within feminism, the labour movement and socialism, forming an influential and long-lasting coalition of women, though as we shall see, it came to represent very different values in the changed atmosphere of the inter-war period.

Despite the foundational standing of Heterodoxy and *The Freewoman* within Anglo-American feminist history, many involved in these circles were initially uncomfortable with the term 'feminism'. Dora Marsden specified that her aim was to use the term 'feminist' in order to revise it. As a London daily reported it,

Miss Dora Marsden, speaking to one of our representatives, half-apologised for the use of that nebulous term, Feminist. 'We recognise', she said, 'that it is a word which carries a good deal of odium; but it has so established itself that we feel there is nothing for us to do but to employ it and to give it a new significance.[52]

Heterodoxy member and *Freewoman* subscriber Beatrice Hale referred to feminism 'by which for lack of a better term we call it, [as] somewhat misleading, the French form lacking robustness to ears attuned to English'.[53] Marie Jenney Howe, wife of the transatlantic social reformer Frederic C. Howe and the founder of Heterodoxy, also felt that 'the term feminism has been foisted upon us' but would 'do as well as any other word to express woman's effort towards development'.[54] In 1914, Charlotte Perkins Gilman (also a member of Heterodoxy) was still referring to 'feminism' within quotation marks, to indicate its uncertain provenance, and she usually qualified her versions of feminism as 'human feminism' or 'the larger feminism' in order to distinguish them from competing versions. Rose Young (1869–1941), a writer and suffrage activist living in New York, perceptively noted that 'Some fear to have the woman question fitted with a name, however expansive, a creed to swear by, hard-and-fast rules to go by, when what is desired is the open mind, ready and willing to abide by the individual's development'. In 1916, feminism was still being called 'a new and most uncomfortable word' by the *Washington Post*.[55]

What was the intellectual and cultural content of this new variant on 'women's rights'? The October 1912 issue of the American monthly, *The Forum*, was devoted to feminism, and the issues surveyed are revealing of what was considered the feminist 'programme' at the time. The issue included a reprint of an article from the *English Review* by the British feminist writer May Sinclair, an article on syphilis, and some other regular *Forum* writers on 'women's issues', but there was an overall lack of focus. A recurrent theme of the *Forum*'s treatment of 'the woman question' in 1912 was maternity – its power to embitter if left unused, and its dominance of women. The editor disliked the violence and hysteria of British suffragists.[56] The picture that emerges of feminism is as a fairly conventional, vaguely drawn position, using the 'English' women's movement to denote sensational radicalism and violence, while America remained safely the realm of 'social feminists' concerned with maternity and purity issues. The feminist avant-garde was portrayed in a single article on Dora Marsden and *The Freewoman*, by another Heterodoxy member Frances Maule Björkman. It acknowledged a new element within the women's movement, illustrated by the 'effort on the part of women to lift themselves forever out of the "servant" class and to place themselves definitely and finally among the "masters"'. However, this could still be read as an isolated 'English' peculiarity.

In Britain, feminism was similarly still contested and used with caution. A 1913 *New Statesman* special supplement on 'the Awakening of Women' sought to divorce this 'awakening' from 'mere *feminism*'. The supplement's Fabian editor, Beatrice Webb, viewed feminism as 'one of three simultaneous world-movements towards a more equal partnership among human beings in human affairs'.[57] Webb's supplement included some established feminists such as Charlotte Perkins Gilman, and its biblio-graphy included a wide range of European and American psychological and sociological thinkers. The main focus of this collection, and of socialist activist Ethel Snowden's 1913 book *The Feminist Movement*, was the eco-nomic status of women. Neither text indicated any avant-garde associa-tions with feminism – Dora Marsden wrote of the *New Statesman* to her American acquaintance, Floyd Dell: 'nothing duller exists in that swamp of dullness – London journalism ... I would lay all my money on Mrs Pankhurst as against Mrs Webb in the cause of the emancipation of women'.[58]

In America in 1913 and 1914, however, *The Forum* began to run strings of articles, for and against, on the rise of the 'free personality' within fem-inism, the centrality of sexual identity and self-willed emancipation to this movement. Bergson, Ibsen and Nietzsche were acknowledged as key forebears to this new 'feminism', and another periodical, the socialist *New Review*, published a 'feminist symposium' in August 1914, welcoming the involvement of men and development beyond suffrage into 'feminism'.

Above all, the transformation of *Harper's Weekly* by its new editor, Norman Hapgood, revealed the extent to which 'feminism' had become an essential ingredient in the modern realm of progressive politics, and could be comfortably championed by a man. Hapgood, already an established figure in progressive circles and previously an editor of *Collier's Weekly*, joined *Harper's Weekly* in August 1913. He immediately commissioned a series of articles on feminist issues – modern marriage, unmarried motherhood, physical freedom and so on. These articles were fore-grounded under full-page headlines such as 'Unmarried Mothers: One Big Job for the Feminist Movement'. Citing Elsie Clews Parsons, Mary Austin, H. G. Wells and Ellen Key, his first-issue editorial, 'What Women Are After', aimed to 'make clear what will be one of the principle purposes steadily pursued by this publication' – the elaboration of a feminism that transcended suffrage to inspire an intellectual and moral revolution.

Hapgood believed that 'the publication that undertakes to express progress can no more leave this movement out of account than it can ignore labor, or the relation of government to wealth'. He called for feminism to be 'discussed constantly' under his editorship, and placed *Harper's* in a periodical community with what he called 'our radical contemporary' the pro-feminist New York paper, *The Masses*.[59] This was clearly a controversial strategy, and stimulated much comment in readers' letters. One reader 'hoped that [Hapgood] has misunderstood entirely the feminist movement; that as a whole it stands for purity and not for adultery'. Feminism was still open to diverse personal interpretations, though its avant-garde connotations were becoming increasingly established. In December 1913, one correspondent wrote, 'How fast the movement grows! I have been away from America only two years, and it already seems intellectually like a different place'.[60] She was impressed by the new willingness to discuss controversial sexual matters, and this had become a clear sign of 'vanguard' feminism. By 1916, feminism had sufficient currency and weight to support its own bibliographies, citing individualist and avant-garde writers such as Rosa Mayreder, Floyd Dell and Mary Austin, and the avant-garde periodicals *The Egoist, The Little Review* and *The Masses*.[61]

Though the term 'feminist' was widely toted, the impact of feminism was initially upon private life and personal practices. There was little organised feminist activism in the United States until early 1914, when the 'First Feminist Mass Meeting' was held in New York. Historian Sandra Adickes situates this meeting, and its follow-up meeting three days later, as foundational for 'the birth of feminism as an expression of the women's movement's rising expectations'.[62] This description implies an untroubled evolution of feminism from the existing women's movement, and downplays the lack of enthusiasm many felt for this novel political formation. For the avant-garde feminists though, this meeting marked a welcome shift in feminism from a concern with institutional reform to a focus upon cultural matters such as women's clothing, and a critical, introspective gaze at women themselves.

The mass meeting was chaired by Marie Jenney Howe, and featured as speakers many Heterodoxy members (some such as Charlotte Perkins Gilman, known nationally), as well as some men, including Floyd Dell and Edwin Björkman (husband of the transatlantic feminist activist Frances Maule Björkman). Topics included women's right to work, dress reform, keeping one's maiden name, women's industrial organisation, and the easing of women's labour in the home. Women's own responsibility for their degradation and emancipation was stressed. Elsie Clews Parsons, also a Heterodite, commented 'The most decided applause was given to various statements to the effect that our idle, parasitical women were our greatest menace. A class war between women *is* no doubt in the order of things. It may be a surprising kind of ferment to the class war at large'.[63]

As Parsons' comment on the class war suggests, many early twentieth-century feminists saw their beliefs as shaped by other 'progressive' or radical traditions – socialism, anarchism, union politics and so on. Amongst socialists, British feminists sustained especially close links with the Fabian Society, which had grown out of the sexual egalitarianism of the Independent Labour Party (ILP) and the Fellowship of the New Life.[64] Dora Marsden described Fabian women to an American colleague as the only group of women other than the feminists who 'profess to be intelligent and advanced'.[65] American feminists were also attached to the Fabians, including Charlotte Perkins Gilman, Harriet Stanton Blatch and, later, Hazel Hunkins Hallinan. Despite the Fabian suspicion of the flamboyant Edwardian avant-garde, Ethel Bradshaw, secretary of the Fabian Women's Group in Bristol, commented in *The Freewoman* that 'most of our members read your paper'.[66]

Feminism provided some with a means to criticise the gender politics of other 'radical' movements. As one feminist wrote in the *New Review* in 1914, 'timid and cautious' socialists would always be suspicious of feminism's class origins, but feminists must continue to organise as socialists, otherwise their freedom would be empty.[67] Multiple commitments were foregrounded, and exclusive loyalty to achieving the vote was not favoured. It was clear to many feminists that suffragists would not fully embrace socialist or labour politics, and that suffrage could be highly conservative.[68] American suffragists only attended to the concerns of working-class women in a sporadic fashion. This perhaps motivated the elaboration of 'feminism' as a space for political argument and identification that did recognise the complex cross-currents of gender and class.

Socialism, however, was only one interest among many. The feminism initiated by avant-garde feminists was characterised by its abandonment of 'rights talk' in favour of an inward gaze, indicating a desire to explore, understand and transform their own desires, drives and frustrations. *The Freewoman*'s editor consciously set out to make feminism 'definitely self-conscious and introspective'. Rose Young was reported in the *New York Times* following her speech at the 1914 'feminist mass meeting': 'To me, feminism means that woman wants to develop her own womanhood. It means that she wants to push on to the finest, fullest, freest expression of herself. She wants to be an individual'.[69] Journalist Rheta Childe Dorr commented on the introspection of Heterodoxy discussions 'We thought we discussed the whole field, but we really discussed ourselves'. She noted that feminism, 'invariably pronounced in small capitals ... was something with dynamite in it, like trial marriage or free love ... It was never a secret doctrine of the suffragists. It is not a doctrine or even a cult. Feminism, like Boston, is a state of mind'.[70] Echoing *The Freewoman* declarations in

Britain, American feminists hailed self-development, individualism and 'personality', and rejected the neglect of self-development embodied in the feminine ideal of self-sacrifice. Edna Kenton, an American *Freewoman* subscriber and experimental theatre writer, argued forcefully:

Feminism is not a concrete thing, to be touched with hands or seen of eyes; *it is any woman's spiritual and intellectual attitude toward herself and toward life. It is her conscious attempt to realize Personality;* to make her own decisions instead of having them made for her; to sink the old humbled or rebelling slave in the new creature who is mistress of herself . . . [71]

Warren Susman's shift from character concerns to 'personality' as a prominent American idiom is evident here. Feminists found the new, introspective language of psyche and personality useful, and put their case in terms of the development of their own personality in order to further their own ends and self-realise to their fullest extent. This included sexual experimentation; as Edna Kenton pithily pointed out, 'feminism will give men more fun', though she herself apparently sustained no sexual relationships with men, and may well have preferred lesbian experimentation to heterosexual.[72]

Many worked with a relatively exclusive, elitist definition of feminism. In her 1914 book, Beatrice Hale saw feminism as 'a child of the few, a product of that minority which has had the leisure and training that make thought and aspiration possible'.[73] Hale identified the leading intellectuals of feminism as Olive Schreiner ('the prophetess of feminism'), Ellen Key and Charlotte Perkins Gilman. The naming of these figures indicates something of the central (always disputed) concerns of feminism, as well as its international scope. There had long been a tendency for the women's movement to refer to its key texts as 'bibles of the women's movement', and a small group of books were regarded as defining the essentials of the movement. Mary Wollstonecraft's 1792 *Vindication of the Rights of Women* and John Stuart Mill's *The Subjection of Women* (1869) had long held this place, but by the late Edwardian period, a new set of books had been canonised.

Olive Schreiner (1855–1920), a South African writer based in London, gained notoriety and success as a 'new woman' novelist with her 1883 *Story of an African Farm*. She also wrote some very widely quoted and reproduced allegories aligned to the cause of women, including *Three Dreams in a Desert* (1890). She was perhaps best known in feminist circles for her 1911 *Woman and Labour*, widely described as a 'bible' of the women's movement and the subject of many 'conversion' narratives. Schreiner claimed that for women, 'all labour is our province', and excoriated feminine economic parasitism. She was vastly critical of women as currently constituted and held the characteristic Edwardian feminist belief that women were responsible for their own freedom, and their continued subordination therefore could be laid at their own door. Schreiner devoted three chapters out of six in *Woman and Labour* (1911) to the issue of parasitism – economic and emotional – and called for women's rebellion against it. The dependence of women on men was morally reprehensible, and had corrupted their character, leaving them, as Schreiner put it, 'effete and enervated' and acting as a 'deadly microbe' on the constitution of the race. Both internal effort and external intervention was needed to overcome parasitism, but 'the will' was seen as the most fundamental site of reform, since 'the ultimate effect of parasitism is always a paralysis of the will'.[74]

Schreiner combined some highly 'advanced' beliefs with a wariness of sexual 'liberation'. Her feminism represents the cautious radicalism of a generation of activists who found the feminist identity appealing, but did not embrace the 'modernism' and radical rupture that it stood for. One *Freewoman* reader, the ILP activist and radical Isabella O. Ford, commented after reading *Woman and Labour*: 'I am so very tired of Woman with a big W that ... I thought it was rather stale'. Schreiner preferred to look backwards, declaring that strong, active women had a racial descent: '*We* are not new! If you would understand us, go back two thousand years, and study our descent; our breed is our explanation'.[75]

Ellen Key's work contrasted sharply to Schreiner's, though she was of the same generation and was also acknowledged as a leading feminist thinker. Key (1849–1926) was a Swedish activist, highly popular in the United States. Like the transatlantic feminist avant-garde, her 'maternalist feminism' travelled beyond national feminist networks. Key's work celebrated women's capacity for sexual pleasure, and their maternal role; she rejected patriarchal control over women's sexual and reproductive choices, and called instead for state endowment of mothers. Her ideas were extremely influential upon the German and Austrian *Mutterschutz* movement. Mari Jo Buhle describes her as 'taking America by storm' following the 1911 publication of *Love and Marriage*, a text which stressed sexual differences above sexual equality.[76] This emphasis on sexual difference distinguishes the trend of American from British feminism, where Key was less widely read and sexual difference remained for many feminists something to be investigated or discarded, rather than celebrated in the traditional terms of maternalism and care.

In writing about female sexuality, Key deployed a language of spirituality, taken up by her American followers. As one put it, 'the female movement is toward fusing, re-forming and organizing with everlasting life. Woman's spirit is the depository of the life-essence'.[77] Key's radicalism lay in her rejection of conventional morality and marriage, and her support for illegitimate children, trial marriage and free unions – for some, this located her within the subversive 'avant-garde'. However, her biological essentialism and support for limitations on women in the labour market could also be read, as Charlotte Perkins Gilman recognised, as profoundly conservative. Gilman preferred to stress the feminist reform of domestic life, and personal liberation. Nonetheless, one suffragist recalled that in 1912, 'everybody who used to read Charlotte Perkins Gilman was now reading [Ellen Key]'.[78]

Gilman (1860–1935) was probably still the most influential figure within American feminism in the early years of the twentieth century, through her prolific journalism, books, lecturing, and national profile, as well as her 'scandalous' personal life. She was popular in Britain, lecturing there repeatedly between 1896 and 1913, and active within the Fabian Society. Her book *Women and Economics*, published in 1898, was enormously influential, immediately published in multiple editions, and widely translated. Her transatlantic influence is clear in her impact upon 'advanced women' such as the British writer Vernon Lee.[79] Gilman argued that economically parasitic women occupied an inferior evolutionary place. This 'sexuo-economic relation' held back the entire race, since masculine advances were always constrained by women's artificially oversexed position. In similar terms to Olive Schreiner, Gilman constructed a narrative for the women's movement ('feminism' not being available as a term when she wrote her major sociological text in 1898) that stressed the natural evolution of the sexes into a complementary, organic unity, if women's economic dependency could be removed.

Gilman published widely in British and American periodicals, and was famous as a pioneer in household organisation. What Gilman later came to term 'the larger feminism' was in some aspects less consciously 'modern' than that of many of her Heterodoxy contemporaries, and matched Schreiner's caution on sexual matters. Her feminism is hard to categorise, and reveals the extent to which 'advanced' views could be held alongside more conventional ones. Though Gilman was understood to 'voice[s] the views of the whole vanguard of Feminism',[80] her commitment to evolution and the civilising mission of women indicates an older, nineteenth century intellectual tradition within the women's movement, largely abandoned by the avant-garde. Gilman described motherhood, in sentimental terms that many later feminists found unacceptable, as 'the sweetest, tenderest, noblest thing we know'. She was against 'irresponsible mothers who promptly turn over the real care of their babies to any ignorant young servant', and those who refused to breastfeed. Gilman ended her association with Heterodoxy when its pacifism conflicted with her support for the United States' involvement in World War One, and she disliked its wartime avant-garde anti-conventionality. But her writings on the ending of women's 'sex specialisation' in housework and childcare were thoroughly radical, and in particular, her concept of psychological, internalised oppression in her widely read short story, *The Yellow Wallpaper* (1899), was in keeping with the emphases of avant-garde feminism. This transnational and diverse group represents those whom American and British Edwardians perceived to be the founding contemporary thinkers of feminism.[81]

In its early formulations, feminism was not, however, simply about 'ideas', but also about creative experimentation. The dancing of Isadora Duncan (1878–1927), for example, created a further channel of transatlantic exchange for 'advanced women' in the early years of the twentieth century. Duncan, born in California, developed a new style of dance that expressed the desire for naturalness and authenticity so prominent in Edwardian culture. Consciously harking back to ancient Greece, Duncan danced barefoot, and wore only a shockingly revealing tunic which allowed her limbs and sometimes her breasts to be seen. She espoused an idea, inspired by Walt Whitman, of 'the new nakedness', expressing 'the highest intelligence in the freest body', which was to be 'the simple unconscious, pure body of woman'.[82]

Despairing of the inability of American audiences to recognise her art, Duncan first travelled to London in 1898, and her style of 'new dance' became critically acclaimed there around 1900. Duncan continued to travel back and forth between Europe and the United States until her death in 1927, inhabiting a transatlantic realm of celebrity that later gave her freedom of movement between America, Europe and the Soviet Union, despite the context of war, and the 'Red Scare' of the early 1920s. In London, she moved in the circles of what she called the 'advance-guard' of the theatre.[83]

The language of feminism was not yet available in the early 1900s, but in her 1903 Berlin lecture, 'The Dance of the Future', Duncan outlined her beliefs in terms that would have been unmistakably read as feminist just a few years later. Adopting the avant-garde idiom of 'will', she wrote that 'the dance should simply be, then, the natural gravitation of this will of the individual'. In a sentimental, pro-maternal style, she argued in terms reminiscent of Ellen Key that 'the new dance is a question of race, of the development of the female sex to beauty and health ... It is the question of the development of perfect mothers ..., to develop and to show the ideal form of woman'. Duncan was probably influenced by the founding of the *Bund für Mutterschutz* in Berlin in 1905 while she was living there. *Mutterschutz* represented a characteristically European strand of the women's movement, calling for free unions, control over reproduction, and state support for all children, including the illegitimate. Duncan was herself to live out these ideals, having two children within fairly short-lived free unions.

Duncan was highly critical of the over-sexualisation of women's bodies, and the way in which this interfered with their creativity. She believed that the dancer of the future 'will not dance in the form of nymph, nor fairy, nor coquette, but in the form of a woman in her greatest and purest expression ... From all parts of her body shall shine radiant intelligence, bringing to the world the message of the thoughts and aspirations of thousands of women. She shall dance the freedom of women'.[84] This placed her far outside of the suffrage struggle; Duncan believed 'we women can get anything in the world we want to without the vote', and she described her own views as 'considerably in advance of the women's movement of the present day'.[85] Her dancing was understood by audiences as utopian, a literal embodiment of aspirations for change carried through the female body. Despite her attempt to de-eroticise the 'new nakedness', Duncan was also associated with scandalously libertine sexuality. Her many love affairs linked her to the idealisation of sexual experimentation that became so characteristic of the later feminist avant-garde.

Duncan's impact was enormous. Marie Stopes described the intoxication she felt after seeing Duncan dance in Munich in 1904.[86] In Britain *The New Age* hosted eulogistic articles about her dancing as a new kind of socialist revolution, of passion and spirit rather than public reform. As one male correspondent argued:

Open a thousand Isadora Duncan schools in England and you may issue advance notices of the Golden Age ... It is time we made up our minds. Is it Bellamy we mean, or this thing that Isadora Duncan shows us? Will you blue-book, or will you dance?[87]

Ruth Slate, a lower-middle-class London clerk, ILP member and *Freewoman* reader, described in her diary going to see Duncan in 1908:

I could not write in cold words an account of that evening – or what it meant to me. I do not think I have ever seen anything more exquisite than Miss Duncan's dancing . . . *And* the audience – the tribute of perfect silence during each dance – the enthusiasm at its close! The whole thing was a revelation to me.[88]

Though she had been read as a kind of socialist, when 'feminist', was coined, Duncan became explicitly celebrated as such. In *Harper's Weekly*, placed next to an article titled 'What is Feminism?', her dancing was described in gushing terms.[89] In Floyd Dell's *Women as World Builders*, Dell wrote that 'it is modern science which, by giving us a new view of the body, its functions, its needs, its claims upon the world, has laid the basis for a successful feminist movement . . . It is to the body that one looks for the Magna Carta of feminism'. For Dell, Duncan symbolised this new attitude towards the body. Feminism, then, was being constructed as creative energy in touch with 'the goodness of the whole body'. Isadora Duncan articulated the possibility of women relating to their own bodies, without reference to the demands of male sexuality or the gaze of men. As Max Eastman wrote, 'All the bare-legged girls, and the poised and natural girls with strong muscles and strong free steps wherever they go . . . owe more to Isadora Duncan than to any other person. The boys too, who have a chance to be unafraid of beauty, to be unafraid of the natural life and free aspiration'. Dance was an important medium for the feminist avant-garde, as the subsequent transatlantic career of Agnes deMille, a choreographer and member of Heterodoxy, suggests. Another Heterodoxy member, Elsie Dufour, pursued a similar barefoot, free-expression dance style to Duncan, interpreting 'the song of the body' through 'the studio of bodily rhythm'.[90]

Alongside the realms of ideas and art, feminism was also intended to signify a new lifestyle for women. Elsie Clews Parsons' anthropological observations in her *Journal of a Feminist* notes her protagonist's involvement in social settlements, journalism and social reform, her college education, and her journeys between the Old World and the New. Her account revolved around the ethnographic curiosities of gender distinctions in clothing, in smoking practices, in sexual relations and social propriety. This was a loosely disguised representation of Parsons' own life, one of relative privilege and independent wealth. Unlike many of her British counterparts, Parsons (1875–1941) was born into an elite family. She was given a higher education in New York at the end of the 1890s, and went on to lecture in sociology and to conduct extensive anthropological fieldwork. Parsons was one of the few avant-garde feminists who seemed to achieve marriage, motherhood, and professional advancement. This was achieved without curtailment of her iconoclastic beliefs, both in her periodical journalism and her sociological books.[91] Even she, however, found it hard to sustain her public voice and circle of avant-garde friends after the changes brought by the war in 1917, and her later career can be seen as a retreat into the scholarly world of anthropology. Her more startling texts such as *Journal of a Feminist* remained unpublished in her lifetime.

Parsons' 'feminist lifestyle' comprised a rejection of the social conventions of clothes – she undressed in front of open windows, went nude in front of her family, refused to wear stockings and skirts on the beach or wear gloves. Above all, she indicated her 'advanced' status by smoking tobacco. Parsons continually referred to the social unease generated by women smoking, and the smoking feminist became 'the object of concentrated attention' in all public places.[92] Smoking had long signified the hallmark of the 'new woman'. Harriet Stanton Blatch noted, as a sign of her 'American' modernity, her penetration of European smoking rooms 'where it was "not customary to serve ladies"'. Floyd Dell welcomed the 'hell-raising' lifestyle of the 'cocktail drinking' feminist, and it seems that drinking was another token of one's emancipated status, at least among American feminists. Some also stressed the 'womanly' work such as mothering that feminists were still engaged in. Echoing the British suffragists pictured in *The Vote* cleaning and baking, Rose Young's article on Feminism in *Good Housekeeping* was illustrated by a portrait of Beatrice Hale, festooned with her three children, apparently lovingly absorbed in motherhood.[93] But most feminists presented the lifestyle associated with their politics as serious and studious.

It was common for Americans to identify two competing strands to feminism – as Charlotte Perkins Gilman named them, the Human Feminists, and the Female Feminists, or for Elsie Clews Parsons, the 'humanist' and the 'greedy, sex conscious' feminist. Gilman and Parsons supported the former, which valued above all the humanness of women, and denigrated the latter, which they believed 'considers sex as paramount, as underlying or covering all phases of life'. A stress on human companionship between men and women was prevalent among 'humanist' feminists; a feminist writer, Evelyn King Gilmore, proudly declared in *Harper's Magazine* that for the 'human feminists', 'women differ from men only in their physical functions ... woman's mentality, virtue, honour and integrity are in no wise different from man's'.[94]

Supporters of the alternative 'female' construction of feminism stressed sexual difference and the need to protect vulnerable women. Katharine Anthony, an American follower of Ellen Key, wrote a laudatory account of feminism in Germany and Scandinavia on the eve of America's entry to the First World War. Anthony divided the feminist movement into national

Figure 4: Elsie Clews Parsons on the beach

traditions – the Anglo-American versus the Teuto-Scandinavian. These loosely corresponded to Gilman's pair, and represented respectively 'the emancipation of woman as a human-being and as a sex-being'. She and other followers supported the latter as that to which American feminists would turn once the vote had been won, and they could devote special attention to women's needs as mothers – and this was indeed loosely what the post-war 'new feminism' came to represent.[95] This 'Teuto-Scandinavian' or 'new' strand of feminism, though less widely recognised than the more controversial avant-garde versions, became increasingly well established as an alternative meaning of feminism. Anthony's optimism about the harmony between these strands, however, was naïve. There was in fact an intense conflict between this stance and other forms of feminism, which was to lead to very damaging splits in the women's movement.

Although these three dominant figures (Gilman, Schreiner and Key) feature large in Edwardian 'feminist' bibliographies and guides to reading, feminist debate was carried out by a host of less-well-known figures, some of whom sustained transatlantic readerships. These figures include Rebecca West, Teresa Billington-Greig, W. L. George, Maude Royden, Edna Kenton and Wilma Meikle. They did not produce the substantial and influential texts that could be called 'bibles' of the women's movement. Some wrote books, but many preferred to use the ephemeral and iconoclastic medium of periodicals to discuss feminist ideas.

Though the term 'feminist' was not well established, the genre of the feminist journal was familiar. Throughout the nineteenth and early twentieth century, the periodical was a popular vehicle for discussion of women's issues. As Philippa Levine notes, within the second half of the nineteenth century 'the principles of feminist journalism emerged as a challenge to and means of circumventing reliance upon male-run papers', and provided women with 'an actively separate literary space'.[96] Levine's survey of British Victorian feminist periodicals suggests a growing mainstream market of women readers in the late nineteenth century.[97] An increasing number of journals combined feminist political comment with domestic content in an attempt to reach these readers. The 1890s witnessed an explosion in 'new woman' publishing. Journals such as *Shafts* (1892–1900) and *Women's Penny Paper* (1888–90) provided a new model of a serious and politically committed 'women's paper', as well as a forum for some of the 'new woman fiction'.

Suffrage journals boomed in the Edwardian period. *Jus Suffragii*, representing the International Woman Suffrage Alliance, was one of the earliest and longest-running of these. Published monthly or quarterly between 1906 and 1929, it offered an internationalist perspective on women's suffrage and peace movements. *Votes for Women* was the most successful suffrage paper in Britain, running from 1907 to 1918 and sometimes referred to as 'the suffragette bible'.[98] The paper innovated in women's publishing through its adaptation of popular journalistic devices to the suffrage cause, including cartoons, banner headlines and 'punchy' style, and its numerous 'conversion' narratives, a key genre of suffrage propaganda.[99] *The Suffragette*, the WSPU successor to *Votes for Women*, was published 1912–15. It was edited by Christabel Pankhurst, and was a forum for populist advocacy of militancy, as well as reflecting Pankhurst's interests in sexual oppression and 'purity'. Both journals carried relatively few substantial articles, and mainly served to report on fund-raising activities, parliamentary developments and demonstrations. 'Vanguard' feminists were scathing about such publications. Helena Swanwick (ironically, herself an editor of a suffrage paper) wrote of the 'deadly monotony of a partisan paper'; Rebecca West wrote:

On September the twelfth I spent one penny on the *Suffragette*, and I got too much for my money. For it was a paper rendered wholly undesirable and to people with a sense of humour and a sense of beauty wholly unreadable ... [100]

Few issues beyond immediate campaigning issues were covered in suffrage papers, though women's sexual oppression, legal position and employment sometimes featured. Beatrice Hastings (1879–1943), a prolific contributor to *The New Age* and an ambivalent avant-garde feminist, noted that if 'persons who think in terms of quality, as well as of quantity' were to consult *Votes for Women*, they would 'discover no single intelligible word – that is, intelligible outside the primitive groove of the W.S.P.U. news of caucuses, amounts of money received, cheerings-on to glory and abuse of opponents ... Its make-up proves that it circulates among the uninformed. Who could care about it?' *Votes for Women*'s high circulation, however, made it briefly a de facto representative of the women's movement.[101]

Women's journals aimed at the mainstream or 'respectable' British women's market were also launched in the early twentieth century, along with the more populist or activist suffrage journals. Alongside its own suffrage paper *The Common Cause* (1909–20), *The Englishwoman* (1909–21) was launched as the National Union of Women's Suffrage Societies' (NUWSS) attempt to provide a women-oriented equivalent of literary-intellectual magazines such as *Nineteenth Century* and the *Contemporary Review*. In the main, however, 'advanced' British readers of feminism turned to the 'radical' and unconventional papers such as the explicitly feminist *Freewoman*, and the *New Age*, edited by Alfred Orage as 'a forum for new progressive artistic tendencies and ideas from "advanced" thinkers'.

Alfred Orage's *New Age* had started life as a Fabian journal in 1907, but became a successful political and literary independent with strong provincial roots.[102] It provided a space for criticism of capitalism to be combined with art, literature and philosophy – a characteristic blend of early modernism. John Carswell describes it as filling a void in journalism, by extending to 'a new, literate, but relatively unprivileged public' a new type of journal: 'The earlier radical press ... had been strident, scandalous, and above all sectarian. *The New Age* was as much a journal of ideas as of comment, and it chimed with the aspirations of thousands of individuals and small groups throughout the country who were uncommitted, progressive and for the most part young'.[103]

It was perhaps the publishing innovation of *The Freewoman* to recognise the unattractiveness of radical papers such as *The New Age* to many female readers, through its lack of interest in the women's movement and condescending tone towards women. The identification of *The Freewoman*, like *The New Age*, as an 'open review' indicated a focus on the cultural and a political non-alignment and elitism which few suffrage journals could accept. Marsden purposely kept the price of *The Freewoman* at 3d, commenting that 'we are not proposing writing for women whose highest journalistic needs are realised at one penny'. Suffragists were incensed by both tone and content. When a writer in *The Morning Post* linked *The Freewoman*'s sexual explicitness to the politics of the suffrage movement, suffragists responded that *The Freewoman* 'no more represent[s] the general opinion of suffragists than, say, the opinions of the Mormons represents the Christianity of the Church of England'.[104] Avant-garde feminist periodical publishing was a highly novel entity in 1911, and struggled to construct a reading and contributing community. After a withdrawal of support from the first publisher and a refusal by the news retailer W. H. Smiths to stock it, *The Freewoman* suspended publication for some time. In its 1913 relaunch, it was foregrounded that '*The New Freewoman* is NOT a Suffrage Paper'. By 1914 its publicity stated in 'modernist' terms that 'It is *les jeunes* who make history and literature and science', in the '*revues libres*'. It continued: 'Even America has realised the importance of these young periodicals, and Chicago alone has more than London'.[105] The editors' gaze, then, had moved from London in 1911 to the United States by 1913.

American interest in feminism was extremely strong, prompting numerous periodical debates and special issues. One commentator noted that 'Our American newspapers are far in advance of the London press in reporting the activities of women, their clubs, organizations, etc., including the woman suffrage movement'.[106] A number of American suffrage journals emerged, and most also hosted debates on feminism. The national suffrage periodical, *The Woman's Journal*, was read in Chicago and on the East Coast with around 5,000 subscribers. This journal was a somewhat staid mixture of suffrage campaign news and commentary on

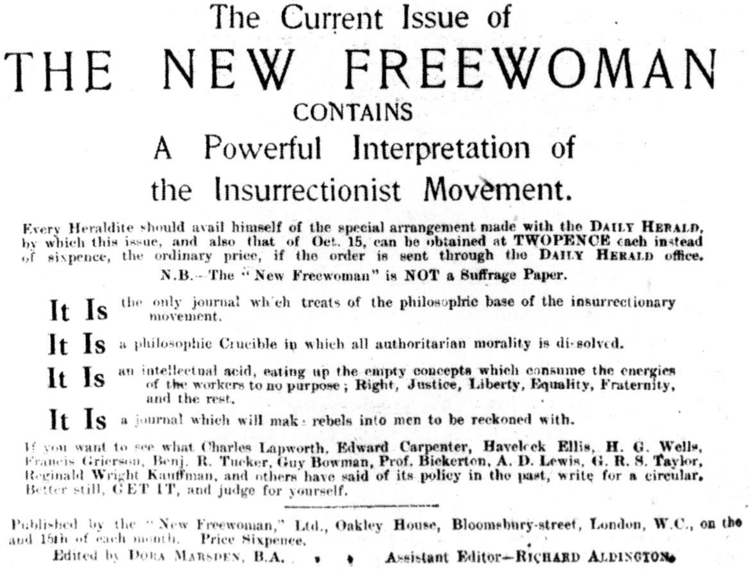

The Current Issue of

THE NEW FREEWOMAN

CONTAINS

A Powerful Interpretation of
the Insurrectionist Movement.

Every Heraldite should avail himself of the special arrangement made with the DAILY HERALD, by which this issue, and also that of Oct. 15, can be obtained at TWOPENCE each instead of sixpence, the ordinary price, if the order is sent through the DAILY HERALD office.

N.B.– The "New Freewoman" is NOT a Suffrage Paper.

It Is   the only journal which treats of the philosophic base of the insurrectionary movement.

It Is   a philosophic Crucible in which all authoritarian morality is dissolved.

It Is   an intellectual acid, eating up the empty concepts which consume the energies of the workers to no purpose ; Right, Justice, Liberty, Equality, Fraternity, and the rest.

It Is   a journal which will make rebels into men to be reckoned with.

If you want to see what Charles Lapworth, Edward Carpenter, Havelock Ellis, H. G. Wells, Francis Grierson, Benj. R. Tucker, Guy Bowman, Prof. Bickerton, A. D. Lewis, G. R. S. Taylor, Reginald Wright Kauffman, and others have said of its policy in the past, write for a circular. Better still, GET IT, and judge for yourself.

Published by the "New Freewoman," Ltd., Oakley House, Bloomsbury-street, London, W.C., on the 1st and 15th of each month.   Price Sixpence.

Edited by DORA MARSDEN, B.A.,   Assistant Editor—RICHARD ALDINGTON.

Figure 5: Advert for *The New Freewoman, Daily Herald*, 6 Dec. 1913

religion, and reports on women's success in the public sphere. It published in a dense typography, and also reproduced material from British papers, including *The Freewoman*. Heterodoxy feminists certainly supported the American suffrage journals; Rheta Childe Dorr became editor of *The Suffragist* in 1913, Rose Young edited *The Woman Citizen* from 1917,[107] and others wrote for *The Woman's Journal*. However, the suffrage press was not ideally suited to conveying feminist ideas, since it sought respectability and largely appealed to conventional public opinion.

More firmly feminist in tone than these suffrage papers was *The Forerunner*, another New York paper, but one with a national readership. This journal – without news-stand circulation, images, and with few adverts – represented the idiosyncratic politics of Charlotte Perkins Gilman, and was enormously influential in shaping American feminist thought.[108] Gilman named herself 'feminist' and 'socialist', though she preferred 'humanist' as her primary identity. Her paper, a monthly mix of fiction, poems and social commentary all written by herself, spanned an ambiguous space between all these identities. Gilman's radical views centred on reform of the home, dress reform, and women's economic and psychological independence. These concerns placed her journal very close to the British *Freewoman*, though it lacked the literary experimentalism and sexual explicitness of the latter, and cannot be easily categorised as 'avant-garde'.[109] *The Forerunner* was important in establishing the intellectual viability of independent feminist journalism, even if not its economic success. The paper probably never had more than 1,500 subscribers, and did not become self-supporting. Nonetheless, *The Forerunner* did inspire discussion circles, and revealed a desire on the part of American readers to participate in a face-to-face 'feminist' community, similar to that formed around the London Freewoman Discussion Circle.[110] It also formed a channel of transatlantic exchange of ideas, as the many letters to Gilman from European readers make clear. One reader, Ada Nield Chew, wrote to Gilman from Rochdale, England, to thank her for the stimulus of *The Forerunner*. Chew was an ILP member, and had heard Gilman speak in 1895. She only obtained *The Forerunner* in 1911, when it was lent by a friend during a seaside trip. Chew wrote, 'I want to acknowledge my debt to you, and to thank you for the 'clear shining' in the midst of darkness which your monthly *'Forerunner'* brings me'. On her first reading,

the sea and everything else was a blank! ... those three days stand out as a landmark in my life. I have, of course, become a subscriber to the magazine, and have eagerly read 'Human Work', 'the Home' and 'the Yellow Wallpaper' (ye gods! How well I understand that sketch!) ... it is not too much to say that you have opened a new world to me. Whereas I was bewildered and hopeless, though blindly in rebellion, now I see light. Whereas I was inclined to blame individuals now I see the cause and am disposed to be patient. Whereas I almost hated men – feeling in some vague way that they were enemies to be fought – now I know why they act as they do. Always a suffragist yet I felt it was not a complete answer to all we women are unconsciously striving after. Of course not! It's but a trifle compared with the whole.[111]

Discussions of 'women's issues' clearly stretched beyond suffrage and feminist journals, and also featured within the periodicals of the labour and socialist movements.[112] The editor of the Chicago/Kansas independent socialist monthly, *Progressive Woman*, perceived the new atmosphere around gender issues; in a letter to Charlotte Perkins Gilman, the editor claimed, 'We are trying to do something new for the women of America ... Our audience is an intelligent one, and is taking eagerly to the newer ideas concerning women'.[113] Debates on feminism also extended to women's magazines like *Good Housekeeping*, political weeklies such as *The New Republic* and *The New Review*, and illustrated monthlies like *The Forum, Current Opinion* and *The Century Magazine. Harper's Bazar* and *Harper's Weekly* were firmly pro-suffrage, and hosted discussions by 'advanced' feminists, though sometimes accompanied by editorial disclaimers.

American feminists were actively involved with contributing to, editing and reading a number of non-suffrage periodicals, including the anarchist paper *Mother Earth* and the fashion and arts magazine, *Delineator*. A 1916 bibliography of 'modern feminism' recommended that readers consult the 'aggressive journals of the Feminist movement' – *The Egoist* (as *The Freewoman* had then become), *The Little Review* and *The Masses*. *The Little Review*, founded by Chicagan Margaret Anderson (1886–1973) in 1914, hosted feminist discussion alongside the poems and literature of the modernist avant-garde.[114] Anderson, a self-identified feminist and avant-garde iconoclast, saw *The Little Review* as a vehicle for self-expression. Her feminism included a commitment to aesthetic sensibility and 'unreality' rather than duty and 'reality' for women. She also supported anarchist politics, and saw herself as a generation away from the social conscience of 'progressivism'. Rejecting heterosexuality and 'impervious to conventional romance', Anderson lived in a lesbian relationship with the *Little Review*'s co-editor, Jane Heap, and combined a pre-eminent commitment to avant-garde art with a highly oppositional and iconoclastic personal life. Her journal was eventually, like *The Egoist*, to suffer from the bullying tactics of Ezra Pound and his circle, and would shift away from the eclectic 'early modernism' towards the more exclusionary 'high modernists' of the early 1920s.

The Masses was a Greenwich Village radical paper, which became closely associated with the avant-garde feminists of Heterodoxy. This monthly, founded in 1911, was allied to the women's movement, with the by-line, 'an illustrated magazine of art, literature, politics and science ... devoted to the interests of the working people'. When financial difficulties loomed in 1912, its editor suggested a merger with the Chicago independent monthly, *Progressive Woman*. This suggests that the female readership was seen as core to the success of *The Masses*. In the end, the collective committee running *The Masses* preferred to continue to publish it alone; Max Eastman (1883–1969), a committed suffragist and feminist, was appointed as the new editor. After a doctorate under John Dewey at Columbia, Eastman had been a prominent founder of the Men's League for Women's Suffrage in 1909. In the years after this, however, he moved towards a feminist identity through his involvement with the artistic and political radicals of Greenwich Village; on his 1911 marriage to Ida Rauh, she retained her maiden name.[115] *The Masses* under Eastman came to inhabit a more flamboyant, cosmopolitan socialist space. It resembled the British *New Age* in its attempt to link art and politics, though its appeal was more popular, and its visual impact more powerful. Though *The Masses* did not pay its contributors or editor, it was swamped with material. *The Masses* printed readers' letters to create an interactive space for debate, and its poems, illustrations and fiction offered a stimulating space for contributors to discuss and depict sexuality, marriage and domesticity. Unlike *The New Age*, it was consistently pro-women's suffrage, and it never adopted the elitist tone of its British counterpart.[116]

Historians have claimed that it was *The Masses* that gave the terms 'feminism' and 'new woman' currency in America; this may be claiming too much, but like *The Freewoman*, *The Masses* had notoriety far beyond its circulation.[117] While *The Masses* was frequently satirical on the question of suffragists' class interests, it stood against the British government's mistreatment of suffragists, and was regarded by activist American women as 'feminist'. The journal's willingness to publicise and support the birth control activism of Margaret Sanger and Mary Ware Dennett indicated this feminist commitment. Despite what Sandra Adickes calls the 'matey, masculine quality' of the editors, a letter from Heterodoxy feminists in the February 1916 issue called them 'genuine warm-hearted feminists'. Adickes' reading of Eastman's editorials reveals what she sees as a paradox in his embrace of 'feminism' and yet his 'contempt for women in their present condition'. This, however, was a prevailing current within Edwardian and progressive era feminism, frequently expressed in terms that on some levels resembled anti-feminism. It is one of the over-arching arguments of this study that the political and cultural discourse of 'feminism' shared many features with that of 'anti-feminism' (unlike the more clearly defined positions of suffragist and anti-suffragist). Beatrice Hale commented on the 'curious cross-currents in the feminist, suffrage, and "anti" camps which cause each body to agree with their opponents on certain points'.[118] *The Little Review*, for example, insisted on reading as 'feminist' books such as the British writer Constance Gasquoine Hartley's *The Truth About Women*, which was, to say the least, highly ambiguous in its commitment to feminism.[119] Some readers of the feminist 'little magazines' found their ambiguity on anti-feminism and anti-suffragism troubling. But for an American reader, Rose Young,

Being an anti-suffragist by no means opposes one to far-reaching feministic conviction as to the individual development of women ... Dora Marsden, the most professedly individualistic woman in England today, the most relentless in her jeers and jibes at the spiritual subjection of women, is harshly, sneeringly anti-suffrage. So is individualistic Emma Goldman in this country ... Being a suffragist by no means implies being a feminist.[120]

Feminism, at least in its avant-garde varieties, thus included elements that had commonly been read as anti-feminist, and the two represent not polarised positions but different positions within a shared discourse about gender. Eastman's negativity towards conventional femininity was thus not unusual and does not point to any misogyny on his part.[121]

Though these key feminist texts and periodicals were highly influential, an equally dynamic, though more ephemeral, feminist intellectual milieu was found within the lectures, debates and discussion circles that were common within the British and American women's movements. There were some key institutions and sites, such as the New York Cooper Union, London's Chandos Hall or the Ethical Institutes, that hosted many lectures and debates. Feminism was described by its proponents as 'in the air', avidly discussed by 'average citizens' in the intimate setting of 'your home town'. The diaries and letters of two London-based *Freewoman* readers, Ruth Slate and Eva Slawson, suggest a very high level of everyday discussion of feminist issues (including free unions, birth control, motherhood and alternatives to it) within non-conformist lower-middle-class radical circles.[122] From everyday suburban teaparties, to discussion groups and experimental theatre, from Glasgow and Leeds to New York's Patchin Place or cheap bohemian restaurants, heated debates on personal liberation were heard.[123]

Sources for this diffuse level of feminist debate are sketchy; Inez Gillmore described her study at Radcliffe in the last years of the nineteenth century: 'Every day, after the comparison of Chaucer notes, during every fallow interval we could find thereafter, luncheon, unoccupied hours, long afternoon periods when college closed late, we talked of the status of women'. Elsie Clews Parsons described an environment in 1914 New York of salons, 'Woman's Clubs', 'feminist discussion parties' and 'talky talky dinners' on feminist issues. Heterodoxy was one among many, though it is the best documented of the mostly short-lived groups that formed conversational communities within the wider periodical communities that framed them. A 'charter member' of Heterodoxy, Clare Mumford, founded another luncheon club, Query, whose members were described by Inez Haynes Gillmore as 'a younger set' of literary and professional women, who gathered to discuss 'feministic' and political issues until the Second World War. Another discussion circle, the Heretics, also discussed feminism with intense interest, and included a number of feminist members – Henrietta Rodman, Freda Kirchwey, Alyse Gregory, Elsie Clews Parsons and Randolph Bourne.[124]

Bourne (1886–1918) was central to the early modernist culture of New York, a writer employed by the *New Republic*, European traveller, and one of the masculine figures who identified themselves as feminists. Suffering spinal tuberculosis as a child, Bourne was a flamboyant hunchback, commonly dressed in a black cloak and a very visible member of the Greenwich Village bohemians. Bourne was close to the left-wing cultural critics found within Columbia University, and gained a high profile through his contributions to the *Dial, Atlantic Monthly* and the *New Republic*. His friendship with Greenwich Village intellectual women such as Parsons and Gregory made him an important interlocutor in avant-garde feminism, and like Floyd Dell, he was comfortable with his role as a commentator on Anglo-American feminism. Though Bourne was ambivalent about the Heretics, he made it clear how essential these discussion groups and their associated periodicals were to Edwardian intellectual life. He wrote to Parsons that he had hoped that the Heretics would 'be one of the few centres of intellectual stimulation which life vouchsafes to me'; when it failed these hopes, he suggested another discussion group, centred on the *New Republic*. It was characteristic for Edwardian political discussion and exchange to be focused by and on a periodical community in this way, and Bourne expressed an optimism of the times when he suggested: 'Wouldn't it be an important thing to do to get a dozen very serious people and deliberately set about learning how to discuss, agreeing on a vocabulary, on categories, practising faithfully until the group was welded together into a real thinking nucleus?'[125]

In Britain, similar spaces of discussion existed. The Fabian Society Women's Groups offered discussion spaces for 'advanced' thinkers, as did the Ethical Societies and the Workers Education Association (WEA). Some discussion groups were based on a transatlantic impetus. Charlotte Perkins Gilman's work, for example, inspired a WEA class led by Ada Nield Chew in Rochdale in 1911. Chew wrote to Gilman, 'there has never been anything which I have enjoyed more, or from which I have profited more. The class has 42 members ... All have books, and as most of them had never heard of the point of view before there have been numerous shocks and violent shakings of prejudices'. Feminism was clearly still a highly controversial subject. This class seems to have had a long influence – during the 1920s and early 1930s, a 'Gilman study group' still survived in Rochdale, studying Gilman and contemporary feminists. Though Gilman's status as the leading American feminist had declined by the

Figure 6: Randolph Bourne, Columbia University Rare Book and Manuscript Library

middle of the 1910s in the United States, her work continued to have far-reaching resonances with some British feminists.

Discussion groups and lecturing at times led to periodical publications – many of the articles in the *International Journal of Ethics* initially came from Ethical Institute lectures. Conversely, periodicals such as *The Freewoman* or *The Forerunner* generated around themselves discussion and face-to-face meeting. This was not a feature of periodical readerships limited to feminist journals – Mary Gawthorpe recalled in her autobiography that as a member of the Labour Church in Leeds, Robert Blatchford's socialist paper *The Clarion* served as a focal point for her activism, and enabled her to meet others: 'We were comrades and we read *The Clarion* joyfully, not as a discipline ... *The Clarion* was a sort of nation-wide club on a non-dues paying basis which united readers everywhere in an atmosphere of camaraderie, whenever and wherever they met'.[126]

Perhaps influenced by such experiences of the substantial nature of periodical communities, the enthusiasm and controversy *The Freewoman* generated among readers inspired the creation of a fortnightly Discussion Circle, meeting in London from April 1912. The Circle seems to have attracted around fifty to a hundred participants, and spawned a number of smaller discussion groups that met at readers' houses. Rebecca West could not take the Circle entirely seriously, writing to Dora Marsden that it was 'like being in church', and suffering from 'an epidemic of kissing'. Others described it as intimidating. One *Freewoman* reader commented: 'I am half afraid of coming [to the Discussion Circle] anyway, as I am shy of clever people. You cannot have any idea of my ignorance, or of the absolute lack of opportunity for mental development I have had since I married and indeed before'.[127] Marsden, however, was so inspired by the development that she encouraged readers in other towns to set up similar circles, and one was advertised in Bristol. The London group provided a nucleus of support when *The Freewoman* ceased publication in 1911, and was important in helping *The New Freewoman* to be launched. The Discussion Circle was also significant in prompting the publication of exchanges and follow-up articles from discussions within *The Freewoman*, and played a key role in fostering experiences of 'collective reading'.

Even outside of such discussion forums, feminist journals may have been read collectively; one reader wrote from Manchester following the first issue of *The Freewoman*, describing how she could not obtain a copy and so went to her local WSPU office, to find a colleague 'sitting on a cupboard reading aloud to her people the Editorial notes on Miss P!! I've really never seen our crowd so excited and moved.' Copies were also passed around – an American supporter, Frances Björkman, described sending 'battered' copies of *The Freewoman* to Floyd Dell. In the United States, many had heard of the journal, but actual copies were precious and passed through the hands of many readers.[128]

Many *Freewoman* readers apparently knew each other personally, and so gained a sense of the 'Freewoman readership' of their location; this may have been particularly the experience of provincial readers of the journal. Winifred Hindshaw was able to comment: 'In Swansea three of us get *The Freewoman*'. Ann Ardis describes the reading communities of suffrage groups as sustained through collective spaces for reading, in informal and formal reading groups; many accounts of 'reading feminism' are similar.[129] For those reading *The Freewoman* under isolated circumstances, it seems to have served as an 'imagined community'. This concept has been characterised by Benedict Anderson as marked by 'deep horizontal comradeship', where members may never know each other, yet 'in the minds of each lives the image of their communion'.[130] Interactivity and responsiveness represent important aspects of the experience of reading feminist and 'advanced' periodicals. *The Masses* and the close-knit Greenwich Village community in which it was based, for example, offered a ready-made discussion circle in its collective editorial meetings. The relatively newly constituted and overlapping political reading communities of the early twentieth century – the feminist, the 'modern' or 'avant-garde', the socialist – were frequently collectively experienced, including discussion and friendship.

CONCLUSIONS: PERIODICAL CULTURE

The late Edwardian world of 'advanced' periodical publishing was an internally focused, complex pattern of ephemeral and under-funded periodical titles. The 'glue' for these intellectual networks was provided by the close personal associations, friendships, and face-to-face opportunities for discussion that flourished within the early twentieth century. This was an environment in which ideological divides were relatively porous, with a rich cross-fertilisation of ideas and discourse shared between periodicals, lectures and debates. 'Left' and 'right' political labels have little purchase on the politics and culture of these groupings.

George Bernard Shaw, looking back to the early days of *The New Age*, described Edwardian periodical culture as characterised by 'splenetic quarrelsomeness and cliquishness'.[131] The small circulation of even the most well-established or notorious of journals engaged in intellectual and political journalism brings into question the historical significance of these 'cliques'. Was 'avant-garde feminism' simply the realm of what Charlotte Shaw, the wife of George Bernard Shaw, described as 'a clever set'? Avant-garde feminists may have shared similar aims to the 'radicals' with whom they shared their public space and intellectual field, in hoping to bring about social change through reaching a small but powerful elite. *The New Age* strategy was assessed by a contemporary, Gerald Cumberland:

the men and women who read [the *New Age*] are the men and women who count – people who welcome daring and original thought ... Tens of thousands of people have been influenced by this paper who have never even heard its name. It does not educate the masses directly: it reaches them through the medium of its few but exceedingly able readers.[132]

This descriptions of 'people who count' may indicate avant-garde feminist hopes for what their lectures, periodicals and activism could

achieve, a strategy quite different to the mass support sought by the suffrage papers. Beatrice Hastings, for example, explicitly sought to bring
'people who matter' into the feminist movement, because she believed that
'Numbers are negligible nowadays. Statesmen know perfectly well how to
control numbers'.[133] She looked for 'the opportunity of joining a real
feminist league, with no calls to glory, . . . no deadly commercial dealings,
no ostrich tactics', in order to prevent the threatened temporary collapse of
the woman's movement. 'People scarcely bother to argue against it now'.

Hastings, a South African journalist closely linked to *The New Age* and
later to the avant-garde artistic and spiritualist circles in Paris, had voiced
her feminist convictions around the issue of women's choices in childbirth.
She claimed to be speaking from experience, though no records survive of
any children she may have had. But she was surprised to find that the
suffrage-feminist circles would not acknowledge her and refused to engage
with this controversial topic. Her book, titled in characteristic avant-garde
feminist terms, *Woman's Worst Enemy, Woman*, was published in 1909 by
the New Age Press. Hastings accused suffrage periodicals of refusing to
review it. Like so many others of the avant-garde, Hastings concluded that
the women's movement needed a new, rejuvenating basis, without needing
to appeal to the conventional values of a mass feminine audience.

This study contextualises 'vanguard feminism' within the 'splenetic'
Edwardian periodical culture as unashamedly elitist and controversialist.
Though only small numbers identified as 'feminists' in the early 1910s,
their ideas gained a relatively high profile; from the moment it was
coined, feminism was a concept that dominated headlines and political
argument, even if few were even clear as to what the term conveyed. It also
had an international appeal. Aided by its construction and development
within periodicals that could easily cross national boundaries, feminism
was widely understood to be a cosmopolitan project, sharing texts and
forming correspondence friendships transnationally. I now turn to one
such avenue of interaction, between Britain and the United States, which
formed a dominant, highly formative transatlantic relationship for
Edwardian feminists.

END NOTES

1. George Burman Foster, 'Philosophy of Feminism', *The Forum*, July 1914,
    10–22, esp. 15.
2. Stephen Koss, *The Rise and Fall of the Political Press in Britain: The Twentieth
    Century* (London, Hamish Hamilton, 1984); David Reed, *The Popular*

Magazine in Britain and the United States, 1880–1960 (London, The British Library, 1997).

3. Jose Harris, *Private Lives, Public Spirit: Britain 1870–1914* (London, Penguin, 1993), p. 5.

4. Joanna Bourke, *Working-Class Cultures in Britain, 1890–1960: Gender, Class and Ethnicity* (London, Routledge, 1994).

5. Michelle Tusan, 'Inventing the New Woman: Print Culture and Identity Politics During the Fin-de-siècle', *Victorian Periodicals Review*, 31:2 (1998); Ann Ardis, 'Organizing Women: New Woman Writers, New Woman Readers, and Suffrage Feminism', in *Victorian Women Writers and the Woman Question*, ed. Nicola D. Thompson (Cambridge, Cambridge University Press, 1999); Ann Heilmann, *New Woman Fiction: Women Writing First-Wave Feminism* (Basingstoke, Macmillan/Palgrave, 2000).

6. Key, *Woman Movement*, pp. 222–3.

7. Harris, *Private Lives, Public Spirit*; David Brooks, *Age of Upheaval: Edwardian Politics, 1899–1914* (Manchester, Manchester University Press, 1993).

8. Laura E. Nym Mayhall, *The Militant Suffrage Movement: Citizenship and Resistance in Britain, 1860–1930* (Oxford, Oxford University Press, 2003).

9. Holton, *Feminism and Democracy*.

10. Peter Conn, *The Divided Mind* (Cambridge, Cambridge University Press, 1983).

11. Sandra Adickes, *To Be Young Was Very Heaven: Women in New York Before the First World War* (New York, St Martin's Press, 1997), p. 10.

12. Christine Bolt, *The Women's Movements in the United States and Britain from the 1790s to the 1920s* (New York, Harvester Wheatsheaf, 1993), p. 215.

13. Walter Lippmann, 'The Woman's Movement', *The Forum*, Aug. 1914, 156; Conn, *The Divided Mind*; J. D. Buenker, J. C. Burnham and R. M. Crunden, *Progressivism* (Cambridge, Mass., Schenkman Publishers, 1977), p. 22; Daniel T. Rodgers, 'In Search of Progressivism', *Reviews in American History*, 10:4 (1982).

14. Floyd Dell, *Homecoming* (Washington, Kennikat Press, 1961), p. 218. The 'progressive era' perception of the urgency and timeliness of reform resulted in some new suffrage arguments. Traditional claims about women's domestic influence seemed unconvincing in the face of the large-scale changes and powers in society. Women felt a more pressing need for political influence, and Nancy Cott identifies a new rationale of voting in order to *preserve* the domestic sphere, from all the threats of cities, big business, immigrants and so on. This argument for suffrage was not found among nineteenth-century suffragists, Cott argues, and represents a powerful impetus for progressive era suffragism – an example of the cross-current of conservatism within 'progressivism'. Cott, *The Grounding of Modern Feminism*, p. 29.

15. Björkman to Jardine, 16 Aug. 1912, MWDP.

16. Buhle, *Feminism and its Discontents*; R. Porter and L. A. Hall, *The Facts of Life: The Creation of Sexual Knowledge in Britain 1650–1950* (New Haven, Yale University Press, 1995).

17. Adickes, *To Be Young Was Very Heaven*.

18. Anthony, *Feminism in Germany and Scandinavia*, pp. 230–1.

19. Susman, *Culture as History*.

20. Cott, *The Grounding of Modern Feminism*, p. 6.

21. Lippman, 'The Woman's Movement', 163; see Stansell, *American Moderns*, on the American 'bohemians' and their engagement with feminism.

22. Schreiner to Ellis, 7 Aug. 1912, in Olive Schreiner, *The Letters of Olive Schreiner 1876–1920*, ed. Cronwright-Schreiner (London, Unwin, 1924), pp. 312–13.

23. Mary (Mrs. Humphrey) Ward, *The Times*, 19 June 1912, quoted in a promotional circular for *The Freewoman* 'Thousand Club' Membership Establishment Fund, Dora Marsden Collection, Manuscripts Division, Department of Rare Books and Special Collections, Princeton University Library, box IV folder 3 (henceforth DMC, with box and folder numbers appended).

24. Benjamin Vestal Hubbard, *Socialism, Feminism, and Suffragism, the Terrible Triplets* (Chicago, American Publishing Company, 1915), p. 144. *The Freewoman*'s circulation, however, was small, probably around 200–2,500 copies of each issue. *The New Freewoman* issued 2,000 copies of early issues, but in August 1913 the editor's accounts show only 266 guaranteed subscribers; Jane and Mary Nicholson Lidderdale, *Dear Miss Weaver: Harriet Shaw Weaver 1876–1961* (New York, The Viking Press, 1970), p. 69. See also Fifield to Marsden, DMC 9 May 1913: II, 30, and G. C. Beresford, DMC May 1912: II, 1.

25. Two in-depth studies of Dora Marsden and *The Freewoman* exist: Les Garner, *A Brave and Beautiful Spirit: Dora Marsden 1882–1960* (Aldershot, Avebury, 1990); Bruce Clarke, *Dora Marsden and Early Modernism* (Ann Arbor, University of Michigan Press, 1996).

26. Sandra Stanley Holton, *Suffrage Days: Stories from the Women's Suffrage Movement* (London, Routledge, 1996), pp. 114–55; Mary Gawthorpe, *Up Hill to Holloway* (Penobscot, Maine, Traversity Press, 1962).

27. Teresa Billington-Greig, 'A Free Feminist Platform', *New Age*, 30 March 1911, 525.

28. Billington-Greig, *The Militant Suffrage Movement: Emancipation in a Hurry* (London, F. Palmer, 1911).

29. See Garner, *A Brave and Beautiful Spirit*, for a biographical account of Dora Marsden's life, and Clarke, *Dora Marsden and Early Modernism*, for an intellectual biography. Marsden eventually retired into seclusion to write philosophy, became psychotically depressed and was held as a patient in a Scottish mental hospital for twenty-five years until her death in 1960.

30. The actress Ellen Terry was offered by Dora Marsden as an example of an existing 'freewoman', apparently on the grounds of her artistic genius,

abandonment of her husband and economic independence. In the United States, Floyd Dell suggested that the IWW agitator Elizabeth Gurley Flynn was a typical 'freewoman'.

31. See Claire Eustance and Angela John (eds.), *The Men's Share? Masculinities, Male Support and Women's Suffrage in Britain, 1890–1920* (London, Routledge, 1997).

32. Sandra Holton notes that relations between 'the WSPU leadership and its male sympathisers deteriorated rapidly from the end of 1911', Holton, *Suffrage Days*, p. 184.

33. *New Age*, 23 Nov. 1911, 95.

34. Schreiner to Havelock Ellis, 7 Aug. 1912, in Schreiner, *The Letters of Olive Schreiner*, p. 312.

35. AH to Marsden, DMC 24 Nov. 1911: III, 1.

36. Clarke, *Dora Marsden and Early Modernism*, p. 13.

37. Edwin Herrin to Marsden, DMC 27 Jan. 1913: III, 2.

38. Gilman, reported in the *New York Times*, 2 April 1914, 11.

39. Elsie Clews Parsons, *Journal of a Feminist*, ed. Margaret C. Jones (Bristol, Thoemmes Press, 1994), pp. 87, 90. On Clews, see Desley Deacon, *Elsie Clews Parsons: Inventing the Modern Life* (Chicago, University of Chicago Press, 1997); 'Feminism a Cry for Better Lovers, Hutchins Hapgood Tells Women', *The Washington Post*, 23 Feb. 1915, 4.

40. Dell, *Women as World Builders*, pp. 19–20.

41. Margaret Marsh has described the 'feminist mainstream' as including suffragists, the women's club movement and temperance/social purity movements, though this would be better termed 'the women's movement' in place of feminism: Margaret Marsh, 'The Anarchist-Feminist Response to the "Woman Question" in Late Nineteenth Century America', *American Quarterly*, 30:4 (Autumn 1978), 534.

42. Stansell, *American Moderns*, pp. 48–53; Francis, *Secret Treachery of Words*.

43. Cott, *The Grounding of Modern Feminism*, p. 15.

44. *Common Cause*, 23 Nov. 1911, 577. Dell identified himself and his *Friday Literary Review* as in the middle of, and even symbolic of, the new 'modern movement', of which feminism was an integral part. Dell, *Homecoming*, p. 218.

45. Mina Loy, 'Feminist Manifesto', in *Modernism: An Anthology of Sources and Documents*, ed. V. Kolocotroni *et al.* (Edinburgh, Edinburgh University Press, 1998). On Loy's engagement with feminism, see Carolyn Burke, *Becoming Modern: The Life of Mina Loy* (New York, Farra, Straus & Giroux, 1996).

46. Aileen S. Kraditor, *The Ideas of the Woman Suffrage Movement, 1890–1920* (New York, Columbia University Press, 1965).

47. See for example Key, *Woman Movement*, pp. 222–3, and Dale, 'The Term "Feminists"', *New York Times*, 25 May 1914, 10.

48. Elizabeth Robins, 'The Feministe Movement In England,' *Collier's Weekly*, 29 June 1907; Mary Louise Roberts, *Disruptive Acts: The New Woman in Fin-de-siècle France* (Chicago, University of Chicago Press, 2002), p. 39.

49. Belfort Bax, *Essays in Socialism, New and Old* (London, E. Grant Richards, 1906), pp. 306–19.

50. Additionally, some Heterodoxy members were or had been active suffragists, mostly with the NAWSA. Judith Schwarz, *Radical Feminists of Heterodoxy, Greenwich Village 1912–1940* (Norwich, Vt.: New Victoria Publishers, 1986); June Sochen, *The New Woman, Feminism in Greenwich Village, 1910–20* (New York: Quadrangle Books, 1972).

51. Schwarz, *Radical Feminists of Heterodoxy*, p. 24.

52. Woman's Future, *Evening Standard and St James's Gazette*, 25 Oct. 1911, 20.

53. Hale, *What Women Want*, pp. vii, viii.

54. Marie Jenney Howe, 'Feminism', in 'A Feminist Symposium', *New Review*, Aug. 1914, 441.

55. Rose Young, 'What is Feminism?' 679; 'When the war ends . . .', *Washington Post*, 1 Oct. 1916, 13.

56. *Forum* editorial, Jan. 1912, 125.

57. Beatrice Webb, *New Statesman*, 1 Nov. 1913, iii.

58. Ethel Snowden, *The Feminist Movement* (London, Collins, 1913); Marsden to Floyd Dell, 10 May 1913, Box 10, Folder 337, Floyd Dell Papers, Midwest Manuscript Collection, The Newberry Library, Chicago (henceforth FDP).

59. Hapgood, 'What Women Are After', *Harper's Weekly*, 16 Aug. 1913, 28–9, and 6 Sept. 1913, 22 and cover page.

60. Anon., *Harper's Weekly*, 30 Aug. 1913, 32; Olga Nethersole, 'After Two Years', *Harper's Weekly*, 6 Dec. 1913.

61. Paul Jordan Smith, *The Soul of Woman: An Interpretation of the Philosophy of Feminism* (San Francisco, Paul Elder, 1916), pp. 65–6.

62. Adickes, *To Be Young Was Very Heaven*, p. 88. See also Schwarz, *Radical Feminists of Heterodoxy*, pp. 27–9.

63. Parsons, *Journal of a Feminist*, p. 78, original emphasis.

64. K. Manton, 'The Fellowship of the New Life: English Ethical Socialism Reconsidered', *History of Political Thought*, 24:2 (2003).

65. Marsden to Edna Kenton, 22 Feb. 1913, MWDP.

66. *FW*, 7 March 1912, 314.

67. Louise W. Kneeland, 'Feminism and Socialism', in 'A Feminist Symposium', *New Review*, Aug. 1914, 442.

68. The British women's suffrage movement, with its roots in the textile towns in Lancashire and in Manchester radical politics, had always sustained good links with working-class women, though not always with the representatives of working-class politics. In the United States, Elsie Clews Parsons pointed out the highly conventional social assumptions of suffragists, who were still strongly concerned with chaperonage and social propriety, Elsie Clews Parsons, 'Feminism and Conventionality', *Annals of the American Academy of Political and Social Science*, 56:145 (Nov. 1914), 48. The example of discipline and organisation provided by massive strikes of women garment workers between 1909 and 1911 did inspire many suffragists to incorporate working-class women, though normally in a tokenist fashion. The Equality

League of Self Supporting Women, founded in New York in 1907, adopted tactics already common in Britain such as mass parades and open-air meetings, allowing more working women to participate, as audiences and marchers. The Equality League eventually however became the Women's Political Union and, like the WSPU, distanced itself from 'class politics'. See Ellen Carol DuBois, *Harriot Stanton Blatch and the Winning of Woman Suffrage* (New Haven, Yale University Press, 1997).

69. Marsden, *FW* 23 Nov. 1911, 3; advertisement in *New Age*, 23 Nov. 1911, 95; Young, *New York Times*, 18 Feb. 2 quoted in Schwarz, *Radical Feminists of Heterodoxy*, pp. 25.

70. Rheta Childe Dorr, *A Woman of Fifty* (New York, Funk and Wagnalls, 1924), pp. 271, 268.

71. Kenton, *Delineator*, 'Feminism will give men more fun, women greater scope, children better parents, life more charm', July 1914, 17, original emphasis.

72. Kenton, *Delineator*, 'Feminism will give...', and Cott, *The Grounding of Modern Feminism*, p. 39; Schwarz, *Radical Feminists of Heterodoxy*, p. 85.

73. Hale, *What Women Want*, p. 6.

74. Olive Schreiner, *Woman and Labour* (London, Virago, 1978; orig. 1911), pp. 82, 121.

75. Ford to Edward Carpenter, Edward Carpenter Papers, Sheffield Archives, Sheffield Libraries and Information Services (henceforth ECP); Schreiner, *Woman and Labour*, p. 147.

76. Buhle, *Feminism and its Discontents*, pp. 39–43.

77. Marian Cox, 'Bergson's Message to Feminism', *The Forum*, May 1913, 552; see also Florence Guertin Tuttle, *The Awakening of Woman: Suggestions from the Psychic Side of Feminism* (New York, The Abingdon Press, 1915), p. 13.

78. Dorr, *A Woman of Fifty*, p. 245, quoted in Cott, *The Grounding of Modern Feminism*, p. 46.

79. Lee, *Gospels of Anarchy*, p. 263; Patricia Pulham, 'A Transatlantic Alliance: Charlotte Perkins Gilman and Vernon Lee', in *Feminist Forerunners: New Womanism and Feminism in the Early Twentieth Century*, ed. Ann Heilmann (London, Pandora Press, 2003).

80. Hale, *What Women Want*, pp. 211–12.

81. Gilman, *Forerunner*, Jan. 1916, 24–5. There is, of course, a wider story to tell about the transnational basis of modern feminism in additional national contexts. W. L. George, for example, in addition, listed the Austrian feminist Rosa Mayreder as a founder of modern feminism, *Atlantic Monthly*, Dec. 1913, 727. Mayreder's *Survey of the Woman Problem* was translated from the German and published in Britain in 1913. In it, Mayreder complained of 'the vulgar mental habits of the present day which tend to confound the superior individual, the man who rises above the average, with the mass'. Feminism was to be an exploration of these superior individuals. Rosa Mayreder, *A Survey of the Woman Problem*, trans. Herman Scheffauer (London, William Heinemann, 1913), pp. vii-viii.

82. Isadora Duncan, 'What Dancing Should Be', in Duncan, *The Art of the Dance*, ed. Sheldon Cheney (New York, Theatre Arts, 1928), p. 73. See Francis, *Secret Treachery of Words*, Chapter 1; Ann Daly, *Done Into Dance: Isadora Duncan in America* (Bloomington, Indiana University Press, 1995).
83. Isadora Duncan, *My Life* (London, Victor Gollancz, 1928), pp. 71–2, 73.
84. Duncan, 'The Dance of the Future' (1903) in Duncan, *The Art of the Dance*, p. 62.
85. 'Interviewing Isadora', *New York Morning Telegraph*, 14 Feb. 1915, quoted in Peter Kurth, *Isadora: A Sensational Life* (London, Little, Brown, 2001), p. 576 n. 37.
86. Ruth Hall, *Marie Stopes: A Biography* (London, Andre Deutsch, 1977), p. 42.
87. W. R. Titterton, 'The Maud Allen Myth', *New Age*, 27 June 1908, 171–2, and 'Isadora Duncan Preaching', *New Age*, 18 July 1908, 226.
88. Tierl Thompson, *Dear Girl: The Diaries and Letters of Two Working Women, 1897–1917* (London, The Woman's Press, 1987), pp. 120–1.
89. *Harper's Weekly*, 29 Nov. 1913, 5.
90. Eastman, in Arnold Genthe, *Isadora Duncan: Twenty-Four Studies* (New York, Mitchell Kennerley, 1929), n. p.; Dufour promotional pamphlet, MWDP, u.d.
91. These include Elsie Clews Parsons, *Fear and Conventionality* (Chicago, University of Chicago Press, 1997); Parsons, *The Old-Fashioned Woman* (New York, Arno Press, 1972; orig. 1913).
92. Parsons, *Journal of a Feminist*, pp. 13–14.
93. DuBois, *Harriot Stanton Blatch*, p. 209; Stansell, *American Moderns*, p. 82; *Good Housekeeping*, May 1914, 681.
94. Charlotte Perkins Gilman, 'As to "Feminism"', *Forerunner*, Feb. 1914, 45; Clews Parsons, 'Feminism and the Family', *International Journal of Ethics* (henceforth *IJE*), Oct. 1917, 52–8; Gilmore, 'Feminism', *Harper's Magazine*, 11 March 1916, 31.
95. Anthony, *Feminism in Germany and Scandinavia*, p. 6; Smith, *Soul of Woman*.
96. Philippa Levine, ' "The Humanising Influences of Five O'Clock Tea": Victorian Feminist Periodicals', *Victorian Studies*, 33 (Winter 1990), 299.
97. Levine, 'Humanising Influences', 302. See also Kate Flint, *The Woman Reader: 1837–1914* (Oxford, Clarendon Press, 1993), pp. 159–60; Margaret Beetham and Kay Boardman, *Victorian Women's Magazines* (Manchester, Manchester University Press, 2001), Chapter 6.
98. *Votes for Women* was originally the organ of the WSPU, but after the expulsion of Emmeline and Fred Pethick Lawrence in 1912, it became an independent weekly or monthly. In 1909 it had a circulation of around 30,000, and at its peak, sustained around 50,000 readers.
99. Flint, *The Woman Reader*, pp. 14, 234–5; Kabi Hartman, ' "What Made Me a Suffragette": The New Woman and the New (?) Conversion Narrative', *Women's History Review*, 12:1 (2003).

100. Helena Swanwick, *I Have Been Young* (London, Gollancz, 1935), p. 231; West, 'On Mentioning the Unmentionable', *The Clarion*, 26 Sept. 1913, reprinted in Jane Marcus, *The Young Rebecca: Writings of Rebecca West 1911–1917* (London, Macmillan, 1982), pp. 202–6.

101. 'To Your Posts, Feminists!' By D. Triformis [Beatrice Hastings], *New Age*, 16 Feb. 1911, 368. Other suffrage papers included *Common Cause*, the journal of the NUWSS, which ran from 1909 to 1920, with editors including Helena Swanwick, Clementina Black and Maude Royden. *The Vote* was the longest running of all the suffrage journals, published between 1909 and 1933 as the official journal of the Women's Freedom League; David Doughan and Denise Sanchez, *Feminist Periodicals 1855–1984* (Brighton, The Harvester Press, 1987), pp. xii, 25.

102. Tom Villis, 'Early Modernism and Exclusion: The Cultural Politics of Two Edwardian Periodicals, *The New Age* and the *New Witness*', *University of Sussex Journal of Contemporary History*, 5 (2002), 1; Wallace Martin, *The New Age Under Orage: Chapters in English Cultural History* (Manchester, Manchester University Press, 1967). *The New Age* sustained a circulation ranging from highs of 22,000 to a more moderate average of around 3,000 each week.

103. John Carswell, *Lives and Letters* (New York, New Directions, 1978), p. 35.

104. Marsden, *FW*, 23 Nov. 1911, 3; Catherine Furley Smith, *The Morning Post*, 26 July 1912, 5.

105. *Daily Herald*, 6 Dec. 1913, 6; Harriet Shaw Weaver Papers, British Library, vol. 57353.

106. Mary Winsor, 'The Militant Suffrage Movement', *Annals of the American Academy of Political and Social Science*, Nov. 1914, 138.

107. *The Woman Citizen* ran from 1917 to 1927, as an amalgamation of *The Woman Voter*, *The Woman's Journal* and *National Suffrage News*.

108. Cott, *The Grounding of Modern Feminism*, pp. 41–2, 48–9.

109. Gilman's exclusive personal writing, editing and publishing of *The Forerunner*, meant that it lacked the crucial sense of community and meeting of like minds that made *The Freewoman* so vibrant and full of contestation. Readers' voices were frequently curtailed by Gilman's editing, and only functioned as a foil to her own views.

110. In May 1914, Gilman reported that a 'Gilman Circle' had been founded in Tacoma, Washington, and that numerous other cities had 'Forerunner Clubs'. (Gilman, *Forerunner*, May 1914 p. 140; see 19 Dec. 1914, Mary Glenhauser to Gilman, Schlesinger Library, Radcliffe Institute for Advanced Study, Harvard University, Charlotte Perkins Gilman Papers, 002727020 (henceforth cited as CPGP).) These may perhaps have been modelled on the Freewoman Circle, which American readers had admired.

111. Chew to Gilman, 10 Dec. 1911, CPGP.

112. The 'radical' papers characteristically combined an interest in the woman's movement with their primary focus on labour questions. Unlike similar papers in Britain, these periodicals were on the whole pro-suffrage, and even

willing to explore 'feminism', as the 1914 'Feminist Symposium' in the *New Review* suggested.

113. Kiichi Kanecko, to Gilman, 24 March 1909, CPGP. Initially titled *The Socialist Woman*, this periodical was published from 1907 to 1914, edited by Josephine Conger-Kaneko and her husband Kiichi Kaneko. It represented the interests of women within the Socialist Party, though it had no official status. By 1910 it had a circulation of 12,000–15,000. Kathleen Endres and Therese Luck (eds.), *Women's Periodicals in the United States: Social and Political Issues* (Westport, Conn., Greenwood Press, 1996), pp. 308–15.

114. Smith, *Soul of Woman*, p. 66. See Stansell, *American Moderns*, pp. 175–6, 197–208; Francis, *Secret Treachery of Words*, pp. 39–75.

115. William L. O'Neill, *The Last Romantic: A Life of Max Eastman* (New York, Oxford University Press, 1978).

116. Rebecca Zurier, *Art for the Masses: A Radical Magazine and its Graphics* (Philadelphia, Temple University Press, 1988).

117. Margaret C. Jones, *Heretics and Hellraisers: Women Contributors to The Masses, 1911–1917* (Austin, University of Texas Press, 1993), pp. 2, 4.

118. Hale, 'Suffrage Cross-Currents', *New York Times*, 30 March 1914, 8. See also Brian Harrison, *Separate Spheres: The Opposition to Women's Suffrage in Britain* (London, Croom Helm, 1978); Julia Bush, 'British Women's Anti-Suffragism and the Forward Policy, 1908–1914', *Women's History Review*, 11:3 (2002).

119. See Clara E. Laughlin, 'Women and the Life Struggle', *Little Review*, April 1914, 20–4.

120. Rose Young, 'What is Feminism?' 679–80.

121. Adickes, *To Be Young Was Very Heaven*, p. 192.

122. Key, *Woman Movement*, p. 64; Rose Young, 'What is Feminism?' 6791; Thompson, *Dear Girl*.

123. Christine Stansell has documented the importance of, and special place given to, 'talk' amongst feminists and radicals of bohemian New York; Stansell, *American Moderns*, pp. 73–4. See also Katharine Cockin, *Women and Theatre in the Age of Suffrage: The Pioneer Players 1911–25* (Basingstoke: Palgrave Macmillan, 2001), on feminist experimental theatre in Britain.

124. Gillmore (Irwin), *Adventures of Yesteryear*, unpublished autobiography, Schlesinger Library, Radcliffe Institute for Advanced Study, Harvard University, Inez Haynes Gillmore Papers, 000605000, p. 208; Gillmore, *Adventures of Yesteryear*, pp. 424–30. See correspondence between Bourne, Parsons and Alyse Gregory, in Elsie Clews Parsons Papers, American Philosophical Society, Philadelphia, PA (henceforth ECPP), and Randolph Bourne, *The Letters of Randolph Bourne: A Comprehensive Edition*, ed. Eric J. Sandeen (Troy, NY, Whitslon Publishing, 1981).

125. Leslie J. Vaughan, *Randolph Bourne and the Politics of Cultural Radicalism* (Lawrence, Kan., University of Kansas Press, 1997). Bourne to Parsons, ECPP 26 Oct. 1915 and 21 Feb. 1916.

126. Gawthorpe, *Up Hill to Holloway*, p. 175.

127. West to Marsden, DMC u.d.: I, 26; Boord to Marsden, DMC 20 April 1912: II, 27. See Garner, *A Brave and Beautiful Spirit*, pp. 73–5; Clarke, *Dora Marsden and Early Modernism*, pp. 73–81; Lucy Bland, *Banishing the Beast: English Feminism and Sexual Morality 1885–1914* (London, Penguin, 1995), pp. 269–71.

128. Miss Allan to Mary Gawthorpe, DMC 27 Nov. 1911: II, 25; Björkman to Dell, 5 Aug. 1912, Box 3, Folder 92, FDP.

129. Winifred Hindshaw to Marsden, DMC 26 Dec. 1911: III, 3; Ardis, 'Organizing Women', p. 193.

130. Benedict Anderson, *Imagined Communities: Reflections on the Origins and Rise of Nationalism* (London, Verso, 1982), pp. 6–7.

131. Shaw, *New Age*, 15 Nov. 1934, 100.

132. Gerald Cumberland, *Set Down in Malice* (New York, Bretano, 1919), p. 130.

133. Hastings (D. Triformis), 'To Your Posts, Feminists!' *New Age*, 16 Feb. 1911, 368.

CHAPTER 2

Transatlantic interchanges and rival storm centres

The collection of 'modern' beliefs about the relations of the sexes that came to be referred to as feminism in the first decade of the twentieth century has largely been read by historians as a product of the suffrage struggle, and the allied nineteenth-century social movements such as temperance, abolitionism, and social purity. One of the purposes of this book is to contest this view, and to uncover the ways in which ideas from a much wider variety of sources were influential upon Edwardian feminists without necessarily originating within the suffrage movement or the wider women's movement. In so doing, I stress the novelty and fluidity of the identity 'feminist'. But there is an additional motivation to this 'uncoupling' of feminism from suffragism, and that is to extend our understanding of political argument within feminism to encompass not just the intellectual landscape of one country, but also the transnational exchanges that shaped political discourses.

An important site of feminist transnational interaction was between Britain and the United States, and this chapter will examine its significance in shaping the feminist intellectual milieu. As we shall see, there has been a tendency to regard Britain as the influential 'storm centre' of the women's movement. Indeed, historians have tended to see Anglo-American exchanges as marked by asymmetry, with American 'behindness' in comparison to Britain becoming a 'hardened trope' not only in the women's movement, but in much broader areas of social policy.[1] Yet the avant-garde strand of feminism suggests a much more even-handed transatlantic heritage, a genuinely Anglo-American intellectual formation.

Transnational interactions are not easy for a historian to gauge and assess – hard questions must be asked concerning the depth and reach of the relationships that can be traced across national boundaries, and the extent to which shared languages took on different shades of meaning in diverse national contexts. Recognising the weakness of simple ideas of 'diffusion' or 'influence', Daniel Rodgers has suggested a framework for assessing the depth of transnational interactions. Interaction commences with the diffusion and sharing of key texts, and deepens via the construction of friendship or professional networks. Relationships become more significant when techniques and practices are shared, and this may include the sharing of languages, or construction of semantic resources that were not previously available. Lastly, Rodgers suggests that transnational associations and co-ordinated political action represent two final steps of deepening. The suffrage movement operated transnationally at all levels except perhaps the fifth of this framework, that of joint political action. Reading matter, strong friendship networks, the sharing of political agitation and publicity techniques and the establishment of international suffrage associations have all been well documented by historians.[2] This chapter traces the transnational exchanges within feminism as emergent and distinct from the transnational movements that initially sustained it (suffrage, socialism, labour politics, anarchism), and assesses the depth of the feminist relationships that emerge.

SUFFRAGE AND FEMINISM TRANSATLANTIC[3]

Historians have been fascinated by the links between America and Britain within the women's movement, though suffrage exchanges have dominated the literature. A shared 'founding moment' for Anglo-American feminists and suffragists was the notorious exclusion of women delegates at the 1840 World Anti-Slavery Convention in London, which prompted American women to organise the Seneca Falls Convention in 1848. Abolitionism was an extremely important transatlantic channel of influence, with Americans seen as both spearheading the anti-slavery movement, and as backward and 'uncivilised' in their racist practices. Though American women took the initiative at Seneca Falls and other women's conventions, the predominant picture that emerges from the historiography is one of British influence shaping the American women's movement. It is clear that American suffragists and feminists did look to Britain as a source of political radicalism and ideas. The British suffrage movement was generally regarded by the American suffragists, whether they agreed with militancy or not, as 'advanced' in comparison to America, though Britain was regarded as a more conservative country. British suffragists and activists continually toured America to raise money and influence public opinion, and British journals were widely read. Activists saw the two national contexts as closely linked. One wrote to Mary Gawthorpe when she left Britain for the States in 1915 that she regretted Mary's move, but only for personal reasons as 'any improvement in the status of women there reacts here'.[4]

How closely linked were American and British periodical communities? American readers were kept well informed of the British press
through the publication of 'mainstream' journals such as *Living Age*
and the *Review of Reviews*, which reproduced articles from leading British
periodicals. Other American periodicals reproduced occasional British
articles, and there were also a number of American editions of
British journals, such as the *Westminster Review*. British journals operated
in a similar fashion; the London edition of the *Review of Reviews*
reproduced American articles for British readers, and American magazines such as *Century* and *Delineator* produced British editions. Avant-
garde periodicals such as Margaret Anderson's *Little Review* published a
regular 'London letter', as well as commentaries on British politics. For
some Edwardian titles, there developed a long-standing tradition of
transatlantic commentary and reproduction, such as the relationships
which existed between the British *New Statesman* and the American *New
Review* and *New Republic*, or the joint Anglo-American publication,
International Studio.

Within the suffrage movement, there is much evidence of interaction,
with subscriptions and exchanges between the journals of the large suffrage
organisations, however diverse their tactics. British suffrage papers, particularly *Votes for Women*, were popular in America. Emphasising the
shared interests of their readerships, the most popular and long-established
American suffrage paper, the *Woman's Journal* (1870–1917), offered a free
year's subscription to *Votes for Women*, *Common Cause* or *The Vote* for
readers bringing in four new subscribers. Articles, cartoons and letters were
frequently exchanged between *Votes for Women* and the *Woman's Journal*,
though the latter, in an attempt to gain authority for the American
struggle, proclaimed itself the 'elder sister' of the suffrage papers to counter
the continual references from British suffragists to their American 'younger
sisters'. British suffrage figures were reported in American papers as sensational figures of innovation and militancy, and American suffragists read
British suffrage periodicals regularly and discussed the suffrage news from
Britain with great familiarity.[5]

Britain was regarded, as American journalist Elizabeth Robins put it, as
'the Mother of the world-wide New Movement', or the 'storm centre'. The
'storm centre' metaphor became very widely used after the start of the
WSPU militancy, and corresponded to a residual sense of Britain being at
the centre of its imperial possessions, a global leader in democracy through
its 'mother of all parliaments', as well as being the most 'advanced' site for
the struggle for women's rights, and in that sense regarding itself as the

Figure 7: *Votes For Women*, 20 Oct. 1911, p. 33 'I had better hurry up and enfranchise the women of my country or I shall get left behind'

most civilised of countries. American 'rivalry' was not welcomed; NUWSS leader Millicent Fawcett was dismissive about the American suffrage movement, branding the United States constitution 'the most conservative on earth'. She stressed the distinctiveness of 'English' national character, and its role in shaping British suffragism. Historians have felt that there was a diminishing British interest in American speakers as the twentieth century progressed.[6] It seems that some suffragists regarded the two national contexts as competing for both contemporary influence and historical legitimacy, rather than genuinely occupying a shared space. Though there was a rhetoric of sisterhood within suffrage periodicals, a strong sense of rivalry also emerges; Annie Kenney, a leading WSPU militant, commented after her 1914 speaking tour of the United States that 'American women are not as free as British women'.[7] British suffragists gave somewhat laboured explanations of why Britain was still at the forefront of the suffrage struggle, despite the suffrage victories in the American Western states.[8] Nonetheless, techniques and practices were exchanged between the two national contexts.

Amongst suffragists, the influence of the British militants on Americans is well documented, and credited for bringing pageantry, picketing and exploitation of the media to American suffragism. Most notably, the daughter of Elizabeth Cady Stanton, Harriot Stanton Blatch, lived in England for twenty years, returning to America to transform the National American Woman Suffrage Association (NAWSA) using British suffragist techniques such as mass parades. Blatch also sponsored the visits of British suffragist speakers, and she recalled the suffrage struggle as one of British influence:

The work of the Pankhursts at home was the inspiration of similar work abroad. The Pankhursts raised the question of votes for women from a movement of polite propaganda to one of the hottest political questions of the twentieth century, not only in Great Britain but in other lands as well. Suffragette methods modified to meet other conditions were adopted in the United States to good purpose. The vote here, as in England, was won by changing a gentle skirmish of words into a bombardment of deeds.[9]

Carrie Chapman Catt (NAWSA president between 1900 and 1904 and from 1915) also carved out a channel of transatlantic influence. Catt visited England and numerous other countries during world tours in 1911 and 1913. She boasted that during these tours she and her colleagues had, in keeping with the American republican tradition, 'left the seeds of revolution behind us, and the hope of liberty in many souls'. But Catt found it startling that overall, 'we have got much more than we gave – an experience so upsetting to all our preconceived notions that it is difficult to estimate its influence upon us'. For all the rhetoric of suffrage as a world movement, it was clearly still a surprise to leading American suffragists to learn from experiences abroad. Convinced of the importance of international exchanges within suffrage circles, Catt acted as the president of the International Woman Suffrage Alliance from 1904 to 1923, and worked closely with Millicent Fawcett of the NUWSS. Additionally, Alice Paul, Lucy Burns, Rheta Childe Dorr and many others provided another conduit of techniques through their work with the WSPU. Burns and Paul returned to America in 1913 to revolutionise the NAWSA Congressional Committee into a separate 'militant' organisation, the Congressional Union for Women's Suffrage (later the National Women's Party). They were perceived as working along 'British lines' in reviving the federal-level suffrage campaign, using flamboyant (but not violent) publicity tactics, and bringing in the WSPU-inspired policy of working against all ruling party candidates.[10]

The Anglo-American relationship, however, was by no means only one of Americans learning from the British example. Some British suffragists even found themselves ostracised by wary American suffragists. Kitty Marion, a WSPU militant deported from Britain in 1915 because of her German birth, wrote of being treated 'like dirt' by Alva Belmont of the Congressional Union who despised Marion's arson tactics.[11] Marion found a welcome instead amongst feminist birth control activists such as Margaret Sanger – feminist transatlantic networks were perhaps less marked by rivalry and suspicion than those of suffrage.

There was also a long tradition of influence from the United States to Britain, and Daniel Rodgers has described two competing tropes or languages available to explain the relationship between North America and Europe. In the first, it was the established, elaborate European institutions and policies that could contribute to the politically corrupt and intellectually arid North America. Conversely, however, there was a language circulating that stressed the democratic, modern 'New World', in contrast to the aristocratic and mired 'Old World'. The 'single tax' speaking tours of Henry George in the 1880s established America at the forefront of social reform. This language was not only available to social reformers; amongst the young 'avant-garde' that saw itself as responsible for creating a 'modern America', there was a strong tendency to emphasise, as Randolph Bourne put it, 'the stifling air and chaos of the old world'. While embracing a cosmopolitan America, and one that could learn from the culture of all nations, Bourne and his peers rejected those who were 'slavishly imitative of the mother country'.[12] Avant-garde circles in the United States were strongly influenced by European developments, but Christine Stansell has argued that this was at the level of inspiration rather than the close working relationships that characterise the transnationalism of progressive reformers.[13]

As we have seen, within the suffrage community, close working relationships were evident and were far more interactive and discursive than a simple account of American imitation of 'England' would suggest. Americans did not widely perceive Britain as a 'storm centre', but rather as a location of stasis for women. An article in the *Woman's Home Companion* argued that 'in England … women are still regarded as subservient to men; while in America women have from the beginning been treated as the equals and companions of men'. Rheta Childe Dorr saw England as 'the country to which most American women owe their legal disabilities'. Europeans treated women as 'the inferior, the chattel, the property of man', she claimed.[14]

Susan B. Anthony visited Britain with other suffrage leaders in the early twentieth century to great acclaim, giving American enthusiasm to a British movement that many felt had 'died down'. International alliances were another area of American innovation, promoted by the establishment of the International Woman Suffrage Alliance (IWSA) in 1904, which held biennial conferences in Europe up until 1914. Americans dominated this activism, and made a strong commitment to such international links.[15] There were also American innovations in media, using the telephone and commercial radio as part of their suffrage campaigns, using sandwich boards, and enacting silent speeches in shop windows both to convey textual messages and to emphasise the censorship they suffered. Some of these innovations remained distinctively American, and were not copied to Britain. American suffragists within the Women's Political Union and the NAWSA, for example, used commercial film to influence popular opinion. Even though Emmeline Pankhurst starred in one of these productions, there is no evidence that British suffragists ever used feature film to reach their audiences.[16] Within the broader women's movement, the historian Christine Bolt identifies the club movement, consumer leagues and temperance as areas in which Britons learnt from America. Through American temperance lecturers in Britain and shared organisations such as the Order of Good Templars, transatlantic temperance networks became very close, though temperance was much less significant to the British women's movement than the American.[17]

Given these kinds of exchanges, different stories can be told about transatlantic influence. Sandra Holton has emphasised the influence of the 'radical tradition' in suffragism, and locates this as a 'cross-national impulse' in which the ideas and influence of Elizabeth Cady Stanton played a key role. Holton rejects the narrative of a one-way importation of practices from Britain into America, and situates suffragism as a genuinely transatlantic phenomenon. The attempt made by Emmeline and Christabel Pankhurst to situate the WSPU as the 'heir' of the radical American suffragist Susan B. Anthony also indicates how significant, in the early years of the century, the American movement was for the British.[18] These radical and revolutionary traditions which influenced Cady Stanton and other Americans help explain why many persistently regarded America as more advanced than Britain in relation to the status of women.[19]

There is evidence from a wide variety of sources that British suffragists and labour activists also drew on this idea. Sylvia Pankhurst had acknowledged in 1911 that though the Americans were inspired by British methods, 'in the early days of our long struggle it was we who drew our inspiration from them. Our movements act and react on each other.' Pankhurst felt that America was more receptive to new ideas than Britain, and even considered emigrating. Likewise Priscilla Moulder, an English factory worker and labour activist, observed: 'I think it is usually conceded that the Americans are generally first in the field with any new enterprise'. She portrayed the English as 'slow-going cousins' of the Americans.[20] Emmeline Pankhurst (with an eye, perhaps, to fundraising) declared 'All my life I have looked to America with admiration as the home of liberty'. Unlike Fawcett, she felt that Americans would encounter less resistance in gaining the vote than British women.

Two understandings of the storm centre emerged in suffrage-feminist literature. Fawcett's sense that Britain was the suffrage 'storm centre' due to it being the most advanced and most civilised of countries, was countered by an explanation implicit in the comments of the Pankhursts, and made explicit by Ethel Snowden, in her 1913 book, *The Feminist Movement*. Snowden, a British socialist and NUWSS agitator who had lectured widely in the United States, considered that Britain was the 'storm centre of feminism'. Nonetheless she felt that: 'The greatest liberty achieved for women up to the present time has been secured in the United States of America. The American woman has long held the title of queen amongst women.' American women's civic and political freedom co-existed with a failure to establish America as a 'storm-centre', Snowden felt, because 'their men have been so eager to give them everything for which they asked that the spirit of discontent has not invaded them sufficiently'.[21] Snowden and others explained the perceived British phenomenon of more 'advanced' feminism in a more conservative society by the greater need women in Britain had for freedom contrasting with the perceived relative emancipation of American women.

American women were not the only 'quicker cousins' that British suffragists encountered; they were also the recipients of 'sympathy, advice and assistance' from Australian and New Zealand women who were already enfranchised. The Australian suffragist Vida Goldstein, for example, toured Britain in 1911 at the invitation of the WSPU. Recognising the 'hierarchy' of claims to be 'progressive' or 'civilised', indicated by progress to enfranchisement, some Americans, Australians and New Zealanders thus chose to emphasise the relative backwardness of Britain compared to Australasia and the American West, where a number of states had enfranchised women by the early twentieth century.[22] In the suffrage realm, there were thus two conflicting discourses at play for Edwardians, one in which Britain served as the source of suffrage impetus, an appropriate role for the 'mother of all parliaments', and another in which colonial subjects progressed faster into 'modernity' than Britain was capable of.

How did these transatlantic networks and metaphors of 'storm centres' influence the establishment of the self-consciously radical 'subset' of Edwardian feminists? Many American texts discussing feminism acknowledged an intellectual debt to British thinkers and activists. Mary Wollstonecraft and John Stuart Mill were acknowledged to be the intellectual harbingers of feminism, though Americans such as Margaret Fuller, the Grimké sisters, Elizabeth Cady Stanton and Lucretia Mott were given equal foundational status. When Floyd Dell wrote *Women as World Builders* in 1913, he conjoined a British and an American 'world builder' in a number of the chapters, linking Emmeline Pankhurst with Jane Addams, and Beatrice Webb with Emma Goldman. Mary Ritter Beard, an American feminist and historian who spent time at Oxford's Ruskin Hall in the early years of the century, outlined a fairly even-handed transatlantic heritage; in writing of 'the nineteenth and twentieth century woman', she quoted Edward Carpenter and Havelock Ellis as key thinkers on the woman question. But the examples she gave of women's liberation were all taken from America, where she felt that enfranchised women had greater scope for political, civic and religious leadership. She ended her two articles with a long quote from Elizabeth Cady Stanton, thus giving the American radical tradition the last word on 'woman's future'.[23]

There was a persistent assumption among American feminists that America was the more liberated country, while acknowledging some British advances in the realm of feminism. Randolph Bourne, for example, on travelling to Britain in 1913 was bleak about British society, which he regarded as stiff, insular and provincial.[24] Nonetheless, his account of British backwardness was crosscut by another narrative, that of the extraordinary explosion of women's activism, both in suffrage and sexual matters. Bourne, who especially appreciated the work of Rebecca West, noted that the British were experiencing 'a courageous and much needed campaign of sex-education. London stood it, and I am ashamed at the ridiculous pseudo-virtue of New York.' In Britain, Bourne noted, subjects such as prostitution and venereal disease, 'tabooed in America', were discussed 'with the utmost freedom'.[25]

Floyd Dell was also positive about the British contribution to the development of feminism, regarding Emmeline Pankhurst's fighting spirit as more admirable, and more representative of women, than Jane Addam's conciliatory politics; he wrote glowingly of Dora Marsden and her 'radical propaganda as feminism never knew before'. The American feminist activist Mary Ware Dennett, in correspondence with the British suffragist Maude Royden, was especially scathing about the American attitudes to feminist concerns such as the birth control campaign. While England suffered ignorance and prejudice in relation to birth control, America suffered prejudice plus restrictive legislation on free speech. Her colleague Margaret Sanger agreed, and felt that it was the English validation of new ideas that carried weight in the United States. She wrote to Edward Carpenter that 'the American people are always so eager to follow in the footsteps of the English, and any idea which has the sanction of England's thinkers and writers is usually taken up here'.[26] Britain might be 'old and weary', but in the realm of feminism, it could still be seen as a 'storm centre'.

Others, however, strongly downplayed or even excluded the influence of British feminists. In Beatrice Hale's account of modern feminism, she stressed the French heritage of feminist ideas, naming Condorcet, Madame Roland and Madame De Stael as feminist forebears. The feminist tradition subsequently, in her view, shifted to America, as the home of democracy and equality, bypassing Britain entirely. She included only one British thinker in her genealogy of otherwise American feminists (the anti-Contagious Diseases Acts campaigner Josephine Butler), and was very disparaging of social attitudes in 'England'. She noted men's ridicule of independent women 'especially in countries such as England where the main struggles are yet to be won'. She concluded that 'where the old sex discrimination is used, as in England ... the day of true understanding between the sexes is further postponed'. Hale's book reads as a conscious distancing of America from 'England'. Other commentators on feminism also tried to focus reassuringly on the fundamentally American nature of the movement, especially during the European war. Katharine Anthony emphasised in her 1916 book, *Feminism in Germany and Scandinavia*, that 'It is still true that the spirit of Susan B. Anthony guides the woman movement of this country to the exclusion of all foreign influence'.[27]

The presentation of the 'New World' as a place of joyous casting off of convention in the name of equality and opportunity was not only available to Americans, but was also deployed within 'Old World' political argument. Dr Kaethe Schirmacher (1865–1930), a German women's movement activist whose historical survey of 'the modern woman's rights movement' was translated and welcomed in the United States, considered North America to be 'the cradle of the woman's rights movement' through the experiences of the War of Independence. She insisted that 'conditions in England are an evidence of how much more difficult it is for the woman's

rights movement to make progress in *old* countries than in new. Traditions
are deeply rooted, customs are firmly established, the whole weight of the
past is blocking the wheels of progress.'[28]

Some British feminists were deeply impressed with the Americans, and
felt Britain to be 'backward' in relation to feminism. It may have been her
theosophical beliefs, well established in the United States, which led
Frances Swiney to claim that 'we find, undoubtedly, the free woman
advancing towards her unfettered development in the United States of
America. In no other country has woman arrived at such a high stage of
social evolution.'[29] In 1898, 'Ellis Ethelmer' wrote that in all the professions, 'the United States have taken the lead in accepting the talent and aid
of woman and in appointing her to public office ... Strangely laggard and
erratic has been our mother-country in this human progression.' A correspondent of Charlotte Perkins Gilman wrote to her in the 1890s 'Alas!
The millennium which you are helping to bring about ... can come about
far more readily and more early in America than here.' Ada Nield Chew, a
women's trade union and suffrage activist who had been deeply influenced
by Gilman, had her *Freewoman* articles reproduced as an NAWSA
pamphlet. She commented that NAWSA 'must be much more wide awake
than our English Suffrage Societies to want to scatter such ideas broadcast!
I hope they will let me have a few copies – with which to shock my
friends.'[30]

America was also a useful symbol of liberation and newness, deployed by
vanguard artists and journalists. In 1910, the painter Jack Butler Yeats used
a transnational contrast in femininity to convey something of modernity,
figured as a 'New Woman':

[The American girl] means to please herself and to be quite frank about it. She is
face to face with herself ... She is the New Woman. Let us prepare her welcome.
So far her kind are but few in number; presently they will come in battalions.
Woman has often dragged down man; these will uplift the world, and they are
American-born ... There cannot be a greater contrast than that between a young
girl in England and a young girl in America. The former is afraid of herself, afraid
of her men, and of life. She turns to the past for guidance while watching the
future with timid hope, her mind being gentle unless her conservatism is
attacked ... The English girl never forgets that she is a woman, while the
American girl would impatiently cast off her womanhood and live in a world
without sex ...[31]

In 1913 W. L. George, a British journalist who had produced numerous
'shocking' articles on 'modern feminism (much to the irritation of

suffragists), described 'the new-woman' as 'one vast, incoherent, lusty shout ... so young in liberty, so American and so intoxicated with novelty'.[32] Like Yeats, George thus saw modern feminism as American in spirit, even if English in origins.

For most avant-garde feminists, it was not the androgyny of American women but the sexual radicalism of American intellectual life to which British feminists were indebted, and which cast serious doubt on British claims to be the 'storm centre'. Stella Browne and Bessie Drysdale, both *Freewoman* readers, commented in 1915 to Margaret Sanger on England as a 'slow little country', inhabiting 'the sleepy air of Europe'. In the transatlantic *International Journal of Ethics*, Browne repeatedly emphasised her indebtedness to the ideas on sexual variation of the American anthropologist Elsie Clews Parsons.[33] A younger generation of feminists came to see the United States as the intellectual centre of feminism during the years that Britain was at war while America was still neutral. Rebecca West portrayed America as a barbaric yet vivid, activist and cosmopolitan country. Americans, she wrote in 1916, 'are not sitting round polished tables in the quiet committee-rooms of an established social system; they are shouting at each other, while a nation is being noisily run up over their heads by workmen who speak so many different tongues that they communicate chiefly by blows'. In such an environment, West acknowledged that ignorance and bigotry could flourish, but nonetheless, women were empowered to act in social and municipal reform with a vision that put British reformers to shame. Wilma Meikle, a suffragist and 'advanced feminist' of a generation who came to define post-war British feminism, saw British feminists as having 'shirked the demand of their souls for a strong philosophy hewed out by sweating thoughts to fit their own needs'. But, she continued, 'When the war is over, and in an impoverished England we are stretching out our hands for the crumbs of mental and material wealth that fall from the banquet of a world-financing America, it is possible that American feminists will furnish us with some common-sense theories of sex'.[34]

The depth of exchange in the first two decades of the twentieth century made transatlantic feminist relationships intense and formative. Key texts were shared between each community, though others (Loy's *Feminist Manifesto*, Parsons' *Journal of a Feminist*) were left unpublished. This suggests some resistance to the circulation of feminist avant-garde ideas, even in the brief moment when they seemed to be in keeping with modernist politics more generally. Transatlantic friendship networks emerged, fuelled by the motivating power of belief in feminist principles, and by the international visits and speaking tours made by feminists, or in some cases their internationally peripatetic existences. The sharing of 'feminist' practices and techniques is less clearly defined than for suffragists, but nevertheless, new practices associated with feminism were copied, even while their national origins were acknowledged. Experiments with raising children outside of marriage (linked chiefly to the German concept of *Mutterschutz*), of retaining one's maiden name in marriage (associated with America and Lucy Stone), of rational dress (associated with America and Germany), of smoking, of novel childcare arrangements, were all debated and shared across national borders by feminists. British writers credited Americans with introducing the practice of deleting 'obey' from the marriage service, practising co-education of girls and boys, and with granting women access to the church as preachers.[35]

In the field of birth control, American feminists were influential upon British activists, though they themselves had been influenced by German and Scandinavian activist immigrants. Margaret Sanger and her contemporaries in the New York trade union, socialist and anarchist movements were thoroughly committed to the birth control cause by the time Sanger fled prosecution and arrived in England in 1914, where she helped form Marie Stopes' campaign.[36] British feminists such as Kitty Marion or Edith How-Martyn found inspiration and new methods in the American birth control movement. For British late Edwardian feminists, the transatlantic community was marked less by the competitiveness of suffrage activists, and more by a sense of feminism as a shared project, drawing on a common tradition.

These practices and friendships were complemented by the more intangible yet still highly characteristic intellectual components of feminism. Psychological introspection, egoism, the rejection of self-sacrifice, the 'Absolute Demolition' of the 'rubbish heap of tradition', as Mina Loy put it, represented an intellectual outlook that was shared, appropriated and reworked across national boundaries. As for transnational 'associations', these did not take the form of formal societies or leagues; instead, periodicals took on this role, giving institutional form, and an interactive, responsive setting to the sharing of ideas and texts.

THE TRANSATLANTIC *FREEWOMAN*

For Floyd Dell and his avant-garde peers, the 'storm centre' of feminism appeared to be located in Marsden's *Freewoman* journal, a self-declared Anglo-American space. He wrote, 'Until *The Freewoman* came, I had to lie about the feminist movement. I lied loyally and hopefully, but I could not have held out much longer. Your paper proves that feminism has a future as well as a past. We needed that assurance.' *The Freewoman* was positioned from its first issue as a cosmopolitan magazine – its initial publicity stated 'It is believed that feminism would be conceived in truer perspective if the English movement could keep in review the forms of activity in which the impulse finds expression in countries other than our own'.[37] Under its initial and subsequent titles between 1911 and 1919, *The Freewoman* serves as an example of the cross-national exchange within avantgarde movements, and specifically, within the earliest formations of twentieth-century feminism.

The Freewoman's blend of cultural, social and sexual commentary appealed to an American feminist readership that was not satisfied by the suffrage papers or other loosely 'feminist' papers like *The Forerunner* and *The Masses*. As one American reader pointed out 'In America there is no *Freewoman*, nor anything comparable with it. Here Feminism seems to have developed along the lines of Suffragism only.' For Marsden, the Anglo-American element was essential for both her British and American readerships. She declared 'I am hoping to be able to make the paper into an Anglo-American Review in a literary sense as well as a commercial. We in England know practically nothing about the new spirit of America ... I think the value of the paper would be increased enormously if it could contain the dual point of view – the different aspects of the same problems debated on the same ground.'[38]

The Freewoman established its initial links with American feminists through the correspondence and growing friendship between Dora Marsden and Frances Maule Björkman, the editor of the New York-based Literature Department of NAWSA, and a member of Heterodoxy. Björkman (1879–1966) was an active NAWSA suffragist throughout the late Edwardian period, despite her doubts about the value of this struggle. She was linked to avant-garde circles through her friendship with many Heterodoxy women, with theatre experimenters such as Jig Cook, as well as through her marriage to the cultural critic Edwin Björkman.

Björkman and her colleagues formed a self-described 'forward' or advanced group within the Literature Department, contrasted to the comparatively conservative NAWSA mainstream. NAWSA was not a cohesive body, having been formed as an amalgamation of the divided suffrage associations in 1890. Historians have seen NAWSA under the leadership of Anna Howard Shaw between 1904 and 1915 as faltering and divided. Faced with vigorous grass-roots activism, the national dimension of suffragism lost focus, and campaigns were largely limited to the state level.

Figure 8: 'Heterodoxy to Marie' portrait of Frances Maule Björkman, *c.* 1920,
The Schlesinger Library, Radcliffe Institute, Harvard University

As a broad church, it contained those who supported the vote alone, and those who identified as feminists, and thus provided space for rebellious and critical factions. Indeed, in 1912 it became official NAWSA policy that its officers could abandon non-partisanship and work with any political parties of their choosing.[39] Where critics, including the *Freewoman* founders, had felt compelled to resign from British suffrage groups on differences of principle and tactics, NAWSA made no such demands. Björkman and others in the Literature Department were able to express their *ennui* with suffrage, their lack of faith in their own suffrage journal, and to publicise *The Freewoman* in a personal and semi-official capacity. Despite the strong dislike of *The Freewoman* expressed by some colleagues, the Literature

Department was able to subscribe to *The Freewoman*, reproduce some of its contents as pamphlets, and use its office as an agency to sell the paper.

In February 1912, Björkman wrote to the British editor Mary Gawthorpe with delight upon her discovery of *The Freewoman*: 'All of us in this office are in a state of delirious joy over *The Freewoman*. It has been really funny to see one after the other of us pick it up casually and immediately become rooted to the spot for hours.'[40] The British editors responded with surprise that suffragists would take such interest in feminism, and noted that *The Freewoman*'s readership in Britain was composed not of suffragists but of 'a quiet thinking class'. Björkman responded with an attempt to situate herself and her colleagues:

[we] are not suffragists 'pure and simple'. Miss [Jessie] Ashley is a socialist [militant suffragist crossed out] with strongly I.W.W. tendencies and insurgent towards the Socialist Party's attitude towards women. Mrs [Mary Ware] Dennett is a Single Taxer with strong Socialist sympathies. I belong to the Socialist Party, but find it impossible to become interested or to have any sympathy with Party tactics ... Really, we are all much more feminists than suffragists, although we are all three anxious to see suffrage put through as speedily as possible.[41]

Björkman initially seemed comfortable with the idea of Britain as the formative 'storm centre' for this new grouping, 'feminism'. The contact with 'England' was a source of new inspiration for her: 'through you [Dora Marsden] and Miss Gawthorpe I feel that I have established my very first connecting link with things in England which have had a vivifying power upon me like nothing I have experienced from my own land'. Publicising the ideas of *The Freewoman*'s editor in a NAWSA pamphlet titled 'Bond-women' enabled Björkman to embrace the 'feminist' identity openly for the first time. She wrote 'the advertisment [*sic*] in the back of "Bondwomen" is something quite new. We've never advertised ourselves before as purveyors of "feminist" literature. I live in joyous anticipation of a protest from some of our members, who take their "suffrage neat" – I'm so thankful to Miss Marsden for teaching me that word – when they learn about the National's *Freewoman* affiliations.'[42]

The distinction between suffragism and feminism remained a troubled one for progressive era activists. One member of Heterodoxy, Winifred Harper Cooley, tried to clarify what she saw as a generation gap between suffragists and feminists:

If the claims of certain advanced feminine thinkers in all countries seem revolutionary and shocking, let me hasten to assert that they are not the claims of

suffragists, *in toto*. All feminists are suffragists, but all suffragists are not feminists ... It is a well established fact that suffrage in itself does not bring about a
revolution ... Woman suffrage to-day rests on a 'safe,' conservative basis.[43]

Cooley's mother, Ida Husted Harper, typified this kind of conservative
suffragism, and it was characteristic of the 'vanguard' feminists that they
should magnify personal rebellion against their parents into a much
broader sign of the times. It remained crucial to conservative suffragists
that they distance themselves from feminism, with its connotations of sex-
antagonism and free love. Björkman commented 'Suffrage here is absolutely booming, but feminism has hardly so much as lifted its head.
Whenever I feel the former to be an insupportably dull and obvious
business, I take a dip into *The Freewoman* and emerge refreshed.'[44] This
correspondence of 1912 represents some of the earliest usage of the term
'feminism' by Americans, suggesting that the term had been given new
currency by its use in Britain. Björkman understood feminism as an
outgrowth of militancy, and was happy to acknowledge that 'There is no
doubt that, whatever its present blunders and short-comings may be, we
American women have much for which we must thank the [English]
militant movement'. But only a year later, another American *Freewoman*
reader Edna Kenton saw the situation in reverse, arguing in 1913 that 'Of
the feminist movement so called suffrage is a tiny part'. It may well have
been *The Freewoman*'s introduction of feminism as a wide-ranging and
established identity which enabled her to make such a claim.[45]

If feminism was in fact the broader concern, it was one that was not
welcomed by many suffragists. While Björkman was clear that *The Freewoman* was 'what we have been dreaming of', she was aware that most
NAWSA members would not identify as feminists. She concluded a letter
to the British *Freewoman* editors with a warning that it should be regarded
as a 'personal and private communication', for the NAWSA 'Headquarters' was far in advance of the Association as a whole in these matters.
Björkman was dissatisfied with the Boston-based NAWSA journal, *The
Woman's Journal*, which she termed 'a puerile little affair' compared to *The
Freewoman*. When the American writer and socialist Upton Sinclair sent
Björkman his *Freewoman* article on 'Impressions of English Suffragism'
and asked her to place it in an American journal, she sent it on to *The
Woman's Journal*, but commented to Marsden 'I no more expect to see it
printed than to find *The Freewoman* embellishing its pages with the
touching pictures of suffrage mothers and babies with which Miss
Blackwell dearly loves to illustrate the Journal'.[46] Björkman laid out her

vision of a suitable periodical: 'One of the dreams of some of us here at Headquarters is a really fine, aggressive [*sic*], uncompromising feminist paper, giving its main attention to suffrage so long as the necessity lasts, and then going on to crystallise the ideals of feminism'. She had written to a colleague about the intellectual poverty of *The Woman's Journal* in 1911, noting, 'We are making a desperate effort this year for new readers – people who have not yet become very much interested in suffrage'.[47] By 1912, she may have hoped that *The Freewoman* could serve her purposes better than *The Woman's Journal*.

Björkman's dissatisfaction with suffrage was profound. She felt her work to be 'idealess', and described her department's literature as giving 'the main suffrage argument in words of one syllable and screaming type on bright colored paper'.[48] Though she wanted to bring working-class women into the 'woman emancipation movement', she was clearly dissatisfied with the 'lowbrow', tabloid-style methods used to gain a mass following. While she saw suffrage as 'a most effective instrument for fomenting general feminine revolt and for focalizing the rising forces of feminine discontent', she was extremely ambivalent about her work with the NAWSA, and open about her disputes with her peers, which centred on what she called 'idealessness':

As editor of the literature department, I confess to a blush of shame remembering all the 'woman in the home, votes and babies, votes for mothers' stuff which we are so disingenuously putting out; but I try to console myself with the thought that occasionally we print something that is REAL – instance, 'Bondwomen'.[49]

Björkman's irritation at the 'mass marketing' of suffrage, and the conservatism of suffragists continually surfaced in her letters to the *Freewoman* office. She had called *The Freewoman* 'almost too good to be true, because none of us felt that we had got far enough to enable such a journal to be born, much less to live'. The American feminist movement, in her opinion, was far less developed than the British. This was a characteristic complaint of American feminists. Alice Groff, a Philadelphia 'woman question' playwright, described her work as 'too radical to be published in America in a journal suited to it', and instead sought a British audience.[50] Upton Sinclair, a regular contributor to *The Masses*, saw *The Freewoman* as uniquely advanced. He became a shareholder in *The New Freewoman* and wrote 'I am intensely convinced of the importance of free discussion of all aspects of the sex-problem. We have no paper on our side which attempts it.'

Despite the impression taken from such correspondence that feminism represented a one-way conduit from 'advanced' Britain to the less-advanced United States, letters from *Freewoman* supporters also show that the American movement was felt to have insights to offer the British, displacing the 'storm centre' metaphor. Björkman, for example, wrote to Marsden: 'From what I hear, I believe that our suffrage movement over here is not quite so much an upper middle-class affair as in England. There isn't after all, the class feeling here that there is there, and the working women and the leisure women mix, on the whole, rather naturally. Also, there is a very general demand for economic independence for women.' American negativity about English class society was an established component of the idiom of the 'aristocratic Old World' versus the egalitarian 'New'. Björkman saw Britain as a realm of the heavy-handed state, epitomised in the British endowment of motherhood controversy (discussed in Chapter 6). She doubted that state endowment would 'find much footing here. For one thing, most of our "revolting women" have been nourished in their insurgency by the works of Charlotte Perkins Gilman; and I think that fact has greatly influenced the development of feministic thought in this country.'[51] Gilman could clearly be placed as on a par with, if not more 'advanced' than, British feminists. Björkman offered to send Gilman's *Forerunner*, as a magazine that Marsden might learn from, or be 'a little amused by'. In a diffident manner, then, Björkman was laying claim to her American contemporaries' credentials as 'revolting women' at the forefront of feminist rebellion. She described to Marsden the sort of readers who might be found for a feminist periodical in '"the Greenwich Village set", a group of young people who live in an old part of New York ... These young people are desperately radical; no doubt you know hundreds very like them – only, of course, it is quite impossible for anyone born out of America to be quite so young or quite so desperate as the American variety.' Though she was ambivalent about their 'desperation', Björkman was clearly laying claim to some kind of 'storm centre' for American radicalism. Björkman also sent Marsden some of their campaign literature, to show her 'how we do it in America'.[52] Again with diffidence, she may have thought that British suffragists had something to learn from American publicity methods.

Dating from late 1912, the American influence on *The Freewoman* became more marked. American readers offered ideas that were key to restarting the journal as *The New Freewoman* in 1913. Charles Hallinan, the Associated Editor of the *Chicago Evening Post*, was credited with the idea of a 'Thousand Club', to gain financial support towards the re-establishment of *The Freewoman*.[53] Marsden hoped to establish a 'friendly rivalry' between American and British supporters, and looked to the United States for many of the testimonials for the relaunch. Testimonials flowed in from readers in Chicago and New York, including the well-known writers Theodore Dreiser and Upton Sinclair. *The Freewoman*'s transatlantic readership was thriving, and American supporters were determined to keep the gendered *Freewoman* title, against the editor's judgement:

The 'emotional push' which landed THE NEW FREEWOMAN on its feet came from a tiny group of American women ... A mightily strong doubt as to whether there existed in what was called the 'Woman Movement' anything of value sufficient to make an effort to give it expression worth while, hung on the energies of those responsible for it, and it was in this doubting frame of mind that the 'American' enthusiasm had its effect: with the result that this new journal came into being ... with the same differentiation as to gender in its title as the earlier paper.[54]

It was American support, then, that prolonged the association between 'feminism' and the literary avant-garde direction in which *The New Freewoman* was heading. Several supporters identified America as the place most likely for it to succeed. Dr Von Bossini, a Chicago probation officer and settlement worker wrote to Marsden 'I do not think it would be difficult to increase the number of your adherents and readers of your splendid paper in the United States. It seems to be the psychological moment, for many American women have been lately forced to take a firm stand towards the questions which you discuss so courageously in *The Freewoman*.'[55] The *Chicago Evening Post* predicted that 'a large and intelligent minority in the suffrage movement in this country is ready for the discussion of something else besides votes', and welcomed *The Freewoman* as the means for this to happen. Another subscriber suggested to the editor that *The Freewoman* be transferred to New York, as a more fitting home for it than London.[56] American readers were not passive receptors of British feminism; it is clear from the correspondence that it was not merely the publishing practices (fundraising and sales strategies, publicity and building of the readership), but also the intellectual content of the journal that had been influenced by Americans. Marsden may have been deeply cynical and disillusioned about the value of the suffrage struggle in Britain, but the clear interest from the American suffragists, and their willingness to engage with Marsden's egoist version of feminism, encouraged her to think that there was still something to be explored in the politics of gender.

Figure 9: 'Heterodoxy to Marie' portrait of Edna Kenton, *c.* 1900, The Schlesinger
Library, Radcliffe Institute, Harvard University

A key figure for the transatlantic exchange surrounding *The Freewoman*
was Edna Kenton (1876–1954), an avant-garde playwright and literary critic
who acted with the Greenwich Village independent theatre, the Provincetown Players. She was part of the close-knit New York feminist
community, as well as being a frequent visitor to Chicago. By mid-1913, she
became seen as the 'representative' of 'the Dora Marsden paper' in
America, and took over its marketing.[57] Kenton's attraction to *The Freewoman* had been through Marsden's editorials, which she lauded in
characteristic 'avant-garde' terms as 'concrete, destructive, no quibbling
with terms or facts, but like Thor's hammer, falling straight'.[58] Though
The Freewoman originated in Britain, its editors continually stressed the
provenance of feminism as an elite, yet worldwide entity. It was perhaps
Kenton's reading of *The Freewoman* that enabled her to perceive England
not as the 'storm centre' of suffrage and feminism, but as part of a global
movement for women's emancipation, using techniques learnt from other

struggles. She felt that not only English women but the 'women of the rest of the world' were part of the 'general unrest that is burrowing beneath old codes, undermining old values and ideals'. The English militants were widely credited with inventing hunger-strikes and other aspects of 'sex-war' – but Kenton situated the hunger-strike as originating in the Russian revolutionary movement. She portrayed feminism not as an English invention, but as a worldwide revolt, of which suffragism was just 'a symptom' and English militancy just a 'detail'.[59] An article in *The Bookman* by Kenton attributed to *The Freewoman* a whole new egoist 'world-view': 'We are just beginning – thanks largely to Dora Marsden and *The Freewoman* – to perceive what the New Woman actually is'. What had 'emerged from half a century of groping' was 'the phrase that would open their new world to women – the magic phrase itself, "I am I" '.[60]

Marsden had been delighted with the publicity given to modern, individualist or egoist feminism in the United States. She wrote in April 1912 to Björkman 'we are very anxious to get *The Freewoman* read and known in America and we are considering the possibility of establishing an agency, especially as the appreciation in America has been very wide-spread'.[61] An article written in the American journal *The Forum* in October 1912 lauded Marsden personally as 'a new prophetess of feminism'. It drew attention to the notoriety of *The Freewoman*, and asserted its utter novelty and radicalism in the world of journalism. British suffragists were described as resisting this new journal 'with all their might', because *The Freewoman* was 'spiking their game'; in other words, *The Freewoman* revealed that women did not want the vote in order to serve mankind more fully, as suffragists, and some leading feminists had argued. Feminism was defined instead as part of the avant-garde project of self-transformation and mastery of 'the will'.

An article in the January 1913 *Current Opinion* situated avant-garde feminists as 'disciples of Nietzsche'.[62] The philosophy of *The Freewoman* was described as 'undemocratic'; it 'discards the ordinary'. There was a fascination with the avant-garde, elitist claim that three women out of four would reject feminism. The 'vanguard' circles of feminists amongst whom these ideas had greatest currency were unashamedly elitist. Dell pointed out that *The Freewoman* was 'frankly a gospel for a minority', and that self-realisation, the exercise of will that only a few could hope for, was at the root of liberation. The mass of women were regarded with contempt. This denigration or dislike of women in her current state of oppression was very characteristic of modern feminism in both countries. In Britain, the socialist-feminist Margaret McMillan regarded contemporary women as

prone to corruption, luxury-seeking and greed, while Olive Schreiner had
characterised them as sex-parasites, degenerate and eventually sterile.[63]
American journalist Mary Ritter Beard had described modern women as
'something between an angel and an idiot – a bundle of weak and flabby
sentiments, combined with a wholly undeveloped brain', while Edna
Kenton noted woman's 'spiritual helplessness, upon which all their other
ineptitudes gather like barnacles'. These represent just a tiny proportion of
comments that could be chosen – yet this is a part of feminist discourse
rarely remarked upon by historians. It is also one of the features of feminism that allies it closely with some anti-feminist texts. While it is clear
that similar claims about women's inferiority can be made with different
intent, Edwardian 'feminist' and 'anti-feminist' sources can sometimes
hardly be distinguished. Dora Marsden was labelled as both, though she
clearly saw herself as a feminist. Others were more ambiguous – the *New
Age* literary editor Beatrice Hastings, for example, used both feminist and
anti-feminist to describe herself, and found the confusion between the two
a productive space for her journalism.[64] This conceptual overlap and
exchange between feminism and anti-feminism is one of the interesting
features of the avant-garde articulation of 'feminism'; it generated great
controversy but also allowed both British and American readers to feel that
they were gaining, as one American put it, 'tanks of oxygen' in comparison
to the confining atmosphere of 'the woman's movement'.[65]

The editors of *The Freewoman* clearly took their American market
seriously, and exploited the *cachet* of being a 'London review'. American
supporters relished the idea of what *Current Opinion* called the 'daring
"humanist" review, the London *Freewoman*'; Alice Groff, for example, was
intensely interested in reaching an English audience, and asked Marsden to
act as her 'English Representative'. 'England' in her letters was double
underlined in an almost fetishised fashion, and she wrote Marsden eleven
letters between August and December 1913, to secure this important link.
In some cases, the invocation of 'England' or 'America' on either side of the
Atlantic implied little concrete interaction, and was simply a gesturing
towards another, imagined space in which feminist ideas or practices could
flourish. W. L. George's comment about the new woman being 'so
American' probably had no substantial meaning but aimed to create
overtones of 'modernity' and liberation around the 'new woman'.

Nonetheless, substantial and ongoing channels of communication and
exchange did exist, and for a brief period, allowed feminists to inhabit a
space that was free of the rivalry and strongly national ethos of the suffrage
movement. These exchanges created the possibility of a shared intellectual

field for feminists, and certainly the 'egoist' ideas of avant-garde feminism were, by 1914, more firmly in circulation in the United States than in Britain. A Chicago contributor to *The Forum* in July 1914 echoed Marsden in his claim that 'Woman's prime function in the social organisation, like man's, is to be a self: this at any cost, even at the price of foregoing her other important function of motherhood ... Woman's primary right [is] full majority and self accountability; full freedom to test her strength as woman and to bring her feminine individuality to supreme and perfect unfolding.' Though Rose Young acknowledged in *Good Housekeeping* that the nature of feminism was still an open question in 1914, she regarded it as beyond question, even for the domestic-oriented audience of this periodical, that feminism concerned individualistic self-development, spiritual freedom, and an end to self-sacrifice.[66]

American readers were treated to a very intense discussion of this strand of feminism. 'Feminism' was a highly marketable – though ephemeral – cultural commodity. It became a staple topic for literary and current affairs periodicals such as *The Forum, Harper's Weekly, The New Republic* and *Current Opinion*. The latter included an article in 1913 billed to 'explain feminism', and thus place the reader 'at the very firing-line of the most thrilling engagement in the war for freedom, which began in the caves and will end with mankind'.[67] Feminism was widely discussed in 'women's magazines', and in the literary and lifestyle supplements to the *New York Times*. In Britain, however, suffrage and its sensationalist violence largely eclipsed feminism, which was rarely debated in sympathetic terms in the literary monthlies or 'women's magazines', and was left to the 'little magazines'.

DETERIORATING RELATIONSHIP

Marsden's commitment to a transatlantic perspective had been a response to the intense American interest in *The Freewoman* and *The New Freewoman*. But there is evidence that the transatlantic friendship with Björkman and others became less close over time. In January 1913 Marsden complained to Björkman that she had not heard from her in a long time. In May 1913, she wrote to Björkman plaintively 'We thought we had lost all you Americans: Chicago, New York, and everywhere else'. While feminist and 'avant-garde' politics had seemed reconcilable and even intrinsically linked in *The Freewoman*, the launch of *The New Freewoman* marked an intensification and elaboration of the avant-garde elements in the journal, at the expense of the feminist. Edna Kenton, whose

literary and philosophical interests made her most likely to welcome the
Max Stirner-influenced *New Freewoman*, wrote that 'The first issue
brought great disappointment and severe criticism, which is slowly
subsiding'.[68]

Marsden asked Björkman to contribute to *The New Freewoman* – but
not on the suffrage question, because 'here, interest in the vote itself is
quite dead'. Björkman declined, on the grounds of the literary-modernist
obscurity of the journal which, following the increasing influence of the
American Ezra Pound as literary editor, gave her a 'hideous sense of
intellectual insecurity':

Apparently my simple Middle Western intelligence is inadequate to grasp the
import of a paper so post-everything as *The New Freewoman*. I have a dizzy sense
of being at sea in a high gale with nothing but a cockle-shell between me and the
briny deep. In reading it, I am oppressed with a truly awful conviction of crudity
and ignorance.[69]

It was not just the obscurity of the journal that troubled her, but also her
sense that Pound's politics of 'imagist' poetry were not in keeping with
feminism:

I wish there were more women contributors, and I could do with considerably less
of 'the white bodies of women'. One is so everlastingly pursued by said white
bodies through literature, and I did hope that *The Freewoman* would furnish us
with a refuge where we could rest secure from them. I am very much interested in
seeing the errotic [*sic*] life of women set forth truly and candidly by women
themselves, but I feel as if I'd had enough of the errotic life of men as set forth by
themselves, and also of what men think of the errotic life of women.[70]

The literary experimentalism that became dominant within the avant-
garde replaced the more overtly political projects of life-style experimentalism and iconoclasm that had allowed feminism to be integral to the
early development of avant-garde movements. The later politics of the
avant-garde left feminists feeling 'dazed', and key figures dropped out of
the project. Rebecca West, though she contributed a story to the short-
lived avant-garde journal *Blast*, preferred in the main to work for more
mainstream British and American periodicals, or to write for the socialist
press. She resigned from *The New Freewoman* in October 1913, declaring to
Björkman that it was 'neither a Feminist nor a constructive paper'.[71]
Björkman answered that she was 'sure that numbers of the Americans
will sympathise with your view ... I have been much disappointed in

Miss Marsden's apparent loss of interest in feminism, and I haven't cared at all for her individualistic philosophy.'[72] Björkman resented what she perceived as a 'take over' by the literary group of Ezra Pound, and she saw Marsden as intellectually isolated within her group of contributors.[73] As another American feminist saw it, 'suffragists withdrew their support from it, it changed its name and speedily disappeared'.

This comment from Heterodoxy member Beatrice Hale was part of a long account of her disappointment in *The Freewoman* in her 1914 book, *What Women Want*:

One or two newspaper writers and minor agitators have ridden their hobby to the point of frenzy and, in the endeavour to lead, have incontinently fallen into a ditch. Among these may be classed Miss Dora Marsden, who recently edited for the few brief months of its existence a little London weekly called '*The Freewoman.*' ... the editor held marked anarchical views, and she rapidly changed from the championship of equal suffrage to a violent contempt for it. Synchronising with this change in politics came one in spirit, the paper became revolutionary and unbalanced in its moral tone.

For Hale, the failure of the paper could be explained by its European origins, the dangers of which, she implied, all cosmopolitan Americans would be aware. Using the idiom of the 'corrupt Old World', Hale wrote that *The Freewoman* 'had fallen into the hands of a tiny and rather decadent group of extreme theoretical anarchists such as are to be found in any European capital, and whose entirely unrepresentative character is familiar to any but provincials. As the little paper dealt, in its later stages, in the most open possible way with sexual problems, it created a brief "succès de scandale" which was immediately seized upon by ingenious anti-feminists and used to besmirch the standing of the great body of suffragists with which it had less than nothing to do.'

Ignoring *The Freewoman*'s humanist subtitle, Hale went on to criticise its alleged antagonism towards men and proposal that women should support their own children. To *Freewoman* feminists, the 'development of individualism was the sole desideratum, and if the good of society ran athwart it, the good of society could be sacrificed. That being so, there was nothing to prevent a "free" indulgence in passion, or maternity, if the individual woman believed the enlargement of her personality demanded these experiences. Hence the prating on "free love" which anti-feminists have so adroitly advertised.' Hale concluded that 'these were the doctrines not of feminism but of anarchy, a philosophy particularly repugnant to the legitimate feminist'.[74]

In her distancing of *The Freewoman* from *legitimate* feminists, Hale recalls the British suffragists who saw the paper as dangerous fodder for the anti-suffragists. But why should feminists be concerned about the opinion of others? As an experimental, modern movement feminism was unconventional, and could exist independent of public opinion. Indeed, the avant-garde evaluation of the impact and prestige of cultural productions was closely bound up with their hostility to the mass reading public, and their cultivation of outrage and rejection by readers. As Pierre Bourdieu has observed, for avant-garde artists 'the only audience aimed at is other producers'; profits, honours and even 'institutional cultural authority' tend to be shunned.[75] Dora Marsden defiantly denied that her journal had any interest in its readers – she claimed, in similar terms to Margaret Anderson of the *Little Review*, that it was written and edited only to please herself. Heterodoxy was itself a self-consciously unconventional group which demanded a certain level of social insouciance from its members. Yet even for Heterodoxy members, the so-called anarchism of *The Freewoman* was threatening. In particular, the paper's subversion of maternalism was singled out as particularly inappropriate for American feminism.

Marsden responded with an editorial on 'Americans and Movements', to answer the heavy criticism she had been receiving from American supporters. She apologised for talking of Americans at all, 'implying that we mean a "people in the bulk", or a "national type", or some other equivalent spook, when all that our experience enables us to speak of is a limited number of persons whose letters bear an American postmark.'[76] Marsden identified the problem with the American supporters as a tendency, like British suffragists, to support a cause and follow a leader. *The New Freewoman*, she argued, 'stands for nothing: it is the flexible frame waiting to be filled with the expression of the constantly shifting tale of the contributors' emotions. It has no 'Cause'. The progressive era, however, was the era of causes, and with this denial of political commitment, and refusal of the mantle of 'prophetess of feminism', Marsden distanced herself from Americans who sought more practical, activist freewomen working in the realm of political leadership rather than philosophical ideas.

CONCLUSION

Overall, *The Freewoman* appears to have been influential in the early stages of development of 'feminist' identity in America, a 'keynote' as Ezra Pound might have described it. It provided a conduit of influence between American and British 'feminists', made particularly distinctive by the sharing of American ideas and expertise with British counterparts, and contributors' refusal to place the 'English' movement as the 'storm centre' of feminism. *The Freewoman* spoke to American ambivalence about militant tactics, which could be divorced by American readers from other feminist concerns and branded 'a merely English detail'.[77] Marsden seemed to be a suitable figurehead for the new movement of feminism – a 'spirit all intellect and fire', as Björkman described her.[78] But *The New Freewoman* did not sustain an Anglo-American perspective; while the first issue in June 1913 included three articles by Americans or American commentators, other issues showed little interest in American affairs. Instead, a strong relationship with French cultural life was developed, with commentaries on French periodicals and 'Paris Notes'. Transnational connections, in becoming more literary, became Anglo-French rather than Anglo-American.

American periodicals continued to be advertised in *The New Free-woman*, but Marsden seemed to find little in American cultural life worthy of comment. She preferred to comment critically on British politics and art, leaving America as a promising empty space, no more than an emblem of intellectual openness and artistic experimentation. Others were much less favourable towards America; it had been through Ezra Pound that Dora Marsden hoped to make a reality of her 'Anglo-American Review', but Pound wrote 'One is not much concerned with American Magazines, any more than one is concerned with the colonial press ... One occa-sionally opens an American periodical in search of the grotesque.'[79] By 1916, he concluded: 'America has ceased to matter ... There are few signs that personal freedom, or the freedom of the Press, or of the arts, will survive West of the Atlantic.'[80] *The Egoist*, though Americans wrote for it and read it, remained in spirit linked to continental Europe rather than the United States. The thrust of Marsden's argument became more negative, against English culture and politics, rather than a genuine engagement with American readers. American dreams of a 'fine, aggressive, uncom-promising feminist paper' could not be realised in *The Freewoman*.

A combination of circumstances led the paper to fail in becoming a genuinely Anglo-American review – the timing of the 1912 bankruptcy of the paper's London publisher, the *ennui* of Dora Marsden in questions of gender, her failure to sustain and capitalise on the enthusiasm of her American contacts. Later, the isolation of the war led to the curtailment of American publicity and sales. It was also perhaps the sense in which feminism had become a more successful and 'mainstream' cultural com-modity in the United States that made it less attractive to the avant-garde.

Feminism had taken on 'American overtones', and this mainstream success made it unenticing as a component of the increasingly aloof European avant-garde. As Ezra Pound made clear, 'American' entities, and those with a 'mass-market' cultural value, were out of favour with modernist elites.

The World War between 1914 and 1918 further disrupted the channels of interaction. British feminists became more closely involved with pacifism, or war work, than with gender politics. American feminists became overwhelmed by the battles around free speech, which state censorship and brutal oppression of suffragists had made a compelling issue. Mary Ware Dennett, for example, had long been a critic of the 'militant' Women's Party in the United States. But in 1917 she wrote to Lucy Burns asking for membership:

> when your work recently resolved itself into a gallant struggle for free speech, I was *for* it ... the great consideration today is free speech. It is the foundation right without which all other rights are mockery. Every drop of revolutionary blood in me boils at the stupid, cowardly, hypocritical attempts at suppression adopted by the administration. Your fight has now become every freeman's fight. I should despise myself if I stood on the outside.[81]

Her criticisms of suffrage and preference for avant-garde feminism had become secondary – and for those who did continue to espouse the radical politics of the avant-garde, the atmosphere became oppressive. Randolph Bourne wrote to Elsie Clews Parsons, 'with these pestilent Vigilantes at work, I foresee a reign of terror for heretic intellectuals.' The correspondence between suffragists also reflects the material disruption of wartime, as news took longer to diffuse, paper was rationed, letters went astray and friendship networks became strained by lack of contact.[82]

Among post-war British feminists, many still believed that America represented 'a young and vigorous nation' which could grapple with ideas in earnest. Americans might be 'violent ... sometimes incredibly naïve and even blatantly ignorant ... but they have the strong right arm and the short, invigorating temper of the housewife', wrote Rebecca West in the *Daily News*.[83] Anglo-American feminist interaction persisted, but via other channels than the avant-garde. Feminists such as Rebecca West, Freda Kirchwey and Vera Brittain continued to write for journals in each country, and to comment on British and American affairs. Personal connections helped to form new spaces for interaction, such as the mentoring of American Hazel Hunkins Hallinan by Teresa Billington-Greig, the emigration to America of Mary Gawthorpe, or Crystal Eastman's marriage to

British poet and anti-war activist Walter Fuller. During the 1920s Eastman (sister of Max Eastman) wrote for the British feminist periodical *Time and Tide*, a journal which also fostered transatlantic connections through its sharing of articles with the American journal, *Equal Rights*.

Time and Tide stressed the continued co-dependence of British and American feminists, their 'passing of the torch' back and forth, as each country encountered waves of feminist advance and anti-feminist backlash. In a 1926 article, the editors prophesied that through American enthusiasm, British feminist 'political lassitude left by the war years' would pass away; it had become a commonplace that the storm centre had moved to the United States, while Britain was in the doldrums: 'For some time now women have been once more looking across the Atlantic and realising that the American movement was a more real, a more alive thing than their own'.[84]

Feminist ideas did not cross and re-cross the Atlantic without undergoing transformations during this process, and the remainder of this study recovers in detail the political argument of the British and American contexts, in order to show the development and hybridisation of 'feminisms'. Certain issues did not easily transfer to other contexts, or took on new meanings where they did cross borders. The components of feminism were distinctive in each country. Feminism was never a static discourse, but a series of more or less fragile 'meaning sets' and coalitions, which were built up in response to the changing political environment. The following three chapters deal with the realms of political argument in which feminist ideas were situated, and the vocabularies on which they drew. Perhaps the most prominent of these was the ever-flexible discourse of individualism – a language spoken by liberals, libertarians, idealists and avant-garde iconoclasts, with widely differing meanings. The following chapter explores how feminists understood and deployed their commitments to individualist self-development for women.

END NOTES

1. Rodgers, *Atlantic Crossings*, pp. 70, 71; Kenneth O. Morgan, 'The Future at Work: Anglo-American Progressivism, 1890–1917', in *Contrast and Connection: Bicentennial Essays in Anglo-American History*, ed. H. C. Allen and Roger Thompson (London, G. Bell and Sons, 1976), pp. 247–8.

2. Daniel Rodgers, unpublished paper, 'Progressivism' colloquium, University of Cambridge, Thursday 13 May 2004. Recent work on transatlantic suffragism includes Holton, 'To Educate Women Into Rebellion', and

Holton, 'From Anti-Slavery to Suffrage Militancy: The Bright Circle, Elizabeth Cady Stanton and the British Women's Movement', in Caroline Daley and Melanie Nolan, eds., *Suffrage and Beyond, International Feminist Perspectives* (Auckland, Auckland University Press, 1994), pp. 213–33; Harrison, *Connecting Links*; Bolt, *The Women's Movements*; Sandra Adickes, 'Sisters, Not Demons: The Influence of British Suffragists on the American Suffrage Movement', *Women's History Review*, 11:4 (2002).

3. Canadian connections are not examined in this study, though they were undoubtedly important for the suffrage movement; there is little evidence that Anglo-Canadian feminist interactions paralleled those between Britain and the United States, though this may be a fruitful area for future research. In terms of American scope, I have limited my study of American feminism to writers and periodicals based predominantly in New York and Chicago, as focal points for avant-garde feminism within the United States.

4. See Elizabeth Robins, *Collier's Weekly*, 29 June 1907; 'The Feministe Movement In England', and 'Why', *Everybody's Magazine*, Dec. 1909, New York. Emmeline Pankhurst toured America in 1909 and 1912. Other British suffrage and feminist notables who visited America included Anne Cobden-Sandersen, Emmeline Pethick Lawrence, Ethel Snowden, Laurence Houseman, Beatrice Harraden and Florence Fenwick-Miller. Hertha Ayrton to Gawthorpe, 28 Nov. 1915, box 5, folder 21, Mary E. Gawthorpe Papers, Tamiment Library, New York University (henceforth MGP).

5. Harrison, *Connecting Links*, pp. 106, 72, 200. See correspondence between Ellen Wright Garrison and Eleanor Garrison, box 41, folder 2, Garrison Family Papers, Sophia Smith Collection, Smith College, Northampton, Mass. I am grateful to Dr Mary Chapman for this reference.

6. Elizabeth Robins, *Votes for Women*, March 1909, reprinted in Elizabeth Robins, *Way Stations* (New York, Dodd, Mead, 1913), p. 101. Teresa Billington-Greig similarly situated Britain as 'the heart of [women's] rebellion that... girdles the earth'. She saw the American feminist movement as learning from British feminists, as well as pursuing their own rebellion, in areas of equal pay and labour organisation. 'The Rebellion of Women', *Contemporary Review*, July 1908, 5; Bolt, *The Women's Movements*, p. 247. See Fawcett's chapter on 'England' in *The Woman Question in Europe*, ed. Theodore Stanton (New York, G. P. Putnam's Sons, 1884), discussed by Sandra Stanley Holton, 'British Freewomen: National Identity, Constitutionalism and Languages of Race in Early Suffragist Histories', in *Radical Femininity; Women's Self-Representation in the Public Sphere*, ed. Eileen Janes Yeo (Manchester, Manchester University Press, 1998), pp. 153–4. Harrison, *Connecting Links*, p. 148.

7. Annie Kenney, *Memories of a Militant* (London, Edward Arnold, 1924), p. 269.

8. Emmeline Pethick Lawrence, 'Across the Atlantic', *Votes for Women*, 11 Oct. 1912, 25.

9. Blatch to Mary Gawthorpe, Aug. 1931, MGP. See Ellen Carol DuBois, *Harriot Stanton Blatch*.

10. Cott, *The Grounding of Modern Feminism*, pp. 27, 25, 292 n. 23. See also Margaret Finnegan's account of how 'English' methods 'helped embolden and revitalise the United States movement', in Margaret Finnegan, *Selling Suffrage: Consumer Culture and Votes for Women* (New York, Columbia University Press, 1999), pp. 51–2. In other key areas for the development of suffragism and feminism, British practices and ideas were also influential: Britain has been seen as the chief source of expertise and innovation concerning the settlement house movement, and women's trades union organisation; Bolt, *The Women's Movements*, pp. 4, 217.

11. Kitty Marion Papers, 7KMA Women's Library, London Metropolitan University.

12. Rodgers, *Atlantic Crossings*. Randolph Bourne, 'Trans-National America', *Atlantic Monthly*, 118:1 (July 1916).

13. Stansell, *American Moderns*, p. 321.

14. 'John Bull's Militant Daughters', *Woman's Home Companion*, April 1914; Rheta Childe Dorr, *What Eight Million Women Want* (Boston, Small, Maynard & Co., 1910), pp. 85, 73–4.

15. Bolt, *The Women's Movements*, p. 241; McFadden, *Golden Cables of Sympathy*; 'Feminism in England and America', *Time and Tide*, 9 July 1926. Though many IWSA members may have come to regard themselves as feminists, the title of this organisation indicates by its singular 'woman' that it was quite distinct from the new affiliation, feminism.

16. On American and British suffrage and anti-suffrage movies, see Kay Sloan, 'Sexual Warfare in the Silent Cinema: Comedies and Melodramas of Woman Suffragism', *American Quarterly*, 33 (Fall 1981), 412–36; Elizabeth Crawford, *The Women's Suffrage Movement: A Reference Guide 1866–1928* (London, UCL Press, 1999), pp. 218–21.

17. Jane Rendall, *The Origins of Modern Feminism: Women in Britain, France and the United States 1780–1860* (Basingstoke, Macmillan, 1985), pp. 254–59.

18. Holton, ' "To Educate Women Into Rebellion" ', p. 229. Patricia Greenwood Harrison documents the 'unreliable memoirs' of Emmeline Pankhurst, in which she claims that Anthony visited Manchester in 1902, and was the inspiration for the founding of the WSPU in 1903. In fact, Anthony did not visit until 1904. The NUWSS also recognised her as a key figure, providing a Susan B. Anthony banner in their parades for American visitors to march beneath. Harrison, *Connecting Links*, pp. 41, 76.

19. Bolt, *The Women's Movements*, p. 235.

20. Pankhurst, *Votes for Women*, 28 April 1911, 495. See also 'In the West the Land is Bright', *Common Cause*, 28 Feb. 1913; George Lansbury, 'A Lesson from America', *Votes for Women*, 10 May 1912, 507. Moulder, *Life and Labor*, Aug. 1912, p. 245.

21. Snowden, *The Feminist Movement*, pp. 69, 17, 76.

22. Marilyn Lake, 'Between Old Worlds and New', in *Suffrage and Beyond, International Feminist Perspectives*, ed. Caroline Daley and Melanie Nolan (Auckland, Auckland University Press, 1994), p. 278. Hale, *What Women Want*, p. 82.

23. Dell, *Women as World Builders*. Mary Ritter Beard, 'The Twentieth-Century Woman' and 'The Nineteenth-Century Woman', *Young Oxford*, Dec. 1900, 101–4 and Jan. 1901, 119–22.

24. Bourne, *The Letters of Randolph Bourne*, pp. 149, 152.

25. Bourne to Alyse Gregory, 1 Nov. 1913, and to Carl Zigrosser, 16 Nov. 1913, in Bourne, *The Letters of Randolph Bourne*, pp. 164, 174.

26. Dell, *Women as World Builders*, pp. 90, 96–7. Dennett to Royden, 26 June 1919, MWDP. Sanger to Carpenter, 13 April 1918, ECP.

27. Hale, *What Women Want*, p. 49. Anthony, *Feminism in Germany and Scandinavia*, p. 10.

28. Kaethe Schirmacher, *The Modern Woman's Rights Movement: A Historical Survey*, trans. Carl C. Eckhardt (New York, Macmillan, 1912), pp. 2, 96.

29. Frances Swiney, *The Awakening of Women, or Woman's Part in Evolution* (London, William Reeves, 1908), p. 252. The occult religion of theosophy was founded in New York in 1875 and became influential upon leading British women such as Annie Besant, Frances Swiney, Charlotte Despard, and many within *The Freewoman* group. See for example Mary Gawthorpe on a 'visionary experience', *Up Hill to Holloway*, pp. 192–3. See Alex Owen, 'Occultism and the "Modern" Self in Fin-de-siècle Britain', in *Meanings of Modernity: Britain from the Late-Victorian Era to World War II*, ed. M. Daunton and B. Rieger (Oxford, Berg, 2001); Joy Dixon, *Divine Feminine: Theosophy and Feminism in England* (Baltimore, Johns Hopkins University Press, 2001). Charlotte Despard, president of the Women's Freedom League, was a committed Theosophist. Her feminism was introspective and spiritual, but unlike the more avant-garde versions of feminism, was not aristocratic. Charlotte Despard, *Theosophy and the Woman's Movement* (London, The Theosophical Society, 1913), pp. 34, 45.

30. Ellis Ethelmer, 'Feminism', *Westminster Review*, Jan. 1898, 57–8. Lucy Bland has suggested that 'Ethelmer' was a pseudonym for Elizabeth Wolstenholme and her husband Ben Elmy; Bland, *Banishing the Beast*, p. 141. Frances Swiney, however, identified Ethelmer as Ben Elmy alone in her *The Awakening of Woman*, 1908. L. J. Mallet (Mrs Charles Mallet) to Gilman, u. d., CPGP. Ada Nield Chew, 6 Aug. 1912, II, 28 DMC. On Chew's life and writings see Ada Nield Chew, *The Life and Writings of a Working Woman* (London, Virago, 1982).

31. J. B. Yeats, 'The American Girl, an Irish View', *Harper's Weekly*, 23 April 1910, 12–13.

32. W. L. George, *Women and To-Morrow* (London, Herbert Jenkins, 1913), pp. 177–8.

33. Bolt, *The Women's Movements*, p. 251. Brown credited Parsons in 'Some Problems of Sex', *IJE*, 27:4 (July 1917), 464–71. See Parsons, 'Feminism and

Sex Ethics', pp. 462–5 *IJE*, 26:4 (July 1916), and 'Feminism and the Family', 52–8. The *International Journal of Ethics* formed an important transatlantic channel for the discussion of feminism after *The Freewoman* became less focused upon feminist issues.

34. West, 'American Women: Their Work as Reformers', *Daily News*, 9 March 1916, reprinted in Marcus, *The Young Rebecca*, pp. 314–17. Wilma Meikle, *Towards a Sane Feminism* (London, Grant Richards, 1916), pp. 95–6.

35. W. L. George, 'Feminist Intentions', *Atlantic Monthly*, Dec. 1913, 722, 725, 723.

36. See Stansell, *American Moderns*, pp. 234–41; Mari Jo Buhle, *Women and American Socialism, 1870–1920* (Urbana, Ill., University of Illinois Press, 1981), pp. 268–80.

37. *New Age* advertisement for *The Freewoman*, 23 Nov. 1911, 95.

38. Clarence Lee Swartz, *New Freewoman* (henceforth *NFW*) 15 Oct. 1913, 178. Marsden to Björkman, 11 Jan. 1913, MWDP.

39. W. L. O'Neill, *Feminism in America: A History* (New Brunswick, Transaction Publishers, 1989), p. 122; Cott, *The Grounding of Modern Feminism*, pp. 28–9.

40. Björkman to the editors of *The Freewoman*, 24 Feb. 1912, MWDP.

41. Frances Björkman to Dora Marsden, 20 May 1912, MWDP. Jessie Ashley was a lawyer, and partner of the IWW leader Bill Haywood. Mary Ware Dennett, formerly a noted arts and crafts leatherworker, worked in the 1910s to secure civil liberties, and women's rights to birth control in the National Birth Control League. See Cott, *The Grounding of Modern Feminism*, p. 90; Constance Chen, *The Sex Side of Life: Mary Ware Dennett's Pioneering Battle for Birth Control* (New York, The New Press, 1996).

42. Björkman to Jardine, 16 Aug. 1912, MWDP.

43. Winifred Harper Cooley, 'The Younger Suffragists', *Harper's Weekly*, 27 Sept. 1913, 8.

44. Björkman to Jardine, 16 Aug. 1912, MWDP.

45. Kenton, 'The Militant Women – and Women', *Century Magazine*, 87 (Nov. 1913), 18.

46. Björkman to Marsden, 25 July 1912, MWDP. The article was, however, published in *The Woman's Journal*, with the comment from Björkman that Sinclair's call for a mass strike of working-class women was 'the direction on which and in which, to me, at least, it is becoming more clear every day, the whole woman emancipation movement must proceed'. *The Woman's Journal*, 10 Aug. 1912, 256.

47. Björkman to Marsden, 20 May 1912, MWDP; Björkman to Grace Seton-Thompson, 15 Nov. 1911, Schlesinger Library, Radcliffe Institute for Advanced Study, Harvard University, Grace Gallatin Seton-Thompson Papers, 000605199.

48. Björkman to Marsden, 25 July 1912, 20 May 1912, MWDP.

49. Björkman to Marsden, 20 May 1912, MWDP.

50. Groff to Marsden, 7 Nov. 1913, 3 Dec. 1914, DMC IV, 4a.

51. Björkman to Marsden, 20 May 1912, MWDP. 'Mothers' Pensions' were in fact enacted in most states between 1910 and 1920, well in advance of their adoption in Britain. Christine Bolt has argued that this is an area in which the United States was in advance of Britain in its 'social feminism', though she ignores the feminist opposition to such measures. Bolt, *Women's Movements*, p. 229.

52. Björkman to Marsden, 20 Dec. 1912, 25 July 1912, MWDP.

53. Marsden to Björkman, 11 Jan. 1913, MWDP.

54. *NFW* 15 Nov. 1913, 203 'Views and Comments'.

55. Testimonials collected in the Dora Marsden Collection, Princeton: II, 24. Perhaps recognising the continuing close ties between suffragism and feminism in the United States, Marsden continued to follow up her WSPU ex-colleagues, mentioning to Björkman her acquaintance with the WSPU activists Alice Paul and Lucy Burns, who had recently returned to the United States. She reported that Paul and Burns' organisation, the Congressional Committee, had asked for a copy of *The Freewoman*, 'saying that they will get subscribers for it and that it will help the Cause greatly'. Marsden cautiously went on, 'It made me fear they haven't seen it, and that they will be shocked by its suffrage attitude, not to say disappointed'.

56. Reported by Marsden to Weaver, 2 Dec. 1912, HSWP vol. 57352, British Library.

57. Forbes Book Publishers, Chicago, to Edna Kenton, 2 Aug. 1913, DMC IV, 10. Kenton was listed in the relaunch publicity as the Honorary Secretary, *The New Freewoman* Committee, New York.

58. Kenton to Marsden, 1 Aug. 1913, DMC: IV, 1a.

59. Kenton, 'The Militant Women – and Women', 13, 18.

60. Kenton, 'A Study of the Old "New Woman"' *The Bookman*, April 1913, 154.

61. Marsden to Björkman, 18 April 1912, MWDP.

62. *Current Opinion*, January 1913, 47–8.

63. McMillan, 'Woman in the Past and Future', in *The Case for Women's Suffrage*, ed. Brougham Villiers, (London, Fisher Unwin, 1907), pp. 106–21; Schreiner, *Woman and Labour*, pp. 82–3.

64. Beard, 'The Nineteenth-Century Woman', *Young Oxford*, January 1901, 119; Kenton, 'The Militant Women – and Women', 15. See Hastings, 'Case of the Anti-Feminists', *New Age*, 29 Aug. 1908. Her readers found it disconcerting – see George Hirst, *New Age*, 17 April 1913, 591. See Lucy Delap, 'Feminist and Anti-Feminist Encounters in Edwardian Britain', *Historical Research*, 78:201 (August 2005).

65. Margery Curry Dell, quoted in Björkman to Marsden, u.d. MWDP.

66. George Burman Foster, 'The Philosophy of Feminism', *The Forum*, July 1914, 18, 22. Rose Young, 'What is Feminism?' 679–84.

67. The Editor, *Century Magazine*, Nov. 1913, 13.

68. Marsden to Björkman, 11 Jan. 1913, MWDP; Marsden to Björkman, 6 May 1913, MWDP; Kenton to Jardine, 6 Aug. 1913, DMC.

69. Björkman to Marsden, 16 Oct. 1913, MWDP.

70. *Ibid.*
71. West to Björkman, 9 Nov. 1913, MWDP.
72. Björkman to West, Oct. 1913, MWDP.
73. Historians have differed over the nature of this 'take over'. Initially, it was read as a typical masculine-modernist colonisation of a women-run paper, leading to the eclipse of those women and their feminist views. See for example Bonnie Kime Scott, *The Gender of Modernism* (Bloomington, Indiana University Press, 1990). More recent work, however, has stressed the long-lasting position of Marsden and Harriet Shaw Weaver as editors of *The New Freewoman* and its successor, *The Egoist*. They have seen the shift to a more literary-modernist form and content as a conscious choice by Dora Marsden, and as not ruling out feminism, which was itself a term used to indicate 'modern' credentials. Nonetheless, though the shift to literary-modernism may have been planned and welcomed on Marsden's part, the perception of a 'masculine take over' persisted among the American readers.
74. Hale, *What Women Want*, pp. 214–16.
75. Pierre Bourdieu, *The Field of Cultural Production*, ed. Randell Johnson (Cambridge, Polity Press, 1993), pp. 39–40.
76. *NFW*, 15 Nov. 1913, 203, 'Views and Comments'.
77. Kenton, 'The Militant Women – and Women', 18.
78. Björkman to Marsden, 12 July 1912, MWDP.
79. 'Bastien Von Helmholtz' [Ezra Pound], 'Review of *Poetry*', *Egoist*, 1 June 1914, 215.
80. Pound, *Egoist*, Oct. 1916, 159.
81. Dennett to Burns, 17 Nov. 1917, MWDP.
82. Bourne to Parsons, 25 Aug. 1917, ECPP. See Mary Sheepshanks to Alice Paul, 16 Oct. 1916, ALC.
83. West, 'American Women'.
84. 'Feminism in England and America', *Time and Tide*, 9 July 1926, reprinted in D. Spender, *Time and Tide Wait for No Man* (London, Pandora, 1984), pp. 264–6. Hazel Hunkins Hallinan, an American feminist activist who became the chairman of the Six Point Group in Britain, described British feminism as apathetic, without new members or direction. But as an American, she felt able to overcome the 'petty frictions' dividing British feminists and thus be more useful to the movement than a British leader could have been. Hallinan, interviewed by Brian Harrison, 8 Feb. 1975, The Women's Library, London Metropolitan University.

CHAPTER 3

Individualism in feminist political argument

The Victorian and Edwardian women's movements can be seen as deeply concerned with what it was to be an individual. The ability for women to be property-holders even if married, to be direct recipients of welfare, or to vote, all reflect a concern with what it was to be an individual that developed over the course of the nineteenth century. Feminist avant-garde thinkers extended this in the early twentieth century to give new attention to the individuality of women and men within marriages and other forms of sexual relationship, within the realm of creative arts, as writers, or within their own psyches. As Rose Young put it, 'One fact that stands out above all ... is the feministic insistence upon the development of the individual ... Every woman who knows much knows that the matter of developing herself as an individual is mainly an inside matter, a spiritual introduction to herself.'[1]

Individualism, in a variety of forms, was thus one of the characteristic underpinnings of Edwardian feminism. This frequently co-existed in tension with commitments to women's social service, their duties to the race, or to an organic society. Understanding the complex intellectual trajectory of individualism is essential to giving a more nuanced and subtle understanding of feminist political thought. An unpacking of 'individualism' is especially crucial to situating avant-garde feminist political argument, since the idea of women as 'an individual' or 'a personality' was extremely important to their constructions of feminism. Nonetheless, 'individualism' remained a broad and ill-defined term, both in Edwardian usage and more recently in feminist theory. Individualism has commonly been associated with a particular discourse, termed a 'liberal feminism' of equal rights and enhanced opportunities for women within the existing status quo.[2]

'Liberal feminism' has operated within feminist historiography as a placeholder for a set of ideas that were not in this period even always identified as 'feminist', and which drew on concepts of sexual difference that do not easily combine with 'liberal' egalitarianism. It refers to the political ideas of the conventional mainstream of the women's movement, those suffragists who sought women's inclusion as citizens, in politics and government. It will be an argument of this study that what have commonly been termed 'liberal feminist' concerns were in fact based less upon an interest in rights and equality, and more upon an uneasy amalgam of ethics of service, duty and self-development. 'Liberal feminism' is an inadequate framework for understanding the very widespread and varied commitments to individualism amongst Edwardian feminists, particularly those who regarded themselves as 'advanced' or 'vanguard' thinkers.

Resituating 'individualism' is made more compelling by the widespread antagonism towards individualism within recent feminist theory. Individualism has come to be seen as antithetical to feminist concerns. The feminist focus on the collective identity 'women' has appeared irreconcilable with concepts of individual uniqueness. 'Feminist individualism' is thus either defined as a historically 'liberal' concern with individual rights, or is regarded as theoretically contradictory. Modern feminist thinkers have articulated an embodied, grounded political perspective, and have challenged the alleged atomism of individualist political theory and the possibility of a 'pre-social individual'.[3] The defining project of feminism has been understood to be a critical examination of what it is to speak as and for women. But feminism is more variable than this would allow – some feminists have rejected the collectivity 'women', and preferred to speak for themselves alone, to deny the saliency of their sex, or their gender, to resist the 'suffusion of sex' which Denise Riley has argued is such a relentless and confining process in the formation of a gendered subjectivity.[4]

Feminist theoretical work can be prejudicial to an historical account of individualist thought within the feminist movement, and has prevented serious analysis of the integration of the two discourses. 'Feminism' – itself a broad and unspecific term – has been opposed to an homogenised and historically unspecific 'individualism', without sensitivity to its diverse meanings. Avant-garde feminists felt comfortable with the term individualism, and used it in ways that complemented or were integral to their 'feminism'. Their individualism was more productive, more closely integrated with their feminism, and more significant than commentators have allowed.

In contrast to 'feminism', 'individualism' was not a new term in this period, but it functioned similarly as an open term, a site of contestation, and a space amenable to appropriation by feminists. 'Individualism' is notoriously slippery to define, and requires attention to historical context. While the force of 'individualism' has been associated in Britain with extremes of political argument, it was not only used by libertarian or anarchist individualists on the political fringes, but was also appropriated by liberals and socialists. In the United States, individualism was a dominant social value of the nineteenth century, understood in Jacksonian terms as the primacy of the self over social institutions. Self-development and privacy, described in de Tocqueville's account of his visit to the United States in 1832, have been core American values for the nineteenth and most of the twentieth centuries.[5]

The term 'individualism' gained political significance as a theory of the limits of state action from around 1880 in Britain and the United States.[6] Indeed, the primary association of individualism in this period was political, specifically, the libertarian individualism of thinkers such as Herbert Spencer in Britain, and in America, Ralph Waldo Emerson and William Graham Sumner. Spencer, the best-known proponent of political individualism, focused on the values of privacy and autonomy. His case for the minimal state rested on a belief in leaving social life to its 'natural' evolutionary processes. Society without external intervention would find an 'ultimate equilibrium' based on reciprocal and perfect liberty for all. Political individualists idealised a personal, economic or civic sphere distinct from the control of the state, wherein individuals could freely compete and develop. The bounds of this realm were contested, but it was associated variously with civil society and the family.[7] These spaces, and not the political realm, enabled self-development. The minimal or residual state retained only a role of contract enforcement and property protection.

Individualism, particularly in the United States, was associated with hostility to aristocratic, arbitrary or hierarchical privilege.[8] However, libertarian individualism implied no interest in egalitarian *outcomes*, nor in the material constraints upon exercising one's rights, and was thus compatible with the inequalities of the free economy. This strand of individualism thus became associated with a celebration of *laissez-faire* capitalism. Spencer's theory of social equilibrium matched the economic equilibrium of nineteenth-century 'Manchester School' political economists. Property had long carried a political and social significance for some individualists; its absence implied dependency, its presence, autonomy. The idea of property 'in the person' was so central that the individualism of Spencer and his followers is sometimes characterised as 'possessive individualism'. The propertyless individual could not be a full individual, nor be a citizen and undertake political responsibilities.

This strand of individualism represented a discourse on which feminists could draw.[9] It motivated campaigns in the second half of the nineteenth century to enact various versions of married women's property acts, aiming to remove the objection that propertyless women could not be voters. The 'liberal feminist' agenda of equality, opportunity and rights – widely read as characterising the feminism of Edwardian suffragists – can be understood as an extension of this individualist discourse to include women. Brian Harrison has argued that 'feminism can be assigned an impeccably Liberal ancestry; British feminists employed Liberal rhetoric, oriented their campaigns entirely towards parliament, and held firmly to Parliamentarism after 1918'.[10] Certainly, the struggle for property and citizenship rights that characterised pre-1914 'liberal feminism' did draw on the universalist discourse of individual rights and equal opportunities related to individualist thought. The American feminist-suffragist Elizabeth Cady Stanton famously appropriated the predominant individualism of American political argument, in her 1892 address, 'The Solitude of Self'. Stanton argued that 'In discussing the rights of woman, we are to consider, first, what belongs to her as an individual, in a world of her own, the arbiter of her own destiny, an imaginary Robinson Crusoe with her woman Friday on a solitary island'.[11]

However, most nineteenth-century libertarian individualists were ambivalent towards feminist aspirations. In his 1851 *Social Statics*, Spencer argued for women's equality with men, but withdrew this in the 1891 edition. Most libertarian thinkers took the male head of household as the representative individual of the entire family, and were hostile to female individuality. Historian Wendy McElroy has traced a late nineteenth- and early twentieth-century libertarian feminist tradition in the United States, but has also suggested that male individualists were predominantly hostile to the inclusion of women. A whole literature of feminist political theory has indicated that libertarian definitions of the individual assumed a male body, and a female-populated private realm of care to release the male individual from physical and domestic concerns.[12]

Though possessive or libertarian individualism has become the dominant strand of political thinking associated with the term 'individualism', in historical terms, other strands have been more influential on feminism, and this has been somewhat glossed over by accounts of this period. The affiliation to individualism within the feminist movement was certainly more complex than a simple 'liberal' individualism of rights and equality. Elizabeth Cady Stanton, for example, went on in 'The Solitude of Self' to commit herself to individualism not only as a natural right, but also as a moral entity, an aid to dignity and character. This suggests the influence of an alternative 'moral individualist' tradition, prevalent within the late nineteenth and early twentieth centuries, associated with idealist political thought.

MORAL INDIVIDUALISM – PROGRESSIVES AND IDEALISTS

The libertarian individualism associated with Spencer in the late nineteenth century had provoked opposition in Britain and the United States that was rooted within the universities and the settlement movement. Idealism, by developing the nineteenth-century commitment to a morality of 'character', became the basis for a new sense of 'moral individualism' that dominated British and American philosophy until the end of the First World War.[13] Idealists, borrowing the organic analogy of evolutionary biology, outlined a 'social organicism' that saw society as a distinct entity from a collection of individuals. Idealist thinkers were highly critical of the abstract, self-oriented versions of liberal freedom that had been philosophically dominant in the nineteenth century.

Idealist social philosophy disseminated through transatlantic networks such as the Charity Organisation Society and the *International Journal of Ethics* and formed a distinctive Anglo-American discourse. William James, in particular, was highly influential upon British idealists and new liberals, and Americans in turn drew on British ideas. In the United States the progressive impulse can be read as incorporating a strand of moral individualism, labelled by the political commentator Herbert Croly 'Constructive Individualism', and inspired by the ideas of American idealist philosophers such as Josiah Royce and William James.

Josiah Royce had inspired his Harvard students, in keeping with progressive era sentiment, to 'do God's service in a world of moral order'. Out of his teachings, according to one student, came a sense of the power of individuals to shape their own lives.[14] Idealist thinkers, however, were ambiguous about their commitment to individualism. Walter Weyl, an influential journalist involved in the *New Republic* journal, rejected American individualism in the sense of 'unalienable rights, negatively and individualistically interpreted'. Instead, he sought 'these same rights ... extended and given a social interpretation'. Many progressives aimed to achieve higher levels of individual self-realisation within a mildly interventionist state, rather than the limited state of possessive individualists.

Idealism had great influence on public debate in Britain and the United States – and on the women's movement – at the level of 'political argument' with which this study is concerned. May Sinclair, a feminist and suffragist writer, explored 'new' idealist philosophy, and writers on women's citizenship quoted idealist philosophers. Idealist language was also found amongst the more advanced feminist thinkers. Charlotte Perkins Gilman, for example, argued in idealist terms: 'The new Social Philosophy recognizes Society as an orderly life-form, having its own laws of growth; and that we, as individuals, live only as active parts of Society'.[15] Gilman and her intellectual peers echoed idealist philosophers in their attempt to reconcile a form of individualism with social interdependency.

Many in the women's movement were attracted by the idealist identification of individual freedom as entailing both external and *internal* liberty. Liberal political thought had tended to limit itself to freedom defined as absence of external coercion; idealists, however, also included psychological factors as potential bars to freedom, and this made for a strong moral element in their philosophy. Self-generated 'unworthy' desires and lusts might impinge on an individual's freedom, and idealists required that each should develop a strong moral control over their own psyches. This interest in the psychological dimension reflects a broad intellectual change in late nineteenth- and early twentieth-century culture. Psychological introspection became validated by not only idealist thought, but also by the relatively new fields of psychology and psychiatry.[16]

Idealists, however, continued to frame psychological states using older languages of ethics and character. They drew on the discourse of character for different political ends from nineteenth-century liberals, regarding it in loosely Kantian terms as the expression of the will of an autonomous moral agent. The British political philosopher Bernard Bosanquet drew from this the belief that the individual must be self-maintained in order to uphold an autonomous will, and that public bodies should teach moral virtues, rather than offer material help against poverty.[17]

This theory was given practical significance by the idealist-influenced Charity Organisation Society (COS, f. 1869), which flourished in the nineteenth century in both Britain and America. It aimed to provide a more systematic evaluation of need for relief, and, through personal visiting, to establish an organic link between the rich and poor and discourage impersonal dependency. COS workers stressed that poverty was normally due to personal moral deficit and choice, rather than environment.[18] Good character, then, was associated with 'restraining one's impulses', and with being responsible for one's own interests (through thriftiness, frugality, enterprise and so on). As characterised by Gareth Stedman Jones, the COS was neither 'old' nor 'new' liberal, but a curious mixture of repudiation

and embrace of modern welfare activities.[19] The organisation was carried
to New York in 1877, and through the next twenty years, to ninety-two
other COS groups in the United States. But by the late 1880s, COS
methods could be seen as outdated in each country. Though its methods
remained influential, the focus of social reform moved to the Settlement
Houses, and, later, to state welfare provision and professional social work.
Nonetheless, the mix of moral individualism, the 'gospel of duty' and
expert, personalised intervention was its lasting contribution to Edwardian
debates on service and citizenship.

As the nineteenth century drew to a close, many American and British
idealists began to think in terms of an organic society, requiring a more
active and interventionist state. This reflected the idealist belief that self-
realisation was intimately tied up with being in a relation of harmony with
the general will, conceived in social organicist terms. Leading COS activists such as Helen Bosanquet (wife of Bernard Bosanquet) began to accept
'man's natural and inevitable dependence upon the community' in spite of
their attention to self-help. Individual effort, it came to be admitted, might
be supplemented by limited measures of state intervention. Stefan Collini
has described how the nineteenth-century association of good character
with self-reliance shifted towards an idealisation of self-development or
self-realisation.[20] This meant for a changed emphasis within moral individualism, towards a stronger emphasis on personal development, which
was very significant for Edwardian feminists.

The shifting emphasis from self-reliance to self-development within the
'moral individualism' of the idealist tradition made it increasingly influential upon the Edwardian women's movement. Though the relationship
between the two was indirect, many associated with the women's movement were linked to this moral discourse by their involvement with the
COS and the settlement movement.[21] Helen Bosanquet sustained a
commitment to women's rights from within the idealist movement, as did
the wives of T. H. Green and D. G. Ritchie. Green himself worked closely
with well-known figures of the British women's movement on issues of
higher education.[22]

Many suffragists in Britain and the United States deployed a vocabulary
that was very similar to that of the idealists to support their arguments.
British writer W. L. Blease used a common suffrage argument in his 1913
Votes for Women, that women's participation in government would be
educative of their moral character. Their vote would substitute direct,
democratic influence for the 'sexually tainted' concept of indirect influence, as well as raising the moral character of politics. The American

pacifist feminist writer Florence Guertin Tuttle (1869–1951) wrote in her 1915 account of feminism 'Society to-day demands service of each individual. Somewhat [*sic*] of one's self each one must contribute to the social machinery – or be a cog in the wheel.'[23]

This idea of a moderately interventionist state prevailed within the mainstream of the women's movement. While the nineteenth-century ethical tradition of the COS was out of favour with most 'vanguard' Edwardian feminists, nonetheless the direction of moral individualist arguments was in keeping with that of the feminist movement. Moral individualism resonated with the widely held feminist sentiment that impetus for change must come from within, and sprang from strength of character. This was already prevalent in the nineteenth-century women's movement; the London-based *Victoria Magazine* argued in 1865 'Woman can be what she makes herself; her power lies within her own grasp, not in what she can prevail upon others to do for her'.[24]

A stress on the development of feminine character – and the self-emancipation this process could entail – persisted within the 1890s 'new woman' debates, and later in Edwardian feminism as an interest in psychological change. A contributor argued in *Blackwood's Magazine* in 1897 that 'the psychology of the feminist' involved 'dissecting [her soul], analysing and probing into the innermost crannies of her nature. She is for ever examining her mental self in the looking glass.' In the 1890s this process was normally understood to be a literary one, epitomised by the 'new woman' novels. But by the later Edwardian period, it had become a personal challenge, and had taken up the vocabularies provided by new theories of psychoanalysis and sex psychology. Marie Jenney Howe, for example, argued in 1914 that feminism meant 'more than a changed world. It means a changed psychology, the creation of a new consciousness in women.'[25] Even where feminists used organicist language, or celebrated communal endeavour, they often retained a language of individuality and introspection. Alice Hubbard, a journalist and writer who was active in the Roycroft Arts and Crafts community, celebrated the feminism implicit in American Women's Clubs. These institutions, she felt, had provided women with 'moral fiber, purpose, courage, determination, power'.[26] These moral qualities have strong nineteenth-century connotations, but for Edwardians were also intimately tied to individuality.

In sum, more interest was shown by feminists in internal transformation than external or political achievements, and this represents an important 'introspective turn' within Edwardian feminism. This trend can be seen in versions of feminism as distinct as Ellen Key's maternalism and Emma

Goldman's anarchist feminism. In 1912 Havelock Ellis approvingly wrote of Ellen Key, in the American edition of her book:

> She is of the opinion that the Woman's Movement will progress less by an increased aptitude to claim rights than by an increased power of self-development, that it is not by what they can seize, but by what they are, that women ... finally count.[27]

The Russian-American anarchist Emma Goldman argued that for women:

> true emancipation begins neither at the poll nor in courts. It begins in woman's soul. . . . [Woman's] freedom will reach as far as her power to achieve her freedom reaches. It is therefore, far more important for her to begin with inner regeneration ...[28]

American journalists began to reflect these opinions. One wrote in a national daily that feminism concerned women's 'great need of freedom, inward, mental, and spiritual freedom from the old sense of inferiority ... Feminism, then, is in essence and fact a spiritual attitude.' In 1915, Florence Tuttle published a book-length investigation into 'the psychic side of feminism' in the United States, in which she argued that feminism 'is an inner revolution before it is an outer revolt, subjective before objective'. Rose Young sought to address this dual focus on individualism and social duty in her 1914 article, 'What is Feminism?':

> Never was there so individualistic a day; never so many people, women like men, bent on self-expression, bent at arriving in truth in their own way – and never was the individual so deeply and humanely concerned for his brother; never was there so general a recognition of the interdependence and coming amalgamation of 'the masses' and 'the classes'; never such sturdy social growth, and blossoming beauty of the social.[29]

Her words echo the concerns of idealists with individual freedom, and their attempt to reconcile this with an overarching 'social whole'. While other strands of individualist thought also focused upon self-emancipation through will, personality or character, what was particularly attractive to the women's movement in idealist 'moral individualism' was the attention to internalised constraints (emotional and psychological) on self-realisation, and the additional belief that self-reliance or self-development should be motivated by the desire to help others and be of service. This was even more influential upon feminism than the liberal/libertarian stress on equal rights and freedom from external constraints which is more usually associated with women's emancipation. Though the early twentieth-century Anglo-American women's movement has been seen as 'liberal feminist', no such clear position existed. It was less a belief in rights and opportunities that predominated amongst Edwardian feminists than the idea that self-development was essential to women for the good of the whole. As Max Eastman noted in 1910, 'I believe that not one-fiftieth of the women engaged in [suffrage] are actuated by a desire to get rights'.[30]

Some wanted the freedom to *serve*: Helen Bosanquet argued in support of feminist reforms that for women, 'without independence there can be no real ability to serve others ... It is only the practice of bearing our own burdens that can maintain the moral strength to enable us to bear those of others.' NUWSS secretary Ray Strachey expressed this in her 1928 history of the women's movement. She acknowledged the influence of 'individualism and love of liberty', but saw as more significant the moral character of suffragism: 'To [suffragists] it was not primarily a fight between men and women, *hardly even a matter of 'rights' at all*. What they saw in [the cause], and what they wanted from it, was an extended power to do good in the world.'[31]

In order 'to do good' or serve, it was widely felt that an examination of women's psyche was needed. The Fabian and feminist writer B. L. Hutchins argued in 1913 'Self-sacrifice has been preached to women for centuries; is it not time to preach self-development? Is not personality the greatest need?' Suggesting the transatlantic exchanges underlying the development of feminist ideas, Hutchins quoted the 'Heterodite', Elsie Clews Parsons: ' "If women are to be fit wives and mothers", says Mrs Elsie Parsons, "they must have all, perhaps more, of the opportunities of personal development that men have" '. The aim of the women's movement, as Hutchins saw it, was internal development and, consequently, external influence: 'to develop a nobler and purer tradition of social life and manners'.[32]

American suffragist Carrie Chapman Catt shared this introspective concern in her indictment of 'women's slave souls'. Using Olive Schreiner's metaphor for parasitism, Catt derided the 'clinging vine' personality, and hoped that women would break through their own cultural dependency, for the sake of their own dignity, and the wider public good.[33] In sum, while feminine good character and self-realisation were not of direct interest to most idealists, the logic of their ideas gave space to women's claims to self-development. The dual focus on self-development and duty suited feminist claims that women would better serve others by expanding their intellectual horizons and political activity.

It was within the feminist avant-garde that these concerns with psychological change and self-development were explored to their fullest extent, while ideas of service and the public good underwent a highly critical examination. Writing in 1909, Ellen Key identified what she critically referred to as 'ultra-feminism' with egoism. This referred to 'the feminism which has driven individualism to the point where the individual asserts her personality in opposition to, instead of within, the race; the individualism which becomes self-concentration, anti-social egoism'.[34] Individualism, within this 'egoist' strand of feminism, was discussed in terms of a rejection of 'rights', anti-statism, and a denial that liberty entailed equality. Above all, the provocative and political discussions of sexuality within avant-garde feminism reveal a new kind of individualism, that did not mesh with the moral individualism of suffrage feminists. The individualism of avant-garde feminists incorporated a similar idiom of personality and self-development, but for quite different purposes from the moral commitment to the good of the whole.

A NEW FEMINIST INDIVIDUALISM?

When Vera Brittain went up to Oxford in 1914, she recorded in her diary a manifesto, written late one night with some fellow women undergraduates, calling themselves 'Young Oxford'. They concluded that 'The age is intensely introspective, and the younger generation is beginning to protest that supreme interest in one's self is not sin or self-conscious weakness or to be overcome, but is the essence of progress . . . The age is in great doubt as to what it really wants, but it is abandoning props and using self as the medium of development.'[35] Similar ideas had circulated amongst 'vanguard' feminists for the preceding half decade. They were most explicitly and fully developed by Dora Marsden, editor of *The Freewoman*, and her circle of readers in Britain and the United States, during the historical moment when feminism connoted an avant-garde and iconoclastic alternative to 'the women's movement'. *The Freewoman* was initially titled *A Weekly Feminist Review* in 1911, became *A Weekly Humanist Review* in 1912, and *An Individualist Review* in 1914, under the title of *The Egoist*.[36] Marsden's first editorial launched *The Freewoman* with a fierce blast of condemnation for 'Bondwomen', on the grounds that they 'are not individuals . . . they round off the personality of some other individual, rather than create or cultivate their own'. She set the tone for subsequent *Freewoman* issues in her propensity to blame women themselves for their subjugation. Marsden incited women to take their freedom, rather than plead for it from men.

> there comes a cry that woman is an individual, and that because she is an individual she must be set free. It would be nearer the truth to say that if she is an individual, she is free, and will act like those who are free. The doubtful aspect in this situation is as to whether women are or can be individuals – that is, free ... Only Freewomen can be free, or lead the way to freedom'.[37]

Marsden was obliquely indicating her scorn of the suffrage-feminist movement with its ideals of self-sacrifice for the cause and renunciation of autonomy into the hands of leaders. She associated suffragism with claiming rights, described as 'nothing more than a collection of fables made up to amuse children in nurseries'. She went on

> A man has a 'right' to what he can get. In a free community no man has any 'rights'; he has what he can make out of his freedom. In an unfree community, the 'powerful' – those who have had the strength, ingenuity, and cunning to establish force to translate their power into domination – dole out 'rights' to a mean and humble rabble, who gratefully accept what is accorded to them, and who but whimper feebly about 'our rights' when the 'powerful' take back what they have given.[38]

Marsden rejected rights as such, and thus opposed libertarian individualism with its framework of rights to defend the individual from the state. However, she shared with the libertarians a faith in property as a material expression of individuality. For a woman to achieve individuality or the status of 'freewoman', she had to 'open up resources of wealth for herself. She must work, earn money. She must seize upon the incentives which have spurred on men to strenuous effort – wealth, power, titles, and public honour.'[39]

These ideas resonated with the egoist theory of individualism that was newly popular in turn of the century Britain and America. The term 'egoism' or 'egoist' came into use in Britain in the early nineteenth century as a political and moral theory of self-interest, used in a similar fashion to 'individualism'.[40] Egoism's foremost proponent was Max Stirner (1806– 1856), whose *Ego and His Own* (later translated as *Ego and its Own*) was first published in 1845 at the height of the German Romantic movement. His book provoked a flurry of responses, including from Marx, Engels and Feuerbach, and then disappeared into obscurity until the late nineteenth century. By 1900, he was again a notorious figure; interest in him arose through a renaissance of interest in egoism in the 1880s, most prominent in the work of American anarchist James Walker, and others associated with the American periodical *Liberty*.[41] This interest was sustained, and is reflected in later texts such as James Huneker's 1909 *Egoists: A Book of Supermen* and Edwin Björkman's 1911 *Something New Under the Sun*.[42]

An English-language translation of Stirner was not published until 1907 (in New York, and 1912 in London), when interest in his work and Nietzsche's was reaching its height. Dora Marsden described the experience of reading Stirner:

From point to point Stirner moves on, deposing all things and all powers in order that he may enthrone the Ego. The entire conceptual world, the complete thought-realm he attacks and overcomes and lays at the feet of the Ego. Morality, religion, God, and man are all brought low . . . The Ego is supreme, and reigns in his lonely kingdom.[43]

Max Stirner's notoriety came from his denial of the existence of abstract and generalised concepts such as 'God, Emperor, Pope, Fatherland'. His radical anti-essentialism implied that one can only know unique human individuals. Essences or general concepts were 'spooks' that prevent one from pursuing self-interest; humans set them up as fictional external compulsions. For Stirner, submissiveness or 'slave morality' was at the root of domination in society: 'If submissiveness ceased, it would be all over with lordship'. The manner in which submissiveness might cease was, however, not through revolution, but through internal and individualised psychological change, a refusal to recognise authority and law, expressed through rebellion and crime. Stirner defined his object as 'not the overthrow of an established order but my elevation above it, my purpose and deed are not political and social, but egoistic. The revolution commands one to make arrangements; rebellion demands that one *rise or exalt oneself*'.[44]

Politics was thus reduced to the social arrangements that might foster individual greatness. 'Exaltation of the self' rested above all, in Romantic terms, on one's claim to uniqueness or 'ownness'. Even freedom was deemed to be a lesser value than this. Genius, defined in terms of self-generated expression of the will, was the most valuable element of uniqueness, and might raise the individual to the status of 'superman'. Within this discourse, there was a tendency to equate individual uniqueness – in theory open to all – with an elitist or aristocratic emphasis on the greatness of the few. Only a minority of egoists or geniuses would throw off servility and learn to use their will. The remainder – the herd – became insignificant. Indeed, the servile condition of most individuals resulted from their collusion with the determination of their lives by outside influences. Their collusion meant that autocratic rule or oppression of the weak was justified.

The tolerance of autocracy, possibly temporary but potentially permanent, distinguished egoists from the majority of anarchist thinkers. In addition, while many anarchists regarded property as illegitimate, Stirner gave it a fundamental status, though in a different sense from 'possessive' individualists. While he accepted that property could become a 'fixed idea' or a 'mania', it was necessary to the first step of becoming an egoist: 'through property our self-will gain[s] a secure place of refuge'. Anything which one used for one's own ends could be regarded as property. The individual was to make society his [*sic*] own 'property', by using it for his own ends.[45]

One's body, however, did not figure as 'property' in egoist philosophy. Max Stirner repeatedly emphasised the corporeal nature of the ego. His concept of the self, or Ego, did not divorce mind and body, or look to some interior essence of 'self'. He was highly critical of those 'spiritualist' or Christian thinkers who 'love only the spirit', cutting themselves 'in half' and exalting the spirit over the body. In contrast, the egoist loves the self, the 'corporeal man with hide and hair'. Stirner argued 'It is only through the "flesh" that I can break the tyranny of the mind; for it is only when a man hears his flesh along with the rest of him that he hears himself wholly'.[46] There was, then, a strongly corporeal element to the individualist literature influential on the egoist 'advanced thinkers' of feminism.

Broadly, Dora Marsden adopted an egoist position from around 1912, after she had moved definitively away from the suffrage movement. Her work as a writer and editor in popularising and developing egoism made it accessible as an intellectual resource for Anglo-American feminism in the period before the changes brought about by the war made egoism politically problematic. This should be seen as a focalisation of concerns with individuality and self-development which had already existed within the women's movement, but which became more pressing as the suffrage struggle became more controversial and less of a unifying force.

The change Marsden sought in women was fundamentally psychological, and in keeping with the introspective turn of Edwardian feminism. Property (or 'owndom') was important to the process of self-development, but secondary to the real goal, the psychological transformation its gaining would entail: 'The Woman's Movement then is the movement amongst women towards the acquisition of property – not as an end in itself, but as the moulder of destiny'.[47] To achieve the power of wealth, the freewoman must cultivate 'the sense of quality, the sense that a woman has gifts, the sense that she is a superior, a master'. Because of this required sense of superiority, Marsden regarded feminism as a doctrine 'so hard on women that, at the outset, we can only appeal to those who have already shown signs of individuality and strength'.

Marsden predicted that only a few women had the capacity to be a freewoman, or would appreciate her ideas: 'at the present time, our interpretation of the doctrine has merely to be stated clearly to be frankly rejected by, at least, three women in every four'. This strand of feminism had no egalitarian commitment to include all women, since this would imply a top-down imposition on women not capable of 'willing' their own emancipation. From the opening editorials of *The Freewoman*, Marsden argued that it was futile to preach feminism to 'women who are essentially ordinary women'. She sought a social and political order wherein 'the gifted might be a natural aristocracy, practising the code of a higher order'. Suffrage feminism was thus working along quite the wrong lines, and implied a dangerous support for equality: 'Men are afraid of all liberty . . . that is why the multitude, when a daring soul has flashed the light of "liberty", immediately caps it with the extinguisher "equality" '.[48]

Marsden's elitist conception of the 'freewoman' was counterposed to the constraining 'mass' features of modern society. Her work echoed a very widely shared cultural and political concern for her contemporaries, a fear of massification. 'The crowd' trope was utilised by many thinkers, most notably Gustave Le Bon in France, Wilfred Trotter, Charles Masterman and Graham Wallas in Britain. For these thinkers, the crowd signified mob mentality, mass consumption and the erosion of the unique in the 'mass' age of modern capitalism.[49] This concern was equally present in the United States. Quoting Emerson, the American critic James Huneker wrote in *Egoists*: 'Is it not the chief disgrace in the world not to be a unit; to be reckoned one character; not to yield that peculiar fruit which each man was created to bear, but to be reckoned in the gross?' A 1913 American dictionary defined the crowd as 'The lower orders of people; the populace; the vulgar; the rabble; the mob'.[50] Marsden drew on these ideas in her disdain for crowd mentality in politics, the servility induced by the state or by concepts of rights, the machine-like nature of industrial conditions that stamped out uniqueness. But she was also no doubt influenced by her own experiences of crowds – both the hostility of crowds towards the suffrage processions in which she had been so prominent only three years previously, and what she saw as the personality-effacing mob instincts of suffrage enthusiasts.

'Personality' – frequently capitalised – was a recurring theme of this set of ideas. On the surface, this could be seen as drawing on the same discourse as that of fostering good character, but with quite different connotations. One can distinguish a 'politics of personality' that grew out of, and yet cannot be reduced to, the 'politics of character' that influenced so much Edwardian thought. 'Personality' and 'character' were frequently used more or less interchangeably, but following Walter Susman, they can be usefully distinguished.[51] 'Character' refers to the more conventional, idealist-influenced moral thought, while 'personality' is used to distinguish elitist and egoist strands of individualism. Both these strands flourished within Edwardian feminism. B. L. Hutchins, a Fabian, *New Age* writer and campaigner on women's work conditions, offers a fascinating example of a blend of these two intellectual traditions, again indicating the free appropriation that could be made of two quite distinct discourses. Her comments on personality as a chief aim of the women's movement were backed up with textual references to Helen Bosanquet's *The Family* (1906) and the work of the COS, as well as avant-garde sources such as Elsie Clews Parsons.

The same moral commitment to self-development that inspired some formulations of 'feminist individualism' could work quite differently when formulated as a concern with personality. 'Character' and 'personality' functioned sometimes as fairly conventional moral terms, sometimes as a means of conceiving radical, iconoclastic personal and social change.[52] Within feminism, the discourses of personality and character shared many features; each deployed the concept of 'the will', and were similarly voluntaristic; use of the will gave individuals the choice – to be free or 'bond'. External constraints would dissolve if one's choice was self-reliance or freedom. Both discourses radically downgraded the significance of 'externals' such as rights, and prioritised introspection and psychological status.

They differed, however, over the question of elitism. Marsden argued that 'only those rare, positive persons whom we call personalities dare claim their kingdoms and claim their own satisfactions. Personality is the living equation of genius.' The political discourse of character included an affinity to social organicism – the moral character of the whole and the individual were interrelated, even though 'circumstances' could not account for character. Personality was more radically individualist, and was to be developed (in Stirnean terms) as self-exaltation, independent of the good of the whole. Marsden's use of personality celebrated uniqueness and genius, and she therefore rejected the entire vocabulary of service and duty that went with many women's claims to self-development in this period. The political order idealised by Marsden and her contemporaries was rooted in personal greatness rather than social interdependence, and this confined their projected utopian order to a very simple, pre-urban, anti-democratic model.[53]

Given the strong Edwardian interest in egoism and the work of Nietzsche, Marsden's use of ideas that can be described as Stirnean is not surprising. But her reading of egoism as compatible with feminism seems to require further explanation. The egoist tradition was ambiguous towards women, and the Nietzschean element of aristocratic individualism was read by Edwardians as overtly inhospitable to women's inclusion as individuals. As Edith Ellis, the wife of Havelock Ellis and a *Freewoman* reader, noted in 1910, 'Nietzsche has little to say of women. He is curiously reticent about them. In his philosophy there is evidently to be no over-woman.' Stirner's work was seen as more favourable to women; in the introduction to the 1912 edition of *The Ego and His Own*, James Walker argued 'Stirner's attitude toward women is not special. She is an individual if she can be, not handicapped by anything she says, feels, thinks or plans. . . . there is not a line in the book to put or keep woman in an inferior position to man, neither is there anything of caste or aristocracy.'[54]

Egoist thought was also associated with Ibsen, and in this form, with women's emancipation. James Huneker paraphrased Stirner to label 'Womanhood' a 'spook', in order to lay claim to a 'feminist' egoism: 'There is no Woman, only a human Ego ... Society, family are the clamps that compress the soul of woman. If woman is to be free, she must be first an individual, an Ego.'[55]

Though his followers read him as a 'feminist', Stirner seems at first sight an unlikely source of ideas for feminists. Yet he was a seminal influence on some within the feminist vanguard, as a letter from Edna Kenton shows:

I read Stirner's Ego five times through before I laid it down for more than over night: then I went off with it to a little solitary island for six months of solitude and tore and clawed at myself – to find myself. Stirner did it – started me.[56]

Kenton went on, 'until the advent of *The Freewoman*, I had not had the same feeling of breathless wonder at the voicing of hitherto unprinted things since reading *The Ego and His Own*'.[57] Kenton had been hovering at the edges of the suffrage movement, but her real commitment was to feminism, developed through her participation within Heterodoxy and reading of *The Freewoman*. Through her success as a novelist and journalist, she was an inspirational founding member of Heterodoxy. Inez Gillmore described Kenton as 'first and foremost' amongst Heterodites;

Gillmore had avidly pursued Kenton's writings in the *Smart Set*, and admired her work on Henry James. Kenton wrote confidently on feminism, and even where she was asked to comment on suffrage, she managed to attach an air of 'the modern' to her contributions. In 1915, for example, she participated in the suffrage special issue of *Harper's Weekly*, with a piece titled 'The Shocking Aspect of the New!' This article conveyed a simultaneous sense of suffrage being an unthreatening goal, while also being insufficient as the prime aim of the women's movement. Kenton was convinced that 'Feminism in its essence – if it is anything – is a great personal, joyous adventure with one's untried self' and she stressed women's own responsibility to grasp this opportunity.[58]

The concept of freedom as a subjective choice, to which external conditions would 'conform' had been hinted at in assertions such as Emma Goldman's, that 'woman is confronted with the necessity of emancipating herself from emancipation, if she really desires to be free'. However, Dora Marsden was perhaps the first to explicitly construct the feminist project in Stirnean terms, and to deny women's duty of service towards larger entities.[59] When the American journal *Current Opinion* ran a biography of Marsden, under the title 'A Feminist Disciple of Nietzsche', the author simultaneously implied that Nietzsche and Stirner were well known to women, and that Marsden's use of their ideas was something extraordinary and novel: '[Dora Marsden], of course, has read Nietzsche and Stirner. So have other women. But not one of them has thus unflinchingly applied the egoistic philosophy to the woman movement.' What resonance did Marsden's ideas have in the wider feminist movement?

Marsden's egoist individualism has been read as alienating suffragists and feminists, and placing her journal in extremist isolation; yet in fact her readership welcomed at least some of her insights. The idea of a greater emphasis on introspection within feminism was especially well received. Isabel Leatham, for example, wrote to thank Marsden for her 'Bondwomen' editorial 'where you make it so clear that woman's bondage in the last resort is psychological, and that only in the freedom of her will lies her true equality with man'. Mary Gawthorpe called for *The Freewoman* to be made 'a fighting weapon for a pure individualism'.[60] The fierce rejection of parasitism that characterised feminist texts of this period resonated with descriptions of 'the freewoman' as financially and emotionally independent. Indeed, Marsden explicitly drew on the 'parasite' metaphor that Schreiner had used so famously in relation to women, though with different connotations from the 'character discourse' of more mainstream feminism. In an interview publicising *The Freewoman* it was reported that

'Miss Marsden described the position of the majority of women as "parasitic"' – both in terms of money, but more importantly, parasitic on others' personality or will.[61] Readers of feminist texts would have been familiar with the parasite metaphor, as well as with calls for a transformation in feminine character; to argue for a new development of personality may have seemed only a small step from this.

The Freewoman thus became a forum for the development of an individualistic version of emancipation, abandoning feminism's moral vocabulary of duty and service. A contributor argued, 'It is morality, with its constraints, laws, punishments, conventions, prejudices and timidities, which spoils life, not unmorality, or even immorality'. Charles Whitby, one of the regular *Freewoman* contributors, and a cousin of Olive Schreiner, argued, 'Morality is, when you get to the bottom of it, mainly, perhaps exclusively, a matter of taste'. No moral or social duty – children, the race, purity, tradition – could be seen as making a binding claim. In its most developed form, this position was associated with a full-blown and amoral egoism. As Marsden saw it:

The objective of the Woman Movement being the development of the individual Ego ... it appeals to the spirit of woman ... it seeks to make them strong in spirit, to rise up and seize the means to their own development ... to throw off external authority and follow the voice within.[62]

This voluntaristic and self-oriented vision raised some problems. An egoistic world in which one must defend one's own interests, and may aggressively encroach on others at whim, seems antithetical to any analysis of society that highlights some groups as systematically discriminated against, and seeks to end such discrimination. *The Freewoman*'s experimentation with individualism and egoism has therefore struck many historians as inimical to feminism. Stirner's amoral vision of a world of self-interested action was hard to render compatible with the highly moralised Edwardian feminist visions of service and the public good. With egoism replacing any kind of 'moral economy', an elitist approach or indeed virtually any self-oriented action seemed to be justified.

Marsden's highly polemical ideas were contested and modified by other contributors. Dr David Eder, pioneer Freudian and socialist, provided a socialist rebuttal of Marsden's individualism in the second issue of *The Freewoman*. Eder rejected the free individual as 'an entity separate from all other human entities, with relationships towards no other individuals, associating with none, linked to no one, bound to nothing. Such freedom of the individual is forever impossible to human beings.'[63] Other contributors supported Eder's position. Millicent Murby, a feminist involved in the *New Age* circle and a translator of Henri Bergson, was also provoked by the individualism of *The Freewoman*:

Surely we have learnt that progress and the whole art of life consist in realising not one's self as an individual only, but one's self as an individual who is one with the society of which he or she forms a part in its past, present and future. The creative output of every individual is to be judged solely from social criteria.[64]

Murby and Eder's contributions forced Marsden to make her position on the subjective nature of freedom clearer. She stated that she did not intend to imply atomism, which was 'not only impossible, it is inconceivable, and no such parody of freedom was ever suggested by the writer of "bond-women". The word "freedom" postulates relationships. It has no meaning apart from them. Alone on a desert island a person can neither be "free" nor "not-free". Dr Eder is thinking of "isolation" which we did not mention.'[65]

Marsden clearly intended her individualism to be compatible with some forms of social relations and entities distinct from the individuals that made them up. She supported co-operation, but on the condition that the agent was 'her own master, master of her own free-will, independent and free to make her own alliances and her own co-operations'.[66] This co-operation was not to be based upon passionate political inspiration, sentiments similar to those inspiring the suffrage agitation:

To how many will the beat of a drum set the heart pulsating to a quicker vibration ... in the passion for causes, in martyrdom, the joy of living is so intense and life so vivid that only the highest form of human love-passion can be compared with them.[67]

Political action was sanctioned in Romantic terms, based on inspiration rather than contract or coercion. As Charles Whitby saw it, 'Nothing really great can be accomplished without passion ... By passion is implied the preoccupation of the personality by a single, irresistible and overwhelming desire. The vast majority of individuals are, needless to say, incapable of passion.' The claim to self-development or personality was justified by the opportunity it gave to 'the individuals who compose societies to become Great'.[68] Despite this elitism, there was one shared, even democratic means of accessing the passion that made individuals great – and that was through the realm of sex.

EMBODIED PASSIONS

It is clear that Dora Marsden and her contemporaries saw the egoist individual (freewoman, or superwoman) not as abstract, of the spirit, but embodied and passionate. 'Ultra-feminists' were notorious for their celebration of diverse forms of sexuality, and frank discussions of bodily functions. Indeed, the multiplicity of types of desire, and questioning of any standards of 'normality' in sexuality came to symbolise individuality within *The Freewoman*.[69] Many feminists welcomed the chance to 'fill their minds' with questions of the body. For Floyd Dell in Chicago, the most remarkable thing about *The Freewoman* was its openness to correspondence on the topic of sex. He wrote about the debates prompted by Marsden's ideas 'it must have done the writers no end of good to express themselves freely. For once sex was on a plane with other subjects, a fact making tremendously for sanity. In this Miss Marsden not only achieved a creditable journalistic feat, but performed a valuable public service.'[70]

This, however, was a feature that many in the women's movement found revolting. So was the sexually liberated new woman or freewoman merely 'libertine' and 'licentious', as Olive Schreiner and Maude Royden felt? Mari Jo Buhle has pointed out that feminists of this period were seeking to understand sexuality as 'the leading indicator of selfhood' or, in later terminology, of subjectivity. They hoped to delineate a female psyche through looking at sexuality, and thus to highlight not only gender differences, but also the transformative power of sexuality.[71] Buhle has described the appropriation of Freud by American feminists to this end. A number of early Freudians were involved with 'advanced' feminist circles, although the 'sex psychology' with which avant-garde feminists engaged was eclectic, comprising thinkers such as Jung, Havelock Ellis and Otto Weininger. Heterodoxy members included Beatrice Hinkle, a Jungian psychologist, and Leta Hollingworth, an early researcher in the field of psychology. Members such as Mabel Dodge conspicuously inhabited and relished the world of psychotherapy; Edna Kenton cynically described the atmosphere in 1915 Greenwich Village: 'Freud and Jung and the minor psychoanalysts were just then beginning to be translated and Washington Square and its many radiating little streets bloomed into a jungle of misunderstood theories and misapplied terms'.[72]

In Britain, many 'advanced' feminists were heavily involved in the study of the psyche. Winifred Hindshaw had studied experimental psychology in Manchester with Samuel Alexander, a philosopher interested in the new pioneering science of psychology and a strong supporter of the women's movement. Two other British *Freewoman* contributors, Barbara Low and David Eder, became prominent psychoanalytic practitioners, with Eder providing some early translations of Freud and experimenting in psychoanalytic methods.[73] The development of Edwardian psychology was part of the intense interest in the nature of the 'modern self' that underlies much feminist and avant-garde thinking of this period. Psychology provided a language and conceptual framework for the Edwardian 'introspective turn', by calling into question the rational, conscious individual.

Though Marsden herself did not to our knowledge sustain any sexual relationships in her lifetime, she clearly intended the discussion of sexual morality to feature large in her journal. This cerebral approach was characteristic of her, as a highly abstract thinker who retreated more and more from personal human relationships. Nonetheless, what seems to have been a non-sexual friendship with Mary Gawthorpe was still intense and stormy, and she was well acquainted with experiences of passion, though apparently not with heterosexuality. Five editorials by Marsden, titled 'The New Morality', ran from 14 December 1911 to 18 January 1912. 'The New Morality' was a euphemism for the new science of sexology. British 'New Moralists' were prominent, with Havelock Ellis and Edward Carpenter exploring sex as central to selfhood, natural and healthy, and politically crucial. By 1910, the movement had gathered force in America, where *The Masses* openly discussed and advertised works by European sexologists, and where the ideas of Freud were increasingly popular.[74] In the first of her 'New Morality' editorials, Marsden portrayed the English women's movement as moving from a 'small' request for political emancipation, into a more radical recognition of 'the disorder of living according to the law, the immorality of being moral, the monstrousness of the social code'.[75] This process was difficult for women because while men had only paid lip service to moral law, women had internalised it: '*Their* moral code has received its sanction and force from within'. Women's self-renunciation had gone deep, leading to a rejection of all sensual pleasures. The religious, ascetic basis of morality must (echoing Nietzsche) be replaced by the 'riotous, passionate, exultant thrill of being'.

Marsden went on in the 'New Morality' series to resist the equation of passion with lust. The 'thrill of being' was not 'the snacking at sex, the dreary, monotonous sounding of one note in sex'. She proposed an ideal of 'sensuous, sensitive, restrained and fastidious men and women'. Sex was important, but 'the turbulent exultation of sense which rushes to work itself out to a swift finish' was not the highest manifestation of passion. Instead, the 'riveted attention' of 'creative vibration' – expressed in

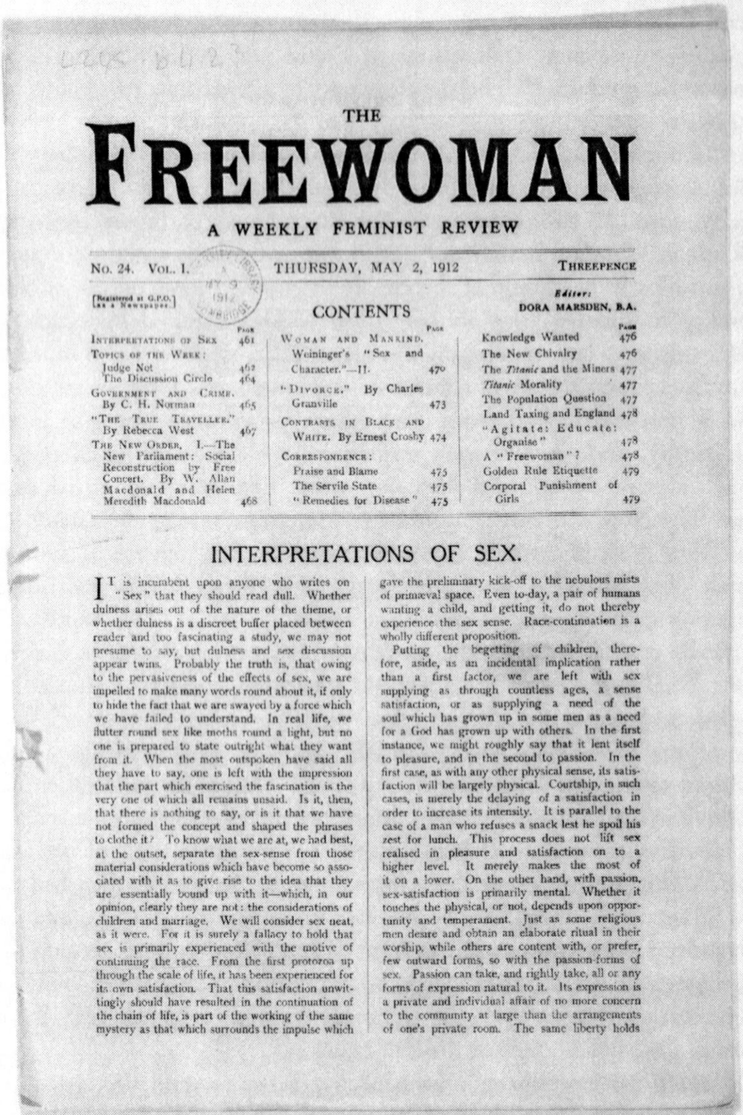

THE
FREEWOMAN

A WEEKLY FEMINIST REVIEW

No. 24. Vol. I.   THURSDAY, MAY 2, 1912   Threepence

[Registered at G.P.O.]
[as a Newspaper]

Editor:
DORA MARSDEN, B.A.

CONTENTS

INTERPRETATIONS OF SEX.

IT is incumbent upon anyone who writes on "Sex" that they should read dull. Whether dulness arises out of the nature of the theme, or whether dulness is a discreet buffer placed between reader and too fascinating a study, we may not presume to say, but dulness and sex discussion appear twins. Probably the truth is, that owing to the pervasiveness of the effects of sex, we are impelled to make many words round about it, if only to hide the fact that we are swayed by a force which we have failed to understand. In real life, we flutter round sex like moths round a light, but no one is prepared to state outright what they want from it. When the most outspoken have said all they have to say, one is left with the impression that the part which exercised the fascination is the very one of which all remains unsaid. Is it, then, that there is nothing to say, or is it that we have not formed the concept and shaped the phrases to clothe it? To know what we are at, we had best, at the outset, separate the sex-sense from those material considerations which have become so associated with it as to give rise to the idea that they are essentially bound up with it—which, in our opinion, clearly they are not: the considerations of children and marriage. We will consider sex neat, as it were. For it is surely a fallacy to hold that sex is primarily experienced with the motive of continuing the race. From the first protozoa up through the scale of life, it has been experienced for its own satisfaction. That this satisfaction unwittingly should have resulted in the continuation of the chain of life, is part of the working of the same mystery as that which surrounds the impulse which gave the preliminary kick-off to the nebulous mists of primaeval space. Even to-day, a pair of humans wanting a child, and getting it, do not thereby experience the sex sense. Race-continuation is a wholly different proposition.

Putting the begetting of children, therefore, aside, as an incidental implication rather than a first factor, we are left with sex supplying as through countless ages, a sense satisfaction, or as supplying a need of the soul which has grown up in some men as a need for a God has grown up with others. In the first instance, we might roughly say that it lent itself to pleasure, and in the second to passion. In the first case, as with any other physical sense, its satisfaction will be largely physical. Courtship, in such cases, is merely the delaying of a satisfaction in order to increase its intensity. It is parallel to the case of a man who refuses a snack lest he spoil his zest for lunch. This process does not lift sex realised in pleasure and satisfaction on to a higher level. It merely makes the most of it on a lower. On the other hand, with passion, sex-satisfaction is primarily mental. Whether it touches the physical, or not, depends upon opportunity and temperament. Just as some religious men desire and obtain an elaborate ritual in their worship, while others are content with, or prefer, few outward forms, so with the passion-forms of sex. Passion can take, and rightly take, all or any forms of expression natural to it. Its expression is a private and individual affair of no more concern to the community at large than the arrangements of one's private room. The same liberty holds

Figure 10: *The Freewoman*, 2 May 1912, p. 461

passion, love, great causes, or religion – was to be explored.[76] Only 'great geniuses' would be able to draw upon most of these spheres of passion; for the rest, 'human love, the greatest common measure of passion, has to open out the way for us'. Marsden therefore declared her 'new sex morality' to be in favour of experimentation, and against 'indissoluble monogamy'. This stance could not lead to excessive promiscuity, because she believed that for freewomen, polygamy was 'a physiological and psychological impossibility'. She depicted genuine passion as 'absorbing, jealous, exclusive, and individual', and therefore naturally monogamous. Despite this, true lovers were ready to change sexual partners once 'psychic communication' was at an end.

The avant-garde feminist assertions about sexuality should be understood in the context of widespread assumptions about 'the sexual nature of woman'. The tendency to comment on 'woman' in the singular had led to numerous generalised assumptions about the nature of feminine desire. One such assumption was that women were more invariable and 'average' than men. Havelock Ellis, for example, in his influential *Man and Woman* argued:

in men as in males generally, there is an organic variational tendency to diverge from the average, in women as in females generally, an organic tendency, notwithstanding all their facility for minor oscillations, to stability and conservatism, involving diminished abnormality.

The criminologist and phrenologist Cesare Lombroso came to a similar conclusion. He argued that 'All women fall into the same category, whereas each man is an individual unto himself; the physiognomy of the former conforms to a generalised standard; that of the latter is in each case unique'.[77] This argument was widely restated and accepted by Edwardian biologists and social commentators.

Amongst 'advanced' feminist circles, this assertion was subverted by those such as Stella Browne, who believed one should 'acknowledge the infinite variety of human nature', and especially the 'great variations of sexual constitution, tastes and temperament'. Similarly, Dora Marsden argued that life was moving from undifferentiation or amorphism in the direction of 'differentiation, articulation, individuality, personality' in all spheres including the sexual. 'A Would-Be Freewoman' agreed, arguing that 'there are hardly two feminine natures alike, and nowhere is the difference between individual women so great, as in this, sexual temperament'.[78] Individualism here represented a rejection of an overarching

and homogenising 'womanhood'. Far from compromising their individuality through their physical nature, such 'freewomen' achieved individuality *through* the creativity of sex. Individual diversity was carried into
the sexual realm. Marsden's view of sexual activity as a 'democratic' means
of 'springing life higher', in which all could participate and potentially gain
access to the 'higher realms' of human experience, was distinctly Romantic,
and she saw sex as part of the creative work that went into the realisation of
individuality.

One feminist writer, Stella Browne, simply stated 'Let us admit our joy
and gratitude for the beauty and pleasure of sex'.[79] Many of advanced
feminist circles, however, found it extremely hard to express any such
emotions, and wrote of their extreme naïvety and inexperience in sexual
matters. Françoise Lafitte, a young French visitor to London in 1912, wrote
of her chance meeting in Hyde Park with a stranger, who kissed her
unexpectedly. She immediately abandoned their shared park bench, but
then spent the whole night worrying about the encounter. 'I was disgusted
with myself; more so next day when I had spent a sleepless night during
which I had felt stark naked in the arms of a naked man and, to my virgin
mind, in such an intensity of feverish contact that the day-dream appeared
actual possession'.[80] In order to 'humiliate' herself, as she put it, and place
the encounter into perspective, she forced herself to go and meet the man
the following Sunday, only to flee on sighting him. Shortly after this, she
fell in love with an American syndicalist, who (quoting Fourier) promised
her a free union but they parted when she became pregnant. There was,
then, both psychological and practical barriers to the enjoyment of the
'new morality,' and birth control debates were the place where these were
most openly confronted.

BIRTH CONTROL AND SEXUAL DIVERSITY

Stella Browne, a Canadian-born but London-based socialist and activist
for women's rights, was a prominent contributor in discussions of sexuality.[81] Browne made bodily integrity a basis for individuality, celebrating
sexual pleasure and rejecting outside influence on women's reproductive
decision-making. Like many other 'advanced' feminists, she demanded
free access to contraception and abortion. The campaign for birth control
had been well established in America and Britain by the time that it came
to be associated with 'feminism' in the early twentieth century. In the
United States, nineteenth-century campaigns for 'voluntary motherhood'
were widespread, mostly resting on calls for sexual abstinence and women's

right to refuse sex. There was some experimentation with the prevention of conception, in the Oneida community's practice of male continence (prevention of ejaculation), for example, or Alice Stockham's 'Karezza'.

The campaign became more political after some American states began to outlaw abortion, and in 1873, the federal government Comstock Act made all birth control information obscene. Despite the reluctance of the leadership of the labour and socialist movements, birth control became the province of activists within the grass roots of these groups, while the women's movement remained relatively silent on the issue. In the early years of the twentieth century, the flamboyant Greenwich Village activists took up the issue, working through their IWW and Socialist Party networks. The socialist Margaret Sanger became a figurehead for the movement after the banning of her column in *The Call* in 1913, which allowed birth control to be framed as a free speech issue. Her arrest and flight to Europe in 1914, and the high-profile prosecution of her husband, in 1915 opened up the campaign, which was taken up by Emma Goldman, Mary Ware Dennett, Elizabeth Freeman, Kitty Marion and Elizabeth Gurley Flynn.[82] The periodicals of the avant-garde and the politically active – *The Masses, Mother Earth* – were strong supporters of Sanger and her journal, *The Woman Rebel* (1914).

Heterodoxy members were engaged in sexual experimentation, though they disappointed Margaret Sanger with their lukewarm response to her campaign, perhaps because heterosexuality was not at the core of their identity. A few, such as the NAWSA activist Mary Ware Dennett, brought a radical commitment to democracy to the birth control campaign, in contrast to Margaret Sanger's determination that medical doctors should be the gatekeepers to the regulation of reproduction. Dennett, like other feminists such as Max Eastman and Elsie Clews Parsons, preferred to liberalise the entire field, providing free access to contraception to all comers. The campaign uneasily combined Sanger's move to entrench (male) health-care professionals and occasional use of racist versions of eugenics, with socialist commitments to anti-poverty strategies, anarchist rejections of the state's involvement in reproduction, and more avant-garde commitments to free unions and experimentation without the responsibilities of childbirth. Within such a complex landscape, the construction of birth control as a feminist issue was somewhat obscured, and even the most controversial, such as Elsie Clews Parsons, only referred to it obliquely and without detail, as 'the spacing of babies'.[83]

Birth control leagues developed across the United States from around 1914, marshalled from 1917 by the *Birth Control Review*. Many activists in this campaign looked to Europe where they felt that nation-states were more liberal, and the devices available more advanced. The issue of birth control in Britain, long discussed by radicals such as Francis Place and William Thompson, had been given a public airing during the 1876–8 prosecution for the distribution of contraceptive pamphlets by Charles Bradlaugh and Annie Besant. It was also dramatised by the clear evidence of fertility control in the declining birth-rate of the middle classes, evident in the 1911 *Fertility of Marriage Census*.[84] The Malthusian League was set up in 1877, and distributed its own periodical, *The Malthusian*, as well as hundreds of thousands of pamphlets urging family limitation. From 1913, their pamphlet *Hygienic Methods of Family Limitation* gave explicit contraceptive advice, though it was aimed only at the married, and was not freely distributed.[85]

Though birth control gained a high profile in the late Edwardian years, there was little comment and involvement from the British women's movement. Millicent Fawcett explicitly denied any link between neo-Malthusianism and suffrage, and was delighted to report that enfranchised women in the Antipodes had a higher fertility rate than disenfranchised British women. Tentative discussions took place in working-class bodies such as the Women's Co-operative Guild, but this did not translate into an active campaign until the 1920s.[86] As in the United States, the idea of voluntary motherhood was popular, but this was more likely to mean chastity and continence than the control of reproduction and free unions.

Influenced by social purity traditions, there was a deep suspicion of the freedom contraception would give men to exploit women sexually within the women's movement. The vanguard 'feminist' movement, however, became explicitly associated with 'free love', inheriting this from the anarchist and free-thought circles with which it had been customarily associated. Mary Knight, a WSPU activist, wrote of the desire amongst 'advanced women' to limit their families. They 'decline to do their duty to anyone but themselves. That is their individualism.' Knight saw greater openness about sexuality and control of reproduction as a transatlantic phenomenon: 'The American girls and the advanced women have brought about this change'.[87] As so often in Britain, the 'advanced woman' was associated with American lifestyles. For Knight, however, this meant the ability to live 'the free bright life' of the spinster, and many feminists extolled the life of the 'bachelor maid'. One 'advanced' feminist and simple life enthusiast, Millie Price, described her ambivalence about marriage; within the context of the 'restless energy' of the Leeds Arts Club and unconventionality of Letchworth Garden City, she wrote,

'I was glimpsing a form of cultured, mentally active, "Old Maid" life that fascinated me'.

Millie Price's male peers in the Leeds Arts Club were also less interested in the spinster life, and preferred the physical. During her formative years in Leeds, Mary Gawthorpe described the married Orage unexpectedly stealing a kiss from her during her involvement in the club. Price herself wrote: 'I offered A. R. O[rage] the service of my mind, but was too often aware that the service of my body would have given him greater satisfaction. He christened me The Ice Maiden. Openly expressing his belief in free love, he was prepared to practice his beliefs.'[88] Sexual experimentation was sometimes a dangerous realm for 'advanced' women.

However, for many avant-garde women, not only the freedom of spinsterhood but the sexual variety of the 'rebel girl' really represented individualism. It was *The Freewoman* that provided the most open of feminist forums in which abortion, masturbation, sexual passion and sexual variety could be discussed, often in conjunction with debates around birth control. Malthusian League activists Charles Vickery Drysdale (editor of *The Malthusian* between 1907 and 1916) and his wife Bessie Drysdale were heavily involved with *The Freewoman* and its Discussion Circle. Charles Drysdale contributed a series of articles on 'Freewomen and the Birth-rate' to *The Freewoman*, provoking a great deal of discussion about birth control. While some argued against limitation of births, they did so from the radical grounds of seeking to destroy 'the whole edifice of life-marriage', rejecting sexual monogamy, and asking for absolute sexual freedom for 'freewomen'. Most however, assumed that 'free working women will, either by natural or artificial means, avoid having children frequently'.[89]

What distinguished feminist individualism was that, birth control aside, women must take absolute responsibility for the raising of their children. Above all, maternity should not serve as a means of obtaining financial support or social status. Marsden argued: 'child-rearing is not the State's business, nor even yet the father's business, but the mother's'.[90] This idea was ridiculed by others in the women's movement, as tending to weaken the involvement of fathers and make women more financially vulnerable, and it reads as an oddity to twenty-first-century feminists.

It was, however, an important declaration of women's individuality, and became widely expressed amongst American feminists. Winifred Harper Cooley argued that in the United States, 'younger feminists' felt that support from a man for 'sexual privileges' or motherhood was 'morally revolting'. Elsie Clews Parsons declared in 1916 that the state should regard the mother as ultimately responsible for her child, and not the father. The unwillingness to accept this 'in certain feminist circles', Parsons put down to 'the persistence of the very institutional ideas about women that feminists in general oppose, the proprietary ideas that make of women irresponsible beings to be cared for'.[91] Given the experiments with raising children as single mothers amongst advanced feminists such as Rebecca West, Isadora Duncan, Mina Loy and Françoise Lafitte – as well as the large numbers who remained childless – they were well aware of the price of 'free' motherhood. Duncan, for example, suffered prolonged postnatal 'neurasthenia' after the birth of her daughter, perhaps in response to the lack of material and emotional support from the child's father. West also complained of personal and professional isolation of motherhood. On finding herself pregnant, Lafitte investigated having an abortion, but changed her mind when she realised she would be operated on by a 'quack' who might injure her and possibly leave her to bear a disabled child. Stella Browne made the difficult decision to have an illegal abortion. Aware of such experiences and prospects, Browne therefore saw sexual choices as an essential part of this Edwardian synthesis of feminism and individualism:

our *right to refuse maternity* is also an inalienable right. Our wills are ours, our persons are ours; nor shall all the priests and scientists in the world deprive us of this right to say 'No'.[92]

CONCLUSION

In sum, the individualism expressed by Marsden and others within the feminist avant-garde was not of a liberal or even libertarian kind – there was no embrace of rights and equality, and little interest in external constraints on individuals. Rather, their individualism was introspective, and highly critical of ideas of women's social service and duties. A shared commitment of these strands of individualism lies in the rejection of egalitarianism, in preference to 'the great individual'. This specific feature was not necessarily opposed to the political ideas of the women's movement, particularly the militant suffragists, who tended to support the idea of exceptional women leading from the front and changing politics through heroic individual interventions. There was nevertheless a divergence between the moral individualist politics of *character* that I argue was associated with suffragism more generally, and the egoistic politics of *personality*. Both emphasised attention towards (voluntaristic) self-development, but constructed quite different political orders on this moral claim, as we shall see in subsequent chapters looking at theories of the state and visions of utopia.

'Egoist feminism' was not an entirely comfortable space, and the logic of Stirner's anti-essentialism led Marsden to come to argue by 1913 in the successor to *The Freewoman*, *The New Freewoman*, that 'accurately speaking, there *is* no "Woman Movement." "Woman" is doing nothing – she has, indeed, no existence.'[93] This was perhaps a response to the retreat of the WSPU from any attempt to construct a mass, popular movement for women's suffrage. As the leadership of the movement was purged, first of the Pethick-Lawrences in 1912 and then of Sylvia Pankhurst and the East London Federation of Suffragettes in 1914, the dominance of Christabel Pankhurst (now based in Paris) was uncontested. Violence grew from window-smashing to arson; Emily Wilding Davison was killed at the Derby of June 1913; forcible feeding became more intense under the continuous release and rearrests of the Cat and Mouse Act. Where Marsden had still believed in 1911 in the power of women's suffrage as 'a really popular agitation', she had come by 1913 to see 'Womanhood' and the 'woman movement' as generalised essences that constrained the individual. And as we shall see below, her analysis of first the industrial unrest of 1914 and then the war only intensified her commitment to egoism.

Individualism of the Stirnean kind had the potential to undermine the collectivised, aspirational function of the identity 'freewoman' that was such a powerful draw for 'vanguard' women. However, 'individualism' as a generic whole should not be blamed for this development. Within Edwardian feminism, individualist concerns from a variety of traditions were deployed in a productive manner. The more controversial thinkers attempted to associate values of individuality and autonomous decision-making with the 'private' sexual sphere. The discussion of the body portrays an attempt to rethink the body as integral, rather than dangerous, to individuality.

This chapter has sketched out the diverse elements of individualist political thought. I suggest that the individualism of avant-garde feminism had distinct sources from the moral individualism influential upon the mainstream of the women's movement. It also differs from the individualism which more recent feminist theorists have criticised as atomistic and disembodied. I argue therefore for a more historically aware understanding of the term individualism in relation to Edwardian feminist thought. The roots of the individualist position embraced by 'ultra-feminists' are not to be found within aspects of libertarian thought, of which later feminists have rightly been critical. Their values might be called the Romantic or egoist values of self-development and uniqueness, rather than values of privacy and *laissez-faire*. The vehicle for these values was not an abstract, pre-social individual, but an embodied, passionate and emphatically sexed individual.

This avant-garde feminist individualism was not aberrant and misplaced, as some commentators have suggested, but should be seen as an engagement with the central discourses of the Edwardian period. The contemporary intellectual context shows widespread concerns over 'the crowd', 'machine-culture', and the growth of state intervention. Other feminist texts show similar (introspective) concerns, particularly a stress on the individual's responsibility to achieve emancipation. The avant-garde thinkers of feminism stressed women's dignity, creativity and self-development, and shared some of these concerns with the more conventional suffrage-oriented women's movement.

There was however no successful and complete assimilation of feminism and individualism; the very nature of these generalised 'isms' rule this out. However, this reading of Edwardian feminism does provide a counter-account to the commonly assumed opposition between feminism and individualism, and a historically sensitive account of the sources of this feminist appropriation of individualism. I turn now to the most directly political aspect of early twentieth-century feminism, the relationship between the individual and the state.

END NOTES

1. Rose Young, 'What is Feminism?' *Good Housekeeping* May 1914, 680.
2. Zillah Eisenstein, *The Radical Future of Liberal Feminism* (London, Longman, 1981); L. Susan Brown, *The Politics of Individualism: Liberalism, Liberal Feminism and Anarchism* (Montreal, Black Rose Books, 1993).
3. Carole Pateman, *The Sexual Contract* (Cambridge, Polity Press, 1988), pp. 184–5.
4. Denise Riley, *Am I That Name? Feminism and the Category of 'Women' in History* (Basingstoke, Macmillan, 1988), pp. 4, 42.
5. Linda K. Kerber, 'Can a Woman be an Individual? The Discourse of Self-Reliance', in Kerber, *Toward an Intellectual History of Women* (Chapel Hill, University of North Carolina Press, 1997), p. 212. The values of individualism were given classic nineteenth-century expression by Henry Thoreau as aloofness and self-expression, and by Ralph Waldo Emerson as dissent, the ability to remain distinct within the crowd. Thoreau's 1854 utopia of backwoods isolation, material autonomy and hard work expressed what came to be seen as the 'rugged individualism' of frontier mentality. Alexis de Tocqueville, *Democracy in America* (New York, Library of America, 2004); Henry David Thoreau, *Walden* (Oxford, Oxford University Press, 1999).

6. It is beyond the scope of this chapter to give a full intellectual history of individualism in Britain and the United States; I give a brief summary of some individualist thinkers, and refer to the extensive literatures available on their ideas. Stefan Collini discusses four historical forms of individualism – political, economic, scientific and moral individualism. Stefan Collini, *Liberalism and Sociology: Liberalism and Political Argument in England, 1880–1914* (Cambridge, Cambridge University Press, 1979). In this chapter, I have explored the (overlapping) political and moral arguments for individualism, with a somewhat narrower scope than Collini's – the former refers to those ideas associated with idealism (used in political rather than philosophical argument), while the latter refers to that concept of the limited state associated with Herbert Spencer and his followers. I have been concerned to distinguish egoist individualism from the core political formation of Victorian and Edwardian individualism, the liberal or libertarian belief in limits to state action.

7. Charles E. Mitchell, *Individualism and its Discontents: Appropriations of Emerson, 1880–1950* (Amherst, University of Massachusetts Press, 1997); Rodney Barker, *Political Ideas in Modern Britain* (London, Methuen, 1978), pp. 52–4; Herbert Spencer, *Political Writings*, ed. John Offer (Cambridge, Cambridge University Press, 1994).

8. Collini, *Liberalism and Sociology*, p. 22.

9. Most notably, the liberal individualism of J. S. Mill drew on many of the same premises concerning privacy and autonomy as Spencer, while maintaining a progressive position on 'the woman question'. See J. S. and H. T. Mill, *Essays on Sex Equality*, ed. Alice Rossi (Chicago, University of Chicago Press, 1970).

10. Harrison, 'The Act of Militancy'.

11. Stanton, reprinted in Mari Jo and Paul Buhle, *The Concise History of Woman Suffrage* (Urbana: University of Illinois Press, 1978), pp. 325–7, esp. 325.

12. Barker, *Political Ideas in Modern Britain*, p. 115; Wendy McElroy, *Individualist Feminism of the Nineteenth Century: Collected Writings and Biographical Profile* (Jefferson, NC, McFarland, 2001); Pateman, *The Sexual Contract*; Naomi Scheman, 'Individualism and the Objects of Psychology', in *Discovering Reality*, ed. S. Harding and M. B. Hintikka (Boston, Reidel, 1983).

13. David and Andrew Vincent Boucher, *British Idealism and Political Theory* (Edinburgh, Edinburgh University Press, 2000).

14. George Herbert Mead, 'Josiah Royce – A Personal Impression', *IJE* (1917), reprinted in Randall E. Auxier, *Critical Responses to Royce* (Bristol, Thoemmes Press, 2000), vol. 2, pp. 295–6. See Josiah Royce, *Lectures on Modern Idealism* (New Haven, Yale University Press, 1964).

15. Weyl quoted in Charles Forcey, *The Crossroads of Liberalism: Croly, Weyl, Lippmann, and the Progressive Era, 1900–1925* (New York, Oxford University Press, 1961), p. 78; May Sinclair, *The New Idealism* (London, Macmillan, 1922); Mary Gilliland Husband, 'Women as Citizens' (a lecture delivered to the Hampstead Ethical Institute), *IJE* (July 1909), pp. 466–76; Gilman, 'The Humanness of Women', *Forerunner*, 1909–10.

16. Stears, *Progressives*, pp. 28–35; Reba Soffer, *Ethics and Society in England: The Revolution in the Social Sciences 1870–1914* (Berkeley, University of California Press, 1978); Nikolas Rose, *The Psychological Complex: Psychology, Politics and Society in England 1869–1939* (London, Routledge, 1985).

17. R. Plant and A. W. Vincent, *Philosophy, Politics and Citizenship: The Life and Thought of the British Idealists* (Oxford, Blackwell, 1984), p. 108.

18. Helen Bosanquet, *The Strength of the People: A Study in Social Economics* (London, Macmillan, 1902), pp. 44, 46.

19. Gareth Stedman Jones, *Outcast London: A Study in the Relationship Between Classes in Victorian Society* (Oxford, Clarendon Press, 1991), pp. 10–15, 256–72. See also Susan Pedersen, *Eleanor Rathbone and the Politics of Conscience* (New Haven, Yale University Press, 2004), p. 91.

20. Bosanquet, *The Strength of the People*, pp. 4, 38; Collini, *Liberalism and Sociology*, p. 28.

21. Millicent Fawcett, for example, lectured for the COS, and *The Englishwoman's Review* strongly endorsed COS policy. Leading figures such as Eleanor Rathbone also worked with the COS or local equivalents in their early years of public work, and endorsed the principles of self-help, moral uplift and thrift. Pedersen, *Eleanor Rathbone*, p. 59.

22. Helen Bosanquet, *Social Work in London 1869–1912* (Brighton, Harvester Press, 1973; orig. 1914), p. 402; Bosanquet, 'The Intellectual Influence of Women', *IJE* (Oct. 1905), 15–24; Olive Anderson, 'The Feminism of T. H. Green: A Late-Victorian Success Story?' *History of Political Thought*, 12:4 (Winter 1991).

23. Tuttle, *Awakening of Woman*, p. 57.

24. Quoted in E. M. Palmegiano, *Women and British Periodicals 1832–1867* (New York, Garland, 1976), p. xliii.

25. Hugh Stutfield, *Blackwood's Edinburgh Magazine*, Jan. 1897, 105, 104; Marie Jenney Howe, 'Feminism', in 'A Feminist Symposium', *New Review*, Aug. 1914, 441.

26. Alice Hubbard, 'Something New Under the Sun', *Harper's Weekly*, 13 Dec. 1913, 6–8. See also Hubbard, *Woman's Work* (East Aurora, NY, Roycrofters, 1908), p. 39.

27. Key, *Woman Movement*, p. xv.

28. Goldman, 'The Tragedy of Women's Emancipation', *Mother Earth*, March 1906, 9–17. See Matthew Thomas on the transatlantic intellectual heritage of anarchist feminism, 'Anarcho-Feminism in Late Victorian and Edwardian Britain, 1880–1914', *International Review of Social History*, 47:1 (2002).

29. 'Some of the Meanings of Feminism', *Christian Science Monitor* 12 June 1914, 23; Tuttle, *Awakening of Woman*, p. 16; Young, 'What is Feminism?' 684.

30. Max Eastman, 'Is Woman Suffrage Important?' 1910, Men's League for Woman Suffrage, MWDP.

31. Bosanquet, *The Strength of the People*, pp. 123; Ray Strachey, *The Cause: A Short History of the Women's Movement in Great Britain* (London, Virago, 1928), pp. 235, 305, emphasis added.

32. B. L. Hutchins, *Conflicting Ideals: Two Sides of the Woman's Question* (London, Thomas Murby, 1913), p. 81.

33. Robert Booth Fowler, *Carrie Catt, Feminist Politician* (Boston, Northeastern University Press, 1986), p. 16.

34. Key, *Woman Movement*, pp. 222–3.

35. Vera Brittain, *Testament of Youth: An Autobiographical Study of the Years 1900–1925* (London, Victor Gollancz, 1933), p. 25.

36. Commentators have read the name-changes of the journal as symptomatic of a linear retreat *from* feminism *to* individualism; see for example Clarke, *Dora Marsden and Early Modernism*, pp. 1–4. My reading in contrast stresses the compatibility, indeed the centrality, of individualism to feminism at this historical moment.

37. Marsden, *FW*, 23 Nov. 1911, 1–2.

38. Marsden, *FW*, 12 Sept. 1912, 321.

39. Marsden, *FW*, 23 Nov. 1911, 22.

40. In common usage, egoism designated 'selfishness', Stefan Collini, *Public Moralists: Political Thought and Intellectual Life in Britain 1850–1930* (Oxford, Clarendon Press, 1991), p. 61. This meaning persisted; W. Lyon Blease described male opposition to feminism as 'practical egoism', in Blease, *The Emancipation of English Women* (London, Constable, 1910), p. 133. But the growing impact of Stirner and Nietzsche's ideas and Ibsen's cultural criticism led in the late nineteenth century to a new understanding of egoism as a philosophy. Egoist philosophy entailed a nihilistic rejection of collective entities such as the state, and of abstract concepts such as 'Justice' or 'Humanity'. Egoism is frequently read as part of the anarchist tradition, but it drew on a wider set of individualist values. Egoists placed no intrinsic value on merely being human – value was *earned* by one's efforts to achieve individuality and express one's will. This resulted not from acting on whim, pleasing oneself, but was found in a 'prescription of law to oneself,' an effect only few could achieve. Max Stirner, *The Ego and Its Own*, ed. D. Leopold (Cambridge, Cambridge University Press, 1995), p. 182. Nietzsche's politics of the 'master race' envisaged 'a tremendous new aristocracy, based on the severest self-legislation, in which the will of philosophical men of power and artist tyrants will be made to endure for millennia' (Nietzsche, *The Will to Power*, quoted in Bruce Detwiler, *Nietzsche and the Politics of Aristocratic Radicalism* (Chicago, University of Chicago Press, 1990), p. 99).

41. In Britain, egoist philosophy made little impact until the end of the nineteenth century. See David Thatcher, *Nietzsche in England 1890–1914* (Toronto, University of Toronto Press, 1970); Steele, *Alfred Orage and the Leeds Arts Club*, p. 52.

42. James Huneker, *The Egoists: A Book of Supermen* (London, T. Wener Laurie, 1909); Edwin Bjorkman, *Is There Anything New Under the Sun?* (London, Stephen Swift, 1913), pp. 28–31.

43. Marsden, *FW*, 8 Aug. 1912, 222.

44. Max Stirner, *Ego and its Own*, p. 16, original emphasis.

45. *Ibid.*, p. 169.

46. *Ibid.*, pp. 37, 31, 81.

47. Marsden, *FW*, 29 Aug. 1912, 285.

48. Marsden, *FW*, 30 Nov. 1911, 21–2; 6 June 1912, 42; 18 Jan. 1912, 161.

49. Graham Wallas, *Human Nature in Politics* (London, Archibald Constable, 1908); C. F. G Masterman, *The Condition of England* (London, Methuen, 1960); Gustave Le Bon, *The Crowd: A Study of the Popular Mind* (London, T. Fisher Unwin, 1896); Wilfred Trotter, *Instincts of the Herd in Peace and War* (London, T. Fisher Unwin, 1916).

50. Emerson, quoted in James Huneker, *The Egoists*, p. 372; *Webster's Dictionary*, 1913, p. 349.

51. Susman, *Culture as History.*

52. Edith Ellis, *Three Modern Seers* (London, Stanley Paul, 1910).

53. Marsden, *FW*, 8 Aug. 1912, 222. Emma Goldman used a similar language of personality. She argued that women's 'freedom, her independence, must come from and through herself. First, by asserting herself as a personality and not as a sex commodity.' Emma Goldman, *Anarchism and Other Essays* (New York, Kennikat Press, 1969; orig. 1910), p. 217.

54. Ellis, *Three Modern Seers*, p. 182. Stirner, *Ego and His Own*, pp. xvi–xvii. Though for Walker, 'the author shows not one iota of prejudice or any idea of division of men into ranks', he overlooks the strong current of anti-Semitism in Stirner's work.

55. James Huneker, *The Egoists*, p. 361.

56. Edna Kenton to Marsden, DMC 1 Aug. 1913: IV, 1a.

57. Kenton, *New Freewoman* circular, 1913: IV, 3.

58. Kenton, 'The Shocking Aspect of the New!' *Harper's Weekly*, 8 May 1915, 434; *Delineator*, 'Feminism will give men more fun, women greater scope, children better parents, life more charm', July 1914, 17.

59. Goldman, *The Tragedy of Women's Emancipation* in Alice Rossi, *The Feminist Papers* (New York, Columbia University Press, 1973), p. 510; *Current Opinion*, Jan. 1912, 48.

60. Leatham, *FW*, 7 Dec. 1911, 54. Gawthorpe to Marsden, 29 Oct. 1912, DMC, original emphasis. Joan Scott's study of Madeleine Pelletier reveals a French version of 'a feminism articulated within the discourse of individualism' in the early years of the twentieth century, Joan Wallach Scott, *Only Paradoxes to Offer: French Feminists and the Rights of Man* (Cambridge Mass., Harvard University Press, 1996), p. 127. *The Freewoman* published an article by Pelletier, and its links with French intellectual life suggest that the intellectual milieu for 'advanced' feminism was not just Anglo-American, the primary focus of this study, but also included French thinkers.

61. Woman's Future, *Evening Standard and St James's Gazette*, 25 Oct. 1911, 20.

62. 'Tiens Ferme', *FW*, 25 April 1912, 457; Whitby, *FW*, 1 Feb. 1912, 216; Marsden, *FW*, 29 Aug. 1912, 285.

63. Eder was an early pioneer in school hygiene in Bow and Deptford. He was also secretary to William Morris' Bloomsbury Socialist League, and one of

the founders of the London Labour Party. See J. B. Hobman, *David Eder: Memoirs of a Modern Pioneer* (London, Victor Gollancz, 1945). David Eder *FW*, 30 Nov. 1911, 33.

64. Murby, *FW*, 28 March 1912, 374.
65. Marsden, *FW*, 14 Dec. 1911, 73.
66. Marsden, *FW*, 29 Aug. 1912, 285.
67. Marsden, *FW*, 1 Feb. 1912, 201.
68. Whitby, *FW*, 4 April 1912, 385; Marsden, *FW* 26 Sept. 1912, 365.
69. Bland, *Banishing the Beast*, pp. 275, 280–7; Lesley A. Hall, "'I Have Never Met the Normal Woman": Stella Browne and the Politics of Womanhood', *Women's History Review*, 6:2 (1997); Hall, 'Stella Browne, the New Woman as Freewoman', in *The New Woman in Fiction and in Fact: Fin-de-siècle Feminisms*, ed. Angelique Richardson and Chris Willis (Basingstoke, Palgrave, 2001), pp. 224–38.
70. Dell, *Women as World Builders*, p. 92.
71. Buhle, *Feminism and its Discontents*, pp. 28–9.
72. Edna Kenton, *The Provincetown Players and the Playwright's Theatre*, ed. Travis Bogard and Jackson R. Bryer (Jefferson, NC, McFarland, 2004), p. 15.
73. W. Hindshaw, 1938. *Reminiscences*. Samuel Alexander Papers, John Rylands Library, University of Manchester. Alexander also taught Dora Marsden, and went on to become her philosophical mentor in her later, more isolated years. In 1913 David Eder became the first secretary to the London Psycho-Analytic Society.
74. Buhle, *Feminism and its Discontents*, pp. 35–7.
75. Marsden, *FW*, 14 Dec. 1911, 61.
76. Marsden, *FW*, 4 Jan. 1912, 121; Marsden, *FW*, 28 Dec. 1911, 102. There is some evidence that Marsden thought the passions of suffrage were of this creative kind, when unstifled by the discipline imposed by leaders. She described her own experiences of hunger-striking and her experiences of 'spirit expansion'. Marsden, *FW*, 9 May 1912, 482.
77. Quoted in Joan Scott, *The Conundrum of Equality*, Occasional Papers (Paper 2), School of Social Science (Princeton, Institute for Advanced Study, 1999), p. 4.
78. Browne *FW*, 18 April 1912, 437, 1 Aug. 1912, 218; Marsden, *FW*, 13 June 1912, 61; 'A Would-Be Freewoman', *FW*, 21 March 1912, 353.
79. Browne, *FW*, 18 April 1912, 437.
80. Françoise Delisle, *Friendship's Odyssey* (London, Heinemann, 1946), p. 185.
81. On Stella Browne see Hall, 'Stella Browne and the Politics of Womanhood'; Sheila Rowbotham, *A New World for Women. Stella Browne: Socialist Feminist* (London, Pluto Press, 1977).
82. Stansell, *American Moderns*, pp. 234–41.
83. Schwarz, *Radical Feminists of Heterodoxy*, pp. 81–2, 84; Chen, *The Sex Side of Life*; Eastman, 'Revolutionary Birth-Control', *The Masses*, July 1915; Parsons, 'Feminism and Sex Ethics', p. 463.
84. See Floyd Dell [?], 'Criminals All', *The Masses*, Oct.–Nov. 1915, 21; Browne, 'The Work of Margaret Sanger: Birth Control in America', *Beauty and*

Health, Jan. 1917; Richard Allen Soloway, *Birth Control and the Population Question in England, 1877–1930* (Chapel Hill, University of North Carolina Press, 1982), p. 125.

85. Lesley Hall, 'Malthusian Mutations: The Changing Politics and Moral Meanings of Birth Control in Britain', in *Malthus, Medicine and Morality*, ed. B. Dolan (Amsterdam, Rodopi, 2000), p. 150.

86. Jeffrey Weeks, *Sex, Politics and Society: The Regulation of Sexuality Since 1800* (London, Longman, 1989), p. 163; Richard Allen Soloway, 'Feminism, Fertility and Eugenics in Victorian and Edwardian England', in *Political Symbolism in Modern Europe*, ed. S. Drescher *et al.* (New Brunswick, Transaction Books, 1982), p. 152. Fawcett probably practised birth control herself, but refused to testify for the defence in the Bradlaugh-Besant trial in 1877. Gillian Scott, *Feminism and the Politics of Working Women* (London, University College London Press, 1998).

87. Mary Knight, 'Woman v. The State', *Westminster Review*, July 1909, 39–40.

88. Unpublished autobiography of Millie Price (née Browne), 'This World's Festival', Margaret Byham Papers, The Women's Library, London Metropolitan University (henceforth MBP), pp. 142, 94–5.

89. Isabel Leatham, *FW*, 4 Jan. 1912, 131; 11 Jan. 1912, 151; E. M. Watson, *FW*, 4 April 1912, 397.

90. Marsden, *FW*, 28 March 1912, 375.

91. Cooley, 'The Younger Suffragists', 7; Parsons, 'When Mating and Parenthood are Theoretically Distinguished', *IJE*, 26:2 (Jan. 1916), 213–14.

92. Stella Browne, *FW*, 1 Aug. 1912, 218.

93. Marsden, *NFW*, 15 June 1913, 5.

CHAPTER 4

The state, the home and nurturing citizenship

In an apparent contrast to the intense individualism of the early twentieth century, the goals of the nineteenth-century women's movement can be seen as centred on what the state could do for women. Campaigns as diverse as women's right to keep their citizenship and property on marriage, their ability to sit on local government bodies, to act as factory inspectors, or to gain the help of the state in their domestic responsibilities, all oriented themselves towards public action. I have sketched out the commitment to individualism amongst 'advanced' feminists as an introspective affair. Nonetheless, the tendency amongst feminists to address themselves to the state persisted alongside this introspection, and provoked intense feminist debate concerning the range and legitimacy of governmental action.

The predominant nineteenth-century libertarian strand of individualism was associated with a strictly limited state, a neutral arbiter, mediating between different interests and guaranteeing private spaces for the activities of individuals.[1] The discourse of 'moral individualism', loosely associated with idealism, came to underpin a conception of a more interventionary, enabling state, though still founded on an individualist basis. At their most polemical, avant-garde feminists rejected both these formations of the state, and dismissed all forms of law, state power and processes of representation. At other times, their individualism proved to be compatible with state intervention. A careful reading reveals quite large spheres which they were willing to allow for state action. The treatment of the state by avant-garde feminists represents a specifically Edwardian individualism, characterised by a curious mixture of distrust of the state and recognition of its enabling power.

This chapter therefore describes the shifting status of state power in early twentieth-century political thought, giving a brief survey of trends in 'new liberal', progressive, and Fabian approaches to the state, before turning to suffrage and avant-garde feminist political argument. The anti-statist current within modern feminism has been seen as opposed to the predominant statism of the Edwardian women's movement. Nonetheless, I conclude with a reading of this political argument as arising from specifically feminist concerns.

THE EVOLVING IDEA OF THE STATE

The Edwardian period in Britain and the United States witnessed a growth in state power, and in its social intrusiveness. The idea of an 'essentially socialistic Great State, owning and running the land and all the great public services' became welcomed by commentators like H. G. Wells, and despaired of by Hilaire Belloc. Given the increasing visibility of social, and particularly urban, problems, Edwardians 'had come to accept that the State must increase its intervention in order to raise up the underprivileged, even though this meant exposing all citizens to greater government activity'.[2] Indeed, the idea of the collective responsibility of the state for the 'welfare' of its citizens has been regarded as a hallmark of twentieth-century progressiveness. Within Fabian socialism, for example, top-down state-led reform was seen as an alternative to class struggle. Progressive reform was to take the form of an expanded state providing a wide range of social goods and services. The trend is evident in Britain within the increasingly interventionist Liberal Party, who came to support the Factory Acts, the Trades Boards Act in 1909, a National Insurance scheme in 1912 and increased state intervention into industrial disputes and social policy. Likewise in the United States, the challenge of the Progressive Party from 1912 and the widespread atmosphere of discontent with traditional methods of governance allowed for experiments with a broader range of state powers.[3]

NEW LIBERALISM

For many feminists, British 'new liberalism' (if women could be incorporated as voters) promised an ideal mode of government, capable of both philanthropy and a maximisation of social efficiency.[4] Feminists, for the most part, expected and required the state to become more proactive in social provision. Their expectations were met by the reforming Liberal governments of 1906–1914. Women had recently come to take a more active role in government, gaining the right to serve as parish, rural and urban councillors in 1894, and county councillors in 1907.[5] Both the personnel of the state, and the concept of its appropriate sphere of influence, were being transformed.

The Liberal Party, in power in Britain from 1906 to 1914, responded to the concerns raised by the Boer War, the growing labour unrest and the increased strength of working-class political representation, by offering a series of social policy measures. Pensions, school dinners, medical inspection in schools, and health insurance all emerged over this period, though this was an ad hoc programme, experimenting with different styles of state intervention. Overall, it amounted to a significant gain in regulatory or disciplinary power by government. The new liberals' progressive agenda required that the state provide a minimum of economic security that would then enable citizens to provide for themselves. In the words of the new liberal theorist, L. T. Hobhouse, the 'civic state' should 'secure conditions upon which its citizens are able to win by their own efforts all that is necessary to a full civic efficiency. It is not for the State to feed, house, or clothe them. It is for the State to take care that the economic conditions are such that the normal man ... can by useful labour feed, house and clothe himself and his family'.[6]

The '*laissez-faire* atomism' of nineteenth-century political theory had been challenged at the end of the century by the social organicism of idealist political philosophy. The state as conceived in Bernard Bosanquet's 1899 *The Philosophical Theory of the State* might step in to remove obstacles to the formation of good character and self-reliance in its citizens, acting as a 'hindrance to hindrances'. T. H. Green introduced 'positive freedom' into the political vocabulary, conveying the idea that the ideal freedoms of individualism might require limited forms of social legislation.[7]

This moderate political individualism envisaged a strictly limited role for the state, but a larger one than the more libertarian individualism of the mid-nineteenth century. Though idealism was an Anglo-American affair, it took contrasting forms in each country. American idealists such as Josiah Royce were less convinced that a centralised state could empower individual and social freedom, and preferred to stress the local 'provinces' of governance where intervention might be appropriate. In contrast, British idealists became more enthusiastic about the central level; D. G. Ritchie's *Principles of State Interference* (1891) sought to dissolve the opposition between the state and individual, and saw the state as a positive instrument for self-realisation. Under this new conception, the state did not function to guarantee privacy, but to foster good character, and this logic opened the way to a more enabling role for legislation.

Influenced by idealism yet also frequently in opposition to it, new liberal theorists evolved a 'social welfare' programme of 'utilising the productive powers of members of society for social purposes'. The new liberals moved

away from the Spencerean idealisation of free competition and thrift, to
focus on maldistribution of consumption power, and the social and economic waste involved in economic competition. The organic metaphor for
society came to imply the need for the state to ensure an efficient and just
distribution of resources across groups. As J. A. Hobson argued, 'In a body
which is in health and functions economically, every cell contributes to the
life of the organism according to its powers'.[8] The head or brain served as a
metaphor for the central organising role of the state in a holistic social body
for idealists and liberals.

FABIAN STATISM

A second, related strand in Edwardian political argument came from the
centre-left Fabian Society, founded in Britain in 1884 to pursue 'ethical',
reformist forms of socialism. It is not easy to make generalisations concerning the Fabian Society's 'approach', since a number of strands are
present in 'Fabianism', often coexisting in tension. Early Fabian work is
located near to the 'philanthropic' concerns of late nineteenth-century
feminism, and was strongly influenced by idealist and other nineteenth-
century formulations of 'good character'.[9] The Fabian focus shifted in the
early twentieth century, as they became more dominated by efficiency and
reformist concerns, often condescendingly described as municipal or 'gas
and water' socialism. This strand of Fabianism was epitomised by the work
of Beatrice and Sidney Webb, though the two strands were never entirely
distinct. In later years, the Fabians became synonymous with a state-
led form of socialism, with a particular focus on local government. For the
Webbs, the state was figured as 'the missing prime mover, the massive
actor and legislator necessary to deal with apparently intractable social
problems'.[10] In 1916, Sidney Webb declared municipalisation and
co-operation to be the two leading characteristic trends in modernity. The
state was the meeting-point of these trends, and was to express both in
harmony.

The Fabian view of the state has been seen as its most distinctive contribution to socialism, and represented a reformist attempt to relate socialism to existing political institutions. It has, however, been associated with
the sacrifice of representation and individual autonomy to efficiency. The
political participation of those whose lives they set out to improve has been
seen as marginalised within Fabianism, which did not promote a politics of
individual agency and action. Dora Marsden argued that the Webbs'
'intolerable itch for managing their fellows is the one thing which breaks

down – almost eradicates – all free instincts'.[11] The Fabians preferred administrative efficiency and pragmatic permeation to inclusion and direct action. The affinities between the radical liberals and the Fabians were thus counterbalanced by their diverse approaches to democracy.

Democracy, consent and participation were core values of new liberalism. The state was to be made more inclusive (perhaps even including women) to match its widened responsibilities. But despite their commitment to democracy, the new liberals also shared with the Fabians a tendency to condone state coercion, if in the interests of the common good. The liberal theorists occupied a precarious position between the traditional liberal promotion of economic competition in conditions of equality of opportunity, and a powerfully interventionist state. State coercion was justified by its moral end. This moral element was entrenched in the legislation of the early twentieth century and made for an element of judgmental intrusiveness in Liberal social policies. The social citizenship conceived of by the new liberals and the Fabians, theoretically open to all, was in fact policed by conceptions of fitness for citizenship. It is worth dwelling on this element of coercion, and its moral overtones, since it was these features of the theory of the state that particularly irritated and provoked individualists, including those of the feminist avant-garde.[12] Nonetheless, the prevalent political stance was one that accepted top-down intervention as appropriate and desirable.

THE AMBIVALENCE OF AMERICAN STATISM

There has been flourishing historiographical debate concerning the decades before the First World War in the United States. This period was viewed unproblematically as a 'progressive era' by historians of the 1950s and 1960s. In the 1970s, however, the defining characteristics of the 'era' came under scrutiny, and historians such as Peter Filene preferred to see 'progressivism' as a historical 'moment', one political formation among many. Such historians have stressed the plurality and fluidity of issue-focused coalitions working within a period in which there was a weakening of party loyalties. The progressive 'era', it seems, cannot be defined in terms of its core commitments or ideologies; any list of 'progressive' tenets would, as Daniel Rodgers points out, contain any number of contradictory positions. Rodgers thus suggests that the search for an ideological framework for 'progressivism' should be abandoned, in favour of attention to the discursive resources of progressives – namely, the 'distinct social languages' or 'clusters of ideas' drawn upon. These include rhetorics of anti-monopolism, of social interdependence, and of social efficiency. While the first is distinctively American, the second two were thoroughly transatlantic in their origins.[13] I make no claims to adequately summarise this complex ideological space, but in what follows, various progressive understandings of the state are traced out, and related to the British context and the American feminist movement.

The United States government, a new colonial power from 1899, intervened in unprecedented ways domestically and internationally, experimenting with new powers of organisation and centralisation. Theodore Roosevelt, president between 1901 and 1909, struggled to centralise political power into the executive, and to extend the bureaucratic power of government. British political ideas – both the nineteenth-century Spencerean and idealist traditions, and the early twentieth-century Fabian and new liberal politics – were influential upon American politics, though they took on different slants in that distinct context. Fabian ideas – initially those associated with the ethical socialism of the early Fabian Society – spread to the United States through the influence of Rev W. D. P. Bliss, and of Robert Woods' description of Fabianism in his 1891 *English Social Movements*. Some prominent Americans were also members of the London Fabian Society. Bliss had founded the Society of Christian Socialism in Boston in 1889, modelled on English equivalents. He later founded several short-lived Fabian Societies, issued Fabian Tracts, and, from 1895, published *American Fabian*.[14]

The later Fabian focus on efficient governance also contributed to the transatlantic exchange in social policy, as prominent British Fabians lectured in America and actively attempted to create a transatlantic sphere of influence.[15] Like these Fabians, American progressives sought to maximise efficiency, stressing the scientific nature of their reforms. They preferred the intervention of the expert or the professional, preferably within a voluntary organisation, to bureaucratic government. The policies of the American progressives have sometimes been characterised as representing a 'new liberalism' (or a 'corporate liberalism'), though marked by a much greater commitment to nationalism than British versions. American 'progressives' resembled 'new liberals' in seeking uplift rather than wholesale social revolution. They described themselves as 'radical without being socialistic' and identified as 'cautious Fabians'.

As in Britain, then, the 'progressive era' in America heralded a more interventionist state, particularly in relation to the power of big business. There was, however, a continuing distrust of power devolved to the state. Reformers campaigned to make government more responsive, through using referenda, popular elections and so on. There was also a persistent reliance upon voluntary organisations, including religious ones, in effecting reform. The idea of a 'service state', popular in Britain, was treated with more ambivalence in the United States. American political culture had become averse to party politics and thus wary of the partisanship of democratic governments. Despite this ambivalence, there were attempts made to enhance the effectiveness of government, to make administration more scientific, and to use this 'enhanced' state as an instrument of social reform. As in Britain, this was particularly directed to experts and elites. The state, in Herbert Croly's ideal, served *and* shaped public opinion, which was to be 'aroused, elicited, informed, developed, [and] concentrated' by elite leaders.[16] Increased social welfare spending was not matched by any accompanying commitment to popular participation. The period did not see an expansion in voting rights except for women's suffrage, initially achieved incrementally at state level. Poor and black voters were increasingly excluded from the franchise, and progressives emphasised economic rights rather than active citizenship.

FEMALE CITIZENS AS 'THE NATIONAL HOUSEKEEPERS OF THE FUTURE'

What impact did this overall shift towards interventionism have on women, and feminist political thought? In broad terms, 'progressivism' should be read as sympathetic to the various American women's movements. Settlement house social work and suffragism were in keeping with the progressive trend towards more responsive, democratic government and greater attention to social harmony and social control. The expanded state institutions took an increased interest in women, given the growing awareness of interaction between efficiency in production and efficiency in reproduction. This concern was deepened by the rhetoric of 'racial degeneration', and perceived familial neglect by working women that prevailed in both countries. Ellen Ross describes the intense social policy pressure exerted upon British women:

What was new in the twentieth century was the exclusive focus on mothers and childcare, the sheer size, number and organisation of the programmes ... and the series of coercive laws that now accompanied the programmes.[17]

Activists of the women's movement in the early twentieth century certainly felt excluded from the state, its law-making and enforcing processes that could be so coercive for women. They identified the law as 'man-made' and oppressive to women. Key politicians and advisors seemed ill-disposed to the greater political *involvement* of women. Though most 'new liberal' progressives supported women's suffrage, they were a male-dominated, upper-middle-class elite, who showed little sensitivity to gender relations. Many leaders (including Woodrow Wilson) were noncommittal on the question of women's suffrage. The progressive approach was open to social intervention by the state, but was nonetheless dominated by a business ethic that placed profitability as the main concern. The municipal politics which were often coded as 'feminine', in contrast, centred on the equation of the home with the wider city, and were dominated by concerns about health and collective interdependence. There concerns were sometimes understood as antagonistic to other progressive agendas, and there was no easy settlement of the differences associated with 'men's' and 'women's' politics.[18]

Nonetheless, most activists of the 'women's movement' remained faithful to the idea of the state, held accountable by a democratic and broad (to varying degrees) franchise. Many clearly felt comfortable with, and sought to expand, the mechanisms of state power, despite the negative experiences of arrested and imprisoned militants. Sandra Holton argues that the radical potential of the suffrage movement lay in its extension beyond the single issue of the vote, into an alliance with progressive politics that required a feminisation of the polity. Appeals to extend the state's work on behalf of women shifted from the mainly nineteenth-century purity and philanthropic concerns to a broader set of policy areas, including industrial protective legislation and welfare issues.[19] Feminists such as Margaret McMillan, an American-born ILP activist and later campaigner for state services for children in Britain, recognised that women expected a new role in the expanded work of the state:

The thinking, wage-earning woman does not wish then to go back, but forward. The State is not a mere name to her – an abstraction. Whether she willed or no, she has had to come into a new relation to it. She sees that there is a larger life, and that she has to become an active and conscious part of it.[20]

There was scope for such involvement as 'private' reproductive and familial decisions came to be seen as legitimate areas of public intervention. The state in America and Britain came to take on an increasing range of 'domestic' tasks, such as the feeding of school children, the collection of rubbish, and widows pensions.[21] Few within the women's movement were critical of these developments. Indeed, many both initiated and sought to capitalise on this developing role for the state, which was widely seen as requiring women's input, to argue for women's citizenship rights. As a contributor to a British symposium on women's suffrage described it:

The most powerful argument for women's suffrage is, I think, the change that is proceeding in the functions of the State. Originally a military organ, the State is on the point of becoming the nerve centre through which the nation's collective thought and will is translated into action ... The work the State did in the eighteenth century was man's work. For the finer work now in hand women's assistance is essential. As long as the State denies women's citizenship it is doing its work with one hand, perhaps the right hand, tied behind its back.[22]

The writer deployed a metaphor favoured by idealist political thinkers, of the state as an organism. From around the end of the nineteenth century, however, women activists offered a new metaphor to lay claim to a public space in which women might be as competent and 'at home' as men – the state as the home or family. This metaphor relied upon a portrayal of the 'public sphere' as populated by the values of the family – the 'mother-instinct of altruism', for example. Charlotte Despard of the Women's Freedom League envisaged a familial and all-embracing state:

The larger life of the future offers [woman] opportunities of service to the great family, the State, which will be then to each of us what it was in the old Greek democracies, mother, father, master, friend.[23]

A contributor argued in *The Vote* 'the State is the family with its boundaries extended, and ... the ethics of the smaller human family must also be the ethics of the larger'. The writer and suffragist Laurence Housman made a similar argument: 'As Wesley said "the world is my parish", so should a woman say "the State is my home". The State should be the home writ large'.[24]

Sustained by the transatlantic links between settlement, suffrage and temperance networks, this language also flourished in the United States from the 1890s. Anna Garlin Spencer, a high-profile journalist, social worker and independent minister, argued to a suffrage audience: 'the State enters "Woman's peculiar sphere", her sphere of motherly succour and training, her sphere of sympathetic and self-sacrificing ministration to individual lives'.[25] Spencer spoke of 'the mother-office of the State', and American reformers tended to speak of the state in the feminine gender.[26] Adopting the same metaphor as British activists, suffragists commonly referred to government or municipal housekeeping; Jane

Addams stated: 'Politics is housekeeping on a grand scale'. Rheta Childe Dorr argued that 'Women's place is Home. Her task is homemaking. Her talents, as a rule, are mainly for homemaking. But Home is not contained within the four walls of an individual home. Home is the community. The city full of people is the Family, the public school is the real Nursery'.[27]

Another suffragist pointed out 'The new truth, electrifying, glorifying American womanhood today, is the discovery that the State is but the larger family, the nation the old homestead, and that in this national home there is a room ... and a duty for "mother" '.[28] Historians have argued that women activists in America were able, through this discourse of familial or 'civic maternalist' politics, to exert considerable influence upon the shaping of social policy in the early Edwardian years. This was less to do with received ideologies of women's special moral influence or separate spheres, and rather stemmed from activist women's daily gendered experiences in the running of the home, as well as from the transatlantic exchanges in social policy thought located within the women's movement.[29]

This maternalist idiom may have been influenced by idealist political thought, with its moral ideal of self-development placed within a collective, communal context. The family was regarded as a key site of character development and altruism. These virtues were the foundation of civic virtues, and the family could be seen as a miniature polis. Idealist philosophy was read and written by activists within the women's movement. Eleanor Rathbone, who became an important post-war feminist leader, studied in Oxford with idealists such as David Ritchie, and was heavily influenced by the tradition set up by T. H. Green.[30] Idealism also informed the social work of women such as Jane Addams in the United States, and in Britain, Helen Bosanquet, Millicent Fawcett and Octavia Hill.[31] While the idealists tended to reject state intervention as destructive of character and responsibility, their ideas of active citizenship and equation of the family and state later came to be seen as consistent with more state intervention. Bernard Bosanquet remained ambivalent about the role of the state, but many of his contemporaries became more enthusiastic. D. G. Ritchie argued unambivalently that 'the State, ... by freeing the individual from the necessity of a perpetual struggle for the mere conditions of life ... can set free individuality, and so make culture possible'.[32] The state, like the family, could be regarded in idealist terms as a moral sphere, though it was distinctive as the realm of the expression of the general will.

In the overlapping feminist, socialist and social policy literature of the early twentieth century, the metaphor of state as home or family was referred to in countless contexts. Though it could be put to use in ways which did not favour women, its prevalence indicates an attempt by suffrage-feminists to appropriate the sphere of governance, and to convey their qualifications to enter this sphere. The metaphor was intended to represent women as active agents of public service, to dispel the portrayal of women as objects of state policy. Margaret McMillan commented:

It is a fashion among pretty writers to say that the Home is woman's true sphere. The pretty phrase is TRUE. Woman's whole mission will probably be found at last to consist in making a great home of the whole habitable planet.

Feminists sought to describe women as taking on the 'public' roles of powerful 'managers' *within* the home, and thus potentially without it.[33] The metaphor gained its strength through translating the structures of sexual difference on which the home was based into the public sphere. This was by no means always a traditionalist or conservative strategy. Domestic interests did not necessarily limit women's political outlook, but could be viewed as a gateway to the wider political world.[34] The idea of the state as home or family retained the woman as homemaker, a powerful and central figure, and set the stage for a widespread pro-statism within the women's movement.

This prevalent pro-statism both motivated and derived from the dominant suffrage question. For most feminists around the turn of the century, a primary demand was for inclusion as citizens within the institutions of the state. Suffrage-feminists 'accepted the terms of liberal political discourse – that power lay in the vote' and thus 'directed the brunt of their attack on the centralised power of the state'.[35] Their demands for inclusion suggest an implicit endorsement of the state, understood as the institutions of governance and legislation. Indeed, many argued for an expanded role for the state, for example in the use of the criminal justice system to police 'purity', or factory inspectors to protect women from sweated labour. One can see the foundations being laid for what Georgina Waylen has described as 'state feminism', a 'benign social democratic welfare state'.[36] Where feminists were critical, they tended to focus on the way the state was run by men, and pointed out the need for women's presence. Some used a straightforward equality argument to demand women's inclusion, or appealed to a common, transcendent humanity.[37] Others took a more instrumental position, and saw women as a beneficial moral influence within politics. Keir Hardie for example argued:

Whilst [women's] influence in politics will be humanising it will also be strengthening, and much of the chicanery and knavery of political life will go down before her direct march upon the actual.[38]

Even more explicitly, Millicent Fawcett maintained 'Women bring something to the service of the state different to that which can be brought by men'. Such arguments based on sexual difference highlighted the moral, emotional or biological divide between the sexes. Implicitly appealing to the prevalent racial degeneration discourse, it was argued 'Woman is the guardian of the divine flame of life, she must guard it more than ever before, and for this reason it is essential that her wishes be consulted, and her advice taken'. Women's 'racial role' thus gave them a political perspective that required inclusion. It is easy to see why sexual difference seemed of more use to the women's movement than appeals to sameness. The 'difference' or essentialist case was intended to oppose those like James Mill, who argued that 'women may, consistently with good government, be excluded from the suffrage, because their interest is the same with that of men'.[39] Sandra Holton links arguments for representation through difference to an alternative conception of the state, which has figured prominently in late twentieth-century feminist political theory, as the instrument of care rather than justice, nurturance rather than control. Holton terms this a 'feminised democracy', and points to both the conservative implications of sexual difference as 'separate spheres', and to the radical potential of a redefinition of the public sphere, a 'domesticated' public life. This was a subversion of the separate spheres doctrine, a threatening and empowering projection of the experiences and expertises of the 'private' sphere onto the public. The home became a site of social agency, and the expertise of the housewife became qualification for the franchise.[40]

Suffrage-feminists thus largely argued that only women could supply the 'mother's instinct' or altruism necessary to the conduct of the state.[41] Little doubt was expressed as to whether state institutions could be compatible with 'women's values'. Some spheres of the work of the state were seen as particularly suitable for the exercise of such values. Ethel Snowden described the function of a Poor Law Guardian as especially suitable for women, as it 'appeal(s) to the mother-soul within her, and give(s) suitable opportunities for the exercise of all her God-given instincts of love and pity'.[42] An idea of feminine citizenship emerged that was qualified for citizenship by possession of a penumbra of qualities associated with nurture and service. Patricia Hollis comments on the way in which local government was used as part of this construction of feminine citizenship:

Local government ... caught up notions of ... service, philanthropy and practical Christianity; and permitted the pursuit of good causes, temperance and liberalism, moral and social purity. It offered multiple languages within which women could advance their rights, plead their cause, pursue their duties, fulfil their mission, and lay claim to full citizenship.[43]

Calls for increased state power and intervention were not only made by suffragists, but also by popular and working-class women's organisations. The British Women's Co-operative Guild, founded in 1883 and representing for the most part working-class women as homemakers and consumers, made a particularly strong case for the 'household' analogy to the state. The Guild provided women with experience of political management, and made some extremely radical demands concerning issues such as divorce, maternity care and household resource management, while promoting an agenda rooted in women's domestic concerns.[44] Rosalind Nash, writing on behalf of the Guild, portrayed housekeepers as 'the very pick of the voters', whose home life led to a natural interest in Factory Acts, Public Health Acts, the land question, and housing.[45] The intersection between public and private was self-evident in the Guild's projection of the public sphere of production onto the home: 'as married working-women we depend, more than any other class, perhaps, on good laws. Our everyday home life is touched by law at every point. Our houses are both our workshops and our homes'. Thus women's organisations argued that the equivalent spheres of the nation and the home required woman's influence: 'not man only, but also woman must develop civic virtues, if the home is to be built on safe foundations'.[46] Many activists of the women's movement argued that women's experience in running homes was parallel to the experience of 'housekeeping' for the nation.

The metaphor of state as family was in use beyond the literature of the women's movement, indicating the impact it had on the prevailing political ideologies. Those who portrayed the state as 'the home writ large', for example, found Fabian statism couched in similar terms. The Webbs referred to the progress obtained through the modern state as 'National House-Keeping'. Their conception of the state and society also matched the emphasis on 'service' found within much feminist literature, and which Susan Pedersen has described as a 'politics of conscience'. The Webbs demanded a reconstruction of society, 'on a basis not of interests but of community of service, of that 'neighbourly' feeling on which local life is made up, and of that willingness to subordinate oneself to the welfare of the whole'.[47] The nurturing construction of citizenship found within feminist texts and based upon mother-souls and feminine altruism meshed with the powerful philanthropic and 'service-oriented' element in the late nineteenth- and early twentieth-century women's movement. Teresa

Billington-Greig, who only a few years later became so critical of the statism of suffragists argued in 1909: 'We have the power of service and of sacrifice ... and out of these we must fashion victory'.[48]

The qualities of service were portrayed as key to citizenship in both Britain and the United States. A suffragist American senator, George F. Hoar, argued in his 1891 pamphlet 'Woman in the State': 'Everywhere that domain of the State which is represented by force is contracting and that domain of the State which is represented by public spirit, by charity, by humanity, is enlarging ... The debate between the advocates of woman suffrage and its opponents is, to my mind, but a contest between two theories of the function of the State'.[49] Ethel Snowden's 1908 pamphlet on 'Women and the State' was saturated by the idea of women's service and sacrifice, and the just call this gave them to representation:

> The State has benefited profoundly from the efforts and sacrifices of its women. Will the State repay these debts with the gratitude which it surely owes by placing confidence in women and giving them a proper place in government? ... The cry for enfranchisement is not the cry of envious women discontented with their sex. It is the expression by women of the desire to be of service to mankind.[50]

However, it was the 'sacrificial' nature of aspects of the suffrage movement that feminists (many of them former suffragists) began to find so repugnant from around 1909, because it had clearly been founded upon a model of femininity that they found personally confining. In that year, Mary Knight argued that 'The self-sacrifice so long preached by the clergy to women, is not acceptable any longer to ... American girls and the advanced women'.[51] Charles Drysdale noted within *The Freewoman*: 'the idea of self-sacrifice, which has always been drilled into women, makes it difficult to convince them that they will serve their country best by looking after their own self-interest more'.[52]

What were the implications of these 'inclusion through difference' arguments? Ironically, there was significant overlap between the arguments offered by the suffragists and those of the anti-suffragists. A parallel 'projection' of the home onto the state was made by anti-suffragists such as Mary (Mrs Humphrey) Ward, in relation to local government. The British 'progressive Antis', led by Ward and committed to a positive 'Forward Policy' in anti-suffragism, sought to define and strengthen the 'proper' channels for women's influence. Local government qualified as a proper channel due to its proximity to 'home concerns', in its focus on social policy, the upkeep of towns, or 'municipal housekeeping'.[53] The two spheres – national and local government – reflected a kind of public/private split, and became seen as gendered, complementary spheres of expertise.[54]

Echoing the feminist 'difference' arguments, the anti-suffragist Violet Markham argued that 'men and women are different, not similar beings, with talents that are complementary, not identical, and that therefore, they ought to have a different share in the management of the State . . . We seek a fruitful diversity of political function, not a stultifying uniformity'.[55] Mary Ward occupied the same ground as those, like Keir Hardie, who ascribed to women a benign moral influence. Ward argued that women should gain 'their full share in the State of social effort and social mechanism. We look for their increasing activity in that higher State which rests on thought, conscience and moral influence', while rejecting their actual participation through voting. For Ward, 'women must claim a right – but only the right to serve'.[56] Women's service was the common ideal that linked the suffragists to the Antis, and both deployed a rhetoric of 'civic-housekeeping', though with different political intent.

Despite their strong case for inclusion, and alternative 'nurture' conception of the ethic of the state, suffragists rarely explored ideas of what made the state legitimate, through what means it should act, or what the boundaries of its influence should be. They have thus at times been accused of having an undertheorised approach to the state.[57] Those identifying as 'advanced' feminists, some of whom also saw themselves as suffragists, were more likely to feel a need to rethink 'the state'. The suffragist, *Freewoman* reader, and editor of *Common Cause*, Helena Swanwick was perhaps unusually thoughtful when she questioned the value of government at all, preferring 'a condition of virtuous anarchy'. But she was clear that feminists 'are having to hammer out for ourselves the right principles of government. We can take them ready-made from no man'.[58] Amongst advanced circles, there was a stimulating intellectual environment, conducive to attempts to reconceptualise the state and its public functions, which provoked some feminists to think critically about political institutions.

POLITICAL ARGUMENT OF THE FEMINIST AVANT-GARDE

The enlarged role for the state described above opened up, for some, the prospect of a 'servile state', where spontaneity and self-sufficiency would be stamped out by an authoritarian state.[59] These ideas were highly significant to a minority within the women's movement, including the anarchist strand and the individualist feminist avant-garde. These anti-statist tendencies have not been commonly linked to feminism, broadly defined.

Intellectual resources drawn upon by feminists, such as the work of Hilaire Belloc, have been neglected due to Belloc's reputation as an anti-feminist conservative. Belloc, a radical-right thinker highly active in the world of 'advanced' periodicals, coined the term 'servile state' in his series of articles on this theme in the *New Age* around 1912. This term and the connotations it carried emerged within the Edwardian feminist movement at around the same time.

The writings of American feminists reveal a continual dialogue between pro- and anti-statist positions. A slightly older generation, including Charlotte Perkins Gilman and Winifred Harper Cooley, was comfortable with a fairly intrusive state underpinning their utopian visions of the good life, particularly in enforcing eugenic marriages.[60] The younger generation's views on the state were more in flux, but were initially quite inclined towards strong governance. Randolph Bourne, for example, though he later came to resent the wartime encroachment of the American government on civil liberties, had been inspired by reading the British writer H. G. Wells to write to his close friend Elsie Clews Parsons:

I cannot see how any resolute social program can ever be put though without some strong party which has a professional attitude towards government or a will towards the Great State.[61]

Parsons, however, was more concerned with 'inner' transformations than Bourne. An anthropologist and thoroughly unconventional feminist, she wrote a fictional account of a feminist observer of American society in *The Journal of a Feminist*. This sharp-eyed account of gender and sexual norms in 1913–14 America offers a subtle account of the intellectual issues confronting feminists, particularly the 'endless little sex taboos' of everyday life. Using the voice of her feminist diarist, 'Cynthia', Parsons noted that until recently, feminists had been so concerned by the 'institutional bondage' of women 'that questions of inner freedom have rarely occurred to them'. This was now to be the new agenda for feminism. In relation to the state, Parsons was sceptical as to whether it could serve women's interests. She was particularly dubious about the prospect of eugenic legislation, which she saw as drastic and repressive, leading to official corruption and heavy-handed moralism. She supported the removal of the state in marriage contracts, to be replaced by a greater awareness of personality as the key factor in marriage. She was sceptical about the idea of 'society', which she saw as a fictional entity used to enforce social norms. Parsons' protagonist took a more individualist line: 'What is society? Isn't it I and you and you and you?'[62]

In Britain, there was a critical response to appeals for women to 'serve the state' amongst feminists. Mary Knight, a WSPU activist, wrote a scathing article in the *Westminster Review*, 'Woman v. The State', in 1909, in which she refused to accept that individuals should subordinate themselves to the needs of the state'.[63] Taking up similar themes, the crisis in the state became a major theme for *The Freewoman*. In the editor's view, seeking the meaning of the state was 'like delving into one of those big boxes which sometimes come on the first morning of this month [April], from which are removed layer after layer of tissue paper and paper shavings to reveal in the depths nothing more than a little mirror, which reflects oneself. The State, likewise, has neither existence nor meaning apart from individuals and groups of individuals'. Faced with the expansion of powers of the state through the introduction of National Insurance in 1912, Marsden accused the Liberal government of inducing servility in the population: 'It would be difficult to find any fifty years in English history which have been so potent to reveal the nature of government as have the six years since the General Election of 1906'.[64] People had learnt to tolerate their enslaved and servile status, and occupied a 'subhuman' position of a 'slavish or sleeping people':

Individual autonomy is disappearing at such a rate that in fifty years we shall be a people in chains. The State is going to regulate who shall be born, whether we are fit to live in the community, and whether we shall reproduce our kind; the State regulates our education, our status and our work; the State is going to settle our wages; and will clap us in prison if we refuse to accept them, and will shut us up in segregation wards if we refuse to work; it is going to doctor us when we are sick, and keep us when we are old.

Marsden argued that the ideal state should be 'no more than a registration machine plus an executive'. She sought to demythologise 'the big looming notion of the State as something which stands over and against individuals' – the organic state, the 'general will' and so on. The 'looming' state was dangerous to individual endeavour, through making it unnecessary or even forbidding it. Marsden had experienced the power of the state ranged against the individual as a suffragette; her arrests, imprisonment and restraint in a straitjacket had left a vivid impression. She had also witnessed the blank columns which suffrage periodicals occasionally printed to show where the state had censored them, and her own publications also ran into censorship troubles. She was convinced that it was political motives that caused the 1912 ban on *The Freewoman* by distributors W. H. Smith's, and when she attempted to restart the journal as *The New Freewoman* it was extremely hard to secure a publisher who was not intimidated by libel and sedition laws. Her own experiences of state regulation thus made her increasingly opposed to any such intervention. She allowed that 'general arrangements, authorised by the consent of the people, the State may make, but it should not meddle with anything that is individual, growing, mobile'. By 1913, she was even questioning the value of a freely undertaken social contract between individuals. In doing so, she alienated the American anarchist Benjamin Tucker who expressed his frustration with the vagaries of Marsden's position.

The incredulity of some readers when faced with the apparent anti-statism of *The Freewoman* suggests how deeply rooted was faith in the state within the Edwardian women's movement. Mary Gawthorpe, an initial editor of the journal, found Dora Marsden's anti-statism hard to credit. She demanded:

Are you really an anarchist? Do you really deny government in the philosophic sense even? ... Do you really regard all men as 'free', remembering that your original appeal to freewomen could, as yet, only be made to one in four women? ... What I want to know is – are you in actuality opposed to Government as Government?

Marsden answered:

We shall make use of Government whenever we can to its own detriment or to our advantage. We shall lose no opportunity of doing it an injury. We work for its destruction ... As for Votes for Women, we think the women will be very quick to see the nature of government. Unless they get it soon (and then forget it) the more thoughtful among them will cease to ask for it. They should battle with Government itself.[65]

The anti-statism of the journal clearly went against the grain of pre-dominant trends in the early Edwardian women's movement, within which most activists envisaged an expanded, and feminised, state of the future.

EUGENICS

It is clear from Marsden's and Parsons' comments that it was the eugenic aspect of state control that they had, by the late Edwardian years, come to find most intrusive and unacceptable. This was a strongly contested issue within the feminist avant-garde, and indeed had been equally high profile within late nineteenth-century 'new woman' controversies. Angelique

Richardson has discussed the pro- and anti-eugenic positions of new woman novelists, and the wider social fascination with biological explanations for social and political circumstances. The many activists of the women's movement involved with social purity campaigns were aware of the eugenic implications of their work. Richardson notes the initial strong resistance to the intervention of the state in sexual matters, epitomised in the 1880s campaigns to repeal the Contagious Diseases Acts. These sentiments, however, gradually faded. Activists of the 1890s and 1900s came to welcome a more interventionist and at times, coercive state that could work along eugenic lines.[66] Sarah Grand, Ellice Hopkins, Frances Swiney and Caleb Saleeby were all prominent within this pro-eugenic aspect of the women's movement. Feminist writers such as Mabel Atkinson, even where critical of the tendency among eugenists to exclude all women from employment and leave them dependent on their husbands, supported the idea of checks on population growth, and inducements to marriage and child-bearing 'among precisely those classes where we desire to encourage it'.[67] Younger generations of feminists such as Eleanor Rathbone also took up this kind of language. The eugenic idiom was widespread, even where the eugenist identity was not embraced.

This preference for a planned, woman-centred eugenic society was opposed by some important figures preceding and within the feminist avant-garde. Mona Caird (1858–1932) was a prominent writer, born a generation before the establishment and naming of the feminist avant-garde, though she contributed to journals of the political avant-garde such as *The New Age*. Influenced by J. S. Mill's articulation of liberal individualism, Caird was active into the twentieth century in the women's movement, but also in bodies such as the Personal Rights Association. She famously questioned conventional marriage in the *Westminster Review* in 1888, seeking 'greater respect of the liberties of the individual' within its bounds. This article sparked an intense newspaper controversy; when *The Daily Telegraph* asked in response to Caird, 'is marriage a failure?', it received a flood of over 27,000 letters. Caird's work was read in both Britain and the United States, and she was described by contemporaries as a 'flaming bomb' of the early feminist movement. Like many of her generation, she supported the suffrage cause and respected the heroism of the militant activists, while rejecting violence as a political tool. Caird emphasised human agency and the environment in the shaping of individuals, displacing the eugenic focus upon biological determinism. Like the later avant-garde feminists, Caird was very critical of the entrenched idea of self-sacrifice in conventional femininity, and the effect this had on women's creative genius. She was also extremely aware of the vulnerability of women to the interventions of the state and its 'atrocious and insulting' laws, imposed by the governing sex.[68]

By 1912, facing the popularity of increased government control over 'the feeble minded' amongst suffragists, the tone of *The Freewoman* was predominantly anti-eugenic – Marsden regarded eugenics as criminal and immoral, the state dangerously becoming the 'very arbiters of Life and Not-Life'. She was unimpressed by eugenic theories of breeding, believing that doctors 'have not yet grasped the elementary fact that the distinctly human thing about the human being is the mind, and that the mind is an individual thing, and will do its own experimenting, even in breeding, by their leave!'[69]

The letters page within *The Freewoman* was a site of debate encompassing all points of view on eugenics, though the overall tendency was critical.[70] Stella Browne, though she later became a member of the Eugenics Education Society, was always highly critical of the misogyny of many eugenicists. She rejected their advocacy of monogamy and marriage as a framework for 'fit' reproduction, as well as the eugenic conception of maternity as a 'duty towards an outside entity'. Her writings in *The Freewoman* and other journals asserted a woman's absolute bodily integrity and right to self-determination, without economic calculations, psychological repression or responsibility to the state determining her choices.[71]

Other avant-garde feminists agreed. Beatrice Hastings, a highly equivocal feminist but a very prominent interlocutor on 'women's issues' in *The New Age*, organised a campaign against the 1912 Feeble-Minded Persons (Control) Bill. She was also well aware of the coercive overtones of the contemporary moral panic concerning 'white slavery', and denounced such state intervention into women's lives.[72] The saliency of their resistance to ideas of women's purity and the need to regulate sexuality was shown when in 1913, Christabel Pankhurst published her notorious book, *The Great Scourge and How to End It*. While many were ambivalent about her arguments, Pankhurst demonstrated the prominence of ideas of chastity and purity within the women's movement that could be construed as supporting an extremely interventionist state. The avant-garde resistance to this was important, and continued to surface within *The New Freewoman* and *The Egoist* in the years preceding the war.

In Britain, the prospect of eugenic legislation by the governing Liberals (given urgency by the Feeble-Minded Control Bill) framed these debates on women and the state, as is clear in the endowment of motherhood issue discussed in the following chapter. However, little legislation emerged from eugenics controversies. In the United States, in contrast, eugenic legislation was more pervasive. In 1907 the state of Indiana authorised the compulsory sterilisation of any 'unimprovable' criminal, idiot, rapist or imbecile in a state institution. In total, twenty-nine states came to permit the sterilisation of the insane and feeble-minded, of which twelve also covered sterilisation of criminals. Many of these statutes did not survive legal challenges, and were quickly overturned; around 6,000 people were sterilised under such legislation. In contrast to the British feminists' ambivalence about eugenics, the American women's movement, and the feminist vanguard within it, produced some strong advocates of eugenics. Margaret Sanger stressed women's agency in regenerating the race, and Florence Tuttle understood feminism and eugenics as part of the same movement. Tuttle preferred positive eugenics to negative, and stressed women's responsibility to educate their children, and public opinion, in the facts of sexual reproduction.[73]

For neither Sanger nor Tuttle, however, did eugenics imply a more interventionist state – Sanger was well aware of how intrusive and coercive the state could be, after her arrest and state harassment for writing about and dispensing birth control. This insight was intensified in the atmosphere of state surveillance and curtailment of free speech during and after America's involvement in World War One. Florence Tuttle was thoroughly committed to a new moral order, in which a eugenic 'ethics of love' would transform society, giving women the power to make their own reproductive decisions. But this was combined with a suspicion of the state, its negative eugenics, and the 'clanking chains' of conventional forms of marriage. She sought only personal or public opinion reform; the individual's relationship with the state was not relevant to her eugenic-feminist vision. The language of American feminists was frequently one of racial advancement, but this certainly did not entail a crude politics of state-led moral intervention.

ELITISM

Despite the misgivings or indifference on the part of many feminists concerning state action, this did not necessarily make for a celebration of the 'grass roots', or a leaning towards anarchism within their political argument. An elitist approach and tendency to dismiss popular political participation spans the Fabian, new liberal, progressive and avant-garde feminist political discourses. The Fabians had tended to regard the poor as positively disqualified from participation. As one commented, it is difficult for their atrophied brains to grasp an idea. Even if they could, their devitalised natures and anaemic bodies would be incapable of working for it. This explains why *no socialist has or ever will come from the slums*.[74]

The Fabian and suffragist Ethel Snowden commented that 'the majority never wants what is good for it; never will keep abreast of the times. The history of the ages has ever been the story of an intelligent minority dragging on the huge mass of an ignorant and unthinking majority'. H. G. Wells' *A Modern Utopia* (1905) portrayed a cult of the intellectual in the rule of the 'Samurai', and in *The New Machiavelli* (1911), Wells was an important transatlantic public intellectual. His articles featured in American and British journals, his books gained a cosmopolitan readership, and he sustained friendships and correspondences with American feminists such as Henrietta Rodman and Madeleine Doty. His political work dwelt on the rule of aristocrats. Wells' utopias 'were inevitably ruled by a special governing order of the best and the brightest'.[75]

Though their motivations and political agents differed, feminists and Fabians shared elitist tendencies; Wells' rhetoric chimed with the feminist aversion to being subsumed under the 'wide-spreading robes of the stupid'. Norman Hapgood, on taking up the editorship of *Harper's Weekly*, explicitly described feminism as an attempt to make women intellectually attractive to 'the superior men of her community'. Exceptional men, he went on, had long recognised the uses of feminism.[76] However, different justifications underlay this elitism. Marsden, for example, saw the domination of the masses as in the legitimate interests of the few who were able to self-develop, those genius 'superwoman' figures; Hapgood saw eugenic justifications; the Fabians saw government by elite, or by experts, as the most efficient form of government, and thus in the interests of the masses.

In broad terms, similar trends can also be seen within the 'new liberal' and 'Progressive' traditions. The judgement of the poor as apathetic and unable to help themselves was widely held, across the spectrum of 'progressive' views. In Britain, David Lloyd George commented: 'If these poor people are to be redeemed they must be redeemed not by themselves, because nothing strikes you more than the stupor of despair in which they have sunk – they must be redeemed by others outside'. American progressive Walter Lippman was unconvinced about the democratic ideal of majority rule, and aimed to increase the influence of intellectuals in American society.

Roosevelt, Herbert Croly and the Progressive Party identified as paternalist 'New Nationalists', highly sceptical about the power and intelligence of public opinion, and preferring that elite leaders would 'mould their followers', 'the plain people'. Croly directed his *New Republic* at his 'exceptional fellow countrymen', and envisaged a top-down reform of governance led by a strong executive: 'We believe in a government of the people, and for the people, but not by the people'.[77]

The American women's movement offered a somewhat different construction of how the state was to engage with society. Avoiding the elitist-nationalist language of Croly, the metaphor of the state as the 'home writ large' gave activists such as Jane Addams a language to talk about the state with reference to the family and the neighbourhood, rather than the nation. Settlement house work had led to an alternative view of how the state should interact with communities. Many within the American women's movement felt that the state should act on the community level, in conjunction with voluntary bodies, and in a way that respected the local distinctiveness of the grass-roots level. However, approaches to state action within the women's movement were also not immune from a certain elitism. The American settlement reformer Vida D. Scudder, who had studied with Ruskin in Oxford, preferred reformation 'from above and not from below'. Charlotte Perkins Gilman was scathing of why social organisation had failed, and why a strong state was needed: 'We can see in the years behind us how our progress was needlessly impeded by the density, the inertia, the prejudice and cowardice and sodden ignorance of the multitude'. This was to be an attitude which survived the democratising influence of World War One, and the attainment of a wider suffrage. In 1920, Heterodoxy member Alice Rohe decried the 'world made safe for mediocrity'; only Heterodoxy provided her with an 'oasis' in the 'great American desert'.[78]

Throughout the first two decades of the twentieth century, then, it was possible to imagine feminism as the province of the gifted, leading from the front, particularly for those in the avant-garde who were concerned with the creative energies of geniuses, 'supermen' and 'superwomen'. Just as the Fabians and new liberals regarded the poor, so avant-garde feminists regarded most women. Rebecca West was happy to acknowledge that the creation of aristocracy was a foremost feminist aim.[79] However, for the Fabians, or Lloyd George, it was precisely their 'elitism', or lack of faith in the initiative of the masses, that prompted them to turn to the state. They envisaged the state as the province of a decisive political elite, experts in human affairs. In contrast, for many within the feminist avant-garde, an elitist position led to an opposite stance, a rejection of the 'servile state'. The state was conceived as an impersonal machine, 'the sum total of servile, obedient, negligible little individuals'. Furthermore, it was argued that women's habit or experience of servility in relation to men made them all the more vulnerable to servility towards the state. Their agitation for the vote was dangerous, as it opened the way for them to be incorporated into a system they would be particularly unsuited to control.

DEMOCRACY AND REPRESENTATION

How did the representative system that was so widely expected to empower women fit into this feminist conception of the state? Teresa Billington-Greig was perhaps the foremost critic of the state within the feminist avant-garde. Despite serving prison sentences in Holloway as part of her WSPU and WFL activism, she became disillusioned with the autocracy and politics of suffrage. Billington-Greig resigned her post, and published in 1911 a devastating critique of the militant suffragists, *Emancipation in a Hurry*, first in *The New Age* and then as a book. She then maintained herself as a free-lance journalist, and developed a new basis for a con-sumerist feminist movement, outlined in her 1912 book, *The Consumer in Revolt*. At the same time, she developed a highly polemical critique of the state, published in articles in the little magazines and radical papers. While she had advocated in 1907 that feminists should establish an 'Independent Woman's Party', she became increasingly disillusioned by the suffragist belief in 'emancipation by machinery'.[80] Billington-Greig maintained that the systemic corruption of representative systems was not just an imper-fection in the British system, but 'inherent in all democratic governing machines'. Without universal ownership of 'a share of power sufficient to ensure self-protection', democracy inevitably meant coercion of some groups – and women, she argued, were especially powerless and vulner-able, both to being coerced and to sponsoring coercion themselves. As Billington-Greig argued, 'The vote in the hands of women trained emo-tionally to self-sacrifice and self-subjection will not be so potent an engine of progress as many women think. The value of a tool depends very much upon the training of the person who uses it. The women of this country have either not been trained at all or they have been trained under systems notoriously bad'.[81] It was their sense of the vulnerability of women to state coercion that made 'feminists' such as Beatrice Hastings strongly suspi-cious of parliament's attempts to end the so-called 'white slave trade', and highly critical of women's apparent support for this kind of 'sentimental', panic-driven legislation. Hastings was also cynical about the value of the mass electorate, which she saw as gullible and easily led. She concluded

'The vote will make no woman free who is not individually free before she gets it. In the direction of cherishing individual freedom lies the work of true feminists'.[82]

Many 'advanced' feminists thus became unconvinced of the value of the suffrage. Teresa Billington-Greig felt that mass suffrage would only exacerbate coercion. Multiplication of voters would reduce the value of each vote and hand power over to the bureaucrats. The only power remaining to voters was that of destruction, of 'dealing death' – like Marsden, in 1912 she supported the use of insurrectionary political violence. Her views on suffrage were echoed by American feminists. Elsie Clews Parsons felt the vote would do 'a little [good], but only a very, very little. It doesn't do men so very much good, does it? It's more important for women to get rid of their petticoats than to get a vote. And it's still more important for them to get a good job'.[83] Dora Marsden, in direct opposition to her suffragist past, came to believe that the democratic control embodied in the vote was illusory:

Our representative system calls itself so, in order to obscure its true intent. It is a cover under which the chains of slavery are forged more finely. It is an ingenious device which makes the people acquiesce in and be the agent for their own subjection.[84]

Democracy, intended to be a guard against the imposition of the 'servile state', became for Marsden the mark of servility. Criticism of democracy was a well-established, though minority, strand amongst Edwardian 'radical' intellectuals, and was based on a variety of concerns. There was an element of fear of the 'uneducated masses' whose democratic participation was likely to introduce more populist and demagogic elements into political culture. Mass democracy, though accepted by most as inevitable, was seen as making politics more impulsive and irrational, especially in the United States. Charles Masterman noted in his 1909 *Condition of England* essay that American democracy had allowed the hysterical 'Crowd' sentiment into politics:

The old discussion by argument, commonplace posters, and literature, even the cheery rioting of rival mobs, is already voted as a thing stale and outworn. Instead, we are to see an effort to capture, not individuals as individuals, but the Crowd as Crowd.

The 'soapbox demagoguery' of the British suffragettes exemplified this trend in England for Masterman, and 'the crowd' was nearly always feminised.[85] Feminist concerns were put in somewhat different terms.

Dora Marsden believed that voting represented an abstraction of the individual from his or her concrete existence, and dangerously reduced the uniqueness of each to a supposedly equivalent and comparable unit, the voter-citizen.[86] 'Great' individuals were valued no more than 'lesser types', and would have to submit to the views of the majority. Majoritarian democracy was thus rejected for its mediocrity. As Teresa Billington-Greig argued in the *Contemporary Review*, 'Under present conditions, control by the multitude must mean control by ignorance, mediocrity and common-place ... The rate of advance under democracy is measured by the average intellect and activity; and with us the average is still low'.[87] Feminists were relatively unconcerned with the effective governing of the polity or the corruption of political culture that exercised other anti-democrats.

Marsden also believed that delegating responsibility was damaging to the self. Furthermore, she and other contributors argued that popular consent was in any case meaningless in the face of the hegemony of the ruling classes; even politicians were simply puppets for the 'real governors – the owners of Land and Money'. Some of the most influential figures associated with the feminist avant-garde thus came to abandon the whole idea of representation. Though Marsden initially allowed that consent could authorise collective action, by September 1912 she argued that

'Government by Consent' would send us off into peals of inextinguishable laughter ... To be governed is to have our lives ordered and controlled, our actions forced, forbidden, or punished, by others. It is to put the directing of our lives under the orders of others. A person who does not resist government is either imbecile or powerless ... What strange manner of person, then, are these ... who agree to have their hands shackled, feet tied, and teeth drawn, *by consent*?[88]

POLITICAL ACTIVISM

Given this analysis, what forms of political activism might be seen as effective or appropriate? Did feminist individualism imply a withdrawal from all collective action? Vernon Lee, converted to feminism by Charlotte Perkins Gilman, concluded that she could see no channel of activism: 'How do you propose to remedy [the woman question]? ... I propose nothing because I do not know'. Lee proposed discussion as the first starting point: 'All these speculations, serious or frivolous, enthusiastic or cynical, serve to plough up the solid, sterile ground of our prejudices'.[89]

Teresa Billington-Greig, in a similar fashion, wanted an extended debate amongst the 'discontented and disgusted feminists – and those who are merely truth-seekers!' While the suffrage struggle, in her opinion, actively blocked this kind of debate, she hoped that 'Organised lectures, discussions and debates on a free platform should prepare the way for a vigorous rational development in feminism, should assist in promoting study and investigation, and in systematising the material already available. A movement of action, would naturally follow this one of thought and inquiry'.[90] These feminists were clearly optimistic about what literary historians have described as the creation of 'counterpublic spheres'.[91] Rather than turning their back on mass audiences and public discussion, they sought to create spaces and institutions of voice from which they could actively engage in challenging the 'mainstream' of political argument. They were clear, however, that the well-established suffrage 'counterpublic spaces' could not host their discussions.

Others did not merely want to influence political argument, but in keeping with egoist politics, sought a less cerebral kind of rebellion. Dora Marsden predicted a grass-roots rebellion, though like many of her feminist contemporaries, she was unimpressed with revolutionary socialist politics. Revolution, as an organised and controlled affair, could not challenge state power. It merely 'reshuffles the cards for a fresh game'. Insurrection, in contrast, 'changes the game'. The anarcho-syndicalist ideal of (industrial) revolt or insurrection was the only option. Marsden called for women to 'join the army of industrial revolt. An organisation of women Syndicalists would do more to hurry the steps of politicians than all their political oratory. If women take up the bolder stand, the politicians will give them the vote, if only in an endeavour to provide them with a harmless occupation'.[92]

Syndicalist ideas resonated with the emphasis in *The Freewoman* on attaining emancipation by one's own efforts, rejecting revolution for rebellion, and gaining economic power prior to political. It was the insurrectionary aspect of syndicalism that Marsden admired; she remained doubtful about the manner in which syndicalists envisaged the working of industrial unions, seeing them as likely to form a bureaucratic and interventionist tier of government. Syndicalism for Marsden was only 'a method, and not an end'. Violent direct action, as in grass-roots industrial action, would allow mastery to be assumed: 'The kingdom of heaven has to be seized by force. A cross on the ballot-paper will not do the deed'.[93]

The British Dock Strike of 1912 was welcomed by Marsden and others as an assumption of mastery that women might copy.[94] The Dublin General Strike of 1913 offered an even more compelling example of how syndicalist methods of insurrection might actually be realised, though Marsden suspected that the ability of the Dublin strikers to take armed action – to access their own 'vital power' – was likely to be 'smothered by the sheer mass of the stupid' – the cost of any mass action. Instead, she argued that the unionist followers of Sir Edward Carson in Belfast were closer to the feminist-egoist ideal – they dealt in arms and force rather than ideas. She therefore called on women and workers alike to realise that 'rebels armed with stones will be clapped in prison, but that rebels armed with rifles will be treated with the respect due to such, and be invited to a conference'.[95]

Along with the armed protester, Marsden idealised the criminal: 'the persons who fill our prisons have followed their bent, and Government has been powerless to stop them'. In particular, the prisoners Marsden most respected were the group she herself had been part of, the suffragette hunger-strikers. Marsden herself had gone on hunger-strike during her imprisonment in 1909 and held in a strait-jacket, though she had not been force-fed.[96] She saw the feminist movement as opening the possibility of women subverting the state, through claiming the right to starve:

The most brilliantly promising manifestation of the human spirit in England to-day is that of the hunger-strikers, who challenge to its extremity the right of the State to coerce, in the region of ideas, or to inflict a punishment of a kind not endorsed by the individual.

Hunger-striking was, in individualist terms

the last weapon of the one against the many. It is the intensive force of the will of the individual pitted against the extensive force of the will of the community ... It is the final retort of a minority to the majority that would govern it without its consent.[97]

It did not matter to Marsden that hunger-strikers did not have this aim, nor that they usually experienced hunger-striking as a collective force. Her experiences and those of her peers within the WSPU had clearly impressed them with the potential of the militant woman's movement; a correspondent referred to the WSPU as 'the forcing house of feminism'.[98] Despite her opposition to WSPU goals, she did not abandon suffrage-feminism, but harnessed feminist activism to her own agenda. Feminism for Marsden was about women's economic independence, which opened up an unpredictable world of opportunities, far removed from the realm of the state:

Women need wealth; therefore they must produce wealth; and what they produce they must receive value for ... These are individual and not collective affairs, and, far from seeking the intervention of the State, the State must be peremptorily forbidden the presumption of interfering in them.[99]

Despite this apparently uncompromising stance, it is curious that avant-garde feminists actually conceded an extensive sphere of collective action to the state. This suggests that Edwardian anti-statism was paradoxically to some degree compatible with the development of an interventionist state. As we have seen, the widespread expectation and desire that the state should act in social and economic policy was reflected across a variety of political groups, including the women's movement. But amongst some feminists, state power virtually replaced male power as most threatening to (women's) freedom. It is intriguing therefore that a thinker such as Dora Marsden did in fact allow quite an extensive role for the state. In *The Freewoman* she argued that the state should maintain an army and navy, though it should not determine the internal organisation of these bodies. Similarly, the state should provide school accommodation, but not determine the curriculum. And most interventionist of all, Marsden advocated the nationalisation of the post office, land and the railways. After some prompting from a pro-state reader, Marsden conceded in the correspondence pages that the state's business was to 'keep open to the people access to the land, and to administer effective punishment to any, whether capitalist or other, who frustrates access' – in sum, to be the agent for important aspects of her vision of social change.[100]

Other radical intellectuals shared Marsden's desire to utilise state action quite extensively, while remaining dubious about its ability to intervene. H. G. Wells' involvement with *The Freewoman*, its Discussion Circle, and his intense, stormy personal relationships with feminists such as Rebecca West made him an important and persistent interlocutor for avant-garde feminists. Wells had advocated substantial powers for the state in the enforcement of a minimum wage, provision of employment and endowment of motherhood in 1912. Yet by 1914, faced by the prospect of war, he felt that 'already there is too much power in [politicians'] clumsy and untrustworthy hands'.[101] Individualists like Wells or Randolph Bourne in the United States oscillated between outright rejection of the state and recognition that progressive social change did require some kind of collective public agency such as the state, industrial parliament or the guild. Individualism, as Stefan Collini has pointed out, was 'a theory of the grounds rather than the frequency of legislation'.[102] It could therefore be deployed to support some forms of state intervention, despite individualists' desire for less government. The strength of avant-garde feminism was that its overall theme was one of wariness of the potentially coercive nature of the state, particularly towards women (as the endowment controversy discussed in the next chapter makes clear). Yet the enabling power of some forms of state action was still explored. Individualism and statism can be described as in persistent but fruitful tension within the feminist movement.

The rejection of the state and the 'service' conception of citizenship by feminists was motivated by their unease at the subsumption of individual rights to the well-being of the whole. The familial metaphor for the state did not seem compatible with a polity that respected citizens' autonomy. Carelessness of individual autonomy pervaded the pro-statist discourse; the new liberal J. A. Hobson, for example, insisted that 'claims or rights of self-development must be adjusted to the sovereignty of social welfare', while Sidney Webb argued that individual rights 'may be inimical to our fullest development or greatest effectiveness'.[103] Women had long been denied the opportunity to self-develop; in 1911 the world of self-development had been opening up to them through practical advances in their education, property rights, employment opportunities, and increased knowledge of birth control. There was also a clearly expanded intellectual realm in which they could for the first time assert their need for, or right to, individual emancipation. It must have appeared highly suspect to avant-garde feminists that opportunities to develop were simultaneously being subordinated to idealist-inspired appeals to service, sacrifice and the interests of society as a whole. Women for too long had been the repository of appeals to the common good, via discourses of the race, conscience, or the family. Though feminists had themselves deployed arguments that drew 'women's interests' and 'the common good' closer, a current of critique was present among feminist thinkers. Some recognised that the role of 'race mother' or, as settlement worker Anna Martin bitingly put it, 'unpaid nursemaid of the State', was not necessarily in women's interests.[104] The feminist critique of male 'protection' of women corresponded to their unease at the state's 'protection' of the individual. In this context, an anti-statist 'anarchist' individualism has some coherency as a feminist position.

However, Marsden's key contribution to feminist thought was her clarification of an idea that was not only implicit in a great number of avant-garde feminist texts, but was also quite distinct from the collectivist and humanist strand in anarchism. Marsden's antipathy to the state came to be combined with a kind of respect for those who ruled ruthlessly and deployed force. No pity for the coerced, or weak, can be found in her writings – especially not for those women she termed 'bondwomen'. Indeed, pity was a suspect emotion for many within the avant-garde, characterising the sentimental politics of suffrage-feminism. Those who allowed themselves to be coerced by the state were to blame for their enslavement:

> The focus for contempt will have moved in a direction which is from 'governors' to 'governed', from the 'tyrant' to the 'tyrannised'. It will be clear that if the governors are cruel as tigers and savage as bulls, they are not contemptible. They are not worms, which is what the governed are.[105]

Marsden's work came to express an extreme egoist rhetoric which began to alienate supporters from across the political spectrum from around 1913. She argued that there was no objection to oppressive rule, because 'those who have had the strength, ingenuity, and cunning to establish force to translate their power into domination' act in their own, egoistic interests. Her concern in *The Freewoman* and its successors was to convince women that they (at least some of them) possessed these personal qualities.

Influenced by the Stirnean and Nietzschean ideas circulating within her intellectual milieu, Marsden argued that government necessarily rested on a threat of force. The 'mere sanitation and administration work' of government 'act as dust in the common people's eyes. They are meant to supply a *raison d'être* adequate to satisfy the blunted intelligence of an enslaved community'. Stirner's insight concerning the state was that its power was sustained through the submissiveness of the governed, rather than actual domination or violence. He drew upon Hegel's account of the lord/bondsman relationship, where significant place is given to the bondsman's recognition of lordship in perpetuating the relationship. Stirner saw state rule also as a form of lordship, resting on recognition of citizens: 'He who, to hold his own, must count on the absence of will in others is a thing made by these others, as the master is a thing made by the servant'.[106] Marsden adopted this argument: 'The person who is responsible for the tyrant is the slave; the person who is responsible for the selfish man is the unselfish man'. She applied it both to the state, and also to male 'lordship' over women. This formed the basis of her argument that women were to blame for male domination; if they would only cease to acknowledge male power, this power would dissolve. Internal psychological and self-sustained bondage was all that held oppressive institutions together.

Applying Stirner's reading of Hegel to feminist concerns represents an important insight. Yet Stirner's violent rhetoric was perhaps less useful than his ideas; Marsden adopted a ranting and extreme tone, and she began to construct a conspiracy theory that abruptly introduced a vicious anti-Semitic element into the journal that seems to have been inspired by her reading of Stirner. Indeed, Stirner's influence seemed to transform Marsden's political ideas in *The New Freewoman* and *The Egoist*. She had previously espoused a society 'where the mass of men are free and equal, working in a social structure from the base upwards'. This vision was compatible with the wide range of socialist, anarchist and progressive positions within her milieu. Marsden had been critical of the WSPU, for setting up a hierarchy 'where only one is free, a few privileged, and the great mass enslaved, working from the pinnacle downwards'.[107] Stirner's vision of social organisation was precisely the latter, based on a conception of only a few gifted individuals capable of acting egoistically. This elitism led Marsden and avant-garde feminists to construct a feminist politics around the concept of the genius or superwoman, which I shall argue to be a narrow and constraining political framework.

Nonetheless, this understanding of woman as *self-enslaved* was one with great resonance both in Britain and America; Floyd Dell approved of Marsden's portrayal of women 'not indeed as the slave of man, but as the enslaver of man, but with the other end of the chain fastened to her own wrist, and depriving her quite effectually of her liberties'. It chimed with the ideas of Charlotte Perkins Gilman and Olive Schreiner. Schreiner famously saw woman as a parasite, holding back the evolution of mankind. The metaphor of woman imprisoned or chained, beating on the door for release, but then discovering that she held the keys herself, was used by Gilman on several occasions.

Such imagery of women as self-chained, or jointly enslaved with men, was not limited to the acknowledged feminist opinion-formers, the 'great' writers like Schreiner and Gilman, but also circulated in lesser-known texts, and in mass-market magazines. In *Harper's Bazar*, for example, the American feminist writer Inez Haynes Gillmore imagined 'woman' chained, but 'as she stands, she kisses the chains which bind her wrists and ankles'.[108] The long history of transatlantic co-operation within the women's movement around the abolition of slavery may have made this a particularly powerful image for both national communities of feminists.

How much resonance did these ideas which mostly originated in Europe have transatlantically? Historians have seen American progressive feminists as increasingly obsessed with working within the framework of the status quo, rejecting anarchism as a dangerous European tendency. Beatrice Forbes-Hale's comments on the anarchist dangers of *The Freewoman* are representative of this. However, there was a strong avant-garde element to feminist thought which did not seek 'respectable' forms of politics, and this is obscured within historical accounts, which tend to conflate feminism and suffragism.[109] Outside of the avant-garde, American women's movement activists were more positive about the state than their British counterparts, and rarely identified as anarchists. Charlotte Perkins Gilman, for example, was keen to deploy state or collective bodies at the service of the public. Gilman argued that social evolution meant that public services such as the school, the church and the army should expand their function. The army, for example, could be used in peace time for 'industrial service'; she felt that public services had come to be 'feminised' by the commitment to 'loving service' within the women's movement.[110] Gilman idealised service and 'duty to humanity', but believed that these could be compatible with justice, rather than self-sacrifice.[111] The American avant-garde itself was certainly no cohesive body, and the predominant political concerns of the women's movement – service, and linking the state to the home – were found amongst self-consciously 'heterodox' feminists.

One way to situate the British feminist rejection of leadership and the state without reading it as a form of anarchism is to read it in the context of their critique of the WSPU. Marsden and Billington-Greig perceived the WSPU's 'hatred of liberty, its littleness of spirit, its cruelty' as parallel to that of government – each institution crushed genius and individuality.[112] They characterised themselves as having been part of a tiny group of Manchester suffragettes which 'as an unholy joke called itself the S.O.S. They were Sick of Suffrage'. The WSPU had institutionalised and perverted the inspired, individually undertaken actions of the hunger-strikers. Emmeline Pankhurst was accused of having 'rid her group of all its members unlikely by virtue of personality, conspicuous ability, or undocile temper, to prove flexible material in the great cause'.[113] Similar criticisms, though made less publicly and with less bitterness, emerged in the United States, where feminists were critical of the 'idea-less' nature of NAWSA campaigning, and largely unconvinced by the charismatic leadership of Alice Paul after her 'apprenticeship' in Britain. Avant-garde feminist debates on the state can be read as an extension of this critical discourse within feminism. Most feminists were content to rest their criticisms upon identifying the feebleness of the vote, and the unlikeliness of it achieving the social goals at which feminists aimed. The feminist 'vanguard' extended the argument to a full-scale critique of government and leadership.

Stirner's insight, that 'slaves' had their fate in their own hands and might declare themselves free at will, seemed to lead to an unattractive, elitist form of feminism. One *Freewoman* correspondent, Frances Prewett, anxiously declared that egoist feminism would leave 'all power in the hands of the strongest individuals'.[114] She preferred to understand government as 'the organisation through which society expresses and enforces its collective will'. Marsden responded that she did not intend 'aristocracy' to mean oppression of the mass, as this inevitably corrupted the great. Indeed, for the strong to *exploit* the weak was to place themselves in their power. In an editorial on 'leadership', Marsden argued that power, genius or Personality (used interchangeably) could not be used *against* others: 'Its legitimate use is to make him [*sic*] a greater soul; its illegitimate is to direct it towards the subordination of his fellows'. Leadership thus represented 'degeneracy', an argument no doubt directed at the leaders of the WSPU. Marsden's appeal to 'freewomen' was spiritual and only secondarily political – to set themselves on 'the path of self-confidence, which leads to the realisation of a man's own Personality – his Soul'.[115] This situating of feminist argument on the spiritual or psychic level was characteristic; many avant-garde feminists were vague about how their politics would be realised at the level of state institutions and preferred to talk in terms of the 'awakening of women' or construction of 'superwomen'.

CONCLUSION

The controversy about the role of the state persisted within feminism into and beyond the war years. As ever, working within an Anglo-American intellectual space, the editor of *Common Cause* published a 'Thought for the Week' from Abraham Lincoln in 1916: 'It has long been a grave question whether any government not too strong for the liberties of its people can be strong enough to maintain its existence in great emergencies'. This quote provoked a horrified response from Oliver Strachey, an NUWSS supporter. He acknowledged that many *Common Cause* readers were afraid of the State 'tampering with the liberties' of its people, but asked that this 'disruptive point' be excluded from debate as too likely to split the suffrage movement. The editor responded with a warning about state interference as one of 'the reefs on which democratic communities have come to grief'. Adopting the idiom of the pre-war vanguard feminists, she stated that 'the defence of our liberties depends upon our own will'.[116]

The feminist movement displayed a longstanding ambivalence about 'the state'. Nonetheless, it is unhelpful to assert a stark or polarised split between pro- and anti-statism. Marc Stears has outlined the lack of a 'knee-jerk rejection or confirmation of the central state' among American and British progressives and pluralists, and instead identifies a willingness to experiment with institutions in order to fulfil more fundamental aims.[17] The same willingness to experiment and subtlety of political argument is found amongst feminists, for whom it was most important to transform women's psyches and aid individual self-development. Feminists aimed to instil in women the confidence and desire to revolt against oppressive institutions, whether within government or suffrage societies, marriages or workplaces. The fact that most within the feminist avant-garde thought that few women had the capacity to revolt, and were not interested in collective institutional change, makes this an elitist political stance that seems to sit oddly with the inclusivity more commonly associated with feminism. However, elitism and a 'vanguard' approach spanned pro- and anti-statist positions, and must be read with sensitivity to their location in an Edwardian intellectual context. Feminists were open-minded about what the state could do for them, and experimented with different kinds of political philosophy. It is a mistake to read their ideas as answerable to any 'feminist principles' such as inclusivity, understood as valid for all times.

The endowment of motherhood controversy of the first two decades of the twentieth century provides an illustration of this experimentation with institutions. State support for mothers, widows or wives was a point at which state power and women's lives might collide. Numerous interests had a stake in this debate, and found common ground in the proposal. The complex overlap of feminist, eugenic, imperial and socialist concerns is a fascinating one, and provides an insight into the dilemmas feminists experienced when theorising state intervention. As a case-study, it sheds light on what kinds of state intervention were seen to be compatible with feminist and individualist concerns.

END NOTES

1. W. H. Greenleaf, *The British Political Tradition: The Rise of Collectivism* (London, Methuen, 1983), p. 19.
2. H. G. Wells *et al.*, *Socialism and The Great State: Essays in Construction* (New York, Harper and Brothers, 1912), p. 42; Hilaire Belloc, *The Servile State* (Indianapolis, Liberty Fund, 1977; orig. 1913); Donald Read, *Edwardian England 1901–1915* (London, Harrap, 1972), p. 87.
3. Sheila Rowbotham, 'Interpretations of Welfare and Approaches to the State, 1870–1920', in *The Politics of the Welfare State*, ed. Ann Oakley and Susan

Williams (London, University College London Press, 1994), p. 19. Morton Keller, 'Anglo-American Politics, 1900–1930, in Anglo-American Perspective: A Case Study in Comparative History', *Comparative Studies in Society and History*, 22:3 (July 1980) provides a comparative Anglo-American approach.

4. Beryl Haslam, *From Suffrage to Internationalism: The Political Evolution of Three British Feminists* (New York, Peter Lang, 1999), pp. xix–xx; Martin Pugh, 'Liberals and Women's Suffrage: 1867–1914', in *Citizenship and Community*, ed. E. Biagini (Cambridge, Cambridge University Press, 1996), p. 62.

5. Women's public participation was insecure; they were excluded from School Boards in 1902, and later from Vestry Councils. As Ethel Snowden described it, women engaged in public service did so in fear of 'arbitrary ousting', Snowden, 'Women and the State', in *Woman: A Few Shrieks!* ed. Constance Smedley (Letchworth, Garden City Press, 1908), p. 132.

6. L. T. Hobhouse, *Liberalism* (London, William & Norgate, 1911), p. 83.

7. Barker, *Political Ideas in Modern Britain*, p. 60; Stefan Collini, 'Hobhouse, Bosanquet and the State: Philosophical Idealism and Political Argument in England 1880–1918', *Past and Present*, 72 (Aug. 1978), 110; T. H. Green, *Lectures on the Principles of Political Obligation*, ed. R. L. Nettleship, vol. 2 (1886), §209.

8. Michael Freeden, 'J. A. Hobson as a New Liberal Theorist: Some Aspects of His Social Thought Until 1914', *Journal of the History of Ideas*, 34:3 (July – Sept. 1973), 430; J. A. Hobson, *The Crisis in Liberalism: New Issues in Democracy* (London, P. S. King, 1909), p. 81.

9. D. G. Ritchie, *The Principles of State Interference* (London, Swan Sonnenschein 1891), p. 148.

10. Beilharz, *Labour's Utopias: Bolshevism, Fabianism and Social Democracy* (London, Routledge, 1992), p. 63.

11. Marsden to Dell, 10 May 1913, FDP.

12. Ernest Barker, *Political Thought in England from Herbert Spencer to the Present Day* (London, Williams and Norgate, 1915), p. 37. Faced with National Insurance, Hilaire Belloc's 1913 *The Servile State* captured a mood of resistance to the moral and 'fiscal' intrusion of the state (Indiana: Liberty Fund (1977)).

13. Rodgers, 'In Search of Progressivism', pp. 123–7.

14. Arthur Mann, 'British Social Thought and American Reformers of the Progressive Era', *Mississippi Valley Historical Review*, 42 (1956), 688.

15. Forcey, *The Crossroads of Liberalism*, pp. 95; Rodgers, *Atlantic Crossings*, pp. 65–6.

16. Buenker, *Progressivism*, p. 12; Kathryn Kish Sklar, 'Two Political Cultures in the Progressive Era: The National Consumers' League and the American Association for Labor Legislation', pp. 36–62, in *U.S. History as Women's History: New Feminist Essays*, ed. L. K. Kerber, A. Kessler-Harris and K. Sklar (Chapel Hill, University of North Carolina Press, 1995), p. 40; Herbert Croly, *Progressive Democracy* (New York, Macmillan, 1915), pp. 303–4.

17. Rowbotham, 'Interpretations of Welfare', p. 21; Ellen Ross, *Love and Toil: Motherhood in Outcast London, 1870–1918* (Oxford, Oxford University Press, 1993), p. 196. See also Dorothy Schneider and Carl J. Schneider, *American Women in the Progressive Era, 1900–1920* (New York, Facts on File, 1993), p. 38.

18. Maureen A. Flanagan, *Seeing With Their Hearts: Chicago Women and the Vision of the Good City, 1871–1933* (Princeton, Princeton University Press, 2002).

19. Holton, *Feminism and Democracy*, p. 21. Purity concerns did not vanish from the feminist agenda but shifted in focus in the twentieth century from rescue work with prostitutes to legislative restrictions on the 'white slave trade'. See Judith R. Walkowitz, *City of Dreadful Delight: Narratives of Sexual Danger in Late-Victorian London* (London, Virago, 1992).

20. McMillan, in Atkinson, *Case for Women's Suffrage*, p. 119. See Carolyn Steedman, *Childhood, Culture and Class in Britain: Margaret McMillan 1860–1931* (London, Virago, 1990).

21. Paula Baker, 'The Domestication of Politics: Women in American Political Society 1780–1920', *American Historical Review*, 89 (June 1994).

22. Dr Gilbert Slater in Huntly Carter, *Women's Suffrage and Militancy: A Symposium* (London, Frank Palmer, 1911), p. 53.

23. Despard, in Atkinson, *Case for Women's Suffrage*, pp. 195–6.

24. *The Vote*, 9 Sept. 1911, 248; Housman, reported in *The Vote*, A. Mitchell, 18 May 1912, 77.

25. Spencer, 'Fitness of Women to Become Citizens from the Standpoint of Moral Development', NAWSA Convention Feb. 1898, reprinted in Buhle, *History of Woman Suffrage*, p. 365.

26. Linda Gordon, 'Putting Children First', in *U.S. History as Women's History*, ed. Kerber, Kessler-Harris and Sklar, pp. 63–86, esp. p. 69.

27. Dorr, *What Eight Million Women Want*, p. 327.

28. Elizabeth Boynton Harbert in *History of Woman Suffrage*, ed. Susan B. Anthony and Ida Husted Harper (Rochester, NY, 1902), vol. 3, 78–9. See Baker, 'The Domestication of Politics'; Patricia Hill, *The World Their Household: The American Woman's Foreign Mission Movement and Cultural Transformation, 1870–1920* (Ann Arbor, University of Michigan Press, 1985).

29. Seth Koven and Sonya Michel (eds.), *Mothers of a New World* (London, Routledge, 1993); Maureen A. Flanagan, 'Gender and Urban Political Reform: The City Club and the Woman's City Club of Chicago in the Progressive Era', *American Historical Review*, 95:4 (1990), 1046; Rodgers, *Atlantic Crossings*, pp. 19–20.

30. Pedersen, *Eleanor Rathbone*, p. 45.

31. Jane Lewis, *Women and Social Action in Victorian and Edwardian England* (Aldershot, Edward Elgar, 1991). On idealist thought, see Collini, 'Hobhouse, Bosanquet and the State'; Plant, *Philosophy, Politics and Citizenship*; Den Otter, *British Idealism and Social Explanation: A Study in Late Victorian Thought* (Oxford, Clarendon Press, 1996).

32. Ritchie, *Principles of State Interference*, p. 50.

33. McMillan, in Atkinson, *et al.*, *The Case for Women's Suffrage*, ed. B. Villiers (London, Fisher Unwin, 1907), p. 115; Jane Addams, 'Why Women Should Vote', *Ladies Home Journal* (1909); Snowden, 'Women and the State', p. 127.

34. Barbara Epstein, *The Politics of Domesticity: Women, Evangelism, and Temperance in Nineteenth Century America* (New York, Columbia University Press, 1981); Levine, 'Humanising Influences'.

35. Susan Kingsley Kent, *Sex and Suffrage, 1860–1914* (Princeton, Princeton University Press, 1987), p. 227.

36. Georgina Waylen, 'Gender, Feminism and the State', in *Gender, Politics and the State*, ed. Georgina Waylen and Vicky Randall (London, Routledge, 1998).

37. Teresa Billington-Greig, for example, argued that 'Woman belonged to the same genus as man ... she was fully human, and human only, not an inferior animal or superior angel but just a common human female'. Quoted in Kent, *Sex and Suffrage*, p. 215. In the United States, these kinds of argument came to distinguish a position termed by its supporters, 'human feminism', opposed by the 'feminine feminism'. Many in the women's movement would use 'difference' or 'equality' arguments according to context. I focus mainly on the 'difference' arguments for inclusion, because these tend to offer a distinct analysis of the nature of the state. Equality arguments tend to accept the status quo and demand women's inclusion, while those that focus on difference suggest the need to change or expand the role of the state, through women's participation.

38. Hardie, in Atkinson *et al.*, *Case for Women's Suffrage*, p. 83.

39. Fawcett quoted in Holton, *Feminism and Democracy*, p. 12. Anna Garlin Spencer similarly argued that women 'give a service to the modern State which men can not altogether duplicate'. Spencer, 'Fitness of Women to Become Citizens', p. 365. *The Vote*, 4 Feb. 1911, 182. James Mill quoted in the *Westminster Review*, Jan. 1898, 53–4.

40. See Holton, *Feminism and Democracy*, pp. 14, 18; M. Friedman, 'Care and Context in Moral Reasoning', in *Women and Moral Theory*, ed. Eva Kittay and Diana Meyers (Totowa, NJ, Rowman and Littlefield, 1987); Carol Gilligan, *In a Different Voice: Psychological Theory and Women's Development* (Cambridge, Mass., Harvard University Press, 1982).

41. Olive Banks notes that feminist strategy proposed 'the attempted invasion of the masculine world not simply by women but, potentially even more revolutionary in its impact, by womanly values'. Banks, *Faces of Feminism*, p. 90.

42. Snowden, 'Women and the State', p. 133.

43. Hollis, *Ladies Elect*, p. 7; Pedersen, *Eleanor Rathbone*, p. 92.

44. See Jean Gaffin, 'Women and Co-Operation', in *Women in the Labour Movement*, ed. Lucy Middleton (London, Croom Helm, 1977); Margaret Llewelyn Davies (ed.), *Life As We Have Known It, By Co-Operative Working Women* (London, Virago, 1977); Scott, *Feminism and the Politics of Working Women*. The Guild was not an explicitly 'feminist' organisation, but many

of its publications and member's narratives show similar themes to those of the feminist movement.

45. Nash, in Atkinson *et al.*, *Case for Women's Suffrage*, pp. 69, 72.
46. McMillan, in Atkinson *et al.*, *Case for Women's Suffrage*, p. 111.
47. *The Crusade*, Aug. 1912, quoted in Lisanne Radice, *Beatrice and Sidney Webb* (London, Macmillan, 1984), p. 194.
48. *The Vote*, 30 Oct. 1909.
49. Hoare, *Woman in the State*, NAWSA pamphlet, 1891.
50. Snowden, 'Women and the State', p. 141.
51. Knight, 'Woman v. The State', 39, 40.
52. Drysdale, *FW*, 21 Dec. 1911, 89.
53. See Hollis, *Ladies Elect*, p. 6. Though Ward was a well-known opponent of women's suffrage, her work with the settlement movement and in municipal government made her influential upon the women's movement. Beth Sutton-Ramspeck gives a sympathetic reading of Ward's 'social feminism', and indeed her explicitly anti-feminist contemporaries saw her as dangerously 'feminist'. Beth Sutton-Ramspeck, 'Shot Out of the Canon: Mary Ward and the Claims of Conflicting Feminism', in *Victorian Women Writers and the Woman Question*, ed. Nicola D. Thompson (Cambridge, Cambridge University Press, 1999); Bush, 'British Women's Anti-Suffragism'.
54. Pugh, 'Liberals and Women's Suffrage: 1867–1914', p. 63; Harrison, *Separate Spheres*, pp. 73–4; Bush, 'British Women's Anti-Suffragism'. For the 'Forward Policy' anti-suffragists, national government, in contrast to local, was concerned with empire, and defence of borders, questions over which physical force might be called in to play. For these reasons, it could not be analogous to the home, nor be under feminine influence. Mary Augusta Ward, 'An Appeal Against Female Suffrage', in *Before the Vote Was Won: Arguments for and Against Women's Suffrage*, ed. Jane Lewis (London, Routledge, 1987), p. 410.
55. Quoted in *The Vote*, 9 March 1912, 233.
56. Ward, quoted in Sutton-Ramspeck, 'Shot Out of the Canon', p. 211.
57. Judith Allen, 'Does Feminism Need a Theory of the State?' in *Playing the State*, ed. Sophie Watson (London, Verso, 1990), p. 21.
58. Swanwick, *The Future of the Women's Movement*, pp. 3, viii.
59. See Belloc, *The Servile State*.
60. See Gilman, 'A Woman's Utopia', and Cooley, 'A Dream of the 21st Century', in *Daring to Dream: Utopian Fiction by United States Women Before 1950*, ed. Carol Farley Kessler (New York, Syracuse University Press, 1995).
61. Bourne to Parsons, u.d. (1915?), ECPP.
62. Parsons, *Journal of a Feminist*, pp. 45, 18, 56–7.
63. Knight, 'Woman v. The State'.
64. Marsden, *FW*, 18 April 1912, 422; 15 Aug. 1912, 243.
65. 'What is Individualism?' Gawthorpe, *FW*, 26 Sept. 1912, 376–7; Marsden, *FW*, 26 Sept. 1912, 379.

66. Angelique Richardson, *Love and Eugenics in the Late Nineteenth Century: Rational Reproduction and the New Woman* (Oxford, Oxford University Press, 2003), p. 46. See also Bland, *Banishing the Beast*.

67. Mabel Atkinson, 'The Economic Foundations of the Women's Movement, Fabian Tract No. 175', in *Women's Fabian Tracts (1988)*, ed. Sally Alexander (London, Routledge, 1914), pp. 277–8.

68. Caird, 'Marriage', *Westminster Review*, 130 (1888); Charles Whitby, quoted in Richardson, *Love and Eugenics*, p. 179; Caird, 'The Militant Suffragists', *New Age*, 14 Oct. 1909, 448; Caird, Women's Suffrage Supplement, *New Age*, 2 Feb. 1911, 1.

69. Marsden, *FW*, 14 March 1912, 321–2.

70. See Marsden's anti-eugenic editorial, *FW*, 25 July 1912, and letters from Stella Browne, *FW*, 1 and 15 Aug. 1912.

71. See Hall, ' "I Have Never Met the Normal Woman" '; Stella Browne, 'Woman and Birth Control', in *Population and Birth Control, a Symposium*, ed. Paul and Eden Cedar (New York, Critic and Guide, 1917), p. 152; Browne, 'Some Problems of Sex', *IJE*, 27 (July 1917).

72. See Delap, 'Feminist and Anti-Feminist Encounters in Edwardian Britain'.

73. Tuttle, *Awakening of Woman*, pp. 123–45.

74. Ruth Cavendish Bentinck, 'The Point of Honour: A Correspondence on Aristocracy and Socialism', in *Women's Fabian Tracts*, ed. Alexander, p. 144.

75. Snowden, 'Women and the State', pp. 124–5; Ruth Brandon, *The New Women and the Old Men: Love, Sex and the Woman Question* (London, Secker and Warburg, 1990), p. 162.

76. Marsden, *FW*, 18 Jan. 1912, 162; Hapgood, 'What Women are After', *Harper's Weekly*, 16 Aug. 1913, 28–9.

77. Lippmann, 'Why Should the Majority Rule?' *Harper's Magazine*, March 1926, 399–405; Lippmann, *Drift and Mastery: An Attempt to Diagnose the Current Unrest* (New York, 1914). See also Mann, ''British Social Thought and American Reformers'; Herbert Croly, *The Promise of American Life* (Cambridge, Mass., Harvard University Press, 1965), p. 449. Croly, cited in Stears, *Progressives*, p. 49. See Morgan, 'The Future at Work', p. 262.

78. Scudder, quoted in Mann, ''British Social Thought and American Reformers'; Gilman, 'A Woman's Utopia', *The Times Magazine*, Jan.–March 1907, repr. in Carol Farley Kessler, *Charlotte Perkins Gilman: Her Progress Towards Utopia* (New York, Syracuse University Press, 1995), p. 134. Rohe quoted in Schwarz, *Radical Feminists of Heterodoxy*, p. 47.

79. West, quoted in Amy Wellington, *Women Have Told: Studies in the Feminist Tradition* (Boston, Little, Brown and Co., 1930), p. 187.

80. Billington-Greig, 'For Sex-Equality', *New Age*, 30 May 1907, 73; 'Feminism and Politics', *Contemporary Review*, Nov. 1911.

81. Billington-Greig, 'A Bombshell for the Suffragists', *Nash's Magazine*, March 1911, 26.

82. Hastings (D. Triformis), 'To Your Posts, Feminists!' *New Age*, 16 Feb. 1911, 368.

83. Billington-Greig, 'Women and Government', *FW*, 21 Dec. 1912, 85–6; Parsons, *Journal of a Feminist*, p. 67.
84. Marsden, *FW*, 18 April 1912, 421–2.
85. Masterman, *The Condition of England*, p. 99.
86. Anne Fernihough, ' "Go in Fear of Abstractions": Modernism and the Spectre of Democracy', *Textual Practice*, 14:3 (2000).
87. Billington-Greig, 'Feminism and Politics', *Contemporary Review*, Nov. 1911.
88. Marsden, *FW*, 26 Sept. 1912, 364, 363.
89. Lee, *Gospels of Anarchy*, pp. 292–3.
90. Billington-Greig, 'A Free Feminist Platform', *New Age*, 30 March 1911, 525.
91. Morrison, *The Public Face of Modernism*.
92. Marsden, *FW*, 8 Aug. 1912; 224; 25 July 1912, 184.
93. Marsden, *FW*, 11 July 1912, 144.
94. Marsden, *FW*, 25 July 1912, 184. See Bob Holton, *British Syndicalism, 1900–1914: Myths and Realities* (London, Pluto Press, 1976), p. 133.
95. Marsden, *Egoist*, 1 Jan. 1914, *NFW*, 15 Oct. 1913.
96. Jardine to Björkman, 23 July 1912, MWDP.
97. Marsden, *FW*, 25 April 1912, 443.
98. AH to Marsden, DMC u.d.: III, 1.
99. Marsden, *FW*, 14 March 1912, 232.
100. Marsden, *FW*, 18 April 1912, 422; *FW*, 4 April 1912, 395.
101. H. G. Wells, *An Englishman Looks at the World* (London, Cassell, 1914), p. 309.
102. Collini, *Liberalism and Sociology*, p. 14.
103. Hobson, 1909, quoted in Read, *Edwardian England 1901–1915*, p. 101; Sidney Webb, 1889, quoted in Beilharz, *Labour's Utopias*, p. 53.
104. Anna Martin's work with the Bermondsey Settlement led her to be critical with regard to the state's policies on mothers and working women. See Anna Martin, *The Married Working Woman* (London, The National Union of Women's Suffrage Societies, 1911); Martin, *The Mother and Social Reform* (London, The National Union of Women's Suffrage Societies, 1913); Ross, *Love and Toil*, p. 197.
105. Marsden, *FW*, 12 Sept. 1912, 321.
106. Stirner, *Ego and its Own*, p. 175.
107. Marsden, *FW*, 2 May 1912, 475.
108. Gillmore, 'The Life of an Average Woman', *Harper's Bazar*, June 1912, 281.
109. Marsh, 'Anarchist-Feminist Response'.
110. Gilman, 'A Visible Evolution', *Forerunner*, Aug. 1914, 214.
111. Gilman, 'Justice Instead of Sacrifice', *Forerunner*, Sept. 1913, 257–8.
112. Marsden, *FW*, 22 Aug. 1912, 264.
113. Marsden, *The Egoist*, 15 June 1914, 223, 224.
114. Prewett, *FW*, 3 Oct. 1912, 393.
115. Marsden, *FW*, 26 Sept. 1912, 366. See Dixon, *Divine Feminine*, on the embrace of spirituality within the feminist movement.
116. *Common Cause*, 25 Feb. 1916, 613; Strachey, 3 March 1916, 652.
117. Stears, *Progressives*, p. 4.

CHAPTER 5

The endowment of motherhood controversy

Avant-garde feminists were well aware that when women talked of their participation in and service to the state, they often meant their reproductive role. Motherhood – its symbolic and racial significance, its failures and consolations – was of intense interest to most feminists, a central issue that they could not avoid – both in intellectual debates and in their own lives. Rebecca West's experiences of 'free union' with H. G. Wells, resulting in her unplanned pregnancy in 1913–14 and many years of struggle as a single mother suggests something of the significance that the economic and social status of motherhood had for those attempting artistic and creative careers in the 'vanguard'. Having witnessed the single motherhood of Françoise Lafitte, a friend from the Freewoman Discussion Group, West had written of the outcast and pariah status of the unmarried mother in early 1913: 'All her life she will be insulted. Men will treat her as though her barriers were down to all comers. Women will not take the trouble to discriminate her from the prostitute. Henceforth she is a broken thing.' She herself became pregnant at the outset of her affair with the married Wells, and had to spend six months of the pregnancy living in secrecy in rural Norfolk. The affair and pregnancy led to a three-year absence from her family home after conflict with her mother, was kept secret from most friends, and left West embittered at the social and economic isolation she experienced. She denied the centrality of motherhood to women's lives, and was highly irritated at the prospect of 'advanced' Edwardians making political capital out of her motherhood. 'Pale Fabians would say that I was the Free Woman and that I had wanted to be the Mother of the Superman', she speculated sardonically, but West herself believed that: 'Life makes itself. I cannot see that childbirth is creative at all, one is just an instrument'.[1] She and other 'advanced' feminists found the sentimentality of many in the women's movement concerning motherhood cloying, and preferred to imagine other destinies for women. Nonetheless, it was clear that motherhood could not be experienced

180

differently until the economics of it were altered, and this topic dominated feminist debates both before and after the First World War, often framed as the controversial question of the state endowment of motherhood.

An exchange between the British suffragist Emmeline Pethick Lawrence and Charlotte Perkins Gilman was published as a pamphlet titled 'Does A Man Support His Wife?' by NAWSA in 1912. It illustrates the lack of agreement on the topic of how motherhood should be supported. Pethick Lawrence was a sentimental writer, and like many suffragists, she waxed lyrical about the transformative power of the 'mother spirit'. In a *Votes for Women* article, she argued that motherhood was analogous to men's military service for the state, and that the state should honour and pay for her labours. Gilman answered in *The Forerunner*. She regarded this position as

of the gravest injury to the very cause it champions. What women need is not to be soothed and kept content in their economic position by any sweeping claims of its world-value, but to learn once and for all that their position is one injurious and degrading ... As long as woman, who constitute half the world, are content to live as private servants to the other half, our civilisation must remain arrested and incongruous as we now see it.[2]

The endowment controversy reveals the difficult choices Edwardian feminists faced when assessing state intervention and women's economic participation. This was particularly so for socialist-feminists, for whom endowment was not only a sex but also a class issue. Their concerns were debated within Anglo-American journals, pamphlets and lectures, along with other controversies such as the role of men in care-work.

Anglo-American debates around endowment provide an opportunity to unpack the anti-statism of avant-garde feminists, in a period when many within the women's movement felt positive about state action on women's behalf. In particular, it illustrates the quite extensive space for state action that was seen as compatible with an anti-statist position. The endowment controversy, which endured in Britain and the United States throughout the first three decades of the twentieth century, was one that demanded discussion of women's public and private roles.[3] As mothers, women could be located in the 'feminine' private sphere while simultaneously performing a 'citizenship' role, their duty to the race. To be a mother was perceived by many feminists as the key feminine social role, though most felt that other roles could complement motherhood. The question of payment for mothering will serve in this chapter as a focal point for discussion about feminist, socialist and individualist constructions of citizenship and the state. The chapter concludes with an examination of the charges – laid against avant-garde feminists sceptical of endowment – of bourgeois elitism and insensitivity to the needs of working-class mothers.

EDWARDIAN WELFARE POLICY AND ENDOWMENT

As discussed in the previous chapter, the Edwardian period in Britain and, to a lesser extent, in America, was one of increased state intervention, particularly in the sphere of 'welfare'.[4] There was, however, no established or hegemonic theory of welfare intervention. Susan Pedersen identifies three contrasting trends in British social policy in this period, corresponding loosely to those identified by Linda Gordon within American social policy.[5] The first policy approach assumed a stable family, maintained by a man and serviced by an economically dependent female. This basis for welfare measures was associated with campaigns for a family wage, and the British Liberal government's National Insurance measures to combat sickness and unemployment of the male breadwinner. Gordon describes this tendency in America as 'overwhelmingly male and virtually ignor[ing] children', and most activists in the women's movement recognised it as against women's interests.

Second, charitable and Poor Law type distribution of social aid was based on principles of self-help and character reform. Assistance was often based on membership of a 'needy category', and entailed individual 'casework' investigation. Seth Koven has described this idealist-influenced approach to intervention as occupying a 'borderland' between state and civil society, a space for voluntary action that both galvanised and constrained women's social intervention.[6] This was a powerful but declining approach in the early twentieth century, when 'professionalisation' and impartiality began to replace such moralised philanthropy (often to the detriment of women's participation in the organisation of social welfare). Third, there was a trend towards direct welfare provision by the state, intended to bypass the familial power structures that placed the male 'breadwinner' as recipient, and direct resources towards those most in need. It was embodied in the public provision of school meals, direct old age pensions, and, potentially, in the endowment of motherhood.[7] This trend was better established in Britain than in America, where the power of state legislatures to experiment with new forms of welfare provision was severely restrained by the ability of courts to judge legislation unconstitutional. But even in Britain it did not imply an all-powerful state; the trend within the pre-war British welfare state was towards discretion at the local level, and use of voluntary organisations. The growing intrusion of the state was thus not that of a monolithic and centralised bureaucracy, but of central supervision and delegated authority.[8]

How did feminists respond to these trends? Most were wary of the family-wage approach, recognising that male power over female relatives could not be challenged by this route.[9] The second charitable and mor-alised approach had previously been supported by activists involved in the Charity Organisation Society and rescue work with prostitutes. The administration of welfare through voluntary groups was still supported by feminists during World War One, as Eleanor Rathbone's work with the Soldiers' and Sailors' Families Association shows. This approach, as well as being under threat from central and local government bureaucrats, also received declining feminist support in the Edwardian period. The third approach of direct state aid (or state-funded aid) to the needy individual was clearly the most attractive to feminist thinkers, and to settlement and social workers. Margaret Llewelyn Davies of the Women's Co-operative Guild wrote in 1915 that it was 'a really bright sign for the future' that women were now demanding a greatly increased scope for state action. She believed that 'Society cannot cure itself, and the last hope, therefore is for the state to attempt a cure'.[10] Endowment, as a sum paid directly to the mother in cash or kind by the state, was intended to be of this third trend, and a positive, empowering development for women.

Endowment of motherhood gained powerful supporters in the early twentieth century, and was developed as part of the transatlantic exchange on social policy. The idea probably originated in Scandinavia, and was also experimented with in Germany. The rise of public welfare provision in European and Commonwealth countries led to widespread comparisons between nations in their treatment of pregnant and nursing mothers. This was motivated by the almost axiomatic belief that, as Charles Fourier had suggested in the early nineteenth century, one should look to the position of women to determine the level of development of the nation. There thus was a strong 'national-interest' element in the literature on endowment, which spread from Europe to the United States in the early years of the twentieth century. Books such as the influential 1906 *Bitter Cry of the Children* by the American-based socialist John Spargo were full of com-parisons between the United States and the welfarism of European countries. Spargo declared, 'we must turn for guidance and suggestion to the Old World' in fields such as child poverty and mothers' pensions.[11] But this was not simply a one-way movement of ideas from the 'old' world to the new. American political cultures was deeply affected by 'maternalism' (whether of progressive or sentimental varieties), and states began to experiment with 'mothers' pensions' from around 1911.[12] These innovations were admired and discussed in Europe, and the whole issue of maternal endowment developed in a genuinely transatlantic intellectual space.

In debating the ambiguous politics of maternalism, many historians have noted the strong element of social control in policies directed towards mothers. A central trope in the deterioration or degeneration discourse was the feckless mother.[13] The British Edwardian infant welfare movement has been described as interventionist and patronising, and endowment risked being tarred with the same brush. Endowment was intended to have the dual function of promoting the interests of women and children, and serving the eugenic agenda of protecting 'the wellsprings of vitality' of the race – the health of women in their reproductive period. Aside from its functional value, endowment could also be perceived as a just claim for wages, a recompense for the services women provided to the community through the bearing and care of the future generations. This latter claim was sometimes made in terms of citizenship – that women had a duty as citizens to produce and care for the next generation, and that the state therefore had a corresponding responsibility to provide for them. Mabel Atkinson, a Fabian supporter of endowment, argued: 'No act of citizenship is more fundamental than the act of bringing into the world and protecting in his helpless infancy a new citizen'. H. G. Wells, a prominent enthusiast for endowment, had argued 'A new status has still to be invented for women, a Feminine Citizenship differing in certain respects from the normal masculine citizenship . . . The public Endowment of Motherhood as such may perhaps be the first broad suggestion of the quality of this new status'.[14]

In its pre-war formulation, endowment in Britain remained a relatively radical policy, supported by a progressive minority, mostly eugenicists and socialists. For many Edwardian socialists, it was a paradigm case of what sort of provision should be undertaken collectively. Since all benefited from the upbringing of future generations, the cost should be borne collectively. Endowment would also strike against the capitalist constraints that had invaded women's reproductive decision-making. Birth control activist Charles Drysdale maintained in *The Freewoman* that endowment was a potential solution to 'the abomination of mixing up sex-love with the cash-nexus'.[15] That all wives were effectively prostitutes, since they had traded their sexual services for financial support, was a common socialist and feminist argument.[16] Endowment, as the influential feminist proponent Ellen Key saw it, was to make women independent, free to choose partners for love.[17] It was particularly popular amongst Fabians; H. G. Wells took up the idea in his 1906 pamphlet *Socialism and the Family*. He deployed the metaphor discussed in the previous chapter, the equation of family and state: 'Socialism, in fact, is the state family'. Such a socialist family was compelled to provide for the most vulnerable, and would therefore support women during motherhood. Wells portrayed childrearing as a social service, undertaken with the intimate participation of the state: 'The State is the Over-Parent, the Outer-Parent. People rear children for the State and the future; if they do that well, they do the whole world a service, and deserve payment just as much as if they built a bridge'.[18] Wells openly assumed that it was impossible that 'women are, or can be made, equivalent economically to men, and that over and above normal citizenship they are capable of bearing and rearing their own children'.[19] (By normal citizenship, Wells apparently meant engagement in paid work.) Endowment was to take over from the wasteful, inefficient and patchy community or family support of children and female carers, and allow the 'trade of motherhood' to be organised more professionally and with better eugenic consequences.

David Eder, a contributor to avant-garde and socialist intellectual circles, took up the idea and produced a pamphlet in 1908 entitled *The Endowment of Motherhood*. He laid out the motivations for the policy, and compared provision in various countries. Such comparison was given significance by the Edwardian panic at Britain being overtaken by Germany and the USA, in terms of trade, population and 'imperial standing'. Endowment thus had a national saliency in this context of Britain's relative decline. Unlike Wells, who had portrayed motherhood as women's 'supreme social function', Eder stressed that motherhood was just 'one of women's many fields of occupation'. Social and eugenic efficiency was presented as the main benefit of endowment, but Eder also mentioned other benefits resulting from the promotion of early sexual unions – discouragement of the evils of masturbation, prostitution, sexual repression and perversion. Endowment would reverse the falling birth rate while simultaneously discouraging venereal disease. Eder sought to link avant-garde theories of sexuality to social policy, in arguing that sexual activity was to be encouraged due to its links with creativity: 'Artistic genius and perhaps all kinds of genius are closely associated with sexual activity'.[20] The knowledge that maternity was to be provided for would allow for greater sexual expressiveness and experimentation, particularly by women.

Eder's work was developed and extended in a Fabian tract of 1910, by the liberal barrister, later an active WSPU supporter, Henry D. Harben, also titled *The Endowment of Motherhood*. As might be expected, Eder's emphasis on creative sexual energy became somewhat submerged by Fabian pragmatism. The overall tone in most texts on endowment was one of promotion of an efficient public health scheme. As Harben put it, 'money spent on the beginning of life is more economical than money spent at the end'. The family was an effective point of intervention for social policy. The high rate of infant mortality, and tendency to chronic ill-health for mothers was deplored.

Eder and Harben saw the home as 'blighted' by 'our modern industrial system'. Yet this blight was to be easily remedied by the provision of a temporary dole on the birth of a child. In Eder's scheme this benefit was to last approximately a year, while in Harben's more cautious scheme, only eight weeks. The possibility that the birth rate might increase was entertained by Harben, but not seen as problematic since more British births would ensure a good supply of Anglo-Saxon population that could be exported to 'the colonies'. The authors identified the limitation and inefficiency of the Poor Law approach to welfare, which could only respond to destitution and could not take into consideration the future welfare of the child.[21] More suitable was the local authority or charitable provision of midwives, advice and milk, but this intervention was limited by its patchwork nature. Universality was becoming a fundamental principle of welfare intervention, and endowment was to be a means of extending this principle into infant and maternal provision. The discourse of citizenship was used to underpin this – as Harben put it, every 'new-born citizen' had a 'birth-right' to adequate care, that the state must guarantee.[22]

Neither Eder nor Harben foresaw that women would be permanently excluded from the labour market as a result of their motherhood. Eder commented 'I have no wish to indicate to women what is their proper sphere; I think they are experimenting to-day, but I have assumed throughout that women, married or not, will enter into all activities in the freest possible manner'. Nonetheless, 'a certain number of women will consecrate themselves to the bringing up of children'. His scheme hovered between the temporary support of women under 'exceptional' circumstances and the support of a number of women as 'professional mothers'.

A strong case was made by such writers, and the British state had been newly ready to intervene in the raising of children in the Children's Act of 1908. The British endowment campaign gathered speed from 1912 when Eleanor Rathbone, a prominent liberal suffragist of the NUWSS based in

Liverpool, took it up.[23] Her research into women's wages had convinced her that women would always be paid less while men could claim to be supporting their families, however haphazardly, through a 'family wage'. She believed that 'Equal Pay for Equal Work' would remain an abstract ideal until the family wage concept was exploded, through the state taking on the care of mothers and children directly. This would sow the 'seeds of divine discontent' that would give feminists their focus for future, post-suffrage campaigns.[24] Rathbone argued that the separation allowances paid to the dependants of men in the armed forces from 1915 provided a model for a post-war universal scheme, and she campaigned to this end throughout the 1920s and 1930s. Her focus on women as mothers, based within the home, was to split the feminist movement, leading to a loss of political voice for feminism in Britain.[25] Endowment was finally successful in Britain, in a limited fashion, in the passing of the 1945 Family Allowances Act. However, as Carol Dyhouse comments, Family Allowances 'were implemented in a way which fulfilled nothing of the radicalism of Rathbone's early vision'.[26] The ending of women's dependency on men was never realised, and following the 1945 Act, the whole vocabulary of endowment disappeared from the social policy vocabulary, and with it, a chief plank in feminist social policy.

In the United States, endowment was successful much earlier than in Britain. Mothers' and widows' pensions had been available in some American states as a means-tested benefit since the second decade of the twentieth century, but tended to be of inadequate value to release mothers from needing to work. As in Britain, socialist groups supported the idea, though endowment tended to be seen in more conservative terms (prefiguring Britain in the 1920s and 1930s, where endowment became associated with pro-natalism). Motherhood was a key element of progressive reform, often constructed in racial terms (the problematisation of 'white sterility', and black mothers' 'fecundity'). Alison Berg has described motherhood as 'a national project of rational reform' for progressives, and notes their tendency to read all women's issues as ones of motherhood, and thus of race.[27]

The idea of 'mothers' pensions' gained popularity as a solution to the inadequacies of day nurseries, and the perceived unsuitability of the workplace for mothers. This was in contrast to British versions of endowment, which tended to stress endowment as enabling women to remain within the workplace between births, supporting their claims for equal pay and discrediting the idea of the family wage. In the States, however, Julia Lathrop, the head of the United States Children's Bureau (established in 1912), supported state payments to keep mothers out of the workplace, seeing the home as their more appropriate sphere. Her stance was in keeping with socialist arguments for endowment; John Spargo had argued for mothers' pensions since 'the effort of society should be to keep the mother in the home with her children'. Convinced of the dangers of maternal ignorance, Spargo supported quite invasive state action to control mothers, including prohibition of work for six to eight weeks before and after birth, and public instruction in the duties of motherhood.[28]

The growing influence of suffrage-feminism came to allow for endowment to be understood as a citizenship claim, arguing that mothers should be seen as 'disabled soldiers', temporarily unable to provide for themselves through their service to the nation. Recognising the unattractive elements of dependency and disability within this imagery, one supporter argued that the endowed mother was not dependent, but remained an independent citizen with 'future citizens at her knees'. Endowment should be a means of support aimed at children, and 'only incidentally for herself'.[29] British activists recognised the dangerous turn within American debates about endowment which seemed to epitomise, as one *Common Cause* editorial put it, 'the possessive and protective theory which some men profess to hold concerning the relation of the male to the female ... We hope that American women will be aroused to a full sense of the ignominious position in which these [endowment] proposals, if carried out, would place them. Any woman who is willing to be stall-fed in this way is showing herself unfit for liberty'.[30]

Nonetheless, the American campaign for endowment became increasingly popular during the World War One years, through the campaigning of voluntary groups such as the National Congress of Mothers, the General Federation of Women's Clubs and the Woman's Christian Temperance Union. Mass market magazines like *The Delineator*, *Good Housekeeping* and *Collier's* supported endowment from around 1912.[31] Forty states had enacted mothers' or widows' pensions by 1920, eighteen in 1913 alone. This relative 'success' made the American mothers' pensions movement influential in turn upon Britain.[32] For many Americans, it was less the British experiments with state welfare provision that were influential, but rather the German and Scandinavian models. The feminist writer Katharine Anthony commented upon the 'backwardness of English legislation in comparison with Germanic and Scandinavian legislation on this subject [of state support for child rearing]'.[33] Nonetheless, Anglo-American transatlantic exchanges remained extremely influential. Harriet Stanton Blatch made a visit to Europe in 1915 and returned to the United States inspired by the endowment policy, particularly in the separation allowances policy. She wrote an influential book in 1918, *Mobilizing Woman Power*, in which she pinned her hopes for the post-suffrage women's movement on its adoption of maternity endowment, as a policy which would make possible equal conditions in the labour market. She was disappointed, however, to find that American feminists divided in a sterile battle between the 'absolute equality' followers of Alice Paul, and the pro-protective legislation activists of the Women's Trade Union League.

Blatch gained little support for her 'third way' in feminism, endowment of motherhood combined with state protection for all vulnerable workers, regardless of sex; endowment controversies illustrate what Ellen DuBois has described as an equality/difference split that became 'a permanent and defining feature of the political landscape' of the women's movement.[34] Endowment was adopted in the United States, but not as Blatch had anticipated. In 1935, it became a federal policy to make cash payments to mothers unsupported by their husbands – a policy which clearly entrenched the idea of female dependence on men. In each country, however, endowment was enacted in a way that inscribed women within the state exclusively as mothers, and gave them lower entitlements than men to other kinds of welfare support. The impact of endowment was not to further the perception of motherhood as a service to the state, but to act as a form of (racially discriminatory) sentimental charity.[35]

THE FEMINIST CASE FOR AND AGAINST ENDOWMENT

Nonetheless, for many feminists, the endowment of motherhood was a policy clearly in women's favour. Feminists had influenced the development of the endowment policy, through their concern with women's autonomy and health during childrearing. Endowment spanned the dual interests of socialist-feminists in class and gender, and it thus came to be seen by Edwardians, as Mabel Atkinson put it, as 'the ultimate ideal of the feminist movement'.[36] Though some members of the NUWSS were less enthusiastic, during the debates over National Insurance schemes in 1911, *Common Cause* declared 'When will [men] see that the care of mothers and babes should be a first charge on the State!'[37] Maude Royden, an editor of the *Common Cause*, saw endowment as the only means to discard the family wage and thus achieve equal pay between the sexes, and this became a key argument for the so-called 'new feminists' of the post-war women's movement.

'New feminism' sought to decentre equality and instead focus on women 'as they really were', in all their particularity and difference from men.[38] Royden argued in the 1917 collection of 'new feminist' essays *The Making of Women* that mothers performed a parallel service to soldiers, and should be paid for this in the same way. She rejected anything 'tainted with the idea of charity rather than of recognition for service given', as well as any element of compulsion in forcing women to tend children. Endowed mothers would be free to share or delegate childcare as long as adequate standards were reached. Nonetheless, she believed that 'women, generally speaking, will make the care of their children the first claim on them during a part of their lives'. This was 'an absorbing duty and not merely an episode'. The Women's Co-operative Guild also welcomed endowment policies. Even critics such as the suffrage playwright Cicely Hamilton saw endowment as 'needful and inevitable'.[39] Victor Gollancz, editor of *The Making of Women*, called for endowment to replace 'equal pay for equal work' as the battle-cry of feminism.

American feminists such as Katharine Anthony, Crystal Eastman, Elsie Clews Parsons (all 'Heterodites') and Harriot Stanton Blatch supported various forms of endowment, probably learnt from British or German examples.[40] As in Britain, endowment was a policy which came to epitomise the divides within feminism, described in the United States as 'human' versus 'female' feminism (though these distinctions were always tenuous). Katharine Anthony was a high-profile proponent of the latter, 'female' grouping. Her book *Mothers Who Must Earn* concluded in 1914 that endowment would keep women out of the workplace in a non-stigmatising way, since it was a universal benefit. Endowment offered a solution to the poverty of mothers and children, and a means of bypassing patriarchal power. Mothers given state support would no longer be dependent upon their husbands, partners or fathers. Their welfare and that of the race was promoted by their not having to immediately return to the labour market after giving birth.

Those we might loosely term 'human feminists', such as Elsie Clews Parsons and Charlotte Perkins Gilman, regarded endowment as a means of solving the dilemma of choosing between maternity and economic independence, though Gilman stressed that endowment should be for the child, rather than the mother. She was very clear that 'maternity should not be considered an economic function'.[41] Despite this proviso, motherhood was treated more positively in the American feminist literature than the British equivalent, and British writers toned down their criticism for the American market. Rebecca West, when writing for an American periodical, modified her former tone of scepticism about the self-sacrificial nature of motherhood, and instead talked of maternal duties.[42] Given this tendency to idealise feminist versions of motherhood, historians, and many Edwardian commentators, have concluded that endowment, as a 'radically mother-centred' policy was in women's favour, and was in essence a 'feminist' reform.[43] It meshed with the predominant statism of the mainstream Edwardian women's movement, as well as with new liberal preferences for efficient intervention and Fabian socialist collectivism.

OPPOSITION

Since historians have tended to regard endowment as a feminist policy, opposition to it from within the women's movement acts as a moment of dissonance that is revealing of feminist encounters with political philosophy. It has been argued that feminists supported endowment since the options of motherhood or work were regarded as mutually exclusive. Jane Lewis has suggested that there was very little discussion of collective childcare in the pre-war women's movement, and thus few alternatives to endowment could be imagined.[44] The debates of the feminist avant-garde suggest a different interpretation. The concept of the endowment of motherhood was controversial amongst feminists, and a rich debate took place over other options – male involvement, childcare and co-operative living, technological alternatives, parents contracts, were all discussed in 'advanced' feminist circles. The case for endowment was intensely debated in a series of editorial leaders within *The Freewoman* from January to March 1912, following the editor's challenge to supporters of the scheme to state their case. Numerous letters, articles and unpublished correspondence continued the debate amongst the British feminist vanguard. Further critical feminist discussion, mostly by American writers, was found within the *International Journal of Ethics* in the years leading up to America's entry to the war in 1917. What, then, were the feminist objections to endowment?

Feminist opposition was generated less by the worthy principles of the scheme (mothers' independence of husbands, greater resources for children) than by the tacit assumptions and asides made by supporters of endowment. For example, while some feminists presented endowment of motherhood using the powerful argument of a citizenship contract, the work of Fabians such as Harben and Wells undermined this interpretation. As discussed above, Harben specifically identified the new-born as a citizen, and thus due care by the state. Yet it is noticeable that no discussion of mothers' citizenship featured in his account. Even more explicitly, H. G. Wells argued in *The Freewoman* that 'Womanhood is not something superadded to the normal citizen; it is something taking up time, nervous energy, room in the body and room in the mind. It is something *carved out of* the normal citizen'.[45] He saw motherhood, or femininity in general, as inimical to citizenship. This recalls some long-standing weaknesses in socialist thought from the feminist perspective – the exclusive equation of citizenship with work in paid employment, and lack of interest in the 'unproductive' work done in the home. The endowment literature tended to reproduce this weakness.

Not only was doubt cast on the compatibility of motherhood and citizenship, but in addition, endowment schemes drew on the contemporary 'feckless mother' discourse. For Harben, endowment was a means of undermining 'the old wives' tales and remedies' of 'ignorant mothers', and promoting 'elementary rules of health'.[46] Indeed, he explicitly listed as a benefit of the scheme that mothers would be deterred from turning to drink. Mothers were not portrayed as citizens, but as ignorant objects of social policy, and it was this paternalistic element of endowment schemes that irritated some feminist commentators. Even feminist supporters such as Eleanor Rathbone were guilty of portraying poor women as unable to speak for themselves, and in need of the mediation of feminists such as herself. Rathbone had written in 1916: 'the wife of the really neglectful or cruel husband is sunk too deep in a sea of physical misery and moral humiliation for her cry to reach the outer world'.[47] Avant-garde feminists were convinced that this kind of rhetoric only increased the status of women as voiceless victims.

Feminist critics also suspected that the endowment scheme would anchor women in the home, and deepen their exclusion from the labour market. Though Eder emphasised that many women would go back to work, Harben in contrast argued that 'the normal place for the mother and the child is the home'.[48] This confinement of mothers was firmly rejected within *The Freewoman*. For the editor, the chief objection to endowment lay in its deprivation of women's ability to engage in money-producing work. Such work would allow them not merely to live, but to 'live upon the value and sale of their labour in the open market, and not in that special incalculable market where all sales are questionable – i.e., that of sentiment and passion'.[49] Once working, women could then consider the question of motherhood from a secure position. 'Cover the cost of your motherhood just as you would arrange for the cost of your holiday' was Marsden's somewhat bourgeois advice. Furthermore, mothers' exclusion from the labour market would not only exacerbate their poverty and dependency, but also made the labour market position of women *in general* more vulnerable. Endowment provision for mothers would tend to undermine all women's status as workers, and was likely to push all into the 'mother category' in the eyes of employers and policy-makers.

Indeed, feminists suspected that a drive towards motherhood (for some) was the unstated aim of endowment as a coercive and controlling policy. This tendency was certainly present in some feminist understandings of endowment. Mabel Atkinson wanted women to 'bear children for the service of the State', as a duty of citizenship. She felt that 'if childbearing is to be protected by the State, it would not be unreasonable for the State to impose on the women who are possible mothers certain restrictions with regard to the activities which they may follow'.[50] Endowment quickly became an argument for restrictions on all women, as *possible* mothers, and not simply an enabling, anti-poverty strategy. As Stella Browne argued in the *International Journal of Ethics*, 'it is only when the right *not* to have children has been firmly vindicated, that its positive complementary right can be established. Under present conditions, maternity endowment would be peculiarly liable to become an engine of exploitation and oppression'.[51]

This control aspect of endowment emerged most strongly in the eugenic arguments of endowment texts, which were full of calls to 'strike at the root of deterioration'.[52] Wells, for example, had argued that 'A woman with healthy and *successful* offspring will draw a wage for each of them from the State, *so long as they go on well*'.[53] Endowment was not therefore a universal and unqualified provision for those in need, but might be withdrawn if mother or child behaved inappropriately. Wells' endowment editorial in *The Freewoman* incorporated a state qualification of fitness for reproduction and a marriage veto on those considered unfit. Later commentators have regarded it as a 'first principle of Wells' socialism' that he sought 'better births, and a better result from the births we get'.[54] Both Wells and Eder proposed euthanasia or the lethal chamber to deal with the 'defective'.[55] Eleanor Rathbone also talked of the excess multiplication of the 'slum population' who were 'physically, mentally or morally degenerate'.[56] Marsden pointedly asked what the standard of eligibility for endowment was, and who was to set it? Would the state restrict the choice of fathers, and what should the mother do if her child was 'poor quality . . . from the particular stock' of her husband? Indeed, it was the prospect of the state using endowment as a tool to guarantee, or coercively induce, 'eugenic' reproduction that caused such opposition amongst avant-garde feminists.

Endowment, as some saw it, was intended not to support women's choices, but to regulate motherhood, incentivising some while restricting others. It placed women in a degrading position; for a correspondent writing under the name of 'Tout Pouvoir', women's citizenship could not be reduced to reproduction without abandoning any kind of citizen status: 'Merely to breed healthy children in order to satisfy the demands of the State seems to me to put woman on a level with a brood mare!'[57] Cicely Hamilton discussed endowment in her essay on 'Women in the Great State', and was left asking 'Is [woman], in short, a personality, or merely the reproductive faculty personified?'[58] Hamilton (1872–1952), a prominent playwright, suffragist and feminist writer, as well as contributor to avant-garde journals such as the *New Age* and the *English Review*, was extremely wary of the state's power to bribe women to bear children, and like many 'advanced' feminists, preferred to emphasise women's right to refuse marriage and motherhood, while offering ambivalent support to the idea of endowment.

This perception of coercion and control was compounded by the unease avant-garde feminists felt at the general nature of state intervention. The anarchist case against endowment was clear. Guy Aldred, a leading anarchist propagandist and supporter of the women's movement, commented in *The Freewoman*

The future free society will have NO *State*. Besides, where everybody has the right to live, how can you endow one person at certain times *for limited periods, apparently, in some cases*? All State endowment schemes are founded on social distrust, and pre-suppose private property.[59]

Total rejection of the state was not necessary however to a belief that dependency on the state was degrading. Rachel Graham, a British *Freewoman* correspondent, based her opposition to endowment on the self-help moral discourse of Victorian welfarism.[60] Dora Marsden also drew on this strand of thought, in deploring the prospect of 'practically all females [being] State maintained from birth till death', whether as state supported children, mothers, or pensioned off after a lifetime of motherhood service. This would lead to women establishing a 'privileged caste', foisted 'parasitically upon the labours of the community', and, she predicted, would inspire a rush into motherhood, and with it a regression of the position of women in society: 'Will not women be able to earn their livelihood by continuously giving birth to a small number of children?'[61] Marsden accused supporters of endowment of reducing feminist demands to superficial economic independence, which in reality meant dependence on the state and confinement within the role of the mother.

Given the tradition of Poor Law welfare relief and compulsory examination of suspected prostitutes emanating from the British state in the nineteenth century, some feminists persisted in regarding the state as overbearing and moralising, a threat to autonomy rather than an enabling institution. Endowment theorists exacerbated this by their lack of interest in women's agency and decision-making; Eder had argued, for example: 'that the women do not realise their own bondage is no reason why we should not attempt to rescue them from it'.[62] Rachel Graham described endowment using a frame of reference clearly drawn from the anti-Contagious Diseases (CD) Acts agitation, as:

very unacceptable to independent women. The State regulation of maternity is as repulsive as the State regulation of prostitution, in fact it is the same thing.

Graham assumed that she and similarly situated women were more capable than the state of choosing their partners, though this was perhaps not to be extended to other 'classes of women': 'I *and others of my class* feel assured that we are capable of choosing our own mates and the fathers of our children. We do not need the State there'.[63]

Opposition to the state examination of alleged prostitutes of the British CD Acts had given feminists a tradition of opposition to the state, and this was still present in the later Edwardian context of 'eugenic' and 'white slave trade' legislation, over which feminists were divided.[64] This libertarian aspect of the CD Acts campaign has been obscured by the efforts of some campaigners within this tradition to use the state's power to police purity and a single moral standard – to protect children, end the 'white slave trade', raise the age of consent, etc. The work of the leader of the Anti-CD agitation, Josephine Butler, was claimed by groups well disposed towards greater state intervention, such as the Association for Moral and Social Hygiene. However, an important counter-discourse in her movement had been opposition to the growth of state regulation. Butler's 1880 pamphlet *Government by Police* argued (in gendered and racialised terms) that the virtues of 'inventiveness, self-protection, and manly self-dependence are being gradually driven out of the people by the delegation of the simplest and most primitive duties of citizens to the agents of the Government'. She praised 'the Anglo-Saxon spirit of mutual protection and responsibility', which had been corrupted by centralisation, bureaucracy, and paternal 'busy over-legislation'. These tendencies, she argued, impacted most upon poor women.[65] A similar tradition emerged within the later feminist avant-garde, provoked by the eugenic elements of endowment.

Elsie Clews Parsons, writing in the *International Journal of Ethics*, formulated this fear of the state's involvement for American and British audiences. Parsons was a supporter of endowment, but in quite different terms from more conventional feminist supporters such as Anthony and Blatch. She was suspicious of the 'greedy feminist' who wanted extra protection for women and the enforcing of 'feminine morals' onto men. Parsons saw state endowment as a temporary or emergency option, suitable as long as women were so handicapped in the labour market, but not in the long term. Ultimately, women had to face the same conditions of parenthood as men: 'The risk of not being able to care for her child herself is the risk an economically independent woman must run. It is the price the theory of free motherhood cannot escape paying'.[66]

Parsons preferred to divide parenting from sexual reproduction, and make the former largely women's responsibility, not the state's or the father's. To determine paternity was a trespass on a key avant-garde feminist tenet – privacy in sexual relations. Parsons' support for sexual variety and her dislike of monogamous marriage also underpinned this belief in the mother's responsibility for her own child. The state could be involved in guaranteeing contracts made between sexual partners and safeguarding children's interests, but not in most cases to support mothers economically. She suggested that women should take out private insurance policies, or, like Marsden, save their salaries, to protect themselves against poverty during maternity.[67]

Parsons recognised that a feminism requiring extra privileges for women might become a form of social control or group tyranny. She was quite negative about the way advanced feminists in New York (probably the Heterodoxy group) were willing to conjoin free motherhood with compulsion over fathers to provide economic support. Beatrice Hale perhaps represented the majority Heterodoxy position in arguing that 'the total elimination of the male's responsibility toward the mother-female is felt by most of us to be fraught with danger'.[68] Hale noted that 'the majority of advanced feminists – Mr Wells being an example – are inclined to lean towards some system of state endowment for motherhood', either by general taxation of all men, or by the specific compulsory payment of husband to wife. Even in 'advanced' feminist circles, then, a critical attitude towards endowment was relatively unusual.

A further feminist objection to endowment was motivated by dislike of the commodification of parenting. Though endowment had been seen by eugenicists as a means of removing financial constraints from women's sexual choices, for many, a payment from the state was equally problematic. Payment was argued to be inappropriate to this kind of service; as Marsden argued 'the best of the worker's work is always unpaid'.[69] Ada Nield Chew (1870–1945), a prolific writer on suffrage and feminism and a rare working-class voice in these circles, expanded upon this argument, noting that since fathering was not paid, why should mothering be? Chew and others argued that the introduction of payments for childcare would place the woman in a position of an employee, and the husband as employer. This was inappropriate to their relations, since the husband could not dismiss the wife, nor the wife have redress against a tyrannical 'employer'. Chew accepted that housework should be paid for whoever carried it out, but placed child-rearing in a different category. 'Women no more require payment for being wives and mothers than do men for being husbands and fathers. The proposal to bribe them to follow natural laws is, in its essence and form, a degradation which could only have emanated from slaves, and which could only be tolerated by slaves'.[70] This could be constructed as a citizenship argument – women's services in caring for children was an element of their citizenship and therefore outside the realm of payment. Ultimately however, avant-garde feminists preferred to see women's citizenship as distinct from their reproductive role, in order to include women without children as full citizens. In contrast to the ideas of many within the conventional mainstream of the women's movement, avant-garde feminists refused to see mothering as giving any extra *qualification* for citizenship, though it might be the source of new political perspectives.

'Advanced' feminists who did reject endowment argued that it was a spiritual issue, symbolising 'the comforts of protection' or the 'greediness' of some versions of feminism, as opposed to 'the harsh responsibilities of freedom'. The essence of endowment was psychological bondage; its tempting comforts would cause women to turn back from the austerities of freedom. As we have seen, Marsden and others interpreted feminism as a psychological, introspective affair, describing the 'genius' of feminism as 'a movement towards fundamental freedom, the freedom of the will'. This introspective turn sat uneasily with the practical, material gains offered by endowment. As Marsden saw it, 'Freedom is an affair of the soul itself. We shall incidentally achieve a material freedom, but this is only a dry husk to the freedom we conceive of.' The material freedom of endowment substituted for genuine freedom, which had to be achieved through one's own efforts, not given out as a dole. Though endowment might aid some women in the short term, it had serious built-in limitations. Marsden concluded 'We must resist the endowment, because it is not good for us. We can effect bolder things'.[71]

In the eyes of Françoise Lafitte, the prospect of state-enforced support from the father of her child was no less demeaning than a dole from the state itself, and made a mockery of her commitment to free sexual union. When, after the birth of her child in 1913, friends tried to take her ex-lover to court to gain child maintenance, she insisted that he

> had not seduced my body. I gave this willingly enough. He won't deny his paternity ... But even if he should give me £500 a week, it would not restore my faith in him. This is where he has raped me. Don't pile insult upon injury by expecting me to retain contact with this man either directly or through the law ... I won't touch his money. If I am to have a child without a father, I shall face the full consequences by myself. As for the law, its rat hunt for paternity just to secure five bob a week is enough to make the angels weep. The law does not interest me; it is mostly sheer anarchy.[72]

She was able to tap into networks of support within what she called 'the Left Wing movement', mostly through her contacts at *The Freewoman*. Despite the hardships of single motherhood, Lafitte entirely rejected her experiences of women's parasitism and sexual dependency – made vivid by her metaphors of women as the boa-constrictor, the leech, the canary bird – in their relationships with men.

In sum, these motives for the rejection of versions of endowment were based on a fundamental commitment to a version of individualism. Marsden believed that having children could and should be an expression of individuality: 'motherhood is the right of every woman who prepares for it, and takes the risks of it; ... it is an individual affair; ... *not* a collective affair'. It is revealing, however, that the individualism found amongst the feminist avant-garde was open to *collective* solutions and state action, where this enabled individual self-development. Faced with endowment, feminist individualists generated some innovative thinking about public provision of childcare, and sharing of domestic labour.

DOMESTIC LABOUR AND CHILDCARE: CONSTRUCTIVE THINKING

One of the most fascinating aspects of feminist debates on endowment is the richness and radicalism of alternatives proposed to it. These range from proposals specifically addressed to the needs of the mother, to broader analyses of domestic labour and the home. These issues were often argued to be key to feminist liberation. Most agreed that domestic duties made self-realisation problematic for women. Late Victorian women regarded the success of the women's movement as largely dependent upon domestic reorganisation. In 1894, a British writer, Mary Gilliland, argued in the *International Journal of Ethics* for co-operative dwellings, nurseries and expert kindergarten teachers, which would enable a simplified, more independent form of family life. This would bring, she argued, inevitable economic independence for women. Under these conditions, 'woman' would 'possess herself', and could then (in keeping with idealist thinking) put herself to the service of her family and her community.[73] In both Britain and the United States, there was a long tradition of co-operative housekeeping projects in the nineteenth century, but it was only in the twentieth century that these became associated with feminist beliefs.

It was Charlotte Perkins Gilman who most closely linked 'advanced' feminism with domestic reorganisation, in her periodical, *The Forerunner*, and her book, *The Home: Its Work and Influence*, first published in 1903. Other members of Heterodoxy also experimented with new forms of domestic organisation. Henrietta Rodman designed a new kind of apartment building, to be run on collective lines.[74] Beatrice Hale proposed that feminist analysis must start with the home, improving its material conditions while also restating women's right to work outside it. Historians have doubted whether the commitment to new forms of domestic organisation from male 'progressive era' feminists really extended to the material, pragmatic realm of who did housework.[75] Crystal Eastman, who had been briefly and unhappily married in 1911, was led to suggest 'marriage under two roofs' in 1923 as an escape from bickering over domestic organisation – feminism had at least by this date given her the conceptual resources to think of such solutions.[76]

Charlotte Perkins Gilman was quoted and echoed by many in Britain. Ada Nield Chew, who limited her family to one child perhaps in recognition of the impossibility of combining larger families with political activism, foresaw the establishment of communal nurseries, and professional cleaning services for all homes. The domestic reformer Alice Melvin argued for 'the Co-operative Colony', with night and day nursery, playground and shared restaurant. Melvin's 'Society for the Promotion of Co-operative Housekeeping and House Service' was said to be 'in touch with hundreds of would-be tenant-members and scores of educated women' who sought to undertake co-operative housekeeping.[77] Mrs A. Herbage Edwards, a British Fabian who in 1914 served on the Fabian 'Committee to Reorganise Domestic Work', commented in *The Freewoman*: 'To be free is to have leisure. And women, as a whole, will have little chance to get free while the large majority are obliged to spend laborious days in feeding their

families and cleaning their houses ... *They have no time to get free*.[78] She
wrote of 'the incessant, insistent meal-getting, dirt-removing toil', which
governed women's position. Some feminists felt that this was women's own
fault, and echoed Dora Marsden's emphasis on internal constraints – this
long-running subtext of Edwardian feminism emerges across a wide variety
of topics of debate. Writing in *The Freewoman*, 'Himandher' perceived the
'problem' of domestic labour as women's own fault, their small-minded
attachment to petty labour:

> when women in general are honestly tired of their subjection to the 'Three F's' –
> Food, Furniture and Floors – they will take a little thought, make a little effort:
> and suddenly, surprisingly, they will be free![79]

For these writers, women's role in domestic labour and childcare was just
another example of self-imposed subordination. Marsden blamed women
for demanding 'two contradictory principles' – freedom and protection.
Women sought freedom from male power, while simultaneously
demanding endowment as liberation from the responsibility of supporting
themselves. That few in the women's movement seemed to perceive this
contradiction clearly motivated Marsden in some of her polemical excesses
regarding endowment. Her language of slavery and degradation was
extreme, but this indicates how important this issue was perceived to be
in defining the focus of feminism. That Marsden saw endowment as
something demanded *by women* suggests how established endowment
had already become in the pre-war period as a policy of the women's
movement.

Others did not blame women for their domestic confinement and
limited horizons, but simply saw domestic labour and motherhood as an
anathema, and a challenge to women's individuality. The American social
scientist Jessie Taft saw motherhood as a fetish, artificially exalted within
society and held to be worthy of complete feminine self-sacrifice.[80] Margaret Anderson, the avant-garde editor of the *Little Review*, made her utter
rejection of her own mother's values, and her own capacity for being a
mother, a core part of her feminist identity. Isadora Duncan, Mina Loy
and Elsie Clews Parsons, all mothers, insisted on their right to independent
creative lives. Writing in *The Freewoman*, Edith Browne saw motherhood
as 'the ruin of intellect and individuality'. Likewise, Helen Winter rejected
the idea of women's maternal *duties*, but with a positive slant of women
developing or affirming individuality *through* motherhood: 'as a freewoman, I refuse to bear children either to the State, or to a man; I will bear

them for *myself* and for *my* purpose! I care neither for the continuance of the race, or the reproduction of any man'.[81]

Winter's comment revealed an appropriation and celebration of motherhood, retaking it from the realm of subservience to men. E. M. Watson, a regular contributor to *The Freewoman* and *The Vote*, (probably Edith M. Watson, legal correspondent for the WFL), made her objection not in terms of the nature of motherhood, but the concept of dependence: 'the love of independence is, and has always been, the ruling passion of my life. I cannot conceive of myself as becoming voluntarily dependent on any person or body of persons.' Marsden made a similar argument with regard to paternal support, declaring: 'What are the responsibilities of the father? Well, that is *his* business ... the freewoman's concern is to see to it that she shall be in a position to bear children if she wants them without soliciting any maintenance from any man, whoever he may be.' This desire for absolute independence was perhaps the most individualistic response to endowment within the journal. Independent motherhood, without support from the father or the state, was argued to be symbolic of being a freewoman. Others, however, remained critical of this somewhat naïve suggestion, arguing that 'Self-supporting motherhood means doing two women's work for one woman's pay'.[82] Solutions lying between the two poles of protected endowment and self-support were explored, including co-operative living, the use of technology, and public provision of childcare. The individualism of 'advanced' feminists did not rule out such collective endeavours, but demanded that all participants in them be defined as individuals, rather than by social categories such as mother and wife.

Supporters of co-operative living argued that it was a means to solve the dilemmas of motherhood, by providing children with better care, and mothers with rest and opportunities to work. 'Advanced' feminists, Fabians, and settlement house workers envisaged expect help and facilities to be at the mothers' disposal in the co-operative colony. Others, like Charlotte Perkins Gilman, expected that mechanical aids, sometimes in individual homes, sometimes deployed in collective living, would be the solution to domestic drudgery. Marsden was convinced that technological advances could achieve a means of feeding babies to replace the breast. She famously argued 'if the feeding of babies is to interfere with the mental development of women, it is the feeding of the babes which will have to give way'. Some argued that what was needed was workplace reform. 'A. F.' argued that workplaces should provide crèche and breast-feeding facilities. Policy towards mothers might even entail a wholesale reform of work practices. After improvements, 'if wage-earning mothers have not time and strength to enjoy their children, the community is working them too hard, and getting more out of them than it has any right to get'. S/he therefore recommended shorter hours.[83]

In tandem with workplace reform, the public provision of childcare was supported by a great many British feminists. They did not agree with those who argued that care in the home was more individual, and better suited to a diverse, individualistic society, since this denied the mother's status as an individual. They sought to move the focus of the argument from the mother, who was better regarded as primarily an individual and a worker, to the child. A number suggested that while endowment of motherhood was restrictive and even coercive of women, endowment of children was entirely appropriate. As one put it, 'May I suggest that the title of the discussion ought to be the State Endowment of Childhood? The State's main concern is with the children, not with the mothers, and provision for proper care ... is only part of a complete scheme of child nurture already begun by free education, school meals and school clinics, which will inevitably be extended and developed in the future.' This formed part of 'a great reconstruction, enabling women to reach our ideal of a livelihood earned by sane, humane activities'.[84]

Similar proposals were made in the United States. Socialists such as John Spargo united with some feminists in calling for more crèche and kindergarten facilities. Beatrice Hale specified in her account of modern feminism that mothers, while devoted to their children, must also pay attention to their own self-development, and their relationship with their husband. Like many other feminists, she welcomed kindergartens, particularly Maria Montessori's 'Casa Bambini', where the child could learn to be 'a little citizen of the world'. The 1911 World Fair in Chicago hosted a much-admired day nursery. But there was also a strong resistance to the idea of collective childcare, private or state run. Julia Lathrop of the Federal Children's Bureau strongly opposed institutional childcare, and perhaps due to the stronger influence of Ellen Key amongst American feminists, many followed Lathrop's lead. Sonya Michel describes the American Day Nurseries movement as stagnated in the progressive era, and largely replaced by mothers' pensions as a policy idea.[85]

Opponents of the endowment of mothers such as Dora Marsden did not disagree with the proposals concerning child welfare, and the new programme of the state it would imply. Despite Marsden's anti-statism, she was happy to agree with a contributor who demanded that the state take on the role of 'over-parent' to all children. The state, for Marsden, might supply 'crèche, kindergarten, school and university ... Even at present, the State, in a fashion, and after a certain age, educates children, feeds them, and is beginning to doctor them. This system must lengthen out in either direction, and broaden and deepen, and so set free the mother ... to do her own work'.[86] Public childcare needed to be supplemented by 'a liberal form of State insurance to cover the period of confinement', plus a guaranteed short maternity leave.

What is clear from these proposals is that the anti-statism that characterised the feminist avant-garde discussed in the last chapter, was tempered by an acceptance of the enabling nature of some state intervention. Endowment of motherhood generated debate and widespread rejection among contributors on the grounds of it being inappropriate intervention by the state. Yet for the well-being of children, most contributors were happy to envisage quite extensive state action.

MASCULINITY AND FATHERING

One of the most radical suggestions to arise out of endowment debates within *The Freewoman* was the suggestion that men should participate in care work. The literature on endowment showed little interest in the role of men. Henry Harben could not imagine that men could provide any care for the family during a mother's confinement, and saw a need for a 'mother substitute' or 'family manageress' to be appointed to each family where the real mother was 'laid up'.[87] David Eder was more perceptive, but still had a limited understanding of what fathers could do. He sought to reassure men that their (very partial) role in childcare would not be usurped by state endowment: 'there is no reason why, just as to-day, they should not take the children out on Sundays, or kiss them before going to the city, or spend odd hours with them in the nurseries'.

Eder's perception of the nature of 'the paternal instinct' was not particularly positive. In a footnote he noted that fathering stemmed from 'love of children, desire to prove virility – showing that man is on a par with any stallion – pride of possession, looking-glass vanity'. He did however outline a more involved role for some men: 'in many of the establishments, to be sure, many of the foster mothers would be foster-fathers, at any rate for children after four or five years of age. My scheme abolishes private nurses and public schools, whilst it seeks to substitute the loving care of men and women, independent of their relationship to the child.' However, this is a single mention, and in no other place did he advocate male involvement in childcare. H. G. Wells specified within *The Freewoman* that 'the role of the

normal father should be, I think, one of friendly advice, and not of legally
sustained intervention'.[88] Wells himself was an irregular father, and
complained of the damage done to his relationship with Rebecca West by
her preoccupation with their own son.

Commentators on endowment perceived the absence of attention to
fathers by endowment supporters. However, the individualist politics of
'advanced' feminism were relatively complex in relation to domesticity and
fathering. A handful of British feminists made the radical suggestion that
men might contribute to domestic work. Mary Gilliland tentatively suggested in 1894 that it might be 'a manly and suitable thing for a man
occasionally to amuse his own children for an hour, or even to put them to
bed, while his wife went out to whatever work or amusement outside the
family round she might desire'. Rachel Graham argued in *The Freewoman*
with some despondency 'We know that [our children] are not entirely
ours and we have hopes that the fathers feel some ties of relationship'.
E. M. Watson was more positive in her arguments for full partnerships in
childcare. She suggested that 'the father's share in his children should be a
ceaseless connection, and he should be granted full facilities, even if
separated from the mother, to see and interest himself in them'.[89]

The acknowledgement of men as fathers and carers was more prevalent
amongst American feminists. Elisabeth Woodbridge, for example, argued
in the *Atlantic Monthly* that 'for many of us, the development of fatherhood has been one of the main lines of social progress'. Charlotte Perkins
Gilman gave an early, if ambiguous, lead on the topic in her 1898 widely
read *Women and Economics*. Gilman believed that 'Man was made part
mother; and so both man and woman were enabled to become human . . .
Both her physical and psychical tendencies have been transplanted into the
organism of the male. He has been made the working mother of the
world.' The language of care was however entirely one of 'mothering', even
when carried out by men; Gilman later came to believe that men had
contributed *too much* care, and women, in their parasitic state, too little,
and in her 1914 lectures on 'the Larger Feminism', she called for less
fatherhood and more motherhood.[90]

In contrast, Beatrice Hale felt that feminism would lead to 'the re-
emergence of the father as a prime factor in the life of the child . . . life will
be happier and more normal for men when they have so rearranged the
scale of their labours and obligations as to have some opportunity for real
companionship with the children whom they have begotten'. Winifred
Harper Cooley expected that 'public opinion in the future will regard men
as quite as essential to the home as are women; and women as quite as

essential to the world as men'. Florence Tuttle called for an end to the 'loud pedal' held down on motherhood, to the exclusion of fatherhood. She called for masculine inputs into child rearing, and not only in the form of cash. She was critical of the attitude to fathers that saw them as 'a kind of animated cash register'. But Tuttle's views on parenting were pronatalist and normalising; she was ready to decry 'those abnormal women who do not wish offspring', and the men who shirk fatherhood. 'Men and women of this type are egoists and uneugenic'.[91] Tuttle would not have favoured the embrace of a liberating kind of egoism within the British feminist avant-garde that enabled them to perceive the limitations of endowment policies.

The NAWSA and birth control activist Mary Ware Dennett suggested within *The Freewoman* that real equality would only come about when men, as parents or state employees in crèches, have 'the opportunity to make up in direct service to the children for the extra work women will always do in bearing them'. Dennett, who had divorced her husband in 1913 and cared for their two children by herself, emphasised that fathers' responsibilities could not be discharged through cash payment. She argued 'Men have been apt to assume that their responsibilities to women and children were wholly discharged by merely paying over cash, without personal service'. This also encouraged men to think of wife and children as possessions. Endowment was just another cash substitute for men's actual participation in childcare. By engaging in housework and childcare, men might cease to think possessively about women, and treat them as equal individuals. Dennett's article countered the extreme individualism of some contributors with a more productive focus on interdependency. Instead of women's dependency on male wage-earners ruling them out of the realm of the individual, relations of interdependence between men and women, based on actual contributions of carework rather than cash, would allow men to become 'complete human beings instead of mere males', and both sexes to gain equal status as individuals.[92]

Dennett's view of what an individual consisted in was not what she termed 'the abnormal individualism' of some feminists, but envisaged a well-rounded and 'truly civilised' human being. She regarded individualism as a necessary staging post for feminism: 'permissible and necessary, just as hospitals and vacations are necessary, as remedial and temporary measures, but cannot be a proper or permanent basis for a normal life'. For Dennett, feminism in the long term represented a socialist agenda of women's labour force participation, production for consumption rather than profit, plus accessible birth control.

CONFLICTS AROUND CLASS

A number of feminists seemed to offer, like Dennett, a unification of feminist and socialist principles without resorting to endowment. But some socialist contributors objected to the apparently bourgeois assumptions that underlay the rejection of endowment. Elsie Clews Parsons had written of a paid-up maternity insurance policy to be given as a wedding present, instead of the 'useless silver'. And 'for girls who do not move in pearl necklace or silver wedding present circles', she felt that parents might instead pay the premiums. The needs of working-class women were not addressed in her account of feminism. Russell Scott, provoked by this class bias, accused *Freewoman* contributors of applying middle-class standards of decency, and ability to save:

> To the women with whom we are primarily concerned, your phrase, 'saving for motherhood as you would for a holiday', can only mean 'saving as you could for a Bank Holiday'. Can they rear children on *these* savings? . . . 'Motherhood' in your columns, seems to mean the bearing of children in a house equipped with a nursery and a servant. You speak of it as a demoralisingly soft job, compared with 'earning' a livelihood. You should try to rear a single baby till the age of two or three without anyone to cook, wash or sew for either it or for you.[93]

Opponents of endowment were accused of overlooking the vital difference to the lives of the poor that endowment of motherhood might make. For Scott, the choice was between payment by the state, by a man, or no motherhood at all; self-supporting motherhood was not available to the mass of women. 'A Socialist' made a similar case in *The Freewoman*, arguing that 'most well-to-do women . . . forget that nearly all women are poor; they do not understand the importance of ten shillings a week' when they oppose state endowment.[94] 'A Socialist' believed both that 'every genuine worker has a right to subsistence wages from the community' and that 'a woman has a right to become a mother and a right to be with her children, without thereby becoming the dependent of some man'. State endowment was presented as the only way to guarantee wages or subsistence with the dignity of 'independence', and to recognise women's devotion of 'time and strength to producing the labour power of the community'.

Nevertheless, not all socialists and spokespersons for working-class women were supportive of endowment. Ada Nield Chew contributed letters and articles to *The Freewoman* that bridged the polarised divide between individualist opponents of endowment and socialist supporters.

Chew supported the ideal of an individual, self-defining and self-supporting freewoman, but located her in a network of social relations and group struggles; her freewoman had class interests. The freewoman's choices were determined by her own psychological make-up *and* by government policy or employment conditions – by both internal and external constraints. She recognised that 'the conditions of life today, more than ever in our history, are complicated and interdependent'; simply asserting individualism was therefore not useful. Instead, Chew sought to analyse why women 'chose' dependence, and how sex defined these choices. Using a figure of speech popularised by Cicely Hamilton's *Marriage as a Trade*, Chew characterised the married state for women as a trade union, where the wife 'earns her living by her sex'.[95] The wife was thus parallel to the prostitute, except in that 'the woman of the streets, who is not bound by the union rules, may sell herself to as many as she pleases' while the wife remains monogamous. Thus the same sexual economy defined both poor and rich women's choices. Chew demanded that all women take their place as producers, break their mental habits of dependence and gain economic independence for themselves and their children.

This stance was incompatible with endowment. Chew stated 'you cannot breed a free people from slave mothers, and husband-kept or state-kept women can never know the meaning of liberty'. Her position revealed the lack of agreement between socialists as to whether women would be primarily mothers or workers. Chew thought motherhood could span both identities; a good mother was not required to sacrifice her life to the tedious tasks of child-raising, but was however expected to provide for her children. This could be facilitated by public provision of care and domestic services.

What distinguishes her ideas from other critics of endowment within *The Freewoman* was that Chew saw the endowment debate as a class debate. In this emphasis, she may have drawn upon the anti-CD Acts tradition, within which some had likewise portrayed what was normally seen as a gender issue (the regulation of prostitution) as a class one. Endowment was, for Chew, a means of restricting the choices of poor women, keeping them from the labour market. Rich women would be unaffected by endowment. In contrast to the poor, they already employed women to carry out the domestic duties that supposedly merited endowment. She believed that endowment supporters preferred not to offer this option to working-class women:

Why not demand the same facilities for poor mothers and children as those enjoyed by women whose husbands are better off? . . . If it is beneficial for well-to-do children to have specially selected women, and specially selected rooms, gardens, and every other facility for healthy growth, it could not be bad for the children of the poor.[96]

Like Eder, she accused middle-class women of hypocrisy in their unwillingness to extend emancipation to poor women, particularly to their own domestic servants. Public provision of childcare and household tasks were being resisted due to a distaste for 'the serving class' receiving any services themselves. Endowment was a less subversive solution that would effectively preserve the status quo, since the amount to be given to mothers was not enough to break their dependency on men. Furthermore, the solution was an individualised one that kept women in the home, divided and dependent. Chew thus placed feminist opposition to endowment in a broader framework of class analysis.

These debates over endowment foreground sensitive issues of class within the feminist avant-garde. 'Advanced' feminists have been accused of thinking in bourgeois terms, but in fact many individuals discussed within this study came from 'insecure' class backgrounds. Inez Haynes Gillmore wrote of her lower-middle-class childhood as 'a long, gray, dusty arid stretch of desert ... We were poor, but not poor enough. That is to say, we were poor enough to be dull, but not poor enough to be picturesque'. Leta Hollingworth told Heterodoxy members of the real poverty of her childhood, and of her dresses made from flour sacks. The advanced feminists of New York and Chicago varied in their class background, and their commitment to the causes of labour. Historians have recorded their work with the Women's Trade Union League, the IWW and so on, and many American feminists perceived a unity of feminism and the labour movement. They also worked for the spread of birth control information among working-class women, and in this probably achieved their most direct influence upon working-class politics and life.[97]

Nonetheless, the feminist avant-garde had few channels for engaging with working-class women and working-class politics. Despite the best intentions of the American Women's Trade Union League, it was a somewhat paternalistic and detached organisation that did not gain a mass following. Beatrice Hale revealingly claimed that 'when feminists speak of women they mean all women, and when they demand a programme of reform they demand it for women as a whole, not for any one class'. In contrast to the British vanguard feminists, there was a denial of the saliency of class amongst American feminists. Greenwich Village radicals were quite isolated from the slum conditions of New York; historians have noted that the activists of *The Masses* preferred to think in romanticised terms of the 'toiling masses' rather than specific classes, and regarded immigrant workers as verging on the exotic.[98] It was perhaps the less flamboyant settlement house workers who attained a greater understanding of and contact with working women in the United States, though these two wings of feminism did overlap to some degree.

The class backgrounds of British avant-garde feminists varied. Dora Marsden and Mary Gawthorpe had emerged from impoverished families in northern English industrial districts. Gawthorpe described herself and a colleague in the Lancashire WSPU organising committee (very probably Marsden): 'we belong, socially speaking, to the working-class, and we have supported ourselves from early years'. Like Teresa Billington, Millie Price and Cicely Hamilton, each had used teacher training as a means to exit this background, joining the 'vulnerable' middle class. Another *Freewoman* reader, teacher, and former Manchester suffragist, Winifred Hindshaw, described herself as inhabiting the 'penniless ranks of the middle classes'.[99] Their status as teachers was based on a class mobility that was newly available to women, and perhaps suggested that class could be transcended. Their background gave them sensitivity to the complex class politics of the women's movement, and each welcomed any sign of rapprochement between the suffragists and the Labour movement.

In 1912, the closeness of the NUWSS and the Labour Party (epitomised in the setting up of an election 'Fighting Fund' by suffragists to support Labour candidates) meant that there was an encouraging atmosphere for those who sought to bring the two movements closer. But British feminists who adopted a progressive stance on the unity of feminism and socialism were compromised by the content and expected readership of the journals of 'advanced' feminism. Dora Marsden commented on the 'new atmosphere abroad in England' that was found within *The Freewoman*, but she regarded *The Daily Herald* (a labour paper founded in 1911) as the vehicle to 'carry [the new spirit] to the Working-Classes', and she did not see *The Freewoman* as likely to be read by them.[100] Furthermore, she and other contributors believed in the necessity for a hierarchically organised society. Marsden agreed with the idea 'that caste is a real thing: that classes should not mix: that lover should find lover on his own level'. This was motivated by a desire to depict 'higher types' and set up standards for behaviour. Marsden's iconoclastic vision of greatness meant that 'types' could not be understood along 'conventional' class lines:

The inverted scale of value which holds good in social class conventions, whereby the parasite is ludicrously considered as of higher class than the producer, has made us fear to speak of class; or, if we speak of it, only to imply that the 'lower' classes are better than the 'upper'. We cannot, however, safely or for long do without appeals to 'class'. For class implies standard, and absence of class implies absence of standard. What holds good in regard to class in the social world at the present is that the standards are wrong, and the consequent class grades obviously ridiculous; but rather than grapple with the standard in order to establish a new one, we indolently reckon that suppression of class will serve the same purpose. It will not ... If, then, we announce our standard, we automatically create our *class* in regard to worth in Being ... This can only happen when 'Rich' men and 'poor' men are abolished and forgotten, when we all earn our means of subsistence ... '[101]

Greatness and genius thus implied the end of the current class system, but also, for some, the birth of a new 'caste' order, relating to 'worth in Being'. The critique of class retained its radical force and the feminist avant-garde was marked by a willingness to work across class lines. But even though many were sceptical of the hierarchies of the class order, there was a widespread fascination with greatness amongst advanced feminists, who continually experimented with ways of fostering genius in women or producing an elite of 'freewomen'.

CONCLUSION

The critics who accused 'advanced' feminists of bourgeois insensitivity had taken some of the more polemical statements of feminists in isolation, and failed to recognise the power of the analysis of motherhood, dependency and state intervention as it developed in the pre-war years amongst 'advanced' feminists. Admittedly, no single position on endowment emerged, and the interest of these debates on endowment lies in the process of contestation, clarification, and space to imagine radical alternatives. The opposition to endowment can give the impression of a somewhat overstated, extreme reaction to what was a fairly modest proposal for short-term maternity pay. With hindsight, the dominance of the inter-war feminist agenda by this single, highly divisive issue suggests that the urgency of avant-garde feminist criticisms was not misplaced.

Emancipation was generally described within 'advanced' feminist circles as giving women the opportunity to escape dependency where they chose to, through labour force participation and psychological transformation. But in the debates described above, some contributors came to see dependency in a productive fashion. Mutual interdependency in the realm of domestic labour was a form of dependency that did not necessarily compromise individuality. Crucially, men were seen as in these relations of interdependence as much as women were, thus problematising the idea of dependency as an exclusively feminine state. As *Freewoman* correspondent Gladys Jones argued: 'When I see a man who is said to support a household of women, I sometimes wonder if it would not be truer to say that they support him, as they dance attendance on his futilities'.[102] Recognition of the household as a realm of interdependency enabled contributors to discuss issues rarely mentioned within the Edwardian women's movement, such as fathering and men's role in housework. The aim was to replace the abstract autonomous individual, or the autonomous male breadwinner, with one that could enter into relations of dependency and nurture without jeopardising individuality. Though operating from an individualist position, many avant-garde feminists used the debates around endowment to discuss key issues of individualism. They challenged the separate spheres economy associated with libertarian individualism, and attempted to imagine an individual who did not require the care and attention of those designated 'non-individuals'. They explored the idea of a mother whose mothering role did not annul her individuality. Parenting was to be a shared role. Through collective childcare and housework, contributors sought to bring 'private' activities into the public domain.

Endowment debates reveal that the individualism of avant-garde feminism was not the doctrinaire sort, fiercely restrictive on state action, found in the work of contemporaries such as Auberon Herbert or Oscar Levy. In contrast, 'advanced' feminists occupied a productive ground between the violent anti-statism of Herbert, and the interventionism of Fabians and new liberals. They conceived of extensive state action, but guarded against coercion of those whom Edwardian welfare policy tended to objectify and control. In this endowment issue, as in others, anti-statism amounted to freedom for the state to act in, effectively, a wide sphere, as long as no element of compulsion of women was involved. Endowment offered an example of why the state's intervention should be opposed, with its moralising, coercive and class-determined character. Public provision of childcare, on the other hand, provided a chance to discuss what the state could legitimately undertake, and was an area in which the state's role should 'broaden and deepen'.

END NOTES

1. West, *The Clarion*, 10 Jan. 1913, quoted in Marcus, *The Young Rebecca*, pp. 140–1.
2. Gilman, 'Does a Man Support His Wife?' NAWSA, New York p. 12.

3. Endowment continued to be an important feminist policy between the wars, becoming virtually the defining feature of the 1920s British feminist movement. See *Common Cause*, 17 March 1916, 648, and Rathbone, *The Disinherited Family* (London, E. Arnold, 1924).

4. In Britain, health and unemployment benefits, old-age pensions, school dinners and the repeal of various punitive Poor Law type measures were all undertaken by the reforming Liberal government of 1906–14. In the United States, federal and state level reformers addressed themselves to child labour, school attendance, mothers' or widows' pensions, food safety and workplace safety. See Koven and Michel (eds.), *Mothers of a New World*; Linda Gordon, *Pitied But Not Entitled, Single Mothers and the History of Welfare* (Cambridge, Mass., Harvard University Press, 1994).

5. Susan Pedersen, 'Gender, Welfare and Citizenship in Britain During the Great War', *The American Historical Review*, 95:4 (1990); Linda Gordon, 'Putting Children First: Women, Maternalism and Welfare in the Early Twentieth Century', in *U.S. History as Women's History: New Feminist Essays*, ed. Alice Kessler-Harris, Kathryn Kish Sklar and Linda K. Kerber (Chapel Hill, University of North Carolina Press, 1995), p. 71.

6. Koven and Michel (eds.), *Mothers of a New World*, p. 96.

7. Pedersen, 'Gender, Welfare and Citizenship', p. 986.

8. Pat Thane, 'Women in the British Labour Party and the Construction of State Welfare, 1906–1939', in *Mothers of a New World*, ed. Seth Koven and Sonya Michel (New York, Routledge, 1993), pp. 343–77.

9. Some thinkers who could be described loosely as feminists did, however, support these measures. Katharine Glasier and Margaret Macdonald of the Labour Party called for men to be paid a family wage, and saw endowment as 'monstrous', a means of undermining union claims for 'fair' wages. See Carol Dyhouse, *Feminism and the Family in England, 1880–1939* (Oxford, Blackwell, 1989), p. 90; Katherine Glasier, *Socialism and the Home* (London, Independent Labour Party, 1909).

10. Margaret Llewelyn Davies, *Maternity: Letters from Working-Women Collected by the Women's Co-Operative Guild* (London, G. Bell, 1915), p. 16.

11. John Spargo, *The Bitter Cry of the Children* (Chicago, Quadrangle, 1968), p. 257.

12. Molly Ladd-Taylor, *Mother-Work: Women, Child Welfare, and the State, 1890–1930* (Urbana, University of Illinois Press, 1994); Joanne L. Goodwin, *Gender and the Politics of Welfare Reform: Mothers' Pensions in Chicago, 1911–1929* (Chicago, University of Chicago Press, 1997).

13. Ross, *Love and Toil*, p. 210; Ladd-Taylor, *Mother-Work*.

14. Atkinson, *The Economic Foundations of the Women's Movement*, Fabian Tract No. 175, p. 21; H. G. Wells *et al.*, *Socialism and The Great State*, p. 44. See Carole Pateman, 'Equality, Difference and Subordination: The Politics of Motherhood and Women's Citizenship', in *Beyond Equality and Difference: Citizenship, Feminist Politics and Female Subjectivity*, ed. Gisela Bock and Susan James (London, Routledge, 1992) for a critical discussion of citizenship and endowment.

15. Drysdale, *FW*, 4 Jan. 1912, 133. Françoise Lafitte had made a similar argument as a speaker at the Freewoman Discussion Circle in 1912. Delisle, *Friendship's Odyssey*, p. 191.
16. Cicely Hamilton famously made this argument in her 1909 *Marriage as a Trade* (London, The Women's Press, 1981), and it came to have a transnational circulation, echoed, for example, by the American feminist Inez Haynes Gillmore, 'Confessions of an Alien', *Harper's Bazar*, June 1912, 280.
17. Ellen Key, *The Century of the Child* (New York, G. P. Putnam and Sons, 1909).
18. H. G. Wells, *Socialism and the Family* (London, A. C. Fifield, 1906), pp. 30, 57.
19. Wells, *FW*, 21 March 1912, 341.
20. David Eder, *The Endowment of Motherhood* (London, New Age Press, 1908), pp. 11, 16, 22.
21. H. D. Harben, *The Endowment of Motherhood*, Fabian Tract No. 149 (London, 1910), pp. 8, 20, 7.
22. Harben, *Endowment of Motherhood*, p. 13.
23. Pedersen, *Eleanor Rathbone*, p. 107.
24. Rathbone, 'Separation Allowances', *Common Cause*, 25 Feb. 1916, 611; 17 March 1916, 647.
25. Pedersen, *Eleanor Rathbone*, Chapter 10.
26. Dyhouse, *Feminism and the Family*; B. Cass, 'Redistribution to Children and Mothers: A History of Child Endowment and Family Allowances', in *Women, Social Welfare and the State*, ed. Baldock and Cass (London, Allen and Unwin, 1983).
27. Alison Berg, *Mothering the Race: Women's Narratives of Reproduction, 1890–1930* (Chicago, University of Illinois Press, 2002).
28. Spargo, *The Bitter Cry of the Children*, pp. 231, 240; John Spargo, *Socialism and Motherhood* (New York, B. W. Huebsch, 1914).
29. William Hard, 'The Moral Necessity of "State Funds to Mothers"', *Survey*, 29 (1913), 773, quoted in Sonya Michel, *Children's Interests/Mother's Rights: The Shaping of America's Childcare Policy* (New Haven, Yale University Press, 1999), p. 80.
30. *Common Cause*, 24 Nov. 1910, 2.
31. Theda Skocpol *et al.*, 'Women's Associations and the Enactment of Mothers' Pensions in the United States', *American Political Science Review*, 87:3 (Sept. 1993).
32. Mothers' Pensions in the United States of America – I, *Common Cause*, 24 Jan. 1919, 490. See also Jane Lewis, 'Models of Equality for Women: The Case of State Support for Children in Twentieth Century Britain', in *Maternity and Gender Policies: Women and the Rise of the European Welfare States, 1880s-1950s*, ed. G. Bock and P. Thane (London, Routledge, 1991), pp. 73–92.
33. Anthony, *Feminism in Germany and Scandinavia*, p. 165.
34. Ellen Carol DuBois, *Harriot Stanton Blatch*, pp. 216–22, 238.
35. Michel, *Children's Interests/Mother's Rights*, pp. 80–3.

36. Atkinson, 'Economic Foundations', p. 23.
37. *Common Cause*, 1 June 1911, 129.
38. For a statement of the divisions between 'old' and 'new' feminism, see Rathbone, in *Our Freedom and its Results*, ed. Strachey (London, Hogarth Press, 1936), pp. 15–76. There were of course no such hard-and-fast divisions on the ground, and individuals frequently worked productively across apparent ideological divides.
39. Royden, in *The Making of Women*, pp. 140, 143; *Common Cause*, 15 June 1911; Hamilton, in H. G. Wells *et al.*, *Socialism and The Great State*, p. 224.
40. Ellen Carol DuBois, *Harriot Stanton Blatch*, p. 216; Michel, *Children's Interests/Mother's Rights*, p. 75. Parsons noted the influence of the war pensions scheme as key to mothers' pensions. Parsons, *Journal of a Feminist*, p. 38. For Eastman's views, see Crystal Eastman, *Crystal Eastman on Women and Revolution*, ed. Blanche Wiesen Cook (New York, Oxford University Press, 1978), p. 57.
41. Parsons, 'Feminism and the Family'; Gilman, 'Maternity Benefits and Reformers', *Forerunner*, March 1916, 65–6.
42. West, 'The World's Worst Failure (VI)', *New Republic*, 4 March 1916, 127.
43. Ross, *Love and Toil*; W. L. George, 'Feminist Intentions', *Atlantic Monthly*, Dec. 1913, 728–9.
44. Lewis, Introduction to Cicely Hamilton, *Marriage as a Trade* (London, The Women's Press, 1981; orig. 1909), p. 5.
45. Wells, *FW*, 21 March 1912, 341, emphasis added.
46. Harben, *Endowment of Motherhood*, p. 16.
47. Rathbone, 'Separation Allowances', *Common Cause*, 17 March 1916, 648.
48. Harben, *Endowment of Motherhood*, p. 22.
49. Marsden, *FW*, 29 Feb. 1912, 281.
50. Atkinson, 'Economic Foundations', pp. 280, 277.
51. Browne, 'Some Problems of Sex', 464–71.
52. Harben, *Endowment of Motherhood*, p. 10.
53. Wells, *Socialism and the Family*, p. 58, emphasis added.
54. Wells, *FW*, 21 March 1912; William Hyde, 'The Socialism of H. G. Wells in the Early Twentieth Century', *Journal of the History of Ideas*, 17:2 (1956), 223.
55. Hyde, 'The Socialism of H. G. Wells', p. 221; Eder, *Endowment of Motherhood* pp. 27–8.
56. Rathbone, 'Separation Allowances', *Common Cause*, 25 Feb. 1916, 611.
57. 'Tout Pouvoir', *FW*, 28 March 1912, 376.
58. Hamilton, in H. G. Wells *et al.*, *Socialism and the Great State*, p. 226.
59. Aldred, *FW*, 18 July 1912, 179, original emphasis.
60. Rachel Graham, *FW*, 11 April 1912, 418.
61. Marsden, *FW*, 29 Feb. 1912, 282.
62. Eder, *Endowment of Motherhood*, p. 69.
63. Rachel Graham to the editors, DMC u.d.: II, 7, emphasis added.
64. Frank Mort, *Dangerous Sexualities: Medico-Moral Politics in England Since 1830* (London, Routledge, 1987), pp. 136–50.

65. Josephine E. Butler, *Government by Police* (London, Dyer Brothers, 1880), pp. 8, 9, 6.
66. Parsons, 'When Mating and Parenthood are Theoretically Distinguished', *IJE*, 26:2 (Jan. 1916), 214.
67. Parsons, 'Feminism and the Family', 52–8.
68. Hale, *What Women Want*, p. 213.
69. Marsden, *FW*, 30 Nov. 1911, 22.
70. Chew, *FW*, 18 July 1912, 169.
71. Marsden, *FW*, 29 Feb. 1912, 281; 14 Dec. 1911, 73; 21 March 191, 342.
72. Delisle, *Friendship's Odyssey*, p. 203.
73. Mary S. Gilliland, 'Women in the Community and in the Family', *IJE*, 5:1, (Oct. 1894), 41.
74. See *New York Times*, 24 Jan. 1915, 9; and June Sochen, 'Henrietta Rodman and the Feminist Alliance, 1914–1917', *Journal of Popular Culture*, 4:1 (1970), 57–65.
75. Stansell, *American Moderns*, pp. 258–9.
76. Eastman, 'Marriage Under Two Roofs', *Cosmopolitan*, Dec. 1923, reprinted in Eastman, *Crystal Eastman*, pp. 76–83.
77. Melvin, *FW*, 11 April 1912, 410.
78. A. Herbage Edwards, *FW*, 7 March 1912, 312.
79. 'Himandher', *FW*, 6 June 1912, 47.
80. Jessie Taft, 'The Woman Movement and the Larger Social Situation', *IJE*, 25:3 (1915), 342.
81. Parsons, *Journal of a Feminist*, p. 86; Burke, *Becoming Modern*, p. 19; Margaret Anderson, *My Thirty Years' War: An Autobiography* (New York, Horizon Press, 1969), p. 4. See also Stansell, *American Moderns*, pp. 246–7. Stansell argues that 'the disavowal of the mother came to be almost a trademark feature of female modernism'. Most avant-garde feminists however had a more complex relationship with motherhood, and recognised that it remained a vivid feature of women's lives, demanding theorisation and policy solutions, rather than outright rejection. Winter, *FW*, 7 March 1912, 312.
82. Bland, *Banishing the Beast*, p. 285. Watson, *FW*, 4 April 1912, 397. Russell Scott, *FW*, 4 April 1912, 396.
83. See Alice Melvin, *FW*, 23 May 1912, 16; and A. Herbage Edwards, *FW*, 7 March 7 1912, 312; A. F., *FW*, 15 Feb. 1912, 252; Marsden, *FW*, 22 Feb. 1912, 262; A .F., *FW*, 15 Feb. 1912, 252.
84. R. J. P. Mortished, *FW*, 28 March 1912, 374.
85. Michel, *Children's Interests/Mother's Rights*, p. 73.
86. Marsden, *FW*, 4 April 1912, 396.
87. Harben, *Endowment of Motherhood*, p. 17.
88. Eder, *Endowment of Motherhood*, p. 57; Wells, *FW*, 7 March 1912, 302.
89. Mary S. Gilliland, 'Women in the Community and in the Family', *IJE*, 5:1 (Oct. 1894), 43; Rachel Graham to the editors, DMC u.d.: II, 7; Watson, *FW*, 14 April 1912, 397.
90. Elisabeth Woodbridge, 'The Unknown Quantity in the Woman Problem', *Atlantic Monthly*, April 1914, 520; Gilman, *New York Times*, 19 March 1914, 8.

91. Cooley, 'The Younger Suffragists', 8; Hale, *What Women Want*, pp. 280, 283; Tuttle, *Awakening of Woman*, pp. 132, 133.
92. Dennett, *FW*, 9 May 1912, 499.
93. Parsons, 'Feminism and the Family', 56; Scott, *FW*, 4 April 1912, 396, original emphasis.
94. 'A Socialist', *FW*, 7 March 1912, 311.
95. Liddington, *One Hand Tied Behind Us*; Chew, *Life and Writings*; Chew, *FW*, 11 July 1912, 150; 18 July 1912, 157; Hamilton, *Marriage as a Trade*.
96. Chew, *FW*, 22 Aug. 1912, 271.
97. Gillmore, 'Confessions of an Alien', *Harper's Bazar*, April 1912, 170; Taft, 'The Woman Movement', 343; Chen, *The Sex Side of Life*; Stansell, *American Moderns*.
98. Hale, *What Women Want*, p. 146; Zurier, *Art for the Masses*, p. 14; Jones, *Heretics and Hellraisers*, p. 54.
99. Gawthorpe, *Eye-Witness*, 23 Nov. 1911, 724; Hindshaw to Marsden, 13 Aug. 1911: III, 2.
100. Marsden to Björkman, u.d. (October 1912?), MWDP.
101. Marsden, *FW*, 16 May 1912, 502.
102. Jones, *FW*, 18 Jan. 1912, 167.

CHAPTER 6

The modern and the pre-modern: feminist
utopian thinking

Thus far, this study has traced the introspective and individualistic turn developed within Edwardian feminism; but the feminist gaze was not only turned inward. Millie Price, a WSPU activist who later became disenchanted with the violence of the movement, inhabited what she termed the 'dream utopian city', Letchworth Garden City in 1906. She described her neighbours as 'Simple-Lifers', pure food enthusiasts and naturalists who wore djibbahs and sandals, ate vegetarian food and sought an individualist lifestyle: 'A few bachelors, intellectuals or artists, lived a monastic life in some of the tiny cottages, often of wood, which were built to suit their fancy and pocket. Self-dependence was the ideal.'' Vegetarianism, sandal-wearing and peasant arts all thrived within a section of the avant-garde who were firmly committed to a personal lifestyle revolution. For some women, a figure like Isadora Duncan represented not just a new kind of artistic interpretation but an example of how they could restyle themselves, released from restrictive clothes and conventions. But as Millie Price's description suggests, it was often easier for men to make this kind of shift than for women. Other feminists were less than enthusiastic about the liberation of sandals and djibbahs, and preferred to imagine automated washing machines.

The intense feminist discussions of the nature of life, work and art led them to think about wider social change and the future, and past, of society – the 'utopian thinking' of the feminist movement. 'Utopian thinking' of one kind or another was central to the feminist movement since it had become widely accepted in advanced circles that the cause of women's discontent and malaise was the ending of her productive role within the household. Text after text lamented the usurpation of women from their central and productive (imagined) role as the home-maker, weaver, baker and brewer. Many felt that women's pre-industrial position gave her honour and authority, and a key role as a 'civilising' force, while modern women seemed parasitic, or exploited in an alienating labour market.

Having framed this question of labour as a central problem of the feminist movement, Edwardian feminists had either to argue for a return to pre-industrial conditions, or a transformation of women's engagement with work. It was this which gave the discussions of the 'simple life' such prominence within the movement. Feminist and 'back to the land' thinkers were brought together not simply by their simultaneous genesis in the early twentieth century, but rather due to the posing of 'advanced' feminism as a question of women's labour.

Avant-garde feminists' focus on the individual and internally generated aspects of emancipation outlined in previous chapters may however seem at odds with the conventions of utopian thinking. The concept of utopian thought is often associated with 'narratives of community' that might oppose 'modern' conditions of 'corrosive individualism and social disintegration'.[2] The possibility of 'utopian thinking' within an individualist framework can appear paradoxical, since individualism or egoism can be read as bereft of a vision of the communal good, and therefore of utopia. However, an individualist perspective may supply a missing element within utopian texts. A recurrent criticism of utopias is that they envisage too little space for individual development and diversity. Virtually all the great utopian texts of the Edwardian and late Victorian period suffered from 'over-regulation' and statism. The tendency towards excessive social control makes 'individualist utopias' particularly fascinating, as sites in which the conflicting needs of the individual and of society are recognised and perhaps resolved.

ARTS AND CRAFTS UTOPIAS

The utopian thought of the Edwardian period seems curiously divided. On the one hand were futuristic, modernist writers such as Edward Bellamy and H. G. Wells, for whom technology and an expanded, centralised state were to transform life. On the other, writers such as the nineteenth-century British evolutionary thinker Samuel Butler were directly critical of machines. He portrayed *Erewhon* as a realm where machines had been banished, and the culture prevailing was 'about as advanced as Europeans of the twelfth or thirteenth century'.[3] William Morris and John Ruskin described a pre-modern, small-scale society of artisans, guilds or smallholders. Morris' 1891 *News from Nowhere* is neo-medievalist, in its celebration of rural life, craftsmanship, and rejection of industrial capitalism. Ruskin similarly advised his followers to 'take an acre of ground, make it lovely, give what food comes of it to people who need it, and take no rent yourself'. This advice sums up many of the themes in the idea of the country as a key regenerative force in society.[4]

Ruskin's work was influential upon feminists, though his concept of gender relations and 'girlish virtue' directly conflicted with the emancipated 'freewoman' of the avant-garde.[5] Similarly, Morris' account of work as pleasure was close to feminist utopianism. However, like Ruskin, Morris saw women as ideally serving men in a continuing domestic role. Their backward-looking vision was often associated with a lack of interest in the emancipation of women, but was nonetheless influential upon feminists.

Other British socialist texts showed similar pastoral themes to Morris, though they were frequently more directly practical and programmatic. Robert Blatchford's *Merrie England* denounced the factory system, the ugliness and pollution of the industrial counties, and called for a self-sufficient agricultural economy. Guild Socialist theories of decentralised industry, craftsmanship and workshop self-government flourished before the First World War, and these themes were discussed in the 'neo-medievalist' *New Age*. These ideas also resonated within American socialist circles; Eugene Debs, leader of the Socialist party and presidential candidate between 1900 and 1920, acknowledged the influence of *Merrie England* upon his beliefs. British and American Edwardian periodicals advertised 'simple life' and Garden City initiatives, as well as manuals with titles such as 'The Simple Life on Four Acres' and 'Three Acres and Liberty'. The American labour movement was imbued with ideas of a golden age of non-alienated craft-labour, in which women featured large. The first issue of the Chicago working women's periodical, *Life and Labor*, for example, showed on its front plate a young woman knitting, with the title 'When Work Was Pleasure'.[6]

The British arts and crafts movement, inspired by Morris and Ruskin, prompted a similar movement in the United States. Journals such as *Craftsman Magazine* and *International Studio* (produced jointly in Britain and America), and communities such as the New Clairvaux in Massachusetts, the Roycrofters in New York State and Julius Wayland's Ruskin Co-operative Association in Tennessee drew on the neo-medievalism of British thinkers, as well as the utopianism of Henry Thoreau and Ralph Waldo Emerson, to construct a simplified alternative way of life. American simple life enthusiasts credited the 'English' garden cities movement with initiating a simplification of city life and 'back to the land' experiments and in spreading these principles to the United States.[7]

Land served as a site for the coalescence of a number of political anxieties in Britain and the United States, both on the part of the conservative elites (who sought to stabilise society through land ownership, and achieve greater self-sufficiency in food production) and radicals or socialists (for whom land symbolised freedom from capitalist social relations). Rural-utopian literature and political argument was surrounded by a penumbra of other cultural and political activities and activism, including Guild Socialism, the arts and crafts movement, back-to-the-land experiments with smallholding, and the early development of the open-air and folk culture movements. These politically and socially diverse movements with their common interest in 'peasant' culture and society clearly drew inspiration from different sources; some sought merely to supplement industrial capitalism, others to replace it. Yet in their culmination in the Edwardian period, one can trace out some common motivations for this desire to restore something of the spirit of the pre-modern. What was it about the turn-of-the-century experience that made this fascination so widespread? Popular interest was captured by land reform, whether through taxes, nationalisation or smallholdings. Land – and the peasant arts that Edwardians associated with a rural lifestyle – was not just a 'Social Question' but also served as a vehicle for ideas of cultural and political reform, and personal development.

The simplification of life inspired a range of alternative and utopian movements, such as Tolstoyan communities in both countries. Fabians, Tolstoyans and anarchists influenced by Peter Kropotkin displayed great interest in farm colonies and the decentralisation of industry. Kropotkin was highly influential upon the 'simple life' tendencies amongst anarchists, and his work was widely read in this period; his *Fields, Factories and Workshops* was in its sixth English edition by 1909. Kropotkin influenced both British and American anarchists, and was cited and admired by prominent leaders of the American women's movement such as Jane Addams. He bemoaned the transformation of artisanship into workers who were 'mere flesh-and-bone parts of some immense machinery; having no idea how and why the machinery performs its rhythmical movements'.[8] Instead, Kropotkin idealised the Middle Ages: 'humanity has never known, neither before nor after, a period of relative well-being as perfectly assured to all, as existed in the cities of the Middle Ages'.

Kropotkin expected the future to bring an integration of manual and mental work, a decentralisation of industry and the combination of agriculture and artisanship in 'worker-controlled federations of self-governing workshops and rural communes'. He sought intensive horticulture, produced for the good of the community rather than the individual, and he was suspicious of the 'Nietzschean individualism' that inspired avant-garde utopians, including feminists. Many anarchists welcomed aspects of machine production, provided machines were socially owned. Most fundamentally, the anarchist 'simple life' was communal and propertyless.[9] Many anarchists, then, saw property as one of the most immoral aspects of modern civilisation.

In Britain, the writer C. W. Stubbs had published his influential *The Land and the Labourers* in 1885, popularising 'cottage farming and co-operative agriculture'. For a late Victorian such as Stubbs, his concern with the divorce from the soil and the pauperisation of the labouring population was primarily moral, but in quite different terms from the anarchist. Stubbs believed that small-scale agriculture 'exercises a very beneficial influence upon the moral character of the agricultural labourer'. In language resonant with Victorian self-help and thrift discourse, he proposed that landed property 'imparts a higher sense of independence and security, greater self-respect, and supplies stronger motives for industry, frugality and foresight than any other kind of property'.[10] He therefore remained broadly confident in the Victorian moral framework. His concern with the social balance of property-holding was influential, and is found again, though expressed in much shriller, apocalyptic language, in the Edwardian distributivist ideas of G. K. Chesterton and Hilaire Belloc.

Belloc and Chesterton rejected the capitalist order from an individualist point of view, as well as the proposed socialist visions of the future. They were influenced by debates generated by the social encyclical *Rerum Novarum*, issued by Pope Leo XI in 1891. In this document, regarded as the basis for Catholic social thought, the pope sought to defend the 'isolated and defenceless' working class, in the face of the monopoly economic power of the capitalist elites. He called for widespread property ownership, limitations on state power, and strengthened private associations, particularly the family. This entailed supporting the working classes 'in reasonable and frugal comfort'.[11]

Belloc and Chesterton built their social reform agenda from the pope's concerns. They felt that the combination of limited ownership under capitalism (and thus limited *economic* freedom), with near universal *political* freedom, made for an unstable equation. The discontented working class was likely to demand a state-led socialist solution to their economic subordination, thus ushering in the 'servile state'. Property should therefore be made more widely available, to enable social cohesion and the avoidance of servility. The contrast between Kropotkin and these thinkers of the 'radical right' show how similar lifestyle projects could be framed in politically diverse ways, and in the first two decades of the twentieth century, had no fixed political valency.

The 'simple life' eulogised in so many 'progressive' and socialist texts was understood by most Edwardians, in contrast to their Victorian predecessors, as aiming at a harmonious, authentic self. The language of thrift and industry came to be replaced by that of originality, connection and balance associated with a peasant lifestyle. Handicraft and small-scale living, according to the British Guild Socialist A. J. Penty, would make man 'once more simple, harmonious and whole'. Historian Jonathan Rose links this objective to a distinctive Edwardian characteristic, a desire for fellowship and personal intimacy across class or racial divides, through the development of nostalgic versions of 'organic communities', mostly ancient Greek or medieval.[12]

The dancing of Isadora Duncan, for example, was read as articulating a utopian imaginary expressing the 'natural' physical and aesthetic life of ancient Greece. Duncan stressed the link between her dance and a holistic 'Nature', bringing flowers and icons of a simpler life into her stage routines. She dressed in Greek-style tunics, even to formal dinners, and based one of her dancing schools in Athens, in a conscious tribute to the ancient world. Even where her feminism was read as forward-looking, it was to a thoroughly pastoral future. Max Eastman described her as looking not only back, but 'forward into the future – farther, I suppose, than Greece, to a time when man shall be cured altogether of civilisation, and return to his natural home outdoors or on the green surface of the earth'.[13] Similarly, the experimental theatre embraced by the Greenwich Village radicals within the Provincetown Players had 'Back to Greece' as their slogan, understanding this to be an appeal to the Dionysian spirit of playful, liberating, expressive drama.

The Middle Ages were equally favoured, through the perceived strength of its religious forces for social unity. The Catholic Church was conceived by neo-medievalists in Britain – spanning the Gothic revivalist A. W. Pugin, Guild Socialist J. N. Figgis, and the Catholic distributivists Belloc and Chesterton – as key to social harmony. Even those who did not seek a religious revival frequently used the Catholic Middle Ages as a vehicle for visions of social renewal. Huntly Carter, a *Freewoman* and *New Age* contributor, eulogised the social unity of medieval monasteries and cathedral building:

In this vast and comprehensive building they harmonised the whole available resources of culture; brought into tune the many and varied forms of art and science; composed a symphonic poem of stone, wood, metal and glass ... and they did all this as a natural result of the Medieval condition and scheme of life, of the Medieval mood.'[14]

Resonances of this can be found within the women's movement; Olive Schreiner used the same cathedral building parable to exemplify social organicism in her 1911 *Woman and Labour*: in constructing the Gothic cathedral, 'each laboured in his place, and the work as completed had unity; it expressed not the desire and necessity of one mind, but of the human spirit of that age'. Many feminists were comfortable with the backward gaze to the 'Middle Ages'. The 'maternalist feminist' Ellen Key celebrated 'the finest life of freedom and culture of the Middle Ages' for women as an unsupported aside, suggesting that this statement was accepted 'common sense' for her contemporaries. Key wrote of the 'union of handicraft and art' in which lay 'the superiority of antiquity and of the Renaissance'. Explicitly quoting Ruskin, she argued for all work to become 'art', though she rejected the avant-garde emphasis on egoist self-development that was associated with this. *Votes for Women* had idealised 'medieval feminists', seeing their achievements as parallel to those of suffragists in the twentieth century.'[15]

The women's movement hosted a great variety of ways of thinking about the past and the future. Two dimensions will be outlined and contrasted here. A pro-technological vision of the modern world formed a well-established part of American feminist discourse, and to a lesser extent, the British. Larger numbers of British feminists were however fascinated by ideas of the pre-modern world as one in which women could live fuller, and fulfilling, lives. These ideas also circulated, but were less well established, in the United States.

FEMINIST UTOPIAN THINKING

Edwardian feminist and suffragist writers outlined schemes of emancipation, personal harmony and social reconciliation via new forms of living and working arrangements, ranging from modern co-operative farming to 'neo-medieval' communities. The early years of the century were strongly marked by a sense of epochal change. Millie Price wrote of the 'restless energy' of experimental circles in Leeds in around 1903: 'The building of Utopian communities was in the air'. Many Leeds Arts Club participants firmly believed in the 'simple life': 'A. J. Penty brought his Ruskinian ethics ... in producing furniture of simple, undecorated and unpolished woods'. Price described how Penty and a friend 'furnished themselves in a cottage, as an example of what craftsmanship can do, and there in the country, lived for a while an austere Thoreauesque kind of life'.[16]

A description from Mary Gawthorpe, who had been a close friend of Millie Price during her years in Leeds, gives a sense of the pervasiveness of such goals within the progressive community from which most 'advanced' feminists came. Gawthorpe described a visit to some Oxford socialists, Willie Roberts and his sister:

> Mr R. is a grave, middle-aged unmarried gentleman, and one of the most cultured beings (in the broad sense of the word) I have ever met. Mr and Miss R. are most earnest students and disciples of John Ruskin. They not only read his works but show their love for his teaching in their lives. Their aim in life is to be 'cultured' in the sense which means 'Be sufficient to yourself' and they have a lively faith in the blessings that will accrue to humanity if all the people can be got back on the land again. Thus so far as they are able, their lives and living are marked by the greatest simplicity.[17]

American progressives and radicals made similar experiments. Floyd Dell, for example, before moving to Chicago and taking up with avant-garde circles, briefly took up truck farming in Davenport with George Cram Cook, the actor who was to found the Provincetown Players. Their experiment was based upon 'a vision of living from the farm and having leisure for literary works', but the realities of 'insects and frosts' soon defeated them.[18]

These experiments with a 'simple life' were practical rather than imagined; the Edwardian women's movement generated only small numbers of specifically utopian novels.[19] The overtly utopian project, along the detailed lines of H. G. Wells or Bellamy, was not attractive; it was a stock feminist response when questioned about the future that they declined to prophesy, preferring to release women from present constraints, but making no further claims about the future.

Those who regarded themselves as a 'vanguard' of feminism were perhaps more willing to speculate about the future. It was an important aspect of *The Freewoman*; suggestions of new names for the resuscitated *Freewoman* in 1913 included *The Prophet* and *Tomorrow*. The fascination with 'back to the land' schemes, reform of the home and the significance of technology debated within this journal and other sources gives an unparalleled insight into the cultural and political influences upon Edwardian feminists.

Two aspects of utopian thinking can be teased out of feminist writings. There were strong links between the women's movement and the 'simple life' movement. Mary Neal was a prominent member of the WSPU and also a founder of the English folk song and dance revival. In her settlement work, she worked closely with Emmeline Pethick Lawrence, Constance Lytton, and others who later became WSPU supporters. Neal promoted ideas of national renewal through rural influences upon city dwellers. Evelyn Sharp (sister of Cecil Sharp) and Lilah McCarthy of the Actresses' Franchise League, were also both 'Folk revivalists' and supporters of the women's movement. Jan Marsh has documented how women were intimately, if conflictually, involved with the arts and crafts movement and 'back to the land' initiatives.[20]

A typically rural vision of the feminist future was held by the Scottish anarchist-feminist Lily Gair Wilkinson. She argued in her 1913 pamphlet, *Woman's Freedom*: 'while there are men and women who hold from others the means of life – the rich surface of the earth and the means of cultivating that richness – so long there will be no freedom for the others who possess none of it all'. She proposed a 'return to a simpler and more wholesome kind of life, in which physical needs will be provided for rather by handicrafts and agriculture than by the complex machinery system of labour in crowded cities.' Her focus for feminist emancipation was not women, but men:

in free communal life, it will be found, not that women are to be emancipated by becoming lawyers and doctors and what not, but that men are to be emancipated by withdrawing from such abnormal occupations and returning to home and garden and field as the true sphere of human life.[21]

In the United States, the leatherworker and designer Mary Ware Dennett was a prominent member of the arts and crafts movement in Boston, as well as a reluctant suffragist and enthusiastic 'advanced' feminist. She had studied at the Boston Museum of Fine Arts, and saw 'arts and crafts' and feminism as vehicles for profound social change, though she was also aware of the limitations and potential conservatism of the former.[22] 'Simple' clothes were a typical vehicle for a greater naturalness and authenticity for women that harked back to an imagined ancient past. As Margaret Anderson described feminist dress reform in *The Little Review*, 'There's something about the new style that points to a finer naturalness ... I don't know why, but I want to use the word "true" about the new clothes. They're so much less dishonest than the old, padded ways – the strange, perverted, *muffled* methods ... We may become Greek yet'.[23]

But despite these intellectual and personal points of overlap between feminism and the 'simple life', there is much less evidence amongst

Americans of the rural utopianism common amongst British feminists. American utopianists may have stressed ecological goals, but did so from within predominantly urban visions of the future.

While 'back to the land' and 'peasant arts' themes were popular within the women's movement, the 'advanced thinkers' of feminism frequently posed an alternative future, of a highly technological, urban lifestyle. Feminism was, for many, something new, and the backward gaze was unhelpful. Teresa Billington-Greig wrote scathingly of the 'cranks' at the fringes of suffragism, including 'the back-to-the-land-to-keep-poultry-and-bees Crank'.[24] Charlotte Perkins Gilman, the most productive of feminist utopists in this period, argued that women's emancipation 'cannot be found behind us. It is not reversion which is needed – there is no going back to an earlier and "simpler" condition – we must go on to a later and better one.' Her American peers felt similarly; one wrote 'Spinning wheels are now quaint articles of bric-a-brac which cost a good deal and gather dust ... We can no more bring [old fashioned home-provisioning] back into the home than the home-made tallow dips, which once illuminated it rather dimly.'[25]

Perhaps because women had stereotypically been associated with the 'simple' and the 'natural', feminists were less prone to celebrate the simple life. Much feminist utopian thought supported the use of technology to enhance women's position, rather than seek a return to machine-less agriculture. A writer in the American journal *The New Review* argued that 'Feminism is the result of human energy set free by machinery to find new outlets in a rapidly developing civilisation'. Likewise, Edna Kenton idealised the 'quickening force' of 'rapid transit, the telephone, telegraph, wireless, newspapers, increasing club and social life, the yeasty ferment of cities'.[26] She was derisive about the revival of women's craftwork as a means of liberation, and attributed this trend to women's nervous energy created by domestic confinement:

[woman] reaches out in desperation and snatches the old handicrafts back under the guise of definite art ... It is likely that the spinning-wheel and the loom may be the next futile scheme for keeping women busy in the modern home.

Historians characterise women's utopias of this period as complex, urbanised, and technologically advanced. The development of technology was usually combined with appreciation and sustainable use of the natural environment, but was a far remove from the peasant farming advocated by others.[27]

CAPITALISM, PROPERTY AND POWER

Debates amongst feminists strongly reflected these themes of simplicity and self-sufficiency. Through their social critique of Edwardian society and the capitalist economy, many feminists sought redemption from the capitalist machine economy. Their concerns echoed Kropotkin, but showed greater sensitivity to the situation of women workers. Dora Marsden for example described capitalism using the parasite metaphor commonly ascribed to women in this period: 'capital is insatiable; it is not a necessity of wealth, but a ghastly, poisonous fungus which has fastened upon wealth and which is rapidly crushing it out of existence'. It was women who were particularly vulnerable to the 'inroads' of capitalism, and in a particularly intimate, bodily fashion: 'Peasant women sell their hair; foster-nurses their nourishment; recently a woman put up her entire person for sale for any purposes whatsoever'. Women emerged as particularly exploited and disinherited within the capitalist system. Rebecca West, *The Freewoman*'s assistant editor, focused on women's relation to industry: 'How could a feminist worship the industrial system? It makes the same demand from women as does the home – physical drudgery, combined with mental inertia.' She felt that if work was not a realm of artistic expression, it became immoral. Another *Freewoman* writer, Françoise Lafitte, recalled the power such ideas had for 'advanced women': 'the idea of severing myself from the machine age, of attempting to live otherwise than for money was irresistible'.[28] Lafitte was a young French socialist-feminist who came to London and became a single mother after entering a short-lived 'free union'. She later became involved in a 'Tolstoyan colony' through the Freewoman Discussion Group.

In Anglo-American avant-garde circles, the industrial 'machine' served as a trope for political and industrial slavery. Women were seen as having the power to break free from the machine economy. The Greenwich Village avant-garde magazine *Judy* put it in libertarian terms:

For so many centuries men have attempted to get redress of grievances by further elaboration of governmental machinery ... Each little statesman and noisy politician adds his greaseless cog to the already over-burdened wheels. Machinery! Always more Machinery! Women come to world problems with a freer touch. Their stroke is more bold, more direct, more amateurish.[29]

Advanced feminists on both sides of the Atlantic agreed that the industrial 'herding' of men to serve machines was paralleled in democracy, where men were 'herded' to vote, and would be represented by those who cared nothing for their interests. They were sceptical therefore about the suffrage struggle and the good it would do women. The entire economic and political superstructure was seen as corrupted by the coercion of capitalist industrial machine-based production, and by the coercion embodied within the democratic system of representation. At the level of bringing about change, many could not accept anything but individual revolt. Any other movement for social change might either compromise individuality, or be unable to challenge the power of the capitalist order. Government intervention fell into this category of ineffectiveness against capitalism. Dora Marsden rejected the state's ability to do anything to change the economic order:

the capitalist system being what it is [politicians] would be powerless to effect anything more than the slow-paced 'reform', of which the sole aim is to make 'men and masters' settle down in a comfortable but unholy alliance ... Every modern State is in pawn, in debt up to the eyes with capitalists. The capitalists own the States.[30]

Anti-capitalism was so persistent a theme that, both at the time and subsequently, vanguard feminism has sometimes been misread as socialism. In fact, neo-medieval and 'back-to-the-land' discourse provided a site for anti-capitalist rhetoric that was distinct from socialism. Feminist utopian thinking amongst 'vanguard' circles differed from Edwardian socialist utopianism in its rejection of co-operation as a guiding principle in society, and fellowship as an end. Many feminists, particularly *Freewoman* contributors, preferred a more individualist future society, comprising not only autonomy in work, but also a political and personal autonomy. Morris or Blatchford's vision of complex interdependency was not favoured, and a more radically 'simple' life was preferred. Rural and craft themes were by no means exclusively allied to forms of collectivism, but they can be seen as one of the points at which 'individualist' and 'collectivist' concerns coalesced.

For a significant number of feminists, socialism did offer the best prospect of social change. One *Freewoman* correspondent, Isabel Leatham, argued that women formed the 'reserve army of cheap casual labour' on which capitalism depended, therefore 'the complete emancipation of women would be impossible without Socialism'. Most however were strongly critical of the gender politics of socialism, and Leatham admitted that 'it would be possible to have Socialism with only a shadow of freedom for women'. This was an important and persistent concern for many feminists, including Heterodoxy member Crystal Eastman, who argued that feminists should not wait for the 'social revolution' to bring them their freedom, but should form a distinct movement. Yet for Marsden and others, socialism failed to work as an alternative, since it would fatally compromise individual freedom: 'Like Capitalism, [socialism] regards the "People" in the bulk, and arranges for them in the bulk; and in the interests of the bulk ... it sacrifices the idiosyncrasy of the individual'. Therefore, 'We are faced not only with the problem of ridding ourselves of capitalist control. We have to dodge the proffered alternative, that of State control. We stand between the Devil and the Deep Sea. There can be no more common ground between State Socialists and Individualists than there can be between Capitalists and Individualists.'[31]

This position led to a curious ideological resemblance between avant-garde feminism and the 'anti-feminist' distributivists, Hilaire Belloc and G. K. Chesterton. Their individualism, combined with their idealisation of 'property as a buttress for personal dignity and creativity' and the agrarian past, made their anti-socialist discourse appealing to some feminists. Belloc and Chesterton in fact shared an intellectual milieu with some avant-garde feminists – their journals were in dialogue, shared readers and contributors, and were sometimes published or subsidised by the same individuals. *The Freewoman* and the *Eye-Witness*, for example, shared a publisher, contributors and readers – in other words, inhabited the same periodical community. Reading periodicals in their intellectual communities rather than as singular entities can throw up some surprising alliances and shared concerns.

The appeal of 'Catholic individualism', however, was compromised by its approach to women. Belloc's idea of the 'working man's dignity' was based upon his power as 'householder and head of a family'. The problematic 'near universal political freedom' he identified ignored the exclusion of more than half the adult population from such freedom; women's lack of political rights was not seen as a significant 'instability' in the contemporary order. He specifically defined universal property ownership as based on family, not individual, property-holding.[32] Chesterton summarised his beliefs as the idea of 'private property universal but private, the idea of families free but still families, of domesticity democratic but still domestic, of one man one home'. Chesterton felt that women should have 'despotic power – not democratic power. Give Mrs Pankhurst a throne, not a vote.'[33] This idealisation of male patriarchal control of the home and trivialisation of women's political ambitions conflicted with feminist 'vanguard' politics, but did not preclude some common ground between the two. There was a breadth and eclecticism to 'advanced' feminism which has sometimes been hard for historians to make sense of, but which must be acknowledged in feminist cultural politics.

POSITIVE CONSTRUCTION: 'LAND-CULTURE AND HAND-TRAINING'

Motivated by their critique of the existing economic order and by the limitations of alternatives, feminists sought to resolve the tensions for women between self-realisation, work and domestic duties both in theoretical terms and in their everyday lives. A 'simple life' without excessive luxury and possessions, organised along communal lines, seemed to meet this need. In part this was a feminist question because, as one *Freewoman* contributor saw it, women found the simple or communal life particularly difficult. George Frankland sought to ease women's domestic tasks with a simple regime, yet blamed women's intransigence for the lack of progress towards it. He felt that women tended to work 'in old-fashioned and wasteful ways', and asked 'Are we yet ripe for co-operatively dwelling together? And, especially, are our women-folk yet ripe?'[34]

Many looked beyond living arrangements and diet, to the radical reorganisation of the entire economic organisation, and in particular, the nature of work. This interest in the external environment was in keeping with the introspective turn that characterised their thought. As Marsden put it, 'Man finds his complexities in himself, and not in his social organisation. That requires to be as simple as man can make it.' How to simplify life, on a broader scale than domestic reform, was a rich topic, prompting speculation upon the overall future development of society. In place of factory production, feminists sought to describe new ways of working that would neither exploit in economic terms, nor aesthetic. Work was conceived as a key channel for the individualist utopian project, and ideally allowed the worker to make 'concrete in objective form the positive qualities of his own personality [and] ... a re-affirmation of his own individuality'. Labour and property-holding implied self-realisation. Edith A. Browne commented: 'Any woman who is earning a pound a week is in a position to think as she likes, and to do as she likes.'[35]

So what were the ideal forms or characteristics of work? Olive Schreiner simply asked that all fields of dignified labour be open to women, and eloquently argued that women must work, even if 'each in her own minute sphere', in order to save themselves from the passivity and degeneration that went with the retreat of work from the modern home.[36] Marsden was more specific about the nature of work. She identified two tendencies of human enterprise, one to make work easy, the other to make work into pleasure. She argued that the latter enabled 'a man to impress upon [his materials] a likeness of the quality of his own personality ... He sought to recreate something of himself, his preferences and his tastes in the work he did.'

But during the course of the industrial revolution, the tendency to 'make work easy' had overwhelmed the pleasurable. She rejected utopian thinkers who prioritised leisure over work: 'What is this demand for leisure? It certainly is not an opportunity of doing nothing. It is, in fact, a demand for opportunity for self-realisation ... For self-realisation, work is required ... Art and work cannot be separated without complete disaster both to the artist and the worker'.[37] The artist was not, therefore, confined to the 'leisure sphere' of fine arts. Agriculture, carried out in smallholdings, was an exemplary sphere of 'artistic' self-realisation and productivity.

This concept of productivity combined with beauty can be found within British economic literature, epitomised in William Morris' 1884 essay, 'Useful Work Versus Useless Toil'. Morris contrasted the corrupt life of luxury to the 'manly and uncorrupted life', drawing upon a common eighteenth-century association of women with luxury.[38] Despite this gendering, it was the productive nature of agriculture that made it so attractive to feminists, and socialists; one *Freewoman* contributor specified that farming was a solution to the fact that 'only a small proportion of [women] are producing necessities'. All 'unproductive' workers were regarded as living immorally, as parasites, since they were dependent upon the necessary goods produced by the productive. For women, this was a particular trap, since social convention made it easy for them to shirk their duty to work, and become unproductive parasites. For Ada Nield Chew, work for women and men should be 'a human, economic necessity, to last their lifetime, *as a due to society*, and not merely as a pastime'.[39]

This emphasis on productive work contrasted with other Victorian and Edwardian utopias. Many utopian texts sought to de-emphasise work, cutting it down to a few hours a day. Still more anticipated the use of labour-saving devices to make work easy. As H. G. Wells asserted, 'A fully developed civilisation employing machines in the hands of highly skilled men [sic] will minimise toil to the utmost'. He therefore argued 'Not a Labour State do we want, nor a Servile State, but a powerful Leisure State of free men'.[40] The enormously influential utopia of the American Edward Bellamy, *Looking Backward, 2000–1887*, portrayed work as a relatively minor part of life. Though participation in the 'Industrial Army' was central to his conception of citizenship, such work was only to last from the age of twenty-one to forty-five, and retirement was seen as the best time of life. Many agreed that the production of useful things should be mechanised in order to be quickly completed, leaving time for the production of beautiful things. This view seemed to prevail amongst Edwardians, with the 'leisure-state' and promotion of free time gaining ground over Morris' vision of universally productive work; even Morris had admitted that 'labour-saving machines' might be useful.

In contrast, feminists identified a duty to work in a manner that aided one's own individual development and was productive and creative. The emphasis on leisure and ease within much utopian literature was unhelpful to their central problematic, the parasitic woman. Utopia was summed up as 'open air, healthful work, simple foods, and a convinced morality'. For Marsden, this style of work was explicitly linked to the pre-industrial period. The 'thousands of years' preceding the industrial revolution 'led to land-culture and hand-training, and the highest manifestations of art the world has seen'. She idealised the simplicity and creativity of the 'little village communities' of ancient Greece, and Britain's 'culminating era', the Elizabethan. Widespread land ownership was the most significant feature of this latter period and earlier: 'In that Golden Era which lies behind us, in the fifteenth century, when men were well-fed and well-clothed, in the seeding-time of that wonderful outburst of the human spirit which we call the English Renaissance, *all men had land*'.[41]

Utopian conditions of universal land-holding would encourage diversity and individuality, since each was free to do with their land as they chose. Dora Marsden decisively placed property, specifically property in land, at the heart of the ideal economy, this being understood as the only means to self-development. 'The propertyless person is in the power of those who retain the property, and is a "wage slave", no matter how loudly he denounces wage-slavery'. The freedom to own property was an essential part of selfhood, and thus an essential element of feminism: 'Ownership is synonymous with worth. A man (a woman) is worth just what he owns. The more extensively he owns, the more augmented is his worth, his power.' Dora Marsden thus harnessed the concept of a simple agricultural society not only to artistic creativity, but to the diversity and personal freedom she associated with individualism. Conditions of 'free will' would lead 'back to the land. Back to freedom. Away back from the petrifying noise and ugliness of the towns. Back from the great factory. Back from machinery. Agriculture is the basis of free society'.[42]

Only self-sufficiency, gained through smallholdings of land to which everyone was entitled, would foster the necessary diversity and free choice of life-style that her belief in individualism demanded. Agricultural society and universal property in land would permanently disable the industrial economy, since none would leave their land to work the machines. Under this scheme, property did not function as producers' medium of exchange, but had a spiritual or symbolic role, as 'the refuge of souls'. Marsden considered that workers should live by barter rather than 'sale of themselves' in a self-sufficient economy. Rebecca West challenged Marsden on this issue:

the idea of producing all one's food from one patch of ground is preposterous. Is the Evesham market-gardener to stop producing the best plums in England and grow inferior potatoes? Is the Sleaford farmer to stop producing the best potatoes in England and grow inferior plums?[43]

Marsden's response was that 'efficient' exchange took second place to individual autonomy:

As for the Evesham plum-grower and the Sleaford potato-man, ... we think it would be well for them to remember is that they are not philanthropic institutions, but that their first duty is to themselves, and, much as the rest of the country may appreciate Evesham plums, it would appear their wisest course to make sure of their corn and let the plums follow after.[44]

Marsden's individual plots represented not efficient food production, but an individual 'soul's refuge'. Many other British 'advanced' feminists stressed the power of a return to the land, though they constructed this in different terms from Dora Marsden. The neo-Malthusian activist Bessie Drysdale regarded agriculture as a particularly appropriate sphere for emancipated, educated women. Drysdale looked forward to the transformation of the weak and anaemic to 'healthy, joyous, and muscular young women'. She did not have in mind the small-holding peasant economy idealised by some, but a more intensive and effective model: 'Farming must be scientific, rational, and more on intensive lines'. Smallholdings were only acceptable on a broader co-operative basis, where many farmers would share the costs of machines. During World War One, such ideas became more widely realised; women's agricultural potential became more high profile, and was discussed in practical terms in professional women's journals such as *Modern Woman and Her Work*, or in patriotic terms in suffrage journals.[45]

'PEASANT ARTS'

In addition to agriculture, craftwork or handicraft was another sphere where feminists felt that the artistic impulse might be authentically expressed. Teresa Billington-Greig recalled the 'green-stained oak and the Poole pottery that graced the simple-life homes of those days'. Emmeline Pankhurst had run what Billington-Greig called an 'arty-crafty business' in Manchester, before suffrage became her dominant concern. Muriel Ciolkowska, *The Freewoman*'s Paris correspondent and a contributor to the *New Age* and *Little Review*, wrote two articles for *The Freewoman* in 1912 titled 'On the Utility of Art', describing a theory of artistic culture intimately bound up with 'manual crafts'. Her ideal was 'a poor peasant's home' expressing 'well-ordered simplicity, the right thing in the right place, nothing superfluous'. She rejected machine production since it could not express character and personality.[46] Ciolkowska expected women to play a large part as 'social reformers through the artistic principle'. Their contribution in craftwork was extensive, and she designated knitting, lace-work, embroideries, wicker, cane, and rush plaiting as channels of self-development. The conservative potential of this project emerged within her articles; in seeking to resurrect and value women's 'traditional arts', Ciolkowska risked perpetuating their artistic and economic isolation.

Josephine Baker, secretary of the Peasant Arts Fellowship outlined her vision of women's work in an agricultural utopia in glowing terms:

> The old peasant life, as it owed its earliest inception to women, so it gave them the fullest satisfaction and scope: it was, and still is, the particular form of civilised life that fits them. Its variety was very great; it was a round of beautiful and enjoyable arts, each one of which was a healthy exercise and a mental training, and all of which eked out, recreated and harmonised one another ... It underlay all the great ages of art, Greek and Gothic alike ...

Baker used this vision to attribute inventiveness and creativity to women, meeting a common anti-feminist criticism that women lacked these features. She concluded that 'The entire fabric of civilisation is everywhere traceable to the needs of women, and to their inventiveness in subserving them'.[47]

Yet she also preserved features of the arguments of anti-feminists, admitting that women did not specialise, and were essentially generalists.[48] For Baker this fact explained why 'women find little satisfaction in an industrial life, and yet feel cramped and denied their full development if confined to a modern home life'. Like Olive Schreiner, she argued that modern industrialism had supplanted the home, and in doing so had taken away women's creative sphere. Unlike Schreiner, however, Baker felt that these old skills could be revived, within an overall gendered division of labour. She hoped to 'recover for women their own work, and [give] them again that possibility of a natural and beautiful occupation of which modern industrialism has robbed them'. Women's work in the home, as epitomised in peasant communities, was 'what women are born to do, are happiest in doing and realise themselves most fully when they have done'. Her final call was for a 'right to a specifically woman's life, not a man's'.[49] This was a controversial position, unlikely to find much favour amongst avant-garde feminists. Marsden, in particular, argued for a transcendence of the division of labour Baker had emphasised, and for a more diverse and individualised approach to work. Baker's contribution makes clear the divergent ideas concerning an 'agricultural utopia' within the feminist movement.

REALISATION

How might such 'peasant lifestyle' utopias be achieved? Sidney Webb admitted his admiration for schemes such as 'the creation of peasant proprietorships', or the restoration of 'village industries'. Nonetheless, he concluded in a 1906 pamphlet, 'well-meant endeavours to set back the industrial clock are ... foredoomed to failure'.[50]

Some *Freewoman* correspondents took a similar position. For a number of them, the problem lay not with *content*, but with the *practicability* of the proposed transformation to an agricultural utopia. They pointed out the unrealistic and backward-looking nature of the agricultural utopia:

The present-day tendency, far from being one of industrial decentralisation that the reversion to a system of handicraft would demand, is one of constantly accelerated centralisation. The continued existence of this system demands the rapid invention of new and more perfect machinery ... Our needs today are far greater than those of the handicraftsmen of old. We have grown accustomed to a comparatively high standard of comfort, and retrogression is impossible.[51]

Ada Nield Chew, whose own working-class origins had left her critical of the drudgery of 'simple' homes, also reflected upon the complexity of modern life:

A moment's thought will remind anybody that these needs could not be supplied, even for ourselves alone, individually. .... Our food comes from many lands, and the combined labour of thousands of people is necessary before it stands on the table ...[52]

A weakness of much of the simple life utopian thinking of the feminist movement was a refusal to confront issues of social interdependence and raised standards of living. While most accepted that the past could not be revived as such, others idealised the autonomy of 'the simple life' without any concession to the complexities and material conditions of modern society. Some were forced to scale down their claims to a practical rather than utopian level. Muriel Ciolkowska recognised that 'we cannot hope to resuscitate peasant costumes and other lost symbols, for what is dead can be stuffed, but not revived'.[53] She merely hoped to 'revive the manual crafts' and reform women's dress to express harmony, simplicity and festiveness.

A *Freewoman* correspondent wrote to propose the formation of a 'sub-group' of the Freewoman Discussion Circle, in order to discover 'what steps of a positive and practical kind have been attempted' to realise the revival of manual crafts.[54] The editor responded that such a group was in process of formation, led by the author of the New Order Tracts, Helen Macdonald. She had stressed the centrality of a 'right to land' which was irrespective of sex in her writings in *The Freewoman*, and sought to realise this through the establishment with her husband of a short-lived vegetarian Tolstoyan colony around 1911. The 'New Order' colony consisted of a cottage and 'huge wooden shack' near London, and a house in London. Amongst others, Françoise Lafitte, H. G. Wells and Rebecca West were involved in what Lafitte described as an appalling unfurnished and 'promiscuous' environment. The colony was short-lived, with cash-flow problems blamed on a sum of money mysteriously lost with the *Titanic*, but its existence does indicate a desire to act on the local level to realise these ideas.[55]

Marsden's own wider vision of social change was more ambitious, and less straightforward to realise than domestic or diet reform. She left unexplored the 'engine for social change', and rejected ideas of social evolution that were common in utopian texts. Instead, she preferred to think that individual rebellion would usher in the new society:

the land might be seized simply by groups of armed men, as it was in Mexico. During the next strike groups of men might settle themselves on the land and refuse to be moved.[56]

Marsden's vision of occupation by groups of armed *men* seemed to displace women from this social revolution and this caused controversy amongst her readership. *Freewoman* correspondents and other feminists were not united in a celebration of agricultural life; some had serious misgivings. For many, agriculture without machines implied hard labour, positively ruling out individuality. Rebecca West argued 'You think of the land as something that only has to be scratched affectionately to give a living; something no more exhausting than keeping a dog. I believe it to be nothing of the sort, but to be as absorbing and jealous as every kind of work must be. Ecstasy if you love it, hell if you don't.' Françoise Lafitte commented 'Back to the land we must go, but this does not mean that we should scratch the earth with our hands, if we could get electric ploughs!'[57] Rachel Graham argued:

I allow that tending a machine is a menial task which no one could love; but then so are many things which must be done, such as cleaning roads, collecting or destroying refuse, mining, etc. I cannot picture a time when these services will not be needed; ... would each individual get his own coal, clean up his portion of the earth, and with a few tools do all the other menial tasks necessary to his comfort? I do not see that an individual could live at all independently. I do not think that work has been a pleasure in the past, excepting as it is to-day, to the lucky few.

Graham, a persistent interlocutor of Dora Marsden's (but for whom no other historical record survives) positively relished the aid of machinery in raising the standard of living:

I look forward to a time when the machine is the slave of man, doing all the monotonous, unintellectual labour, and so leaving us some leisure for doing tasteful things. The machine, the means by which man shall realise his power and his destiny. I confess that I get somewhat confused with the propositions of the ideal state as expounded by some writers in *The Freewoman*. I ... get a vague and muddled impression of human life in the future, under some new order, when we shall be eating uncooked vegetables and fruit, practising in our spare time the simple crafts as a diversion from the compulsion to produce individually the rude necessities of life. To my simple mind, this will be sinking back into a primitive state ...[58]

In response to the criticisms of her 'neo-Luddite' utopia, Marsden did move towards a compromise over her rejection of machinery. She allowed that some mechanical aid might be used to lighten the labour:

Mechanical contrivance has done much to assist man, and has given him considerable insight into the material side of things. A mechanical appliance, specially devised to serve *a man*, to assist what he designs individually, is a most valuable thing, of high worth, *as his servant*.[59]

This allowance for some assistance from tools did not, however, meet all the objections to the simple life. Not only was agricultural life of dubious comfort, but the status and role of women within it was uncertain. There was no convincing evidence that women would be better off in the agricultural de-industrialised world, and much to suggest that they would be worse off. H. G. Wells had recently published in Britain a collection of essays, in which he contrasted his (typically statist) utopia with the 'normal social life' of the agricultural past. Wells associated such 'normal social life' with an 'atmosphere of hens and cows and dung, . . . incessant toil, [and] servitude of women'.[60]

Marsden defiantly sought to revalue Wells' 'normal social life': 'The only safe society of freemen is that which Mr Wells has christened, with admirable precision, the Normal Social Life. This, and this alone, in our opinion, will guarantee free will to men.' But what of women? She and other feminists took the position that women were in fact better off in peasant or farming communities, and that Wells was wrong to associate such communities with women's subordination. Marsden claimed that 'industry, undegraded by machinery, is woman's natural province. Spinning, weaving, pottery, and the rest, were the outcome of woman's instincts.' She also noted that her vision did not require all to be farmers: 'If agriculture again became the basis of the country's well-being, subsidiary crafts, with their specialised skill, would spring up in harmonious service with it. The wheelwright, the smith, the carpenter, the quarryman, the builder, the barber, and the tailor would satisfy the needs of the village communities.'[61] The working life of her utopia, however, seemed singularly focused on traditionally male occupations. As the envisaged life of her 'village communities' was elaborated within *The Freewoman*, the role of women became more obscured.

Marsden's idealisation of fifteenth-century 'universal' land-holding made no mention of women's exclusion from such property-holding. Nor did she note women's absence from her pantheon of the 'great thinkers' of the 'English Renaissance'. Women, by implication, appeared to be excluded from both the artistic and practical handicraft roles within the village communities. It seems inevitable that where freedom and self-development is viewed as a function of production and not consumption, women will be excluded unless special attention is given to their inclusion in systems of production. 'Neo-medieval' and 'peasant arts' feminists had gone some way towards this, with their description of women farmers, spinners, and potters, but their commitment to women's participation as producers was not secure, and women quickly became invisible within the idealised village community.

Finally, the debates revealed some recurring problems for an allegedly individualist utopian society. Marsden's work reveals a tendency to authoritarianism that pervades much utopian thinking. Despite her fervent individualism and genuine commitment to freedom from state control, Marsden was not immune from calling for such control where it might solve anomalies in her social order. This was noticed by Rachel Graham, who pointed out the tension between a stateless society, and the need to allot land on Marsden's scheme: 'How is the land to be divided up and what authority will keep the reserve land for the unborn?', she asked. The static nature of an inalienable allotment of land was in tension with the need to allow individual personal development and growth. Furthermore, land was a limited resource, while population might increase exponentially. Marsden responded 'When the population approaches the limit of what the land will bear, means should be taken to limit the population'.[62] Ironically, Marsden did not hesitate to allow state control at the intimate level of reproductive decision-making. The attempt at positive utopian thinking revealed Marsden's commitment to individualism to be less secure than it had appeared, and indicates a perennial problem of authoritarianism within utopian literature. Overall therefore, Rebecca West regarded a socialist economy as more conducive to individualism than the uniformity and stasis of peasant agriculture:

It seems to me that the Socialist method of recognising that we all possess 'living' property – the faculty of cultivating the land, it may be, or weaving beautiful cloth, or bringing up children, or curing illness – and rewarding us all alike is preferable to your method of dumping us all down on the land irrespective of our different suits. It is more spiritual. It is more compatible with free-will.[63]

There was little resonance for these ideas amongst American feminists, and on this issue the transatlantic conversation was relatively sparse. Despite the popularity of the simple life and craftwork amongst Americans, West's call for the socialisation of labour and property was perhaps the dominant tendency in the United States. An American feminist social scientist, Jessie Taft, for example, explored in some depth the nature of medievalism for women, and came to highly critical conclusions. Taft had written a Ph.D. thesis on the nature of the women's movement while working in Chicago with George Herbert Mead. She argued in the *International Journal of Ethics* in 1915 that the women's movement had to unite with that of labour to end women's ambiguous status as 'neither wholly mediaeval nor wholly modern'.

Taft recognised the attractions of the 'medievalism': 'The self-centred, self-supporting, well-nigh independent [family] unit of medieval times' gave its members an immediate, authentic and direct experience of life.

However, she was critical of the kind of women produced by such institutions: 'Just in so far as society has been able to preserve the feudal family,
it has also succeeded in preserving the feudal woman and until within the
last few years all women have been theoretically of the feudal type'. Taft,
like many of her American peer group, was sceptical about looking
backwards: 'no amount of superstitious worship is going to restore the
mediaeval situation ... the home is no longer individualistic and the
control over its interests is no longer within the power of the individualistic
woman'.[64] Utopian concepts of modernity, then, revealed some major
transatlantic divergences within 'advanced' feminism. American feminists
were much less vocal within the debates over 'back to the land' than their
British counterparts, despite their involvement in the Arts and Crafts
movement, and were largely sceptical about the abandonment of
machines.

CONCLUSION

Placed in their intellectual context, it seems clear that these 'peasant lifestyle' themes were fairly conventional for a period fascinated by the pre-
modern, handicraft and artisanship. 'Peasant arts' and 'back to the land'
feminists joined a well-established British trend in their neo-medieval
crafts-based utopias. What was unusual was the attempt to think through
women's position in such utopias; few neo-medievalist utopian texts were
seriously concerned with women's role, and tended to see women only in
terms of their motherhood. Much contemporary utopian thinking, feminist and non-feminist, confined women to domestic roles, and situated
motherhood as their key role in a new society. Perkins Gilman's *Herland*,
for example, prioritised the mothering role, to the extent of removing men
from the reproductive process. 'Women' and 'mothers' were inter-
changeable in her writing. Her 'A Woman's Utopia' opened with: 'Never a
voice from a woman to say how she would like the world. The main stream
of life, the Mother, has been silent.' One feminist had pointed out in
irritation in the *International Journal of Ethics* that utopists were only
interested in 'married women, usually with young children', while the
category of unmarried women 'is never considered in any scheme of society
nor allowed for in any proposed Utopia'.[65]

A notable feature of the feminist utopianism discussed above, however,
is the absence of the woman figured primarily as a mother. Avant-
garde feminists seemed uninterested in the role of mothering, though
childcare was key to some of the more practical reform schemes. However,

it became difficult for feminists to retain women in focus without this mothering role. Neither could women feature as consumers, another common 'feminine' role, since the neo-medieval utopian literature on which feminists drew explicitly denied significance to the consumer identity. The literature typically gave priority to the producer, and the *process* of production, rather than the consumer and the product. As producers, women tended to simply slip out of the discussion or to take on fairly limited, gender defined roles.

Some general and speculative conclusions about the nature of avant-garde feminists' engagement with modernity are thrown up by this neo-medievalist utopian thinking. There seems to be a paradoxical combination within the feminist avant-garde of a (Romantic) idealisation of the pre-modern, and a modernist individualism with a focus on one's destiny lying in one's own hands. Though I have described Edwardian feminist utopian thinking as in keeping with its intellectual milieu, I think that this combination requires some further explanation. Individualist values were at the heart of 'advanced' feminist discourse. The Middle Ages were frequently characterised as anti-individualist, as in Oscar Wilde's 1891 individualist polemic.[66] The medieval represented a realm of violence and unfreedom, of feudal politics, strictly imposed values, and contempt for individual needs and desires, particularly for those of women. Why, then, were pre-modern guilds, peasant communities and craftspeople the vehicle for some feminist Edwardian utopias?

This trend can be attributed to a nostalgia, described by John Gross as a 'political cul-de-sac' of backward-looking 'Merrie Englandism', that simply turned away from modernity.[67] The widely felt need in Edwardian times to simplify and control life, and move to national or personal self-sufficiency, was prompted by (and coexisted with) a reality of increased social interdependence. Such interdependence, epitomised by urban living, was also accompanied by increased social anonymity. A desire for fellowship or community may have motivated this nostalgia, as Jonathan Rose has argued, and many of the more collectivist utopias described above display this theme. A. J. Penty appeared motivated by an anxious desire for control and simplicity when he argued:

To medieval social arrangements we shall return, not only because we shall never be able to regain complete control over the economic forces in society except through the agency of restored Guilds, but because it is imperative to return to a simpler state of society ... When any society develops beyond a certain point, the human mind is unable to get a grip of all the details necessary to its proper ordering.[68]

Penty explicitly rejected the association of modern values such as individuality and original vision with handicraft. He argued in 1907 that craftsmanship was about learning the *right* way to work, according to a 'tradition of craft design as it existed in the Middle Ages'.[69] It was emphatically not about modern innovations on medieval crafts that might express the modern self.

I argue, however, that 'back-to-the-land' feminists were motivated less by a nostalgia for the community, intimacy and fellowship that modernity could not provide, and more by an interest in specifically modern values. *Freewoman* contributors, with other Edwardian contemporaries, deployed the Middle Ages as a background on which to project modern concerns. One such set of concerns was the determination to live an authentic life, to gain real experience and see life 'in the raw'. Within the avant-garde feminist movement, there was a strong sense that, as Inez Haynes Gillmore put it, women 'were studying a second-hand world ... we were getting our life in translation, ... we never had a real face to face encounter with it'. Gillmore, a 'Heterodite' and journalist, asserted dramatically that 'all women were Helen Kellers', living lives that were 'sifted, strained, twisted, warped, compressed, prettified, decorated, falsified and expurgated'. Likewise the British writer Cicely Hamilton argued in 1912 'We have the accumulation of generations of artificiality to throw off – of artificially induced virtues as well as of artificially induced vices'.[70] Values of autonomy and personal authenticity were prioritised within the feminist movement.

One way to express this was through projecting these values back onto the pre-modern. 'Advanced feminists' were not alone in this, and, arguably, all utopian writing projects contemporary values onto a fictional past or future. Commentators have seen the neo-medievalist William Morris in this light, linking his utopian vision to modern values.[71] The pre-modern ancient world or Middle Ages served utopian thinkers' needs as an open-ended 'repository of desire', a heuristic for thinking through the relations between the individual and society. For Edwardians, the pre-modern age embodied both a critique of the massification of modernity, and a symbolic site for modern values. Handicraft was not just a rejection of factory work. The unique objects produced by crafts-people were regarded as instantiating a thoroughly modern 'unique and highly differentiated individuality'.[72] 'Free cities' and villages symbolised a (fictional) politics of small-scale communities, freed from the top-down oppression epitomised in the modern bureaucratic state, and thus able to innovate and represent in a modern style.

On an individual level, the peasantry was intended to represent personal sovereignty, perhaps in a similar fashion to the 'frontier farmer' ideal of the American West. An association was made between an imagined peasant lifestyle and the modern positive evaluation of an authentic, genuine, and original sense of personal identity – in other words, a strongly individuated self. The highly mediated nature of modernity, in the sense of experience governed through the medium of entities outside an individual's control, gives rise to a desire to gain access in a non-mediated way to some form of the 'real' or 'first hand', and through this to more entirely 'be oneself'.[73] As Graham Wallas argued, 'all our impulses and instincts are greatly increased in their immediate effectiveness if they are "pure", and in their more permanent results if they are "first hand". Modernity can be defined as an experience of chaos and ephemerality, which motivates a search for authenticity.[74]

This is not a rejection of the experience of modernity, in the sense of nostalgia for fellowship, but a necessary element of the project of modernity. Mary Gluck has argued that the pre-war avant-garde was shaped by an organicist attachment to 'a golden age of harmony in some distant past, to be recaptured and reexperienced in some distant future'. This was a theme that resonated strongly for advanced feminists. The values that were being sought by the avant-garde and feminists – the unique, the 'first hand', the authentic – were modern values. This cluster of what Marshall Berman has called 'authenticity' concepts can of course be associated with different things – as the twentieth century progressed, the authentic and real became associated with the mechanistic and the functional. But in Britain prior to the First World War, the 'real' was more commonly seen as the primitive and the natural.[75]

Authenticity in lifestyle and personal identity might thus be achieved in a literal sense by back-to-the-land schemes, or more subjectively, by access to the primitive states of the unconscious; genius, discussed in the next chapter, might arise from either route. Access to the authentic and genuine was important to avant-garde feminists since women seemed pre-eminently artificial creations. Their attraction to individualism was partly through its attention to uniqueness, and to the liberation of the 'real', unmediated individual. Dora Marsden's preoccupation with personality was on these grounds: 'Personality ... stands for the *first-hand* revelation of the nature of things in the soul of the individual'.[76] This helps make sense of why individualists would support apparently communitarian projects of 'village utopias'. The motives were not those of fellowship, but rather a desire to gain access to an authentic, autonomous way of life. It also makes sense of why, in contrast to most women's utopias, a backward-looking utopian scheme was preferred by many in the 'vanguard'. The agricultural 'normal social life' had been associated by H. G. Wells with the subordination of women, but as a back-drop for the modern values of uniqueness, authenticity and individuality, it became relevant for feminist appropriation.

As in much utopian literature, this projection of modern values and desires onto the pre-modern was an uncomfortable device, embodying a tension between historical reality and fictional symbolism. When examined as a genuine historical entity, the medieval period was clearly not the location of high levels of political, economic and personal freedom. Utopian literature based upon backward-looking visions is perhaps always vulnerable to such tensions, and feminist utopists are no exception. They produced 'philosophical' projects, vehicles for the discussion of individualist and feminist values. The communities described within this project were deliberately vague, probably not intended as realistic proposals. Avant-garde feminists worked towards not a blueprint for a new society but an exploration of the values underpinning self-fulfilment, and a raising of the aspirations of women. They combined a backward-looking, politically unrealistic and naïve celebration of the Middle Ages with a progressive commitment to new forms of gender relations and ways of realising the 'authentic self'. Overall, the contributions discussed above were problematic, inconsistent, historically misleading, yet represent an important strand of feminist thinking about modern values, through the heuristic device of the pre-modern.

END NOTES

1. Price, 'This World's Festival', p. 115. The unconventionality of these simple life enthusiasts in fact went beyond what the garden city founders were willing to accept. Price recalls being 'accosted by Sir Ebenezer Howard himself and begged to desist. We were, he remonstrated, giving his garden-city a bad name as a home for cranks' (p. 116).
2. Barbara Sicherman has argued that American women, being excluded from the tradition of American individualism and leadership, were more likely to envision collective solutions to social problems. Sicherman, in *Gender, Class, Race and Reform in the Progressive Era*, ed. Noralee Frankel and Nancy Shromm Dye (Lexington, University Press of Kentucky), p. 129.
3. H. G. Wells, *A Modern Utopia* (London, Chapman and Hall, 1905); Edward Bellamy, *Looking Backwards, 2000–1887* (London, Constable, 1888); William Morris, *News from Nowhere: Or An Epoch of Rest* (London, Penguin, 1993); Samuel Butler, *Erewhon* (New York, Airmont Publishing, 1967; orig. 1872), p. 53.

4. Ruskin quoted in W. H. G. Armytage, *Heavens Below: Utopian Experiments in England 1560–1960* (London, Routledge, 1961), p. 290. See also Jan Marsh, *Back to the Land: The Pastoral Impulse in England, from 1880 to 1914* (London, Quartet Books, 1982).
5. See John Ruskin, *The Works of John Ruskin*, ed. E. T. Cook and A. Wedderburn (London, George Allen, 1905); Jennifer Mclloyd, 'Raising Lilies: Ruskin and Women', *Journal of British Studies*, 34 (1995).
6. Robert Blatchford (Numquam), *Merrie England* (London, The Journeyman Press, 1976; orig. 1893). Charlotte O. Schetter, *Life and Labor*, Jan. 1911.
7. Eileen Boris, *Art and Labor: Ruskin, Morris, and the Craftsman Ideal in America* (Philadelphia, Temple, 1986); Randolph S. Bourne, 'An Experiment in Co-operative Living', *Atlantic Monthly*, June 1914, 823–31.
8. Paul Avrich, 'Kropotkin in America', *International Review of Social History*, 25:1 (1980); Peter Kropotkin, *Fields, Factories and Workshops Tomorrow*, ed. Colin Ward (London, George Allen & Unwin, 1974), p. 24.
9. Ward, in Kropotkin, *Fields, Factories and Workshops*, p. 201; Ruth Kinna, 'Kropotkin's Theory of Mutual Aid in Historical Context', *International Review of Social History*, 40 (1995), 268–70. Wilkinson, *Woman's Freedom*, p. 13.
10. C. W. Stubbs, *The Land and the Labourers* (London, W. Swan Sonnenschein, 1885) p. 23.
11. Leo XI, *Five Great Encyclicals* (New York, Paulist Press, 1939; orig. 1891).
12. A. J. Penty, *The Restoration of the Gild System* (London, New Age Book Dept, 1906), pp. 10–12. See Jonathan Rose, *The Edwardian Temperament, 1895–1919* (Athens, OH, Ohio University Press, 1986), pp. 201, 60.
13. Eastman, in Genthe, *Isadora Duncan*, n.p.; Daly, *Done Into Dance*, p. 90.
14. Carter, 'The Recovery of Art and Craft', *New Age*, 1 Dec. 1910, 116.
15. Schreiner, *Woman and Labour*, pp. 140–1; Key, *Woman Movement*, p. 12; Ellen Key, *The Younger Generation* (London, G. P. Putnam's, 1914), p. 235; 'Mediaeval feminists', *Votes for Women*, 4 July 1913, 587.
16. Price, 'This World's Festival', pp. 92, 91.
17. Gawthorpe, DMC, 24 Sept. 1912: III, 11. See also Gawthorpe, *Up Hill to Holloway*, pp. 211–12.
18. 'Floyd Dell', *The Bookman*, March 1923, 68.
19. Gilman's *Herland*, and Inez Haynes Gillmore's *Angel Island* are the most prominent utopian novels written by feminists. Charlotte Perkins Gilman, *Herland, The Yellow Wall-Paper, and Selected Writings* (New York, Penguin Books, 1999); Inez Haynes Gillmore, *Angel Island* (New York, Holt, 1914). Nan Bowman Albinski, *Women's Utopias in British and American Fiction* (London, Routledge, 1988) discusses some less-well-known women's utopian writings.
20. Marsh, *Back to the Land*.
21. Wilkinson, *Woman's Freedom*, pp. 12, 15.
22. Chen, *The Sex Side of Life*; Georgina Boyes, *The Imagined Village: Culture, Ideology and the English Folk Revival* (Manchester, Manchester University Press, 1993); Boris, *Art and Labor*, pp. 37–41.

23. Anderson, 'Incense and Splendor', *The Little Review*, June 1914, 2.
24. *The Hour and The Woman*, ed. Teresa Billington-Greig and Maude Fitzherbert, WFL Occasional Papers no. 1, p. 14, Teresa Billington-Greig Papers, The Women's Library, London Metropolitan University (henceforth TBGP).
25. Gilman, 'A Woman's Utopia', in Kessler, *Charlotte Perkins Gilman*, p. 134; Jesse Lynch Williams, 'A Common-sense View of Woman Suffrage' in NAWSA, *Woman Suffrage: Arguments and Results, 1910–11* (New York, Kraus Reprint, 1971), pp. 3–4.
26. Louise Kneeland, 'Feminism and Socialism', in 'A Feminist Symposium', *New Review*, Aug. 1914, 443; Edna Kenton, 'The Militant Women – and Women', 16–17.
27. The distinction between these two aspects of utopian thinking should not be overstated, however; the two informed each other, and sometimes achieved a reconciliation of aims. Many American craftsmen and agrarian enthusiasts supported the use of machines or 'new industrialist' techniques to bring individual expression into industry; Boris, *Art and Labor*, pp. 47, 31.
28. West, *FW*, 14 March 1912; Delisle, *Friendship's Odyssey*, pp. 186–90.
29. 'S.', 'Alice Breaks the Looking Glass', *Judy*, July 1919.
30. Marsden, *FW*, June 20 1912, 83; and *NFW*, 1 Aug. 1913, 62.
31. Leatham, *FW*, 21 March 1912. Eastman, 'Now We Can Begin', *The Liberator*, Dec. 1920, repr. in Eastman, *Crystal Eastman*, p. 53; Marsden, *FW*, 15 Aug. 1912, 243–4.
32. Belloc, *Oxford and Cambridge Review*, Aug. 1912, 76.
33. John McCarthy, *Hilaire Belloc: Edwardian Radical* (Indianapolis, Liberty Press, 1978), p. 279; G. K. Chesterton, *What's Wrong with the World* (San Francisco, Ignatius Press, 1987), vol. 4, 145.
34. Frankland, *FW*, 4 July 1912, 137.
35. Marsden, *FW*, 5 Sept. 1912, 303; *FW*, 22 Aug. 1912, 261; Browne, *FW*, 25 Jan. 1912, 188.
36. Schreiner, *Woman and Labour*, p. 143.
37. Marsden, *FW*, 22 Aug. 1912, 261, 262.
38. Morris, *News from Nowhere*, pp. 287–306. The association between women and luxury was strong, suggested by Olive Schreiner's description of the female parasite in orientalist terms as 'bedecked and scented', sexually dissipated and bejewelled, Schreiner, *Woman and Labour*, pp. 81. Charles Masterman in a 1909 essay also feminised luxury. Masterman, *The Condition of England*, pp. 26, 28. The association of women with luxury and degeneration contrasts with, and probably motivated, the active interest within the women's movement in the simplification of life.
39. Drysdale, *FW*, 3 Oct. 1912, 393. Chew, *FW*, 11 July 1912, 150, emphasis added.
40. H. G. Wells *et al.*, *Socialism and The Great State*, p. 35; Wells, *An Englishman Looks at the World*, p. 94.
41. Marsden, *FW*, 5 Sept. 1912, 303, 304; emphasis added; 26 Sept. 1912, 364.
42. Marsden, *NFW*, 1 Sept. 1913, 104–5; 1 Aug. 1913, 62; *FW*, 15 Aug. 1912, 244.

43. Marsden, *FW*, 15 Aug. 1912, 244; 12 Sept. 1912, 324; West, *FW*, 5 Sept. 1912, 312.
44. Marsden, *FW*, 5 Sept. 1912, 302.
45. Drysdale, *FW*, 3 Oct. 1912, 393. *Common Cause* published an issue dedicated to women on the land in under the banner headline 'Pro Patria', 24 March 1915.
46. Billington-Greig, unpublished memoirs, p. 91, TBGP; Ciolkowska, *FW*, 25 July 1912, 192–3; 8 Aug. 1912, 225–7.
47. Baker, *FW*, 21 March 1912, 347.
48. The Edwardian anti-feminist G. K. Chesterton commented, for example, that women 'should not have one trade but twenty hobbies'; Chesterton, *What's Wrong with the World*, vol. 4, 116.
49. Baker, *FW*, 21 March 1912, 347.
50. Sidney Webb, *The Difficulties of Individualism*, Fabian Tract No. 69 (London, The Fabian Society, 1906), p. 13.
51. Newfield, *FW*, 12 Sept. 1912, 326–7.
52. Chew, *FW*, 11 July 1912, 149–51.
53. Ciolkowska *FW*, 25 July 1912, 193.
54. Edwin Herrin, *FW*, 1 Aug. 1912, 216.
55. Delisle, *Friendship's Odyssey*, pp. 186–90.
56. Marsden, *FW*, 5 Sept. 1912, 304.
57. West, *FW*, 5 Sept. 1912, 313; Lafitte, *FW*, 12 Sept. 1912, 329.
58. Graham, *FW*, 22 Aug. 1912, 276.
59. Marsden, *FW*, 15 Aug. 1912, 244, original emphasis.
60. H. G. Wells *et al.*, *Socialism and The Great State*, quoted in *FW*, 27 June 1912, 103.
61. Marsden, *FW*, 29 Aug. 1912, 285; 5 Sept. 1912, 302.
62. Graham, *FW*, 5 Sept. 1912, 314; Marsden, *FW*, 6 June 1912, 42.
63. West, *FW*, 5 Sept. 1912, 313.
64. Taft, 'The Woman Movement'.
65. Gilman, in Kessler, *Charlotte Perkins Gilman*, p. 135; White, *IJE*, 22:3 (April 1912), 332.
66. Oscar Wilde, *The Soul of Man Under Socialism* (London, Arthur L. Humphreys, 1904), p. 217.
67. On Chesterton's utopianism, see Gross, *The Rise and Fall of the Man of Letters* (London, Penguin, 1991), p. 238. See also Christopher Shaw and Malcolm Chase, *The Imagined Past: History and Nostalgia* (Manchester, Manchester University Press, 1989).
68. Penty 1919, quoted in Williams, *Culture and Society* (London, Chatto and Windus, 1958), pp. 187–8.
69. Penty, *New Age*, 26 Sept. 1907, 349.
70. Gillmore, 'Confessions of an Alien', *Harper's Bazar*, April 1912, 170–1. Stansell suggests that this was a widely held value amongst the 'bohemian' avant-garde, who sought 'vital contact', mainly with working-class people. Stansell, *American Moderns*, p. 61. Hamilton, in H. G. Wells *et al.*, *Socialism and The Great State*, p. 238.

71. For David Harvey, Morris' celebration of simplicity of design prefigures the modernist Bauhaus design ideology David Harvey, *The Condition of Postmodernity* (Oxford, Basil Blackwell, 1989), p. 23.
72. Ruth Levitas, *The Concept of Utopia* (London, Philip Allen, 1990), p. 181. See Sharp, *New Age*, 20 June 1907, 117, for a critical review of these concepts.
73. Marshall Berman's study of the 'politics of authenticity' identifies a cluster of expressions that signify this desire for authenticity that so characterises modernity, including those that have surfaced frequently in this study: individuality, self-development, self-realisation. Marshall Berman, *The Politics of Authenticity: Radical Individualism and the Emergence of Modern Society* (London, George Allen and Unwin, 1971), p. 1.
74. Wallas, *Human Nature in Politics*, p. x; Harvey, *Condition of Postmodernity*, p. 10.
75. Mary Gluck, 'Toward a Historical Definition of Modernism: Georg Lukacs and the Avant-Garde', *Journal of Modern History*, 58:4 (1986). David Harvey associates the genuine with vital force, a primitive, Dionysian and thoroughly Edwardian association. My discussion draws on Harvey's periodisation of modernity, in *Condition of Postmodernity*.
76. Marsden, *FW*, 8 Aug. 1912, 222, emphasis added.

CHAPTER 7

The genius and the superwoman: feminist appropriations

'The feminist movement has evolved its superwoman ...'[1]

While eulogies to the premodern age now read as a curious route to affirm modern values, the utopian thinking discussed above has more resonance today than another discourse of 'modernity' which became associated with feminism – that of the genius or 'superwoman'. Indeed, one of the most challenging features of avant-garde feminism for the historian is its identification of the ideal feminist subject as a 'superior being'. This chapter asks why the idea of the genius or superwoman was so compelling and central for Edwardian feminists. The Victorian and Edwardian debates on genius have generated a recent feminist commentary on how women have been excluded from the canon of the great, but this literature has not examined how the women's movement positively engaged with what it was to be a genius or superwoman.[2] 'Genius', however, was not just another concept in the arsenal of the anti-feminists, but was foundational to some constructions of feminism. Teresa Billington-Greig proposed in 1911 that the feminist movement of the future must be 'a movement to make possible supermen and superwomen'.[3] This was not an isolated statement, but a persistent interest in Anglo-American feminism.

In characteristic terms, Florence Tuttle argued that feminism 'will have its most direct racial results in a keener appreciation of genius in the young and a more widespread appreciation of its value to society'. Isadora Duncan's language was saturated with a sense of the coming new age of superwomen. She wrote of the perfectibility of the 'dancer of the future': 'Her movements will become godlike', and she would be a 'perfect mother'. The role of the women's movement today was to 'prepare the place for her. I would build for her a temple to await her', Duncan wrote in 1903. Yet the question of women's genius continued to be a contested one; Rebecca West noted in 1912 that 'the worst of being a feminist is that one has no evidence. Women are capable of all things, yet, inconveniently, they will not be geniuses.' In 1925, the American journalist Sylvia Kopald was still asking 'where are the female geniuses?'[4]

The fascination with genius and the superwoman throughout the Edwardian women's movement has been seen as an aberration, clearly at odds with the feminist keystone of equality, and only of interest to isolated and 'marginal' groups. Some have seen it as prompted only by the anti-feminist argument that no women had been geniuses – feminists were simply responding to this agenda, and were not themselves interested in the idea of genius. Another interpretation is to see the feminist fascination with genius not as elitist, but as an equality strategy; as the historian Flavia Alaya saw it, 'feminists seemed obliged to justify the social and political *equality* of women ... by proving the capacity of women to be *exceptional*'.[5] If some women were exceptional, then all deserved political rights and social freedoms.

While this may have been a strategy for some Edwardian women, it gains explanatory force through posing Edwardian feminist concerns in terms that are comprehensible and attractive to us a century later. Yet equality was not foundational to Edwardian constructions of genius. Some feminists had a genuine belief that progress would only arise from exceptionality, and was therefore key to feminist hopes for social change. I aim to contextualise this belief, showing how in keeping it was with Edwardian political argument, while also suggesting some of the difficulties this entailed. Previous chapters have outlined the individualist, anti-statist politics of avant-garde feminism. This chapter completes the examination of the political argument of Edwardian feminism, by exploring the contested construction of the superwoman-genius, as the political and creative agent within this feminist politics. In doing so, it extends an overarching theme of this entire study – the diverse ways in which feminist thinkers engaged with self-consciously 'modern' explorations of the self.

THEORIES OF GENIUS

The roots of Edwardian theories of genius can be found in the intellectual prominence of the idea of elite rule in the nineteenth and early twentieth centuries.[6] This aspect of the literature on genius was concerned with the central political issues of how society should be organised around 'greatness', and how genius could be harnessed to the needs of a race or nation. A. R. Orage, editor of *The New Age*, wrote that 'the question to be asked of every institution is whether it makes for the creation of a superior type'.[7]

These comments capture the focus of much political and utopian thinking of this period. Innovation was to come from the front, from a few gifted individuals. Edwardians witnessed the development and popularisation of what might be called 'aristocratic' political thought, celebrating the contribution of 'the great man', and denigrating the servility of the herd, most notably in the brief *aube-de-siècle* popularity of thinkers such as Friedrich Nietzsche and Max Stirner.

The concept of a genius was never clear for the Edwardians – it was a period of shifts in meaning. The idea of the genius as a uniquely gifted individual had become significant from the mid-eighteenth century, and later became a key concept of Romantic thought. It became associated with the sublime, with lack of interest in material possessions and unconventionality. Genius-status was potentially available to all, an inclusive concept to which all might aspire. It was thus used in progressive discourse as a concept with democratic potential, and this persisted into the nineteenth century. The genius was to act as an agent of social renewal.[8] This well-known idea of Romantic genius is the starting point for understanding the more elusive Edwardian concepts of genius.

In the mid- to late nineteenth century, a changing conception of genius can be perceived, typified by the work of the British scientist Francis Galton. Galton's 1869 study, *Hereditary Genius*, attempted to redefine genius from a universal human capacity to an embodied type, found within certain 'great' families. Genius was thus shifting from a broad aspirational ideal towards a much more limited and elitist concept of individual greatness. This 'closing down' of genius was also heightened by Galton's belief that 'high reputation is a pretty accurate test of high ability'. He could not allow that genius capacities might be suppressed by environment, arguing that 'if a man is gifted with vast intellectual ability, eagerness to work and power of working, I cannot comprehend how such a man should be repressed'. The common argument from the women's movement, that women's genius existed but had been stifled, was thus ruled out; for Galton, if women were not eminent, it was definitely because of lack of *ability*.[9]

Genius was also shifting from a spiritual or poetic ideal towards an empirical, measurable one. Galton's work suggested that genius could be confirmed by skull size, skin and eye colouring and so on. This quantification and narrowing of genius was continued into the Edwardian period by the work of Havelock Ellis, a pre-eminent British contributor to the new science of sexology, whose work had achieved wide circulation in the United States from around 1895. Ellis' 1904 study of British genius gave an account based upon flows of 'mental energy' and development of the nervous system. He defined genius, somewhat vaguely, as 'a highly sensitive and complexly developed adjustment of the nervous system along special lines'. It took the form of 'intense cerebral energy', directed along a 'limited path'. Mechanical imagery conveyed his meaning: the 'cerebral energy of intellectual reaction' was like 'a high pressure tension' that might 'fall out of gear' if the 'expenditure of tissue' was not constantly repaired.[10]

Ellis was at root committed to the empirical and hereditary model of Galton. His work indicates another shift in the discourse of genius, from the unconventional, excessive Romantic genius to a more conventional idea of eminence, measured by public recognition. 'Eminence', indicated through being listed in the *Dictionary of National Biography*, gave Ellis his population of geniuses. But his concept of genius still had clear links to the constellation of ideas associated with Romantic genius. Like the Romantics, Ellis felt that the genius was an 'exfoliating' agent of 'life renewal', and his account of genius was associated with strong passions, imagination, the unconscious, and sexual drives.[11]

Sexual energy or, as it was sometimes described, 'vital force', was a more successful idiom than the mechanical analogy described above, and references to 'vital force', 'life force' or 'energy' are common in Edwardian descriptions of what it was to be a gifted person or a leader. Vitalism can loosely be described as the postulation of a 'life force' additional to mechanics or chemistry as an explanatory device in science. It had been discarded as a scientific theory for Edwardians, but remained influential as a social ideology. Since 'cerebral' or 'nervous' energy could not be easily described, 'vital force' or 'sexual energy' provided a means of understanding what distinguished the genius from non-genius. Ellis argued 'In men the sexual instinct is a restless source of energy which overflows into all sorts of channels', and he described creativity as 'a male secondary sexual character, in the same sense as a beard'. This of course excluded women, whose sexual energy was to be directed towards carework. Ellis' account of British genius gave a ratio of one eminent woman to every eighteen eminent men; genius was possible in women, but rare.[12] Having devoted pages in his earlier study of the sexes, *Man and Woman*, to describing women's docility, receptiveness, inattention to detail etc., he noted rather nervously: 'No inferiority is hereby attributed to women. It is perhaps even possible to attribute an equality of genius to women if we are prepared to recognise that quality outside the spheres of art and science in the wider spheres of concrete life.' Such feminine genius, he argued, was found in social work, and in love. Ellis preferred to see women's genius as complementary to the male, operating in the spheres men could not access. This was in part due to women's 'dispersal' of energy or 'vital force' through reproduction:

The claims of reproductive and domestic life are in women too preponderant and imperious to be easily conciliated with the claims of a life of intellectual labour ... Among British women of genius very few marriages take place during the period of great reproductive energy.[13]

A 1913 investigation into 'the sexual correlations of poetic genius' published in the *English Review* concluded 'In woman, the continual recurrence of physical crises ... does not allow the phases of internal sensibility ever to pass into the second rank; and the effect of this is ceaselessly to deteriorate and divert her poetic genius'. Though sexual energy in men was closely related to genius, women's link to the sexual sphere disqualified them from genius. This can be attributed to the way gender functioned in theories of genius as an organising metaphor; 'genius' was a concept in transition, and the distinction between non-genius and genius was not clearly defined for Victorians and Edwardians. Where gender was used as a metaphor for genius, it gave clearer definition to the distinction between genius and non-genius, since it was a less nebulous concept. Where a distinction or categorisation is weak or not evident, or rhetorical power is needed, an organising metaphor can be brought to bear. Gender was a well-recognised dualism that could shore up less well-recognised ones. As Edwardian sexologists described it in 'vital force' terminology, femininity was 'anabolic', a preservative or 'storing' force that directed them towards reproduction. Masculinity by contrast was 'katabolic', a destructive or 'spending' force, which held the creative potential that underlay genius. Cesare Lombroso, in his study of genius, had described women as 'conservators': 'Like children', he argued, 'they are notoriously misoneistic; they preserve ancient habits and customs and religions'.[14]

This belief was widely held by both feminists and non-feminists. Millicent Murby, a feminist *Freewoman* and *New Age* contributor, argued for example that 'the male function animates and vivifies – the female enfolds and nourishes and plays the great constructive part'.[15] The idea of genius as a channelling of the (male) life-force in the nervous system was not compatible with the idea that women's life-force might be similarly channelled; gender functioned as a discursive framework that helped organise the boundaries of 'genius' to the exclusion of women.

ANDROGYNOUS GENIUS

Although Ellis was clear that genius 'while by no means confined to one sex, is yet predominantly associated with one sex', he followed popular theories in accepting that there was an element of androgyny in genius:

In persons of genius of either sex there is a tendency for something of the man, the woman, and the child to coexist ... Genius carries us into a region where the strongly-differentiated signs of masculinity or femininity ... are of little significance.[16]

Ellis' concession to androgyny resonated with the development of a distinct theory of androgynous genius by Otto Weininger, an Austrian theorist of genius, in *Sex and Character*. Weininger denied that genius was hereditary, and offered a competing theory to Ellis and Galton. His popular study, published in English in 1906, had sought an explanation for genius in the distribution of what he referred to as sexual plasms M and F – entities that can be seen as vehicles for the gender differentiated 'vital force' described above. Weininger believed that all individuals were bisexual, in that all were made up of different proportions of male and female plasm: 'Any individual, "A" or "B", is never to be designated merely as a man or a woman, but by a formula showing that it is a composite of male and female characters in different proportions'. This allowed a 'mathematical' construction of sexuality, according to a formula of the proportions of M and F in each partner:

For true sexual union it is necessary that there come together a complete male (M) and a complete female (F), even although in different cases the M and F are distributed between the two individuals in different proportions.

While Weininger was commonly regarded by his contemporaries as insane and was entirely rejected by 'respectable' suffragists in Britain and America, he captivated avant-garde thinkers. He was quoted by feminists with fascination, though not universal approval, and some chapters of *Sex and Character* were reproduced in *The Freewoman*. W. L. George argued within an American journal, 'the Feminists argue that there are no men and that there are no women; there are only sexual majorities. To put the matter less obscurely, the Feminists base themselves on Weininger's theory, according to which the male principle may be found in woman, and the female principle in man. It follows that they recognize no masculine or feminine "*spheres*", and that they propose to identify absolutely the conditions of the sexes.' Though George was probably overstating the case,

Weininger offered a solution to 'the woman question' that feminists found it necessary to address; as Charlotte Perkins Gilman pointed out, he carried 'the ultra-masculine view of woman' to its logical conclusion, and therefore had to be engaged with. Weininger had argued, 'So long as there are two sexes there will always be a woman question, just as there will always be the problem of mankind ... Truth will not prevail until the two become one, until from man and woman a third self, neither man nor woman, is evolved.'[17]

The idea of the third sex was not a new one, but Weininger brought it to a new level of visibility in European and American thought. His work was frequently cited and discussed in radical periodicals such as *The New Age*, and was referred to with familiarity, needing little introduction to readers. Why did his 'algebra' of sexual desire have such an impact on Edwardian intellectual life? There was a radical potential to Weininger's theory that made it extremely attractive to all kinds of progressive thinkers. Weininger regarded homosexuality as natural, and argued that all should be free to find their complementary partner in a love marriage, even if this was a person of the same sex: 'the only logical and rational method of treatment for sexual inverts would be to allow them to seek and obtain what they require where they can, that is to say, amongst other inverts'.

His postulation of 'a permanent bisexual condition' allowed him to argue that sexual differentiation was arbitrary, and he vividly described the process of crude, dualistic sexual differentiation as pressing humanity 'as by a vice into distinctive moulds'. What is more, all individuals were subject to 'oscillations' between the plasms, with the female and male aspects of their sexual make-up periodically acting with greater influence. Thus not only were all potentially bisexual, but one could not be sure from moment to moment of one's sexuality; all was rendered fluid and uncertain. He drew on new languages of sexology, avidly discussed in Europe and the United States in the early twentieth century. While 'advanced' feminists recognised sexology as in some senses 'anti-feminist', it could be used to suggest, as Elsie Clews Parsons wrote, 'that sex is not an [in] eradicable, immutable character in any given individual ... The day may come when the individual may be free to express sex, its sex, let us say, when it wishes to ... nor will any individual have to pretend to be possessed of a given quota of femaleness and maleness. This morning perhaps I may feel like a male; let me act like one. This afternoon I may feel like a female; let me act like one. At midday or at midnight I may feel sexless.'[18]

However, Weininger's discussion of human character was less motivated by the sexual reform agenda than by an interest in the 'higher individual'; he aimed to write a 'characterology' that would assess what kinds of character features contributed to greatness. He saw the genius as the pinnacle of personal development, latent within all men and achievable by effort of will. In addition, he had concluded that 'homo-sexuality is a higher form than hetero-sexuality', better disposed to genius. The highest forms of evolution would be androgynous, forming a 'third sex'.

This was not an original view, having been argued by Schopenhauer in the first half of the nineteenth century, by Nietzsche, and in Britain by Edward Carpenter in the 1890s. While Carpenter idealised the 'third sex', many commentators argued that 'uranians' were atavistic and degenerate.[19] Weininger's originality was in his assertion that all were to some extent homosexual, and thus all could aspire to genius. Yet he revealed extreme anxiety at the clear implication of his argument, that women could also expect to aspire to genius. Weininger constantly reiterated that the most gifted of men were likely to be those with high proportions of femininity. The genius was one who 'possesses, like everything else, the complete female in himself'. Yet the feminine plasm was *by definition* without any capacity for genius. He argued:

the female must be described as absolutely without the quality of genius ... There is no female genius, and there never has been one ... *and there never can be one* ... A female genius is a contradiction in terms, for genius is simply intensified, perfectly developed, universally conscious maleness.[20]

The tone of this quote shows how disturbing Weininger found the idea of female genius. He took refuge in a fixed gender polarity that denied the gender fluidity of his own theory, arguing, somewhat unconvincingly, that 'in spite of all sexually intermediate conditions, human beings are always one of two things, either male or female'. Weininger arbitrarily decreed that it was not possible for 'M' to exceed 50 per cent in a 'female', though men of the highest type might well have more than 50 per cent 'F'.

Overall, neither Ellis' nor Weininger's theories of genius could accept a feminine subject. They offered contrasting theories of genius, each with 'progressive' potential. Their theories reveal the way in which genius was an uncertain, contested idea for the Edwardians. But they agreed on their exclusion of women – both required a genius who resembled a woman, or took on feminine characteristics, but could not be 'biologically' female. At root, their theories were based on a 'vital economy' of male sexual energy as creative. Women's life force was widely accepted to be of a conservative kind, unsuitable to creative experimentation. Gender provided an organising metaphor for genius, and provoked anxiety when genius was claimed by real women. The response to women's claims through the discourses of genius on offer was to clamp down on women's aspirations through a polarised and arbitrary sexual economy and appeals to gendered 'life force'.

To what extent was this discourse of genius established transatlantically? An article on 'Recent Theories of Genius' published in an American psychology journal in June 1905 stressed the scientific theories of genius such as that offered by Lombroso, complemented by the popular theories of psychology, where genius represented a 'mystical flowering of a mysterious secondary personality', based in the unconscious.[21] Psychology, in its mystical or its scientific forms, was better established in the United States than in Europe, and this made for a distinctive way of examining genius, with less stress on the pathological forms it might take. It was argued in inclusive terms that genius was an 'excess of normal vitality'. Following the influential American psychologist Stanley Hall, it was widely believed that all children would have some degree of genius. There was much conflict over the nature of genius, but most saw it as 'a higher development of healthy, normal functions', rather than the 'neuropathic' explanation of Lombroso.

The theory of genius as insanity did however persist in American intellectual debate; a *Washington Post* 1912 article, quoting British experts Ellis and Henry Maudsley, argued that genius was pathological, but this was a controversial and minority view.[22] A 1913 article in *Harper's Weekly* by H. Addington Bruce (a writer known for his work on the history of women's achievements in America) confirmed the more inclusive view, arguing that geniuses were 'indications of possibilities open to the generality of mankind'. Following the work of British spiritualist F. W. H. Myers, Bruce argued that genius was 'the resultant neither of an inborn abnormality nor of an inborn supernormality', but was 'latent in all normal men and women'.[23]

Other writers on genius used a hereditarian model along the lines of Galton and Ellis. In 1912, the *Washington Post* reported on some research which had traced the lines of descent of 'great individuals' from one original 'Superman'. Florence Tuttle, who portrayed the question of genius as central to feminism, used Galton's work as her key reference point for theories of genius; Galton, Ellis and, later, Karl Pearson, with their shared eugenic-evolutionary theories of genius, were all influential in the United States.[24] Otto Weininger was also read but, as in Britain, was more influential upon the avant-garde and modernist poets like William

Carlos Williams than the scientific community. The popular elaboration of European studies of genius in America was more democratic, and possibly more open to women, than in Britain.

What impact did these theories of genius and 'life force' have on political thought? The shift from a universal to a more elitist idea of genius resonated with, and had perhaps informed, a turn within late nineteenth- and early twentieth-century political thought towards a more aristocratic and elitist form of politics. This was found quite broadly, and in very varying form, in European and American political thought. Elitism characterised American progressives and British Fabians. The exceptional or great individual might provide leadership – perhaps national leadership, or leadership for the whole process of human evolution.

Political thinkers saw the problem of leadership in terms of the move to a wider democracy, and this was a particularly powerful issue in the United States. The progressive era was marked by an ambivalence towards democratic reform. The influential progressive journalist Herbert Croly, editor of the *New Republic*, argued that despite his commitment to democracy, 'the essential wholeness of the community depends absolutely on the ceaseless creation of a political, economic, and social aristocracy and their equally incessant replacement'. He envisaged a 'constructive' individualism, in which an elite could govern through patriotic disinterestedness, with strong executive leadership. William James outlined in 1907 the American 'democratic problem': 'Who are the kind of men from whom our majorities shall take their cue?' He sought elites that would act as 'the yeast-cake for democracy's dough'.[25]

The fascination with elites and aristocracies is unsurprising amongst conservative thinkers who had long held that, as the British conservative W. H. Mallock put it, 'the strongest human powers and the highest human faculties ... are embodied in and monopolised by a minority of exceptional men'. But forms of elitism were also found among more radical and controversial thinkers. Ralph Waldo Emerson had lectured in Britain and the United States between 1845 and 1850 on the topic of genius and 'representative men'. He believed that while genius was only available to the few, it should serve to benefit the many and was dangerous if it did not – a 'New World', democratic version of individual greatness that was characteristic of the mid-nineteenth century. Emerson later wrote of the 'unexpected greatness of the common farmer and labourer'.[26]

Others, however, saw genius and greatness as less quotidian, and more about leadership and superior powers. John Ruskin had proposed in 1860 'the eternal superiority of some men to others, sometimes even of one man to all others'; and thus 'the advisability of appointing such persons or person to guide, to lead, or on occasion even to compel and subdue, their inferiors'.[27] Ruskin, ever ambiguous in his politics, did not make it clear from where this kind of leader would be drawn. Others believed that it was those normally on the margins of politics who might, through their outsider status, gain special political insight. The playwright, Ibsen, an influential figure for the women's movement, believed in a version of aristocratic rule 'from below'. A statement from him formed the masthead of the 1890s British 'feminist' journal *Shafts*:

Mere DEMOCRACY cannot solve the social question. An element of ARISTOCRACY must be introduced into our life. Of course, I do not mean the aristocracy of birth, or of the purse, or even the aristocracy of intellect. I mean the aristocracy of character, of will, of mind. That only can free us. From two groups will this aristocracy I hope for come to our people: from our WOMEN and from our WORKMEN ...

The idea of the women's and working-class movements as seed-beds for a new 'aristocracy' was already prominent in the 1890s, particularly amongst British Fabian and ILP circles. The preference for the rule of experts was not only found in H. G. Wells' fantasies of elite 'samurai', but also flourished in the women's movement on both sides of the Atlantic. Suffragist leaders, while promoting a wider democracy, sometimes did so in terms of a leadership by elite women. Carrie Chapman Catt of the NAWSA described herself as 'an aristocrat with democratic leanings'. She had noted 'I am a *good* democrat in theory but my faith weakens when it meets bad air ... and horrid smells', and she could not situate political virtues amongst working-class or immigrant communities. Feminists such as Mona Caird were also sceptical of the self-knowledge of the 'average woman'. Caird believed that women were socialised to squash unorthodox opinions at the subconscious level. 'Popular suggestion' dominated their emotions and beliefs, and it was only 'an exceptional woman here and there – criticised and condemned by her contemporaries with amazement and horror' who could provide any kind of genuine testimony about woman's nature.[28]

Even critics of egoism such as Ellen Key argued that the women's movement aimed to establish a new kind of 'genius', who would express both male and female attributes. She conceded that 'Individualism is right in demanding ample space for the great personality ... The essence of genius is an overflow of forces, a rapture of inspiration, an infinity, which demands altogether different conditions for its creative power, especially in art, from those applicable to ordinary men.' Key acknowledged the danger that 'the many, "the herd", would outvoice the few with their claims'.[29] Key's concessions to genius indicate how widespread the idiom of elitist, aristocratic thinking had become in this period.

Impetus for the elaboration of elitism amongst some Edwardians can be traced to the popularisation of the ideas of Max Stirner and Nietzsche. For Stirner, oppressive institutions were sustained through the recognition the oppressed gave to the masters and hegemonic institutions. The genius, or egoist, was the individual who did not accord such recognition. To follow one's own impulses gave one absolute freedom from oppression. The entire focus of political change thus lay in the deployment of 'the will' and the agent's ability to self-overcome. Politics could serve the needs of the few, because in them were the seeds of the future, while the rest could be variously disregarded as the 'herd', 'crowd' or residuum, whose utility and fulfilment was unimportant.

Stirner was relatively uninterested in leadership, though he believed that only a few could embody egoist morality. Nietzsche's concept of the *Ubermensch*, however, gave egoist morality a significance for Edwardian readers that was variously interpreted in terms of leadership of the nation, the race, or humanity.[30] Nietzschean and Stirnean rhetoric was widespread in Edwardian texts between 1902 and 1912 – the British editor A. R. Orage declared in 1907, in highly Nietzschean terms, 'All the tragical history of man would be nothing better than a meaningless comedy were it not that such a history can be regarded as the pre-natal condition of a superior and justifying species'.[31] In 1912, Havelock Ellis expounded Nietzsche's ideas in an important series of articles in the American periodical *The Savoy*. Nietzsche quickly became highly influential upon American writers and literary critics, though American disciples had a tendency to read Nietzsche's superman as a biological rather than a spiritual entity.[32] But both American and British interpreters agreed that in order to achieve the superior race, mass struggle was to be abandoned, and the focus of politics was to be internal and individualised. The entire focus of political change thus lay in the deployment of 'the will' and the agent's ability to self-overcome.

The introspective focus of nineteenth-century Romantic genius was combined with Nietzschean aristocracy, to form a more powerfully elitist politics of the Romantic superman. As a *New Age* contributor described it in 1908,

Emerson and Carlyle [taught] that all can be supermen, individualities, representative men. Theirs is the Individualism of the Reformation preached by Luther. The Individualism of Nietzsche, however, is aristocratic. There must be ordinary men if there are to be supermen. Only the latter are the individualists. Theirs is a different morality from that of the masses.[33]

The genius came to be a remote figure, who had overcome weaknesses and constraints through the power of the will. This trend can be summarised by seeing Edwardian ideas of genius as politically on the cusp, between a Romantic idea of the superman as a regenerative life force, to what approached modernist ideas of the genius as a recluse from the intolerable modern world. The Edwardian superman hovered uneasily between these two meanings, drawing on the unconventionality of the Romantic discourse, as well as the aloofness of early modernist ideas. The Romantic 'outsider' who 'exfoliated' society became what some termed a 'superman', an 'illegible authority' who turned his back on humanity.[34]

Nietzschean political philosophy appealed strongly to Anglo-American modernist thinkers, with their focus on the uniqueness and social atomism of genius figures. The idea of the genius, previously an aspirational, even democratic figure, could now be seen as the individual who threw off oppression through the cultivation of 'egoist personality'. This, as we shall see later on, was extremely significant for some feminist thinkers.

SUPERMEN AND SUPERWOMEN

The 'super' prefix was widely used by Edwardians, with references to 'super-athletes', 'super-ladies', 'supermanity', and so on abounding in the periodical press.[35] Walt Whitman had in 1855 eulogised the 'superbest man'. The American anarchist writer James Walker had argued later in the nineteenth century that 'We will not allow the world to wait for the Superman. We are the Supermen'; the term was circulating in American political argument, and became increasingly important in the early twentieth century.[36] 'Superman', a translation from the German *Ubermensch*, became better known among Edwardians through the popularity of Nietzsche and through George Bernard Shaw's adoption of the term in his 1903 play, *Man and Superman*. The American *Reader's Guide to Periodical Literature* listed both 'superman' and 'superwoman' in its indices covering 1905–19, though neither term appeared before or after these dates.

Shaw situated his use of 'superman' as a political move: 'the need for the Superman is, in its most imperative aspect, a political one', posed by the failures of what he termed 'Proletarian Democracy'. The British Fabian writer, Mabel Atkinson, argued that the superman would represent 'a democracy that levels up and not down'; 'supermen cannot be bred in slums', she concluded.[37] This concern with democracy was particularly important to feminists, who felt that their arguments for suffrage were vulnerable to the 'levelling down' accusation.

In the United States, suffragists argued in racial terms that women's suffrage would increase the 'American-born vote' and decrease 'our uneducated and foreign-born vote'. In Britain, Dora Marsden argued that suffragism 'has to find its defence against the criticisms which are attacking popular democracy … [because] the immediate application of feminist ideals would bring to democracy a preponderating volume of its supposed dangers and difficulties'.[38] The superman and superwoman were used as utopian devices, to describe a democracy of superior types that was not threatened by the uneducated (feminised) masses. But this was a minority usage; most who used the idea of the superman took it to be an anti-democratic ideal, a means of bypassing democracy and constructing a new and frequently aristocratic utopian order.

Two key explanations can be offered for the resonance 'the superman' had in the Edwardian period. First, it can be seen as a political and aesthetic reaction to the massification of modern life.[39] There was a strong concern among Edwardians that the higher elements of life should not be swamped by the increasing massification of political and cultural life. The growth of the mass was found in a great variety of guises – in the 'yellow' press and its development of mass advertising, in urbanisation, and the mass education. The actual and threatened expansions of the suffrage had made a reality of mass politics; in the United States the immigrant vote epitomised the democratic dominance of the uneducated.

Dislike of these developments was widely expressed; the New Liberal political theorist Graham Wallas, for example, was anxious about the effect on politics of 'working men who have passed through the standards of the elementary schools, and who live in hundreds of square miles of new, healthy, indistinguishable suburban streets'. Wallas was part of a group of elitist liberals, many of them Fabians. This group continued a trend in nineteenth-century liberalism, in seeing democracy as incompatible with personal liberty and efficient public service. Reba Soffer has outlined this and other strands of Edwardian thought that were critical of mass democracy, and embraced an elitist solution. She describes the growth of an elitist social psychology, led by William McDougall and Wilfred Trotter, whose political aim was to declare democracy to be incompatible with the crowd instincts of human nature.[40] Likewise, a critique of democracy came from the biological evolutionary thinking of Galton, Karl Pearson and other eugenicists.

These discourses were also influential upon the 'advanced' or bohemian thinkers who surrounded and formed the feminist avant-garde. Randolph Bourne, for example, wrote to Elsie Clews Parsons, 'I begin to wonder whether there aren't advantages in having the administration of the state taken care of by a scientific body of men with a social sense, or perhaps rather an aesthetic-scientific idea of a desirable urban life'. He bemoaned the 'sluggish masses that can only be moved by words so vague as not to mean anything' who had come to dominate in a mass democracy. These different permutations of fear of 'the mass' and its new political power made the idea of the superman popular, as a means of transcending or neutralising the masses. Genius clearly had other meanings, and cannot be wholly elided with 'superman'. But genius had perhaps become so conventional through its association by Galton and Ellis with eminence and great families that progressives required a new and more radical, inspirational agent for social change.[41] The superman provided a means for progressives to talk about 'superior types' in a politically neutral way, avoiding the conventionality of 'genius' and the class and 'Tory' overtones of 'aristocratic' discourse.

Second, the interest in 'the superman' was not only a political one, but also spiritual or occult. Historians have traced a rising Victorian and Edwardian interest in spiritual, mystical or esoteric philosophy and practices. A belief in self-transformation and inner exploration characterised many occult groups, within which women found support for their leadership and a willingness to think outside of conventional morality. The self that was to be explored was often understood as multiple or fragmented, made up of many levels of consciousness, though ultimately, in contrast to psychological explorations of the self, the ego remained self-aware and controlling. This preoccupation with consciousness and the self was, for some historians, what made the 1890s and early decades of the twentieth century 'modern'.[42]

Psychology was a related 'modern' discourse that provided a means of investigating 'higher' and 'lower' forms of the self. The language of 'new psychology' and theosophy gave expression to the desire among feminists such as Mabel Dodge Luhan, Charlotte Despard, Frances Swiney, and others in avant-garde circles to explore new stages of mental evolution, beyond consciousness or representing a higher consciousness appropriate to the modern 'super-world'. The development of Edwardian psychology and Edwardian readings of Freudian psychoanalysis framed the interest in superman and superwoman. Psychologists' undermining of the unitary self, however, made this discourse less suitable than esoteric or spiritualist ideas for those who wanted to explore the 'superhuman', since this was usually understood as implying a self-aware, transcendent and 'perfected' individual consciousness, rather than a fragmented one.

In an age marked by competing secular and spiritual claims, George Bernard Shaw argued in *Man and Superman* that life force as the basis of all evolution would 'build up that raw force into higher and higher individuals, the ideal individual being omnipotent, infallible, and withal completely, unilludedly self-conscious: in short, a god'.[43] A key assumption for Edwardian spiritualists was the god-like nature or perfectibility of humans, expressed through the idea of the superman. Amongst theosophists and members of esoteric groups, the idea of the 'Superhuman', 'Higher Self', 'Permanent Self', 'Genius' or 'Perfect Man' had wide currency, and implied a new gender order. Many argued that sex would be transcended by the superman, or even saw the superman as 'feminine', despite the gender dissonance this implied. Florence Farr, a feminist actress, theatre critic and member of the Hermetic Order of the Golden Dawn, argued in *The New Age* that 'the state of consciousness, now identified by leading modern thinkers as the state called superman, is mystically feminine'.[44] As the theosophist writer Frances Swiney saw it, Women 'are the sole means by which human evolution can proceed. Physiologically they are the most complex and highly specialised of organic forms; psychologically they are the most highly evolved.' Portraying herself as 'the prophet of the Superman', she sought 'the full and perfect development of that basic factor – motherhood – upon which the future of the race depends'.[45] Such arguments tended to come back to women as mothers, and this meshed with the widespread belief that women's vital force was 'preservative'.

An additional connotation of 'superman' was one of breeding and racial selection. Writers spanning the political spectrum explored ideas of racial purity, degeneration and regeneration. The Nietzschean superman, and his counterpart, the 'sub-man', provided an avant-garde means of talking about 'degenerates', and the need to select for a racial aristocracy. Dan Stone has charted the links between eugenicists, race theorists and the idea of the superman, and makes a case for a 'widespread acceptance of racial explanations for social and historical processes' in Edwardian Britain.[46] There was a racial element to this political turn towards aristocracy, though some recent historians have suggested that British racial discourse was not dominated by 'scientific racism', but was more multi-faced, working not only to construct and control racial 'others', but also to relate individuals to their past and positively shape their self-identity. Degeneration and race thinking also incorporated a gender dimension. Stone notes the anxiety of such thinkers over the 'new woman' and feminism more generally; Nietzschean eugenicists such as Maximilian Mügge specifically looked for manliness as a key quality for the superman.[47] As we shall see below, this perhaps made proponents of the superwoman wary of the associated vocabulary of racial degeneration, though they retained the language of spiritual or personal regeneration.

Despite its wide usage, 'Superman' was certainly not a word that gained unquestioned acceptance. It seems to have slipped out of usage in Britain after the First World War, when the ' "super" cult, both male and female' became associated with 'the Teutonic lust of world power' and 'the Hun'. A 1921 dictionary described 'superman' as 'a foolish word', used 'to express an ideal very popular with those to whom nature has denied a pair of shoulders and other virile attributes'.[48] Nonetheless, in the years preceding the war the superman was described by the British journal, *The Englishwoman*, as 'humanity's last and noblest aspiration'. Given this interest in the superman from feminists, it was unsurprising that the neologism 'superwoman' soon came into use. It was needed because of the strong masculine overtones of 'superman' – contemporary dictionaries explicitly pointed out that the superman was male.

FEMINISTS AND SUPERWOMEN

In December 1905, writing for the *New York Times Saturday Review*, the British feminist May Sinclair contributed a satirical dialogue titled 'Man and Superman: A Symposium'. She introduced American audiences to a novel term that was already circulating in Britain, 'the Super-Woman'. In vitalist terms, Sinclair defined her as 'that other and not altogether irrelevant expression of the life-force'. 'Superwoman' became increasingly common from around this time. This was perhaps spurred by the construction of the woman question by 'advanced' and feminist thinkers such as Gilman and Schreiner as centrally concerned with women's atavism and its effects in 'slowing down' racial evolution. In 1910, the Bernard Shaw Fellowship in New York could not agree on the nature of the superman, but all reportedly agreed that it was the superwoman who would produce him and who should therefore be the focus of debate.[49] In the following decade, 'superwoman' was still being given a tentative status by quote marks and varying uses of capitalisation, but it had become well established in 'advanced' feminist periodicals and texts, along with discussions of women's genius.

The pre-war prevalence of 'superwoman' indicates the presence of a debate within feminism that has rarely been discussed. In part because it does not fit with our contemporary expectations of feminist principles, we are troubled by the desire within a subsection of the feminist movement to develop a movement for superwomen, an elitist feminism that would meet the needs of 'higher types'. The debates on the superman and genius discussed above help to contextualise this interest in the superwoman, and suggest that it was very much in keeping with the political argument of the time. The editor of a 1917 British feminist text argued 'The greatness of a society increases in proportion to the number of individuals who are perfectly developed'; many feminists saw it as their goal to conceive of such a society. An American follower of Ellen Key and Henri Bergson termed the whole 'world-wide movement for women's freedom' as one of the evolution of genius.[50]

This focus was motivated for some by their strong sense that the expansionist powers of the state and the law needed to be resisted. The anti-statism that Chapter 4 showed to be characteristic of the feminist avant-garde could easily translate into various constructions of aristocratic elitism. Self-described British 'feminist' W. L. George argued in the American press that 'Every man is in himself a minority, and is opposed to the law because the law is the expression of the will of the majority, that is to say, the will of the vulgar, of the norm'. His feminism, therefore, was a kind of Nietzschean anarchism, and he saw rejection of 'the crowd' or 'the norm' as one of its major elements:

Resignation, humility, and self-sacrifice have for a thousand generations been the worst vices of woman, but it is apparent that at last aggressiveness and selfishness are developing her towards nobility.[51]

There was a surprisingly robust engagement with the question of genius, and desire to rise above the 'vulgar' crowd within the Edwardian women's movement. Some were motivated by a sense that women of genius were those who felt most keenly the confines of women's position. The suffragist Helena Swanwick argued: 'the woman who suffers most [from the tyranny of conventional femininity] is the biggest woman. The world suffers too, from the stunting or warping or exasperation of its strongest and most original female minds.' She felt that feminism should be addressed to these exceptional women, and should organise society to meet their needs. In this context, 'superwoman' could stand in as a potential subject for feminist aspirations. Feminists sought to use the discourse of Romantic genius, associated with the regenerative power of 'life force' and exercised by outsiders, to indicate their aim to transform society. Feminists, especially those of avant-garde inclinations, aimed to position feminism as a movement for social renewal, and 'genius' and 'super-woman' were attractive as concepts that conveyed this. Mary Austin, a Heterodoxy member and acknowledged 'authority' on feminism, published a 1912 novel titled *A Woman of Genius*, tracing 'the personal phases of genius' in one woman's quest for sexual and personal liberation.[52]

As we have seen, for most Edwardians, genius was emphatically gendered as masculine. However, writers such as Helena Swanwick sought to enlarge the spheres in which genius might operate, and thus make it more amenable to feminist ends. Swanwick, whose own pacifist and suffragist career was highly political, focused on political rather than creative genius, and argued: 'it seems very likely that [women] have genius in directions hitherto almost forbidden to them; I mean in organisation, and leadership, and in the power to govern'.[53] Feminist writers had started to think through what feminine versions of greatness and creativity would look like, through the concepts of the genius and the superwoman. Some sought to move the debate away from the Romantic or modernist trope of the lonely, tormented creative genius, resisting the closing down and narrowing of the idea of genius. Feminine genius was to look quite different, and might include such lowly, practical talents as that of organisation. Florence Tuttle argued that 'social creativeness is quite as important as the expression of artistic or inventive power'. The modern geniuses were to be settlement workers, prison reformers and the like.

In general, though, the rhetoric of the superwoman avoided such prosaic concerns, and provided a means for Edwardian feminists to signal their lack of interest in the 'trivial', mass, everyday politics of the suffrage, and address what was portrayed as a more fundamental level of 'self-emancipation'. This represents, I have argued, an 'introspective turn' in Edwardian feminism, a desire to seek liberation through internal transformation of one's psyche and sexual being. Emancipation, for many, depended on voluntaristic entities such as will and character. Though gaining political rights and equality with men were important concerns, they were in some sense subordinate to women's need to exercise will and develop personality. The Romantic ideal of self-overcoming within the genius literature resonated with feminist thought. Many significant feminist (and anti-feminist) texts of this period stress women's responsibility (or inability) to overcome their weaknesses and self-imposed constraints. In Olive Schreiner's influential *Woman and Labour*, for example, three out of six chapters are devoted to a discussion of 'parasitism' and the corrupted character of women; emancipation therefore lay in a determination to seize for oneself an independent lifestyle. Otto Weininger had argued, 'Who is the enemy? What are the retarding influences? The greatest, the one enemy of the emancipation of women is woman herself.'[54]

Though Weininger was recognised as an anti-feminist, his charge and his fascination with genius found resonance within the feminist movement, particularly within *The Freewoman* journal. As an American journal put it, 'the superwoman is the ultimate expression of that new philosophy of feminism preached by the daring "humanist" review, the London *Freewoman*'. The editor argued 'We consider that only those women who are gifted to the extent of genius can be Freewomen, and all the rest must be Bondwomen, i.e., followers, servants'.[55]

Contributors felt that modern conditions of 'mass-values' worked against genius. Charles Whitby bemoaned 'the sacrifice of the great to the small, the exceptional to the mediocre, the superman and superwoman to the manikins of both sexes'. Whitby pointed out 'the wretched life of the typical man of genius' under the current democratic and utilitarian politics of mass-values, and argued instead that 'those for whom [happiness] is synonymous with *ecstasy* shall set the tune of life'. An American correspondent, Edgar Ansel Mowrer, used *The New Freewoman* to bemoan 'The Dearth of Genius', in an age obsessed by its production. Another noted 'In *The New Freewoman* ... overmen have at last found an organ in which they can express their views'. With greater sensitivity to the gendering of superhumanity, Françoise Lafitte noted in her autobiography that her feminism was motivated by 'the comedy of superman toppling over underwoman'. She had come to believe in the motto: 'no common good without grand individuals', and this had led her to the Freewoman Discussion Circle.[56]

The Freewoman's stance was based upon a passionate and spiritual ideal of genius. Since the journal was independent and committed neither to suffrage nor democracy, it could consider radically elitist or inegalitarian political orders. The content of *The Freewoman* was saturated with the idea of 'great personality'. As Marsden put it, 'Moral institutions are dissolved, not by the multitude, but by the higher moral consciousness of the few. A handful of moral, thinking, articulate freewomen are more than a multitude of the unmoral, inarticulate bond. In these things the battle is decided by rank and not by numbers.'[57]

So how could women free themselves of their internal psychological constraints? According to Marsden, nothing but 'the sense that she is a superior, a master can give her the strength [to become a freewoman]'. Though she accepted that some external conditions had to be met, she was vastly more interested in the internal question of genius. If one had genius, one could undertake the hard and solitary process of self-transformation. She defined genius as an expression of 'Being' or alternatively, a form of passion – sexual passion, or passion arising from political action. Marsden's own experiences suggested that 'passion inspired by a Cause' might lead to higher forms of consciousness and vision, and she gave an account, in mystical terms, of her own prison experiences of revelation, probably while *hunger striking*:

Shut up for the night in the cell, suffering acute physical pain, with the quiet came an extraordinary sense of 'spirit' expansion. The sensation of increased size was the first marked, but this was followed by the sensation of unlimited power. There was, too, a conscious sense of lightness of weight, and a distinct 'seeing' of the atmosphere in vibration. The whole was suffused with the consciousness of calm, radiant, abiding joy. The entire experience lasted, how long cannot be stated, but it was extended enough to appear 'long'. It was extended enough for the mind to be able to move round in it and get its bearings.[58]

Like many influenced by vitalist and esoteric ideas, Marsden deployed a vocabulary of the 'super-world', similar in form to Havelock Ellis' description of genius as flows of nervous energy. Marsden also described the political recognition process Stirner had outlined as one of the same kinds of energy flows; she pointed out the waste of energy caused by rage against tyrants, energy better spent on self-transformation. One had a duty not to use up one's energy in useless opposition to the masters, but rather to make oneself a master. Marsden's somewhat vague definitions of the superwoman or freewoman were not intended to set up a broadly available and accessible concept of genius. She argued that 'great numbers of individuals are born without any creative power in regard to any sphere of life whatever', and reminded readers that 'not for one moment do we wish to support the view that all women will be free, any more than all men are free ... a feminist must make her appeal to freewomen, and not to "ordinary" women'.

Nonetheless, her version of the superwoman emphasised the power of sexual experimentation to allow a transcendence of the ordinary spheres of life; As Havelock Ellis had emphasised, it was possible to achieve higher states of consciousness or being through the power of sexuality. It was an important aspect of the *Freewoman* project to throw off the respectability and sexual conservatism that suffrage-feminists favoured. Fearful of anti-feminist comments about licentiousness and sexual disorder, few Edwardian suffragists were willing to risk their cause by commenting on women's sexuality, and preferred to emphasise women's civic responsibilities as mothers and workers. In contrast, the *Freewoman* version of the feminist-superwoman emphasised the power of sexual experimentation to allow a transcendence of the ordinary spheres of life; sexual energy, akin to vital force, was perceived as 'the democratic passion' which was 'within the reach of all' as a 'means of springing life higher'.[59] The superwoman thus fluctuated between an inherent 'superior type', marked off from the herd once and for all, and an embodied, sensual state of being that was accessible to all who chose to experiment with their sexuality.

The superwoman reflects the sense that 'the woman question' was above all one of feminine character or personality. The vote might be granted by external bodies, but it would do little to change women's position until women themselves had changed. Edna Kenton concluded:

The revolt of women is in reality as much against Woman as Man – both of those are capitalized impersonalities! The Woman movement is as much an expression of her self-contempt as of her aspiration.[60]

This question of character reveals a different set of concerns to those normally associated with the predominant suffrage-feminism of the period. As we have seen, rights were frequently not sought as just ends in themselves, but as tools to self-development. Charlotte Carmichael Stopes (mother of Marie Stopes) characteristically noted in 1911 that the strongest argument for the vote was the need 'to develop our individuality, to perform our duty, to fulfil our responsibility'. Another commentator described the vote as 'a staggering blow' to women convinced that they were the inferior sex.[61]

Suffrage, then, still provided a framework for understanding feminine psychological change for many in the women's movement. But avant-garde feminists, however, found one of the chief motivations for their interest in a superior elite of women in their negative experiences of the militant suffrage movement. Many had been or still were members of the Women's Social and Political Union (WSPU) or Women's Freedom League in Britain, while in the United States, the NAWSA continued to host some highly critical members. The British 'militant' groups can be seen as influenced by the shift towards 'aristocratic politics', and yet working in ways antagonistic to it. The aristocratic politics described above strongly emphasised the difference a few, committed individuals could make to the course of events, and one of the attractions of militant action to Edwardian women was their belief in the political impact of the few. The few would redeem the many, and the complete commitment of a select elite was preferred by the WSPU leadership to mass politics. A similar stance was taken by their National Woman's Party 'counterparts' in the United States. Moreover, the embrace of violent direct action could also be seen as a means of self-transformation. In overcoming timidity and the norms of feminine passivity, one might move closer to the ideal of the transcendent super-woman. In Nietzschean sounding terms, Christabel Pankhurst proclaimed 'It is slave morality that the militant women have denied and defied – slave morality according to which active resistance to tyranny is the greatest crime that a subject class or a subject sex can commit'.[62]

This power of militancy to create 'superwomen' and root out 'slave morality' was compromised, however, by the organisational demands of the suffrage groups. The 'militant' movement had served to crush the sense of self-worth and individuality that direct action might have developed, by demanding absolute obedience and self-subordination from its followers. Activists were required to act in a disciplined, regulated manner that allowed for no discovery of personal 'genius'.

The less dictatorial suffrage groups (NAWSA, NUWSS) were held by feminists to be guilty of conservative politics, an unwillingness to challenge conventions in regard to women. Suffragists of all affiliations continued to deploy the very discourses of femininity that governed the internalised subordination of women – the appeals to self-sacrifice, and to femininity expressed in attractive dress and charming manners. It was Dora Marsden's disgust at these constraints that led her to quit the WSPU and establish *The Freewoman*. Militant action had first led her to believe in her own powers of intervention in politics, and then crushed her hopes. She and other feminists resented the internalisation of the psyche of obedient 'follower' and thus gained an interest in self-transforming 'superwomen'. Through a critique of the methods of the suffragists and their democratic aims, *The Freewoman* came to adopt an anti-democratic stance, preferring great individuals to the mass, equalised unit of 'the voter'. Marsden concluded 'It is a contemptible weakness on the part of the intelligent to suffer themselves to be made insignificant under the wide-spreading robes of the stupid'.[63]

This kind of outright elitism might be thought to have become unsustainable in the wartime atmosphere, when the common sacrifices and contributions of 'the people' became emphasised in political argument. But it remained an important theme for feminists. Stella Browne, for example, retained the characteristic avant-garde feminist belief in elites, in her favourable review of Anthony Ludovici's 1915 book, *A Defence of Aristocracy*. She was, of course, critical of Ludovici's overt anti-feminism, but did not feel that this ruled out his proposed 'true aristocracy' – instead she argued in 1916 that such an aristocracy would only evolve if the feminist/eugenic principles of 'free sexual selection by women and voluntary conscious maternity' prevailed.[64]

This stress on elitism led to some pessimism about the possibility of change among women; contributors seemed to despair of women's capacities as superwomen. Dora Marsden's first editorial had commented: 'There must be, say ten [freewomen] in the British Isles'. These ten had a duty to develop one's genius, even if at the expense of others. Marsden explicitly accepted as moral the coercion of the many by the few, arguing that it was justifiable 'because *it is by way of the few that come those innovations which later will be the higher law for the many*'.[65]

RACE AND GENIUS

These voluntaristic understandings of 'genius' led some to despair of women ever attaining creative expression and fostered an exclusive form of feminism. An intersecting realm of exclusion which sheds light on the role genius played in feminist political thought is that of race and racial thinking. The racial construction of Edwardian genius and, specifically, the anti-Semitic thought found within avant-garde feminism is an important context for understanding the purpose of greatness and leadership for Edwardian thinkers. In a period commonly characterised as the 'golden age' of popular imperialism, the construction of an individualist feminist identity as 'superwomen' was likely to be informed by racial thinking.[66] Mary Johnston, for example, an American author and suffragist, explicitly linked the two at a suffrage rally in 1913. She claimed: 'Thinkers of today ... aim toward race quality rather than quantity. If you want to have a super-race you must have a superwoman first.'[67]

Indeed, theories of genius and race frequently relied on similar accounts of 'civilisation' and 'progress'; Ellen Key noted that 'genius is always a miracle, but one that has been prepared: we do not expect a Darwin from Tierra del Fuego or an Eskimo Dante'. Recent histories of the women's movement have charted the 'imperial politics' that informed the British feminist project, and have highlighted the racial hierarchies found in both British and American feminist thought.[68] The question of race also raises the issue of what was considered 'progressive' amongst Edwardians. Historians have shown how deeply implicated in imperial, national and race politics were 'progressive' movements at the time. Even where empire itself was not an issue, the imagery drawn from imperial experiences and race-thinking was used in a vivid manner, as an organising metaphor for gender relations. Israel Zangwill (a WSPU supporter and prominent novelist), for example, used race to attribute an 'oriental' passivity and backwardness to anti-suffrage women:

The bitterest enemy of woman is not man – it is woman, alas. A number of ladies declare they do not want the vote. Poor things! There are ladies in China who are content to have their toes crippled. There are ladies in Turkey who are satisfied with a quarter of a husband, or even an nth share of a husband.[69]

This comparison was also useful in order to suggest the appropriateness of granting women the vote *against* the wishes of some, or possibly the majority, of women, with its implicit comparison to the imperial powers banning foot-binding in China or polygamy in Turkey against the wishes of these 'deluded' populations. Within the British women's movement, support for the British Empire was widespread; empire could function as a realm of expertise for women.[70] A *Common Cause* editorial of September 1911 made this point, deploying the language of racially defined 'stages of civilisation': 'The world has no greater problem to solve than that of the relation between races at different stages of civilisation. It is however a problem which women are more capable of solving justly than men.'

Empire could be conceived as a larger 'moral economy', judged on the comparative position of women, with white, Anglophone women comfortably at the highest level of moral development. Similar rhetoric was found within the American women's movement, which was perhaps more strongly defined by racial thinking. The racism of suffragists, their willingness to accommodate southern white women's opposition to black women's suffrage, has been well established. Some feminists used the popular slavery metaphor for women's oppression, belittling the oppressions of race in comparison to gender. Alice Hubbard argued that early feminists were 'striking off bonds more difficult to remove than those which bound black slave to white owner'. She claimed that women's 'servitude' was 'far more insidious and detrimental to man's progress than was openly acknowledged slavery'.[71]

Arguments concerning feminism and women's suffrage were frequently made in the name of the race, without much attention to the nature or boundaries of this entity. Some of the most significant thinkers and statements of American feminism strongly stressed the racial element; Charlotte Perkins Gilman's work frequently drew on discourses of racial degeneration/superiority. Her utopian novel, *Herland*, for example, talked of the inhabitants of Herland as 'of Aryan stock', and therefore having been 'in contact with the best civilization of the old world'. Florence Tuttle wrote in 1915, 'the question of feminism becomes not a woman's problem but a race problem', and her entire book on feminism revolved around feminism's beneficial racial impact. In keeping with the turn towards aristocratic and eugenic thinking, she anticipated that 'a new aristocracy will then be formed with a new pride of pedigree, a new hope of descent'. For both these thinkers, women were racially backward or less evolved, and the interests of 'the race' required her to catch up with men. The modernist poet Mina Loy likewise wrote of the 'race-responsibility' of the 'superior woman'. One can read their ideas as humanist, the reference to the race meaning a universal humanity; Gilman described herself as a humanist in preference to a feminist. But nonetheless a discourse of what some historians have described as 'scathingly ugly racism' persisted within the American suffrage and feminist movements.[72]

In general, and in contrast, British feminists were both less interested in, and more critical of, issues of 'race'. Dora Marsden chided a reader for referring to sexual matters as 'oriental', and *The Freewoman* provided a space to rethink the standard metaphors of sexual slavery attached to 'the orient'.[73] Most contributors were also deeply sceptical about empire. For Marsden: 'To our mind, [the empire] is in an advanced state of decay, and probably the next fifty years will see its complete break-up ... The Empire is really a symptom of degeneracy rather than of development. Empires have been in at the death of most great civilisations.' In contrast, she believed that a stateless 'simple' civilisation 'would contain potentialities of the higher development of the human soul, which are the causes of great civilisations'.[74]

Individual 'greatness of Being', for Marsden, underlay 'great civilisations', rather than some racial essence or imperial domination. Egoist individualism was clearly a position that encouraged scepticism about claims made for 'the race'. Feminists may have been aware that their claims about women's emancipation were blamed for racial degeneration, and they therefore avoided adopting this language. They preferred to construe 'the woman question' as, above all, of feminine character, without locating 'character' within degenerationist debates. The emphasis was on women's own renovatory power to bring on the age of the superman or super-woman.[75]

The influence of *The Freewoman* upon American feminists like Rose Young was to introduce an alternative mode into American feminism, one that thoroughly rejected talk of 'the good of the race', or 'race mothers'. Citing Dora Marsden, Young argued emphatically in *Good Housekeeping*,

At no other angle of attack on the preconceived idea does the new faith [feminism] more urgently hurl itself than at the historic regard of woman as mere race agent ... The matter of developing herself, as an individual is mainly an inside matter, a spiritual introduction to herself. The social hope must rest with the individual development being self-sought by each and every woman. To attempt to herd women into a woman's movement for the race's sake, a movement bounded and defined by set purpose from the very start-off, would be to keep on treating women as sheep – and the race like a stepchild.[76]

Nonetheless, Young's article was graced by pictures of mothers and babies, and a portrait of Ellen Key, the Swedish feminist for whom the racial role of women was paramount, and who was enormously popular in the United States – an example of the multivalency of periodicals texts, the meanings of which are governed not only by what the text says but by editorial decisions about juxtaposition and illustration. In more general terms, Young's reading of Dora Marsden and defence of individualism was submerged by the general trend towards 'race thinking' within American feminism.

'Advanced' feminists' fascination with Max Stirner and Otto Weininger reveals another racial dimension. Rather than imperial concerns with 'lower' and 'savage' races, *The Freewoman* hosted anti-Semitic debates, on the significance of 'the Jew' for English identity and politics. This aspect of the journal has been curiously passed over by other commentators, who have read it as 'untainted by corporatist, racist or jingoist complicities'.[77] This reading erases the violent anti-Semitism that occasionally emerged within feminist circles. Why was it acceptable within the Edwardian women's movement, and within 'progressive politics' more generally, to excoriate 'the Jew' for a variety of social ills?

Within the British women's movement, Judaism was sometimes portrayed as a root cause of women's subordination. In 1898 'Ellis Ethelmer' described 'the dark tenets maligning womanhood' within 'Mosaism'. Twelve years later, Florence Farr made a much more explicitly *racial* anti-Semitic argument that identified racial groups rather than simply religious influence: 'The degradation of women in the past originated in the region

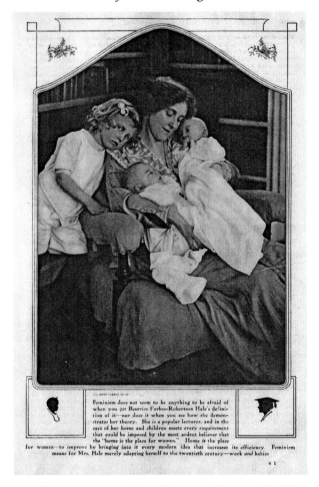

Figure 11: British feminist Beatrice Forbes-Robertson Hale, pictured with her children in
Rose Young's article, 'What is Feminism?' *Good Housekeeping*, May 1914

of the country around Mount Ararat. The lowering of their status occurred
when the white tribes adopted the Assyrian Semite's Scriptures.' She called
for 'white women to fight now, and at last rid their sex all over the world of
the ignominy of this false doctrine [of the Semites]'. Farr's pamphlet is
revealing, since she attempted to position it as reflecting 'the modern
woman'. She was a contributor to *The New Age* and an active participant in
the 'radical' periodical communities that helped shape 'progressive'
Edwardian thought. Her comments indicate how widespread and acceptable an anti-Semitic stance was in these circles.[78]

Greenwich Village bohemians expressed similar sentiments. Randolph Bourne described a meeting of the Heretics Club in 1915: 'The speaker was a shiny, sleeky little Jew. Really the Jew aesthete is beyond endurance. The rolling vulgarity of mind that ran beneath his impeccable language and historic command!' He complained of the atmosphere of 'Jewishness' at the New York periodical *Seven Arts*, and talked of founding 'a more indigenous paper'.[79] Amongst many avant-garde feminists, however – in contrast to other texts of the women's movement – anti-Semitism was presented in more symbolic terms. It represented a critique of capitalism rather than a critique of the treatment of women. Marsden articulated this stance relatively late in the journal's publishing life, perhaps under the influence of the anti-Semitism of Max Stirner, for whom 'Jews' represented materialism.[80] In a violently worded editorial in September 1912 she warned against

the speculations of Jewish money-lenders who batten upon English poverty. A war with Germany would not be a war between Germans and English ... It would be a war between money-lending German Jews and money-lending Jews in England ... Now the Jews are establishing a still more intimate form of coercion, the Spy – called an inspector ... A usurious Jew might set an Englishman to remove offal, spurn him with his foot, lash him with thongs, and spit in his face, and the Englishman would lick the grasping hand.[81]

Françoise Lafitte agreed, though she argued in a letter to Marsden that while the Jews were responsible for the horrors of capitalism, this was the fault of the Christian anti-Semites. She described the Jews as 'the pocket-pickers', yet went on, 'what else could the Jew do, save hide his tactics from the Christian, who was denying him the land and thus seeking to crush him, racially, from the face of the earth? I am no Anti-Semite – I want to bring some Jews in to the New Order as soon as possible.' This letter of 24 June 1912 was perhaps stimulated by Marsden's reference in early June to usury as 'the un-Christian latter-day fungus'.[82] This exchange, preceding the editorial of September 1912 by some months, suggests that Marsden's anti-Semitism was not an aberration on her part, nor lifted wholesale from Max Stirner, but was a theme widely expressed and discussed within the feminist intellectual community. It also suggests the complexity of such a discourse, which could be both progressive and conservative, and sometimes quite friendly to Jewish 'emancipation'.

The publication of some chapters of Otto Weininger's highly anti-Semitic *Sex and Character* in *The Freewoman* confirms the interest, though British anti-Semitism was rarely expressed in the dangerously obsessive sense common in continental Europe. The frequently feminised qualities of 'the Jew' – imitative, parasitic and uncreative – corresponded to those of 'bondwomen', and was therefore a rhetorical device to indicate dislike of capitalism and a critique of conventional femininity.

DEBATING THE SUPERWOMAN

If conventional femininity was the problem, how much did the super-woman or genius come to be an androgynous figure or a 'third sex'? Marsden believed that superwomen would consider 'their sex just as much an incidental concern as men consider theirs'. Perhaps influenced by theosophy, though she was critical of its spiritualism, she argued that 'the next development of man would be towards the man-woman, and the woman-man'. The idea of androgyny had a history not only in con-temporary theories of genius, but also within the women's movement, that gave such a statement a wider resonance. It had long been held by some feminists that an end to sex-differentiation was the goal of feminism. Charlotte Perkins Gilman, for example, held that through women's eco-nomic parasitism upon men, women become highly sexually specialised, to the detriment of 'the race'.[83] Gilman relished the idea of hermaphroditism and parthenogenesis. She wanted 'to blend the opposing sex-tendencies of two animals into the fruitful powers of a triumphant race', a process already begun by men's willingness to adopt feminine 'anabolic force' in learning to love and care as a father and husband. As usual, American feminists were more open to imagining new masculinities than their British counterparts.

Nonetheless, for Gilman, though there might be a temporary reaction amongst more androgynous women to abandon marriage and choose a more 'masculine' lifestyle, she continued to believe that marriage and motherhood were the 'common duty and common glory of womanhood'. Other feminists were sceptical about the rhetoric of androgyny. Ellen Key argued emphatically that her talk of the full development of human per-sonality in the genius did not mean a fusing of the sexes. Marsden also felt that the attainment of genius could not mean an elimination of sexual differentiation and energy; as for the Romantics, sexual energy was a key element to genius. Genius arose out of (yet ultimately transcended) phy-sical sexuality. Sexual difference remained crucial to this process, and the androgynous ideal represented an impossible reversal of evolution: 'It is not possible for this differentiated life to fall back into the undifferentiated whole'.[84] So the superhuman individual remained in the main imagined as gender-differentiated. The interaction of the sexes, with a simultaneous *intensification* of male and female capacities, was to act as the genesis of genius.

Avant-garde feminism, however, also hosted and debated the ideas of those individuals who identified as or spoke for 'Uranians' or homosexuals. These individuals found Weininger's concept of androgynous or bisexual genius productive, and offered a competing definition of 'the genius' to Marsden's. Harry Birnstingl (an architect, writer on social affairs, frequent *Freewoman* contributor, and speaker at the Freewoman Discussion Circle) saw genius as related to bisexuality, and expected the superhuman to be an androgen. Birnstingl pointed out that sex differentiation in 'all modern movements' was on the wane. He believed that 'all the great men who have hitherto been the triumph of the male sex are just those very ones who were most womanly'. 'Genius is typical of sexual inversion' he went on, and 'often come[s] from the ranks of Uranians ... by reason of their dual natures'. Birnstingl was clearly influenced by Weininger, though he was critical of his 'mathematical method'.[85]

Birnstingl's arguments were echoed by the lawyer and transgender activist Thomas Baty, who advertised his 'Aethnic Union' in *The Freewoman*. This group explicitly rejected sexual differentiation, which was argued to submerge 'the mind in a wave of that autocratic sternness which one has been taught is the ideal of the masculine, or of that narrow triviality which one is (less successfully) taught to consider the mark of the Feminine'. Baty, who later edited the long-lived journal, *Urania*, made clear his dislike of the gendered dualisms of society:

In the dress they wear, in the games they play, in the occupations they follow, in their very food and drink, it is constantly borne in upon people that they must assimilate themselves to one or the other imperfect type.[86]

Like Birnstingl, Baty idealised 'the idea of the soul undwarfed by sex', and saw androgyny as the direction human evolution towards a higher race would take. He explicitly included 'female androgens' in his ideal: 'Penthesilea, Sappho, Pallas Athene'.

Nonetheless, it is clear from asides made within this series of articles that the imagined androgen was, as it had been for Weininger, a male with a high proportion of feminine qualities or 'plasm'. This was a problematic identity for the women's movement. The androgynous genius tended to be *like a woman*, rather than genuinely feminine. As one male contributor put it, 'A man of genius may be feminine, but he must *not* be effeminate'.[87]

Though androgyny suggests an abandonment of absolute distinctions between the sexes, Birnstingl's articles drew on apparently clear-cut and conventional distinctions between male and female attributes. He suggested, drawing upon Edward Carpenter, that the male homosexual tended to be of 'gentle, emotional disposition', while the female invert was 'fiery, active, bold, and truthful, with defects running to brusqueness and coarseness'. Birnstingl challenged conventional sexual differentiation in his call for the conceptual extension or abolition of the 'pigeon-holes' that classify human gender.[88] But such calls were persistently undermined by the accompanying language of demarcated and opposed sexual difference.

Genius might therefore be conceived along two dimensions, as the 'androgen-homosexual', or the 'superwoman'. Yet neither theory substantially shifted the idea of the genius from the ground it conventionally occupied. The concept of the feminine, intuitive genius-superwoman was premised on the conventional gender economy of 'feminine' qualities of intuition and quick perception and 'masculine' qualities of intellect and strength. In this theory, the foundational concepts of Romantic genius stayed intact. Contradictions existed at the heart of this project, that of drawing upon the discourse of the superman (complete with Romantic ideals and an economy of male sexual energy) to create a superwoman. The second model available, that of androgyny, was perhaps more promising for women's inclusion. However the avant-garde formulation of androgynous genius could not shake off the persistent 'characterology' of male and female essences, that characterised women as unable to be geniuses. The influence of Otto Weininger offered a troubling legacy for feminists and made the appropriation of the idea of androgynous genius difficult. Overall, there was little consensus as to what feminine genius might mean. Some rejected it all together – 'If freedom can only be attained by an infinitely small number of 'Super-Women', it seems to me hardly worth fighting for at all', wrote one suffrage-feminist. Others felt that while they might agree with the politics of the superwoman, they themselves could not qualify. One *Freewoman* reader asked the editor to 'grade the aspiring Freewomen into classes; then I might, perhaps, scrape into the last one by the skin of my teeth. It is so bitter to feel that one hasn't even a sporting chance of ever being free.'[89]

The realm of genius was a site of anxiety for feminists, and Edwardian women more generally, as Regenia Gagnier has argued. Many, feminist and non-feminist, were clearly anxious at the thought of being measured and found wanting according to a standard of feminine genius. They were also critical, however, of the underpinning assumptions of egoism – the idea that genius suffered no external constraints and had no material concerns seemed to imply that someone else, likely to be a woman, would meet the material, bodily needs of the genius. Rachel Graham argued in *The Freewoman* that the artist required someone else to do his [*sic*] 'menial work' – and thus all could not qualify for the egoist vision of creative genius.[90] Graham perceived the carelessness concerning the subordination of others that was at the heart of avant-garde's attraction to the idea of genius. There was a fundamental tension between the claims of the many over the few in the concept of a superwoman or genius, a tension that reflects the ambiguity of 'genius' – between the Romantic agent of renewal and the modernist aloof and transcendent genius.

CONCLUSIONS

We have seen how in the years directly preceding the war, Edwardian political thinkers became preoccupied with the impact of the few and the great. This concern was expressed by some within the feminist movement, in the belief that the best feminist strategy was to concentrate on the gifted few, to encourage them to fulfil their potential, and thus perhaps to lead the way to a broader female emancipation. What lay at the heart of this method was the belief that the constraints on women were mainly internal. External constraints existed, but the real problem was internalised within women. An American paper, *The Forum*, saw this as the most distinctive feature of advanced feminist thinking. Feminists

came with the incredible heresy ... that the woman movement was nothing if not an effort on the part of the women to lift themselves forever out of the 'servant' class and to place themselves definitely and finally among the 'masters' – using their faculties, like all masters, for the upbuilding and development of their own personalities and the advancement of their own personal aims.[91]

Though presented as a heresy, this belief in self-overcoming was in fact very much in keeping with Edwardian political thought. The discourse of genius offered an ideal language to discuss the voluntaristic process of self-overcoming that many Edwardian feminists identified as emancipation. The genius was the paradigm example of the perfectly individualised, willing ego, succeeding through self-motivation, against strong odds. Genius also provided a basis for criticisms of the modern state and society, and a means to legitimise new models of society. Though external conditions were supposed to be insignificant to the genius, one of the arguments against modern governance was that it would stamp out genius. The need to cultivate genius was used as an argument for small, self-governing communities, inhabited by craftspeople and farmers. The concept of the genius thus linked contributors' negative critique of the state, the celebration of the individual, and the positive utopian thinking of advanced feminism.

Yet how useful was this? At a conceptual level, 'genius' resisted feminist deployment. Gender was such a powerful 'organising metaphor' for genius that it was very hard to change its gender connotations. Feminist attempts to rethink and broaden the concept of genius were very partial, and failed to establish firmly the idea of feminine genius. The prevailing exclusivity of early twentieth-century conceptions of genius and 'the superman' made theories of feminine genius and 'the superwoman' troubling. Though women were paradigm outsiders and thus seemed to fit the bill for Romantic genius, they could not instantiate elite leadership. In fact, they had come to represent the mass and the vulgar, the very features of modern society that the superman was to transcend. The superman's self-transformation was premised on the devaluation of the mass or the crowd figured as female. Gustave Le Bon had argued 'Crowds are everywhere distinguished by feminine characteristics'. Women were widely believed to cluster around the average, to be more invariable than men, lacking the great heights and depths of achievement. As the American psychologist Stanley Hall argued, 'Women go in flocks, and in social matters are less prone to stand out with salient individuality'. Women's agitation to achieve suffrage and freedom to work only emphasised this – they were no longer content with an individualised existence as the 'angel in the home', but sought to join the public sphere 'en masse' as workers and voters. Women's creative work was seen as born of and aimed at 'the crowd', and 'the superwoman', as an entity that transcended the masses, could not be easily 'feminised'. Hall concluded that woman 'is at the top of the human curve from which the higher super-man of the future is to evolve'. But Hall's overall opinion was that women could only be mothers of supermen, and not aspire to superhumanity themselves.[92]

This emphasis on mothering gained ground amongst feminists. An early article on feminism in the British *Westminster Review* had quoted Walt Whitman's *Leaves of Grass* on women's role in creative leadership: 'Unfolded only out of the superbest woman of the earth is to come the superbest man of the earth'. Ellen Key directly echoed Stanley Hall when she argued that emancipated women should seek to nurture 'the completed man – the Superman' through their attention to children.[93] Key's enormous popularity in the United States made her increasingly influential upon the new meanings and resonances within feminism during and after the war.

In both Britain and the United States an increasingly self-satisfied tone of celebration of women's maternal role came to increasing prominence, in arguments for the vote and portrayals of women as citizens. The war years saw an intensified emphasis on maternalism, which proved to be a highly ambiguous concept. While in Britain, appeals to maternal sentiments had been less central to women's activism, in the United States it had long been stressed. Many who had spoken of 'municipal housekeeping' and the state as the home writ large had done so through their belief in the transformative power of maternalism. There had been no stable meaning, however, to this pre-war discourse – it spanned antifeminist and feminist arguments, and could lend weight to internationalist pacifism. But maternalism could also be turned towards a 'patriotic' construction, with mothers having the prime responsibility for the production and socialisation of sons who could defend the nation. This was a reversal of the 'state as the home writ large' argument, which had called for women to emerge from their homes and contribute to the 'public' sphere and creative arts. Instead, civic virtue was 'writ small', as the ideal home was argued to be infused with the values of the state. Women's primary state service became reproductive, rather than an offering of expertise or developing genius in their own right. Their citizenship was to be expressed through the activity of raising citizens, and mobilising for the war.

This did not rule out their genius, but did attach it to some confining gender stereotypes. In 1915 Charlotte Perkins Gilman, who had previously celebrated genius in terms of the 'domestic genius' and 'mother-genius' of women, wrote of an aristocracy of 'Over Mothers' in her utopian novel, *Herland*.[94] And in the same year, Florence Tuttle argued that the paradigmatic feminists were those who 'have fulfilled themselves as wives and mothers and who are now fulfilling themselves still further in some form of socially productive work'. The British suffragist and preacher Maude Royden agreed with the theorists of genius who argued that women were ineligible due to their 'wastage' of life force on reproduction. In 1917 she argued:

We have all a certain vital force, which seeks expression in creation. Some of us have very little, or find life gives it no scope. Some have a force like Niagara, and like Leonardo da Vinci, pour it in torrents along the ways of action, poetry, art. Women's vital force can, and generally does, pour itself into motherhood. Fatherhood costs much less, and the force spent leaves much to spend elsewhere. I think, therefore, that there will always be more 'creators' among men than among women in art, literature, and science . . .[95]

Women's genius, for Royden, was predominantly in the realm of care, and her feminism was concerned with the revaluation of this realm. Royden's stance gained ground in later decades, as the focus of the women's movement shifted from pre-war suffrage to post-war family allowances. It is not surprising, then, that the political discourse associated with superwoman should have become less useful to feminist purposes. Stemming from the set of ideas associated with the 'superman', the superwoman could not throw off the resonances that made it an opaque, muddled concept. It came to be transformed towards its late twentieth-century meaning, to indicate the Herculean combining of work and motherhood duties by some women. As Crystal Eastman wrote in 1918, ambitious women, 'if they also have the normal desire to be mothers, must make up their minds to be a sort of superman, I think'.[96]

I have argued that 'genius' seemed to offer some tempting features for feminists, and progressives more widely – specifically, it offered a politically neutral means of talking about leadership and aristocracy. But with regard to gender it was not neutral at all, nor amenable to successful appropriation by feminists. It addressed few of the interesting questions of why some women might not achieve 'personality'. No means could be suggested for achieving personality, let alone genius. 'Genius' remained an ideal, supposedly attainable by the few but without explanation as to how they had got there. The feminist ideal of the superwoman provided an enigmatic and confining intellectual framework, and did not easily weather the changes brought by World War One.

END NOTES

1. *Current Opinion*, Jan. 1913, 47.
2. Most notably Christine Battersby, *Gender and Genius: Towards a Feminist Aesthetics* (London, The Women's Press, 1989). Cf. L. D. Derksen, *Dialogues on Women: Images of Women in the History of Philosophy* (Amsterdam, VU University Press, 1996); Flavia Alaya, 'Victorian Science and the Genius of Women', *Journal of the History of Ideas*, 38:2 (1977).
3. Billington-Greig, *The Militant Suffrage Movement*, p. 213.
4. Alice Hubbard, 'Something New Under the Sun', *Harper's Weekly*, 13 Dec. 1913; Tuttle, *Awakening of Woman*, p. 22; Duncan, 'The Dance of the Future', 1903 in Duncan, *The Art of the Dance*, p. 63; West, *FW*, 3 Oct. 1912, 390; Sylvia Kopald, in *Our Changing Morality: A Symposium*, ed. Frida Kirchwey (London, Kegan, Paul, Trench and Tubner, 1925), p. 110.
5. Alaya, 'Victorian Science', p. 268, original emphasis.
6. This chapter will focus on the narrow question of the political implications of genius, rather than its medical or scientific constructions. On the relationship

of genius to Social Darwinism and eugenics, see George Robb, 'Race Motherhood: Moral Eugenics Versus Progressive Eugenics, 1880–1920', in *Maternal Instincts, Visions of Motherhood and Sexuality in Britain, 1875–1925*, ed. A. S. Holmes and C. Nelson (Basingstoke, Macmillan, 1997); Mathew Thomson, ' "Savage Civilisation." Race, Culture and Mind in Britain, 1898–1939', in *Race, Science and Medicine 1700–1969*, ed. W. Ernst and B. Harris (London, 1999).

7. A. R. Orage, *Nietzsche in Outline and Aphorism* (Edinburgh, Foulis, 1907), p. 51.

8. Howard Mumford Jones, *Revolution and Romanticism* (Cambridge, Mass., Harvard University Press, 1974); M. H. Abrams, *The Mirror and the Lamp: Romantic Theory and the Critical Tradition* (Oxford, Oxford University Press, 1953).

9. Francis Galton, *Hereditary Genius: An Inquiry Into its Laws and Consequences* (London, Watts, 1950; orig. 1869), p. 318.

10. Jay Hatheway, *The Gilded Age Construction of Modern American Homophobia* (New York, Palgrave, 2003), p. 149. Ellis and his wife, Edith Ellis, were *Freewoman* readers, part of its avant-garde network of sexual radicals. They were however ambivalent about the journal's content but willing to help make it known and speak at the Freewoman Discussion Circle. Havelock Ellis, *A Study of British Genius* (London, Hurst and Blackett, 1904; orig. 1901), pp. 227, 229, 203, 229.

11. Battersby, *Gender and Genius*, p. 102. See also Andrew Elfenbein, *Romantic Genius: The Prehistory of a Homosexual Role* (New York, Columbia University Press, 1999); Mumford Jones, *Revolution and Romanticism*, Chapters 9 and 10, and contrasting earlier meanings of genius, discussed by Kineret Jaffe, 'The Concept of Genius: Its Changing Role in Eighteenth-Century French Aesthetics', *Journal of the History of Ideas*, 41:4 (1980); Logan Pearsall Smith, *Words and Idioms: Studies in the English Language* (London, Constable, 1957; orig. 1925).

12. Havelock Ellis, *Man and Woman: A Study of Secondary and Tertiary Sexual Characters*, 8th edn (London, Heinemann (Medical Books), 1934), p. 360; Ellis, *British Genius*, pp. 10–11.

13. Ellis, *Man and Woman*, p. 436; Ellis, *British Genius*, pp. 158, 159.

14. Prof. Remond, 'The Sexual Correlations of Poetic Genius', *English Review*, July 1913, 587–8; Patrick Geddes and Arthur Thomson, *The Evolution of Sex* (London, 1889); Ethel B. Harrison, *The Freedom of Women: An Argument Against the Proposed Extension of the Suffrage to Women* (London, Watts, 1908), p. 22; Cesare Lombroso, *The Man of Genius* (London, Scott, 1891; orig. 1863), p. 138; cf. Alaya, 'Victorian Science'.

15. Millicent Murby, *The Common Sense of the Woman Question* (London, New Age Press, 1908), p. 55.

16. Ellis, *Man and Woman*, pp. 435, 434.

17. Caleb Saleeby referred to Weininger's work as 'evidently insane'. Nonetheless, Saleeby's *Woman and Womanhood* prominently advertised Weininger's work on its front page (London, William Heinemann, 1912).

The American Journal of Sociology admitted his flashes of genius, but called his work in general 'poor, obscure, illogical, and stupid' (May 1906, 843). W. L. George, 'Feminist Intentions', *Atlantic Monthly*, Dec. 1913, 721, original emphasis; Gilman, *Critic*, May 1906, 414. Weininger, quoted in *FW*, 2 May 1912, 471.

18. Otto Weininger, *Sex and Character* (London, Heinemann, 1906), pp. 36, 34; Bland, *Banishing the Beast*; Hatheway, *Modern American Homophobia*, pp. 111–55; Parsons, *Journal of a Feminist*, p. 91.

19. Carpenter published *Homogenic Love and its Place in a Free Society* in 1894, a pamphlet of the Manchester Labour Press (London, Redundancy Press, 1980; orig. 1894). See also Edward Carpenter, *Love's Coming of Age* (Manchester, Manchester Labour Press, 1896); Edward Carpenter, *The Intermediate Sex* (London, George, Allen & Unwin, 1908); Battersby, *Gender and Genius*, Chapter 11 on 'The Third Sex'.

20. Weininger, *Sex and Character*, pp. 114–15.

21. I. Woodbridge Riley, 'Recent Theories of Genius', *Journal of Philosophy, Psychology and Scientific Methods*, June 1905, 345–6. The article credits most of the work on genius to European theorists, including Edward Carpenter, Frederick Myers, Francis Galton and Karl Pearson.

22. 'Is "Genius" Same as Insanity?' *Washington Post*, 28 Jan. 1912, 4; 'Genius Not Disease', *New York Times*, 9 July 1912, 8.

23. H. Addington Bruce, 'Genius – a World-Old Problem Viewed in the Light of Modern Psychology', *Harper's Weekly*, 9 Aug. 1913.

24. 'Family Rules World', *Washington Post*, 31 Dec. 1912, 1; Tuttle, *Awakening of Woman*, p. 67.

25. Samuel E. Ewing, 'Ralph Waldo Emerson and the New Aristocracy: Greatness and the Great Man in Democratic Society', Ph.D. diss. (Harvard University, 2003); Croly, *The Promise of American Life*, p. 454; William James, *The Social Value of the College-Bred*, in James, *Writings, 1902–1910* (New York, The Library of America, 1987), pp. 1246, 7.

26. W. H. Mallock, *Aristocracy and Evolution* (London, Adam & Charles Black, 1898), p. 379. This was explicitly identified as a 'Tory' position by texts such as J. M. Kennedy's *Tory Democracy*, 1911, or A. Ludovici's *A Defence of Aristocracy: A Textbook for Tories*, 1915; Emerson, quoted by Andrew Delbanco in Ralph Waldo Emerson, *Representative Men* (Cambridge, Mass., Belknap Press, 1996), p. xi. See Victoria Olwell, ' "It Spoke Itself": Women's Genius and Eccentric Politics', *American Literature*, 77:1 (March 2005).

27. John Ruskin, 'Unto this Last', in Ruskin, *The Works of John Ruskin*, p. 74. George Bernard Shaw tried to capture this convergence of progressive and conservative opinion around the idea of aristocracy in a lecture on Ruskin's politics, which he labelled 'Tory oligarchism' or equally, 'Tory Communism': the two could not be easily distinguished. G. B. Shaw, *Ruskin's Politics* (London, 1921), p. 30.

28. Catt, quoted in Fowler, *Carrie Cat*, p. 77; Caird, 'The Lot of Women', *Westminster Review*, July 1910, 57.

29. Key, *Woman Movement*, p. 53; Key, *Younger Generation*, pp. 243–4.

30. See Thatcher, *Nietzsche in England*; D. Stone, 'An "Entirely Tactless Nietzschean Jew": Oscar Levy's Critique of Western Civilisation', *Journal of Contemporary Modern History*, 36: 2 (April 2001), 271–92; Detwiler, *Nietzsche and the Politics of Aristocratic Radicalism*. Most contemporaries drew their interpretation of Nietzsche's superman or (as it was still referred to in 1908) 'beyond-man' from *Thus Spake Zarathustra* (see A. C. Pigou, 'The Ethics of Nietzsche' and A. W. Benn, 'The Morals of an Immoralist: Fredric Nietzsche. II', *IJE*, 18 (April 1908) and 19 (January 1909)). *Zarathustra* was one of the earliest works of Nietzsche translated into English in 1896.

31. Orage, *Nietzsche in Outline and Aphorism*, pp. 43–4. Also quoted in Thatcher, *Nietzsche in England*, p. 249. See also James L. Walker, *The Philosophy of Egoism* (Denver, Katherine Walker, 1905), a text which claimed to be an independent American account of egoism.

32. Patrick Bridgwater, *Nietzsche in Anglosaxony: A Study of Nietzsche's Impact on English and American Literature* (Leicester, Leicester University Press, 1972), pp. 150–1.

33. Dr Angelo S. Rappoport, *New Age*, 26 Sept. 1908, 429.

34. Barbara Will, *Gertrude Stein, Modernism and the Problem of 'Genius'* (Edinburgh, Edinburgh University Press, 2000), pp. 1–7.

35. A 1921 dictionary noted that the word 'superman' 'has led to any number of nonce formations of which the language is getting very tired'. Ernest Weekley, *An Etymological Dictionary of Modern English* (London, John Murray, 1921).

36. Walker, quoted in James Huneker, *The Egoists*, p. 370.

37. G. B. Shaw, *Man and Superman* (Westminster, Archibald Constable, 1903), p. 196; Atkinson, *IJE*, 18:3 (April 1908), 309, 310.

38. Max Eastman, 'Is Woman Suffrage Important?' (1910), Men's League for Woman Suffrage, MWDP, p. 3; Marsden, *New Age*, 23 Nov. 1911, 95.

39. Cf. Thatcher, *Nietzsche in England 1890–1914*, pp. 272–3.

40. Wallas, *Human Nature in Politics*, p. 4; Soffer, *Ethics and Society in England*; Trotter, *Instincts of the Herd*.

41. Bourne to Parsons, ECPP, u.d. (1915?). Tom Steele has argued that the superman fulfilled the aspirational needs of '*petit-bourgeois* intellectuals, denied the opportunity of constituting themselves like gentlemen'. However, he sees both 'gentleman' and 'superman' as inhospitable to women. Tom Steele, 'From Gentleman to Superman: Alfred Orage and Aristocratic Socialism', in *The Imagined Past: History and Nostalgia*, ed. C. Shaw and M. Chase (Manchester, Manchester University Press, 1989), p. 123.

42. M. F. Bednarowski, 'Women in Occult America', in *The Occult in America: New Historical Perspectives*, ed. H. Kerr and C. L. Crow (Urbana, University of Illinois Press, 1983), pp. 179–88; Owen, 'Occultism and the "Modern" Self', pp. 87, 74.

43. Shaw, *Man and Superman*, p. 114.

44. Farr, *New Age*, 6 June 1907, 92. By seeing the superman as a state of mind rather than an individual, Farr was able to claim it for women. On Farr's

journalism, see A. Walton Litz, 'Florence Farr: A 'Transitional' Woman', in *High and Low Moderns*, ed. DiBattista and McDiarmid, pp. 85–90.

45. Swiney in Carter, *Women's Suffrage and Militancy*, p. 63. Cf. Bland, *Banishing the Beast*.

46. Dan Stone, *Breeding Superman: Nietzsche, Race and Eugenics in Edwardian and Interwar Britain* (Liverpool, Liverpool University Press, 2002), p. 93. Interest in race should not however be overstated. Peter Mandler has recently argued that English national character was conceived of in non-racial terms and that degeneration fears were much less prominent in Britain than in continental Europe. Mandler, 'The Consciousness of Modernity? Liberalism and the English National Character, 1870–1914', in *Meanings of Modernity*, ed. Daunton and Rieger, pp. 71–96.

47. For both sides of the debates, see Thomson, '"Savage Civilisation" Race, Culture and Mind in Britain, 1898–1939'; D. Pick, *Faces of Degeneration: A European Disorder, c. 1848–1918* (Cambridge, Cambridge University Press, 1989); Maximilian Mügge, 'Eugenics and the Superman: A Racial Science and a Racial Religion', *Eugenics Review*, 1 (1909), 184, quoted in Stone, *Breeding Superman*, p. 73.

48. 'The Fallibility of the Term "Super"', in the *Anti-Suffrage Review* (March 1915), p. 22. Weekley, *Etymological Dictionary*. The association between genius and homosexuality had persisted from the nineteenth century, and also permeated the idea of a superman.

49. Sinclair, *New York Times*, 1 Dec. 1905, 813; 'Superthoughts on the Superman', *New York Times*, 17 Jan. 1910, 2.

50. Royden, *The Making of Women*, p. 13; Marian Cox, 'Bergson's Message to Feminism', *The Forum*, May 1913, 557.

51. W. L. George, 'Feminist Intentions', *Atlantic Monthly*, Dec. 1913, 723. The quote marks indicate how inadequate 'feminist' and 'anti-feminist' are to describe the politics of a writer like George, who used many 'anti-feminist' arguments in order to make 'feminist' points. George, 'The Downfall of the Home', *Harper's Magazine*, June 1916, 49.

52. Swanwick, *Future of the Women's Movement*, p. 14. Austin described in *Harper's Weekly*, 29 Nov. 1913, 5. Mary Austin, *A Woman of Genius* (Old Westbury, NY, The Feminist Press, 1985; orig. 1912).

53. Swanwick, *Future of the Women's Movement*, p. 147.

54. Weininger, *Sex and Character*, p. 45.

55. Björkman, *Current Opinion*, Jan. 1913, 47; Marsden, *FW*, 30 Nov. 1911, 21.

56. Whitby, *FW*, 18 April 1912, 425–6, original emphasis; Mowrer, 'The Dearth of Genius', *NFW*, 1 Dec. 1913, 232; Chancellor, 'The Angel Club', *NFW*, 1 Oct. 1913, 144; Delisle, *Friendship's Odyssey*, pp. 180–1.

57. Marsden, *FW*, 18 July 1912, 164.

58. Marsden, *FW*, 23 Nov. 1911, 2; Marsden, *FW*, 9 May 1912, 482.

59. Marsden, *FW*, 23 May 1912, 2.

60. Kenton, 'Feminism Will Give', *Delineator*, July 1914, 17.

61. Stopes and Clifford Sharp in Carter, *Women's Suffrage and Militancy*, p. 48.

62. 'Militancy', Christabel Pankhurst, *The New Statesman*, special supplement on 'The Awakening of Women', ed. Mrs Sidney Webb, 1 Nov. 1913, xi.

63. Marsden, *FW*, 18 Jan. 1912, 162.

64. Stella Browne, *IJE*, 26:3 (April 1916), 431.

65. Marsden, *FW*, 25 April 1912, 444, emphasis added.

66. As Joan Scott has argued, 'Individualism was not only a masculine prerogative; it was also racially defined'. Scott, *Only Paradoxes to Offer*, pp. 10–11.

67. *Washington Post*, 4 March 1913, 3.

68. Key, *Younger Generation*, p. 246; Rosalyn Terborg-Penn, 'Discrimination Against Afro-American Women in the Woman's Movement, 1830–1920', in *The Afro-American Woman: Struggles and Images*, ed. S. Harley and R. Terborg-Penn (Port Washington, NY, Kennikat Press, 1978); Vron Ware, *Beyond the Pale; White Women, Racism and History* (London, Verso, 1992); Antoinette Burton, *Burdens of History: British Feminists, Indian Women and Imperial Culture, 1865–1915* (Chapel Hill, University of North Carolina Press, 1994); K. Malik, *The Meaning of Race: Race, History and Culture in Western Society* (London, Macmillan, 1996); Ann D. Gordon (ed.), *African American Women and the Vote, 1837–1965* (Amherst, University of Massachusetts Press, 1997).

69. Malik, *The Meaning of Race*, p. 116. See also Paul Peppis on the uses of imperial and nationalist ideas within modernism and the 'avant-garde', Paul Peppis, *Literature, Politics and the English Avant-Garde: Nation and Empire 1901–1918* (Cambridge, Cambridge University Press, 2000); Israel Zangwill, in Atkinson, *Case for Women's Suffrage*, p. 204.

70. Laura E. N. Mayhall, Philippa Levine and Ian C. Fletcher (eds.), *Women's Suffrage in the British Empire: Citizenship, Nation and Race* (London, Routledge, 2000).

71. See Nancy Caraway, *Segregated Sisterhood: Racism and the Politics of American Feminism* (Knoxville, University of Tennessee Press, 1991), Chapter 5; Alice Hubbard, 'Something New Under the Sun', *Harper's Weekly*, 13 Dec. 1913, 6.

72. See Gail Bederman, *Manliness & Civilization: A Cultural History of Gender and Race in the United States, 1880–1917* (Chicago, University of Chicago Press, 1995); Tuttle, *Awakening of Woman*, pp. 12, 164; Caraway, *Segregated Sisterhood*, p. 140.

73. A reviewer of international affairs responded to a Chinese women's suffrage initiative with a recognition of the need to rethink 'the orient': 'The very thought of Women's Suffrage in China is enough to shake our oldest illusion about the Far East in fragments to the ground'. In her view, the Chinese were 'not the imperturbable, reactionary race our travellers have told us about'. G. L. Harding, *FW*, 7 March 1912, 319.

74. Marsden, *FW*, 26 Sept. 1912, 364.

75. Lyn Pykett discusses this dual concern with degeneration and regeneration in *Engendering Fictions: The English Novel in the Early Twentieth Century* (London, Edward Arnold, 1995).

76. Rose Young, 'What is Feminism?' 680.

77. Christine Stansell has argued that anti-Semitism was prevalent in progressive era American society, but was mitigated for the avant-garde by their secularism and agnosticism. Stansell, *American Moderns*, pp. 62, 67. On anti-Semitism in Britain, see Bryan Cheyette and Laura Marcus (eds.), *Modernity, Culture and 'the Jew'* (Cambridge, Polity Press, 1998); David Feldman, *Jews and Englishmen: Social Relations and Political Culture, 1840–1914* (New Haven, Yale University Press, 1994); Clarke, *Dora Marsden and Early Modernism*, p. 57.

78. Ethelmer, 'Feminism', 50–62; Florence Farr, *Modern Woman: Her Intentions* (London, Frank Palmer, 1910), p. 8. A series of articles on the Jewish Question in *The Eye-Witness* in 1911 suggests this was a common topic of Edwardian political argument. The participation in the resulting correspondence of two Jews, David Eder and Arthur Lewis (also *Freewoman* correspondents), reveals a relatively untroubled intellectual relationship between Jewish intellectuals and the 'anti-Semites'. See also the use in Schreiner's *Woman and Labour* of images of 'the little asthmatic Jew', in contrast to the 'great, almost naked, white bodies' of 'Saxons', Schreiner, *Woman and Labour*, pp. 213, 161.

79. Bourne to Parsons, 15 Nov. 1915, 9 May 1917, ECPP. Christine Stansell describes American 'bohemian' circles as filtering out the more virulent elements of religious and racial bigotry, though still hosting 'rising anti-Semitism'. Nonetheless, the overall atmosphere of the American avant-garde was tolerant, echoing the inclusion and cosmopolitanism called for by Randolph Bourne. Stansell, *American Moderns*, pp. 23–4; Bourne, 'Trans-National America'.

80. Stirner saw his audience as exclusively non-Jewish, declaring 'you, my dear reader, are at least not a full-blooded Jew'. He divided the world's civilisations into three phases, with the 'Negro' stage at the base, then 'the Mongol', and finally 'the Caucasian'. Stirner, *Ego and its Own*, pp. 36, 85.

81. Marsden, *FW*, 12 Sept. 1912, 323.

82. Lafitte to Marsden, DMC 24 June 1912: III, 5; Marsden, *FW*, 6 June 1912, 42.

83. *FW*, 16 May 1912, 503; Charlotte Perkins Gilman, *Women and Economics: A Study of the Economic Relation Between Men and Women as a Factor in Social Evolution* (New York, Harper and Row, 1966), pp. 31–2.

84. Gilman, *Women and Economics*, pp. 127–30, 245–6; Key, *Woman Movement*, p. 53; Marsden, *FW*, 23 May 1912, 1–2.

85. Birnstingl, 'Interpretations of Life', *FW*, 6 June 1912, 50–1, and 13 June 1912, 70–1; 25 Jan. 1912, 189–90; 8 Feb. 1912. Other contributors found Weininger's formulae useful; one, a biological male, asserted that contrary to somatic appearances, 'I am about 80 F and 20 M'. 'Scython', *FW*, 22 Feb. 1912, 274.

86. Baty, *FW*, 22 Feb. 1912, 26.

87. Whitby, *FW*, 18 Jan. 1912, 167–9.

88. Birnstingl, *FW*, 4 Jan. 1912, 128; 8 Feb. 1912.

89. E. M. Watson, *FW*, 21 Dec. 1911, 91; Helen Hamilton, *FW*, 21 March 1912, 352.

90. Regenier Gagnier, *Subjectivities: A History of Self-Representation in Britain, 1832–1920* (Oxford, Oxford University Press, 1991), p. 217; Graham, *FW*, 5 Sept. 1912, 313–14.
91. *The Forum*, Oct. 1912, 457.
92. Le Bon, *The Crowd*, pp. 21, 17; Hall, *Adolescence*, pp. 565, 561. Cf. Kopald in Kirchwey, *Our Changing Morality.*
93. Ethelmer, 'Feminism', 59; Key, *Century of the Child*, p. 105.
94. Margaret L. Woods, 'Supermanity and the Superwoman', *Nineteenth Century*, 66 (Sept. 1910), 534; Gilman, *Herland, The Yellow Wall-paper, and Selected Writings*; Gilman, 'Genius, Domestic and Maternal', *Forerunner* (July 1910), 5–7.
95. Tuttle, *Awakening of Woman*, p. 13; Royden, *The Making of Women*, p. 50.
96. Eastman, *Crystal Eastman*, p. 47.

CHAPTER 8

Feminists and the impact of world war

From 1914, the idea of superman or superwoman took on very different connotations, as the political argument of both British and American radicals became dominated by the ongoing experiences of war. As one British commentator put it in 1917, 'Our Superman fades before our eyes ... The war ... is the answer to the scientific sentimentalists, like Nietzsche and his followers, who talk about slave-morality and crowd-instincts.' The writer preferred to celebrate the 'ordinary men and women who are braver and more generous than the dominating aristocracies and high chivalric groups of the Past'. Talk of women's genius returned to the confining idea that the production of men and women was the creative genius of women; this argument was used to account for women's 'natural' opposition to war.[1] Similarly, the utopian ideas of a pre-modern, stateless pastoral society did not resonate with the conditions of war. Lifestyle radicalism, political argument, publishing, and cultural innovation were all transformed during the war, leaving a very different landscape for feminists to inhabit.

For many progressives, peace and the solution of conflict by international treaties had been a lynchpin of their political thinking. Nonetheless, when war came in 1914, many peace advocates found that it was a cause they could support. The government of Woodrow Wilson remained neutral between 1914 and 1917, but managed to present preparedness for war and intervention as compatible with the principles of progressive politics. Wilson highlighted the potential of war to modernise government, to promote internationalism and bolster civilisation founded on 'American values'. Socialists believed that the war programmes would promote industrial democracy; many radicals and liberals were convinced that American intervention would promote democracy in the rest of the world. However, when the Americans did enter, there was a prevailing atmosphere of intimidation, conformism and extreme intolerance of dissent.[2] Where the pre-war political argument around the role of the state had stressed its welfare functions, it was surveillance that became characteristic of the wartime state. This development was fostered by the 1917 Espionage Act, and its extension in the 1918 Sedition Act. Utterances which criticised the American government in any sense, regardless of the relationship to war, became illegal; Sedition Act measures led directly into the 'Red Scare' in the years following the war.

In 1914 Britain, political radicals faced a more polarised ideological landscape, and a swifter need to take sides. Historians have pointed to the starker, more abrupt changes in British society and political argument caused by the outbreak of war, in contrast to the relative continuity of the United States. Many Fabians (including H. G. Wells) and the Labour Party leadership quickly came to support the government at war. The Independent Labour Party opposed the war, and was relatively marginalised as a result. Its members and other radicals, Quakers and guild socialists who opposed the war felt themselves under threat in Britain, faced with anti-German public opinion, as well as the harassment of the Defence of the Realm Acts and censorship of the press. They organised the Union of Democratic Control and the No Conscription Fellowship in response to the war. Both these groups gained the support of some suffragists and feminists, and both suffered intense surveillance and persecution by the authorities, and some resentment from public opinion.[3]

Historians have argued that the broad coalition of support for the war in the United States and Britain was constructed in part through the adoption of gendered imagery and language. Concepts of masculinity and femininity were powerfully harnessed to ideas of citizenship, militarism and democracy in order to justify and sanction the war activities of governments. Proponents of war suggested that it would virilise American and British men, who were dangerously degenerate and addicted to 'feminine' luxury. Opposition to the war was painted as 'petticoat' behaviour, and the suppression of dissent was framed as a suppression of 'unnatural' gender orders. As Kathleen Kennedy has argued, women opposed to the war found themselves deemed subversive as much for their transgression of the norms of maternal, patriotic femininity as for the actual content of their opposition. Accusations of feminine 'subversion of the state' were frequently linked to those of sexual 'degeneracy'.[4]

In both countries, war paradoxically not only destabilised gender relations, but also intensified the symbolic significance of gender differences. Starker gender boundaries were redrawn, and the idea of a homosocial political community was foregrounded. Constructions of World War One militarism were infused with a fear of the authority and influence of women over the character of men. Of course, some women found war conditions an opportunity for transgression, and for the lessening of gender inequalities, but in the main, the rhetoric of war intensified traditional appeals to vulnerable/dangerous femininity and virile masculinity. War, which historians have tended to see as a major factor of gender instability and sexual disorder, should also be understood as working to stabilise certain conventional representations of gender. There was, as Patrice and Margaret Higonnet have argued, an illusion of change, as the dynamic of gender subordination shifted in a 'double helix' movement to revalue the changed practices of wartime. In the end, this resulted in a strong preservation of the relative status of men and women.[5]

THE WOMEN'S MOVEMENT AND WAR

Within the women's movement, there was a diversity of responses to war and its gendered imagery. Some suffragists were swept into war relief work, judging that this could break the deadlock of Liberal opposition to granting them the vote. The WSPU and the NUWSS both suspended their campaigns and offered their services to the government, despite the tensions this caused within these bodies. Millicent Fawcett, in particular, pushed for an unrelenting patriotism, which provoked mass resignations of the officers and executive of the NUWSS in early 1915. Pro-war NUWSS members worked to promote not only women's voluntary war service, but also to construct suffragists' role as advocates for the neglected non-combatants – working, for example, to safeguard women's employment interests or to resist the reintroduction of Contagious Diseases legislation. Some pro-war WSPU members found their pre-war militaristic rhetoric compatible with a wartime pro-militarism, and adopted a violently jingoistic platform. Emmeline Pankhurst, who during the suffrage struggle had lyrically promoted 'the joy of battle' as something women should embrace, threw her energies into supporting recruitment into the services and war work.[6] *The Suffragette*, renamed *Britannia* in 1915, strongly promoted patriotic rhetoric.

Faced with this landscape, many other British women activists felt misgivings. The Women's Co-operative Guild and the East London Federation of Suffragettes were initially critical of the provision made for women whose precarious economic situation had been upset by the war, and remained uneasy about militarism. Pacifism was an option for some, though most activists experienced high levels of doubt and disorientation in the atmosphere of patriotism. At the outbreak, one wrote in the

Woman's Dreadnought: 'At one swoop our sense of judgement and our sense of proportion seem to be swept away ... It takes all our moral strength to pull ourselves together ... We must keep perfectly clear in our minds that this war is wicked'. Nonetheless, she went on, 'Our whole nature is crying out, trying to believe that there is such a thing as a righteous war, and that this is one'.[7] The *Women's Dreadnought* remained ambivalent towards the war until 1917, when the Bolshevik revolution prompted its name-change to the *Worker's Dreadnought*, and a shift towards a more vigorous demand for a negotiated peace.

Within the WSPU, even the loyal Annie Kenney wrote of the reaction to the Pankhurst abrupt shift to support the government: 'This autocratic move was not understood or appreciated by many of our members. They were quite prepared to receive instructions about the Vote, but they were not going to be told what they were to do in a world war'.[8] New suffrage groups – the Suffragettes of the WSPU and the Independent WSPU – were formed to resist the Pankhurst focus. Another grouping, the United Suffragists, was formed just before the outbreak of war. Its founders aimed to continue active militancy without the violent extremes of the WSPU. This group was small, but continued to produce the former WSPU paper, *Votes For Women*, under the proprietorship of the anti-war Pethick Lawrences. The war caused a decline in the intensity of the campaign and a poor financial climate for suffrage campaigning, but did not entirely crush suffrage activism in Britain.[9]

While the Women's Freedom League and these new suffrage groups continued to campaign for suffrage and to provide a forum for peace activism, some found suffrage an unhelpful platform on which to pursue peace activism. The women-only Women's International League (WIL), founded after The Hague conference, provided some focus for British feminist activism especially in Wales, Scotland and the provinces.[10] Feminist internationalism grew in significance and provided a continuing forum for transatlantic interaction, despite the national differences amongst feminists. The pacifist Charlotte Despard became remote from her leadership role in the Women's Freedom League. Other anti-war suffragists such as Helena Swanwick, Catherine Marshall and Maude Royden migrated into the Union of Democratic Control, where women's political representation was linked to a wider debate about citizenship and military action. Nonetheless, women's claims were seen by some as subordinate to what was perceived as the more pressing issue of anti-militarism.

The suffrage organisations in the United States were also divided by the war. The reformist suffragists of the NAWSA, in the main, were comfortable with offering war work services. But in contrast to most British suffragists, many did not feel that they had to suspend their campaign during the war. There was an intensification of suffrage campaigning as the National Woman's Party (NWP) (which did not itself take a stance on the war) began more aggressive invasions of public space in the form of picketing the White House. American 'militants' made no direct link between suffrage militancy and war militarism unlike their British counterparts in the WSPU, and their actions were quickly read as anti-war. Following the government's decision to arrest, imprison and force feed the picketers from June 1917, the suffrage campaign changed its profile; in the context of war, suffragists' association with 'treasonous' activity caused conflict and loss of focus in the women's movement.

The anti-war sections of the American women's movement, while not in the majority, were vocal. Anti-war female Quakers and suffragists were involved in a number of mixed-sex peace organisations, but their frustrations at the lack of concern over women's interests within such groups led to the establishment of the Women's Peace Party (WPP) in 1915. The WPP was initially founded by the New York suffrage-feminists Crystal Eastman and Madeleine Doty. They sought the support of eminent suffragists such as Carrie Chapman Catt, and drew together a wide range of women, from temperance activists to those in the labour movement. As a broad coalition, attempting even to unite pro- and anti-suffrage women, the WPP was a fairly cautious body, and did not sponsor a programme of *active* opposition to the war, though local groups did go further. Nonetheless, its first act was to send a delegation to the peace conference in The Hague in 1915. Headed by Jane Addams, the American delegation was the largest and the most influential. Faced with practical restrictions on the participation of suffrage-feminists from combatant countries, Americans showed a willingness to take leadership within what was left of the international networks of suffragism. The question of strategic priorities and how to balance the claims of pacifism over suffrage was however extremely contentious for the WPP. It split in 1917 over uncertainty whether to highlight anti-war beliefs, or whether to foreground women's war work for the sake of advances in the suffrage campaign. Leaders such as Catt calculated that pacifism would harm the women's suffrage cause, and so retreated from it. The American women's movement faced intense divides between women activists, coupled with bitterness about the 'peacetime pacifists' who had abandoned the cause of peace for expediency, as a means of compelling suffrage victory.

AVANT-GARDE FEMINISTS AND WAR

There was a long-standing propensity towards pacifism and internationalism amongst 'advanced' feminist circles in both Britain and the United States. Figures such as Crystal Eastman, Florence Tuttle, Alice Hubbard, Fola LaFollette, and Elsie Clews Parsons in the United States, and Olive Schreiner and Helena Swanwick in Britain had long made their views clear on the masculine nature of war. As early as 1908, Alice Hubbard, who was to lose her own life crossing the Atlantic when the *Lusitania* was torpedoed in 1915, had written: 'There will be no war when the right of franchise is given to women, for their hearts say that any honorable compromise is better than to kill and slaughter and slay humanity ... Woman has so far gained hers without carnage, and the methods she has used for herself will be effective for all mankind'. Olive Schreiner's *Woman and Labour* had firmly declared women's natural pacifism. Women had a highly intimate experience of war, Schreiner argued, because they had borne and raised the fighting men whose lives were to be lost. Women's superior knowledge of the 'history of human flesh' made it impossible for them to go to war. This, Schreiner believed, was one of the few significant differences between the sexes.[11]

Schreiner's statement of pacifism was influential, but certainly not definitive. When faced with war between 1914 and 1918, avant-garde feminism produced a range of responses. American feminists were perhaps more united in their opposition to the war than their British counterparts, though Heterodoxy was split. Individuals such as Rheta Childe Dorr and Charlotte Perkins Gilman found their support for the war made their position uncomfortable and resigned from the group. Gilman had opposed what she saw as the masculine egoism of the Spanish-American war of 1898, but the First World War appealed to her sense of the need to preserve 'civilisation' against the barbarism of 'the Hun'. Heterodoxy hosted some pacifists, though other members claimed to inhabit a middle ground of 'mildly radical sympathies' without being full pacifists.[12] Pacifist or not, the club came under surveillance, and began to shift its meeting place each week to avoid harassment. Critics of the war suffered personal isolation as well as attention from the secret services. Fola LaFollette suffered from a painful social ostracism on account of her beliefs. Others found conflict within their own homes. From 1917, Elsie Clews Parsons excluded her own husband who was serving in the army, as well as all others in uniform, from her home.

Prominent radicals such as Max Eastman, Rose Pastor Stokes, Kate Richards O'Hare and Emma Goldman were arrested during this period;

Goldman was deported. *The Masses* retained its prime place as the voice of avant-garde radicalism, and it was eventually closed down under the Espionage Act in 1917. Following the Bolshevik revolution, labour activism had become intensely threatening to the United States government, and where feminists were aligned to the radical labour movement, they became increasingly harassed. Some new journals were founded to resist the atmosphere of intimidation and censorship, but were themselves vulnerable to repression. From its foundation in November 1916, the New York periodical *Seven Arts* became an important mouthpiece for opposition to the war, with the close involvement of Randolph Bourne. Edna Kenton was part of the advisory board, and others from *The Masses* and feminist circles were contributors. *Seven Arts* did not however foreground concerns over gender and was more closely identified with the nativist cultural movement than with feminist politics. The journal preached the regeneration by cultural means of the nation, but its anti-war focus alienated all financial backers and it was forced to merge with *The Dial* in October 1917.

Some feminists sought to work within the framework of peace organisations, despite their limitations. Crystal Eastman led the New York City branch of the WPP, and used it as a radical platform. Despairing of the national WPP's unwillingness to challenge preparedness, she and a group of feminist peers diverged in policy and created a distinctively feminist forum within this one local branch. In January 1917, they founded *Four Lights*, a short-lived bi-weekly feminist-pacifist periodical. Its large, rotating editorial committee included many Heterodoxy members and feminists – Edna Kenton, Lou Rogers, Freda Kirchwey, Madeleine Doty, Florence Tuttle, Anne Herendeen and Mary Ware Dennett were all closely involved. The journal offered an unusually anti-conventional voice during a period of intense pressure to conform. It aimed 'to voice the young, uncompromising women's movement for peace and humanity', and welcomed divergent views to its pages. Following in the tradition of independent feminist journals as opposed to the campaigning suffrage papers, *Four Lights* did not aim at institutional cohesion, and pursued an ironic, humorous tone in its attempt to lift the lid on public debate. Restoring some transatlantic connections, the editors published press clippings from European papers to give an alternative narrative of the war to that conventionally available in the United States; they also stressed the gendered nature of war. *Four Lights* problematised Wilson's claims to be going to war for democracy's sake by constantly reminding readers that women, workers and African-Americans were not included in American versions of democracy. It reprinted the conventional news under mocking new headlines in an attempt to raise readers' awareness of the manipulative process of opinion formation in the United States. *Four Lights* was distributed free to other newspapers, and to all members of the New York City WPP. Its stance on the war led to it being declared treasonous by the Department of Justice, and it was suspended from October 1917, with just one farewell issue in June 1919.

Four Lights' editors and others such as Elsie Clews Parsons, Elizabeth Freeman and Fola LaFollette also became involved in the 1917–18 People's Council of America – an organisation which combined pacifist campaigning with attention to suffrage, labour rights, anti-lynching, and birth control. But most found their feminist interests subordinated to socialism and peace within these kinds of groupings. While the People's Council had a generalised commitment to democratisation, little mention was made of women's specific demands for democracy.[13]

Anglo-American feminists who became involved in anti-war activities experienced a sense of having to choose between anti-militarism and the politics of gender. Many of those who chose the former did not return to feminist politics after the war, and this contributed to the loss to feminism of its connotations of avant-garde revolt. The restrictive atmosphere of wartime Europe and America brought to an end the unique conditions of a relatively free press, and intensely felt political commitment allied to intellectual and artistic creativity. As America entered the war, Randolph Bourne complained of the move amongst feminists such as Henrietta Rodman away from sexual unconventionality. Rodman, accused Bourne, was 'discovering that there are so many radicals today that to be radical is to be conventional. Back to the old homely virtues for her, the dutiful wife, the monogamic home, the twain who have become one flesh ... Henrietta is a perfect barometer of the swing of ephemeral vanguardism'.[14]

Another loss to feminism was its sense as a movement that intimately involved men; within the realms of international institutions, periodicals and discussion groups, men became less prominent as feminists during the war. Peace activism came to dominate gender activism, and 'woman' took on new semantic force as a term that connoted pacifism. While in 1915 Jane Addams had taken a male secretary, Louis Lochner, to the Hague Peace Conference, such involvement of men became rarer as the war progressed. Women found single-sex organisations such as the WIL or WPP more congenial to work in, as apparently sympathetic bodies such as the People's Council proved to disparage feminist concerns and paid their women organisers lower wages than their male counterparts. Ideologically, the arguments made about women's natural propensity to peace, and the sense that war resulted from masculine psychological characteristics, drove men and women apart and made it unlikely that they could see their interests unified under a single identity such as 'feminism'. The Heterodoxy writer Mary Austin, for example, argued in 1918 that war represented 'masculinity run amuck' and was created 'in the very center of male consciousness'.[15] Such arguments, and the single-sex institutional frameworks of peace work, alienated 'male feminists'.

ARGUMENTS AROUND WAR AND PEACE

Much of the historical work examining feminism during World War One has focused on the institutional channels through which it was expressed, rather than the ideas and arguments of individuals, and the period seems to demand acquaintance with a plethora of new acronyms and affiliations in which feminists seem to have become submerged. Those who have examined the political argument and ideas of wartime feminism have either assumed that feminism would naturally evolve in the direction of pacifism, or have argued that the war brought about a 'fatal abandonment' of pre-war feminist ideas in favour of a confining separate spheres ideology.[16] Maude Royden, a consistent and active pacifist, argued in 1917 that 'war, and the atmosphere engendered by war, are the inveterate foes of feminism'.[17] However, a more complex relationship with war is evident in the intellectual history of feminism. Certainly, the war clearly changed the terms in which feminism could function as an identity. An examination of feminist political argument can show some unexpected continuities and intellectual affinities thrown up by the war – feminism was resilient in some directions, while undergoing important changes in others.

As we have seen, many Edwardian women argued that war was due to a masculinisation of politics, which only women's inclusion could avoid. And for many, it was women's qualities as mothers which qualified them to envisage a new world order – historians have described motherhood as a fluctuating and ambiguous discourse, but one which became the primary way of talking about women during the war. In typical terms, Mary Austin described the world as 'a very feminine place, a mother's place, conceptive, brooding, nourishing' to construct her opposition to the war and reinvention of nationalism. Helena Swanwick took up similar ideas in a series of pamphlets published by the Union of Democratic Control.[18] Maternalism and a critique of 'male politics' could be used both to support an internationalist-pacifist stance and to underpin pro-war patriotism. The competing nature of these two options dominated the women's movement, leading to an exclusion of the avant-garde feminist idea that women might live creative lives that did not involve physical reproduction.

Maternalism, however, was certainly not the only reason for a pro-war stance; other leading activist women such as Harriet Stanton Blatch supported the war on feminist principle. She commented: 'I am red hot for war. I want ten million men put on the firing line as soon as they can be got there and I want women organised by women to enter on work here and free men for the army'. Her support came from her belief that 'feminism is at stake in the conflict between the allies and Germany . . . The nations in which women have influenced national aims face the nation that glorifies brute force'. Blatch also saw the war as an opportunity for collective effort by women: 'war compels women to work. That is one of its merits'. Through their paid and unpaid employment, the war did give women opportunities to work in new ways which did not only cast them as mothers, though historians have stressed the fragility of the esteem gained by women war workers.[19] During her travels in Britain and France in 1915 Blatch perceived women flourishing as citizens and 'national servants'. In an interesting inversion of the usual gendered vocabulary of war, Blatch foretold that war would make women virile, bring them out of the isolated home, and modernise their labours.

Faced with the apparent enthusiasm for war on the part of some (perhaps most) women, pacifist-feminists were forced to re-evaluate Olive Schreiner's declaration of women's natural opposition to war. Helena Swanwick recalled that she had to remind herself 'how utterly foolish was the talk of ' "Woman this and Woman that" . . . In one sense, men had made the war. But they couldn't have made it, if the mass of women had not been admiringly, even adoringly, with them'. One Finnish feminist despaired of the 'masses of women' who, sheep-like, had supported their governments across Europe. Women handed out white feathers in England, she noted, while 'from Germany we hear women's voices chanting hate, hate, as persistently as the men's'.[20] She was astonished that suffragists had joined in with the war effort, though she found some comfort in the 1915 Women's Peace Conference. In England, she found that 'the entire woman movement is absolutely halted by [the war]'. There was, then, an atmosphere of despair amongst feminists, which only became more intense once war was declared.

However, the claim that war worked against all the goals of feminism certainly did not resonate with all avant-garde feminists. Mary Austin argued that war would aid sex emancipation because it exploded 'the superstition that the work a human being may do in the world is determined by sex'.[21]

War, then, could represent a transformation of gender norms, and while
Austin was unsure of what the aftermath would be, she was confident that
women's work would never be the same. She also saw war as aiding the
feminist fight for control over reproduction 'by lifting the taboo on sex
intelligence'. War had given a new prominence to how sex was understood,
and a new willingness to discuss its effects openly.

In Britain, this novel openness to discuss sex in the context of war was
welcomed by avant-garde feminists, though it tended to be expressed
within new forums, outside of the pre-war 'advanced circles'. Stella
Browne's interests in sexual psychology and birth control led her from the
Freewoman Discussion Circle towards the activities of the British Society
of the Study of Sex Psychology (BSSSP).[22] This forum for investigation,
founded in mid-1914 and meeting throughout the war, hosted a variety of
enthusiasts and activists, including many interested in homosexuality.
Browne described them in 1918 as spanning Socialists, psycho-analysts,
humanists, birth control and divorce law activists, eugenists and medical
doctors.[23] The Society was open to men and women on the same terms,
and sought to increase the 'sympathy, clarity and equality in the relations
between the sexes'. Such commitments would probably have been
described as feminist if outlined in 1910 or 1911. But while Browne
acknowledged that the women's movement had enabled the BSSSP to
exist, she did not term it 'feminist' when summarising its activities in 1918.
Her interests had moved on and feminism in Britain, split between confining versions of 'old' and 'new' feminism, no longer provided the frame
for these kinds of interests in sexuality and the new morality.

Browne had retained a highly critical attitude towards the war. During
its duration she remained in London and became a regular contributor to
the transatlantic *International Journal of Ethics*. Through this journal, she
retained her links to an Anglo-American space of political argument.
Browne condemned the spirit of aggression and militarism of the war years,
and preferred to unite the individual self-determination which had long
been stressed by 'advanced' feminists with civic and international
co-operation.[24] Nonetheless, she was happy to attribute the spirit of aggression to Germany, which she deplored as the initiating nation in the war.

In contrast, Dora Marsden, living somewhat remotely from the effects
of the war in Southport, Lancashire, developed a startling support for the
war in *The Egoist*. As war broke out in 1914, Marsden used an editorial to
comment on 'women's rights' in the context of war. She regarded the onset
of the war as ending once and for all the controversies about women's
rights to vote, since war demonstrated that rights are conceded not on the

basis of justice, but 'when exhaustion compels one body of combatants to ask for terms'. As usual, she had no patience with those within the women's movement, or the 'humanitarian, pacifist, proletarian, Christian believers', who asked for rights from legislatures or courts.

Might was right, she believed, not in terms of overt violence, but as an expression of 'the inner spiritual flux of might'.[25] Women, she argued, were something like small states in the international polity – under current arrangements, they were the counters which great states/men shuffled around in order to augment their own power. Until they took on their own 'great state' or Napoleon-like powers, women could not act or influence affairs; and she continued to believe that it was only extraordinary women who would possess 'the unique something which sets straight for individual power'. As ever, her arguments came down to an assertion of elite qualities that set a few women apart.[26]

Marsden felt that women's non-combatant role in wartime made a mockery of their political claims – rather than exercising self-defence, they were left to knit socks, while men went to the defence of their country. Ironically echoing the physical force argument of the 'Antis', she felt that only by asserting physical force could women depart from their 'normal womanly protected sphere'. To her readers, this inevitably would have conjured up visions of suffragette militancy, but Marsden denied that militants had ever confronted or realised the real power of their actions. Instead, she claimed, they relied on passive womanliness at the heart of their protests. Marsden perhaps had in mind the embrace of suffering by the ever-womanly suffragette bodies that was epitomised in force-feeding. She preferred women to serve as active combatants, though inspired by egoism rather than patriotic sentiments.

Marsden did not find war and aggression to be problematic qualities, arguing rather that 'our antagonisms are teeming with vitality: they possess the vitalising hardness by resisting which we brace ourselves'.[27] Peaceful conditions governed by law could only be achieved when force was so overwhelming that no resistance could be organised. She therefore identified violence as a pervasive feature of all societies, but a feature that only became visible during war conditions. In Nietzschean terms, Marsden argued: 'Law does not replace violence: it merely gives information detailing the manner in which violence shall be directed'. It was the prerogative of states to exercise violence in such a manner that might be called justice, and far from expecting a state-less utopia, Marsden's thinking seemed to have moved on to a vision of greater states competing in the world order to impose their will. Her feminism had led her to this point, but had become almost invisible in the process; Marsden spoke of this wartime revision of all understandings of rights and justice as proceeding over 'the feminist corpse'. It was clear that for Marsden, feminism and 'advanced women' no longer connoted an alternative to 'the "rights-claiming" women'. While she was still interested in gender issues, and keen to pick holes in woolly arguments about women and their natural pacifism, her utopianism had faded and become a Stirnean egoist-realism, in both international relations and gender relations.

Marsden's ideas had little resonance amongst other Anglo-American feminists and in Southport she became a more marginalised figure, geographically and intellectually. Her mental health began to deteriorate, and she retreated even further from human contact by moving to a remote Lake District cottage. In 1935, Marsden was committed to a mental hospital where she remained until her death. The strain of living according to the ethics of feminist egoism had been at a high personal cost, and despite her charisma, Marsden's following had evaporated. Nonetheless, the ideas of avant-garde feminism did not entirely fade away in the changed atmosphere of Britain at war; they are clearly present, for example, in Wilma Meikle's 1916 book titled *Towards a Sane Feminism.*[28] Her plea for 'sane feminism' was a vanguard call for women to abandon domesticity and motherhood as their ideals. In keeping with her avant-garde predecessors, Meikle saw the vote and higher education for women as relatively trivial issues. Education was felt to be a chimera that would lead women into poorly paid middle-class professional careers while real independence lay in the economic gains possible within business. Like Dora Marsden, Meikle was scathing about the image of women as peace loving, preferring to stress the diversity of women that made generalisations impossible.

What is gone, however, from Meikle's account of feminism is the avant-garde emphasis on creativity, art, and playful sexuality. Meikle, who was around ten or fifteen years younger than most of the 'vanguard feminists', had lived as Rebecca West's companion when West's son was born, but had quickly been ousted by a jealous H. G. Wells. Perhaps reflecting on West's experiences, she christened the avant-garde generation of feminists as the *hetair*, 'obsessed by passion', whose free unions were with men who 'entered these free unions in a Piccadilly spirit rather than in the Puritan spirit of protest which these emancipated women demanded'. Her verdict on the feminist avant-garde was that times had moved on: 'The *hetair* have done service by insisting on the need of sexual freedom for women and trampling on their elders' squalid belief in sexual sacrifice'. But she felt their task of generational hubris had been supplanted by yet another group, the 'youngest' feminists, who placed work above sexual satisfaction. Meikle's feminism was strongly shaped by her sense of age and generation rather than 'the will' and individuality as the distinctive features of the 'freewoman'. Her ideal was the young business woman, who could participate in 'civic and industrial life without the interruption of sex bickerings'.[29] Along with sexual experimentation, elitism had also faded from this strand of feminism. Meikle claimed that she was no longer satisfied with a feminism by which 'a small body of adventurous women for a time turned the world upside down'. She still disdained 'the great mass of mentally flaccid women' but felt that they could not be left out of feminism, and must be 'prodded into activity'.

TRANSATLANTIC INTERACTIONS IN THE WAR YEARS

Meikle's work was welcomed in the United States by Randolph Bourne; he christened it 'the later feminism'. Continuing the transatlantic conversation of the pre-war years, Bourne noted that *Towards a Sane Feminism* was 'so novel in its scathing wit and its high good humor of irreverence that I can imagine it taken with some resentment by the more studious American feminists'.[30] But the transatlantic relationship did not sustain 'the later feminism' as it had done for earlier feminisms; Meikle's work was barely reviewed in the United States. The shared intellectual space had not evaporated, but it had lost something of its intensity and good humour.

Some transatlantic channels of influence can nonetheless be traced out. The Women's Peace Party was in part inspired by the American speaking tour of the British feminist Emmeline Pethick Lawrence, and there were persisting interactions between British and American activists over the issue of peace. Transatlantic travellers such as Harriet Stanton Blatch continued to travel back and forth – her tours of Europe in 1915 and 1918 spurred her first to support the war on feminist grounds, and later to deplore it as intrinsically male. The Anglo-American lecture circuit continued to promote a shared transatlantic intellectual space for all shades of opinion. Supporters of the war such as the Pankhursts and Annie Kenney stressed the importance of carrying American public opinion, and continued to shape their campaigns as Anglo-American through their transatlantic speaking tours.

Nonetheless, the international women's organisations that might have given clearer leadership and cohesion to the movement were nervous of too radical a position, and key individuals such as Carrie Catt and Harriet Blatch at least initially supported the war and preparedness. The IWSA, for example, organised a peace manifesto and Women's Peace Meeting to push for conciliation or arbitration – but its leadership declared itself willing to offer their patriotic services in times of war. Internationalism thus temporarily lost ground, both in institutional and intellectual terms.

Though international organisations and committees seemed to have lost their way, periodical publishing continued to be premised on transatlantic interaction. When Mary Austin analysed women and war in *The Forum*, she confidently quoted British experiences and illustrations for her arguments, without a clear sense that she was referring to a different national context. Prominent British pacifists such as Bertrand Russell contributed to the *Seven Arts*, while British journals such as the *Women's Dreadnought* reproduced anti-war cartoons from *The Masses* and continually reported on the activities of American pacifists. Fred Pethick Lawrence wrote to the feminist lawyer Madeleine Doty in 1917 praising her articles in *The Nation* and giving permission for her to circulate his own pamphlet on internationalism.[31] Inevitably, though, the war disrupted the relationships that had flourished before the war, in logistical and ideological terms. Paper shortages meant that the exchange of periodicals and pamphlets between Britain and the United States was curtailed; *The Egoist* suffered a loss of American readers as a result. The war and its aftermath, ironically, also promoted some interactions through the harassment and deportation of individuals; Kitty Marion was deported from Britain to the States in 1915 on account of her German birth; Elizabeth Freeman, an English-born feminist and Heterodite living in New York, left the country for Britain in 1919 after being investigated by an anti-radical senate committee, as she feared her American citizenship would be revoked.[32] The movement of both these individuals, though not freely chosen, is suggestive of the continuing movement of Anglo-American feminists in these troubled years.

Overall, the American declaration of war in 1917 transformed the landscape in which American feminists operated. Awareness of the pluralistic nature of feminism that had been so evident in the American Edwardian debates began to be eroded. In 1915 there was still a recognition of the many strands of feminism, and the intellectual exchanges between these. Under the heading 'Feminist Movements are Different Abroad', the *New York Times* highlighted the 'outspoken' feminist demands emanating from Germany, Scandinavian lands and other European countries. While the nineteenth-century women's movement had long had nativist overtones, early twentieth-century avant-garde feminists had specifically named nationalism as a 'spook'. But by 1917, feminism had become so divorced from its avant-garde associations that it could be colonised by patriots; the

New York Times headlined the claim that 'Germany Hates Feminism'. The writer celebrated that 'America, reputed throughout the world as the land of feminism, the land of privileged womanhood, is at war with the country in which the claims of feminism are most universally and violently detested'.[33] 'Feminism' had become a bland converse to German 'masculinism'; like suffrage, it represented a site of national rivalry. Readers of the little magazines, who had once welcomed the Anglo-American literary space feminism inhabited, now complained of 'foreign influence'.[34]

NATIVISM AND CULTURAL NATIONALISM

The language of nationalism became insistently present within American political argument. This made more prominent a trend that had influenced progressive thinkers since the early years of the century – a desire to formulate a cultural nationalism that would express the distinctiveness of the United States from the 'old world' of Europe. In texts such as Herbert Croly's *Promise of American Life* (1909), Van Wyck Brook's *America's Coming of Age* (1915), in Theodore Roosevelt's 'new nationalism', or Randolph Bourne's 'Trans-national America' (1916, *Atlantic Monthly*), writers of progressive circles and the avant-garde tried to formulate a novel sense of what it was to be American. Many were comfortable with the nationalist promotion of 'American values' in the world, and with nativist programmes to 'Americanise' and assimilate immigrants. Discourses of Americanisation had long been promoted within progressive liberalism, and were intensified during the war years.[35]

American feminists and suffragists, though frequently critical of militaristic constructions of the nation, took part in this process. They sought a nationalism that could unite individual self-development with the development of a national community and a more confident cultural voice and set of values for the nation. Randolph Bourne tried to express a cosmopolitan nationalism for America which would still allow for opposition to the war and retention of his pre-war radicalism around gender and ethnicity. He insisted that 'No intense nationalism of the European plan can be ours. But do we not begin to see a new and more adventurous ideal?'[36] America, Bourne felt, was to symbolise an intellectual internationalism. Still placing his faith in elites, he charged the 'younger intelligentsia' with responsibility for this.

The suffrage 'mainstream' responded differently to this new agenda. The NAWSA, while it did not go to the extremes of supporting deportation and exclusionary legislation, did shift from being a broad coalition of perspectives that could contain 'advanced feminism' towards a greater conformity to 'American norms'. It instituted an 'Americanisation Committee' to encourage women's work in assimilating immigrants, and portrayed this as an essential part of women's 'war work'. One activist on this committee wrote: 'the woman ... who is the means of converting one alien to become a loyal American citizen ... is in the fighting line as truly as the man who goes to the front'.[37] A new emphasis on nationalism was also articulated by suffragists in Britain; Nina Boyle, a Women's Freedom League activist, for example, declared during the war that 'nationality is the strongest feeling human nature knows, next to the primeval instinct of sex'. Helena Swanwick wrote of her intense feelings of patriotism during the war, which she understood as underlying her pacifism.[38] But the sense of nationalism did not develop into a comparable cultural nativism to that of the United States, and never became a movement that captured the avant-garde in Britain.

For some American feminists, nativism effectively supplanted their focus on transforming gender relations, even though they may not have seen the two as opposed. The feminist-pacifist journal *Four Lights* declared their hope that 'America be true to her destiny, that she may keep forever her place in the sun, the hope of the world'.[39] Contributors continued to focus on gender issues as an important part of how America might distinguish itself. Edna Kenton, an editor of *Four Lights*, wrote within its pages of her disdain for all national boundaries and symbols of nation.[40] But she combined this with a passionate involvement in the strongly nativist Provincetown Players from 1915 and the *Seven Arts* journal from 1916. Both these projects aimed to unite American artists with their communities and express the essence of 'American life'. Kenton apparently saw no conflict between nativism and her pacifist-feminism; 'native', she elaborated, 'meaning always that which is spontaneous, free, liberated and liberating, flowing through and from and again into the people and the nation concerned'.[41] Her understanding of nativism thus united some of the features that had drawn her to egoism – its individualised and self-sponsored version of emancipation – which she now saw as compatible with what Dora Marsden still insisted were 'spooks' – the idea of 'a nation' or 'the people'.

Kenton's involvement with 'nativist theatre' and the Provincetown Players was to last through the war years and the aftermath of the 'Red Scare', and drew her away from the transatlantic and feminist concerns of pre-war years. In ideological terms, nativism encouraged an introspection and cultural isolationism amongst those radicals who had been such active transatlantic communicators.

The newly pressing nature of American and European nationalisms is demonstrated clearly in the later career of Isadora Duncan. She had argued in 1903 that 'the dancer will not belong to a nation but to all humanity', but later had begun to adorn her spontaneous, natural dance technique with tropes of nationalism. Her 1914 rendition of *La Marseilleuse*, draped in red, had evolved by 1917 into a vehicle for American patriotism. In a performance on 6 March 1917, Duncan dropped her red robe to reveal the Stars and Stripes as her undergarment. The orchestra shifted into the *Star-Spangled Banner*, and patriotic hysteria erupted amongst her audience, to the disgust of a reviewer from *The Little Review*. As Ann Daly has written, Duncan had embarked on a second, quite distinctive stage of her career between 1914 and 1918. Peasant dress and pastoral themes no longer seemed relevant, and instead Duncan self-consciously posed as 'Lady Liberty', a symbol of an American heroic nationalism united with motherhood.[42] Gender figured as an important element of nationalism, but tended to be constructed using quite confining tropes, lacking the iconoclasm of pre-war feminism.

As 'Lady Liberty', Duncan had been unseated from the feminist avant-garde by 1917; the feminist journalist Henrietta Rodman disavowed her as 'out of touch' in the *New York Tribune*. Margaret Anderson wrote of how 'Isadora Duncan ran jumped and skipped and stamped and swooned about the stage, dragging with her a body that was never meant to move in rhythmic line, turning music into stories of war and religion'. She saw Duncan as a pseudo-artist, no longer suitable for 'this generation', but instead inspiring 'the mob with the only kind of feeling the mob is ever inspired with'. In their more elitist incarnations, modernists had rejected the sentimentality and obviousness of Duncan's performances, marked as they were by children frolicking with flowers and ferns. 'We all know and share the debt the world owes to Isadora Duncan', concluded Anderson, but modernism had moved on from the idea that 'to feel greatly is to make Art and to put your passion and your anguish into expression is to create. Isadora felt a great deal. She shook her head and arms in such a fury of feeling that she appeared to be strangling'. In the British *New Age*, Duncan continued to be feted into the 1920s; Edward Moore wrote vividly of her brief London appearance in 1921: 'Every public man, every politician, every clergyman, every journalist, should be made to watch her dancing until they began to realise what justice in feeling is'.[43] This, however, was no longer a distinctively feminist vision, and women were, it seems, no longer the expected audience of her work.

Isadora Duncan combined her patriotism with strong support for the Bolshevik revolution in 1917, and like Randolph Bourne and Edna Kenton, tried to make compatible a critical radicalism with the new patriotism. Yet as events in Duncan's life showed, there was a high cost to those who sought to combine pre-war radicalism with cultural nationalism. Isadora Duncan had based herself in the Soviet Union after the war, had married and thus became a Soviet citizen, and opened a dancing school with the support of the Soviet state. When she returned to the United States in 1922 to raise money for her school, she underestimated the political change that had taken place. Despite her earlier role in the nativist movement, she had become seen as a traitorous Bolshevik. Duncan proclaimed herself instead a revolutionist, but this distinction was lost on her audiences. She was forced to cut short her tour, leaving the United States for good in 1923, politically and artistically marginalised. The formalist abstraction of the inter-war artistic avant-garde had no appeal to her, nor she to them. Her final attempt to write in the nativist idiom about 'America' in her essay 'I See America Dancing' offered a racially inflected celebration of white cultural forms, and rejection of the Afro-American influenced dance forms that had supplanted her own dance innovations. Duncan declared: 'Jazz rhythm expresses the primitive savage. America's music would be something different'.[44] Race and nation had replaced gender as the salient point of her politics.

The shifting gender relations of wartime, then, saw the sexually experimental, iconoclastic and individualist 'freewoman' shift to a construction of the capable business girl in the United Kingdom. In the United States, women's liberty became harnessed to the development of nativist cultural forces. Suspicion of the state continued into the war years amongst feminists, but largely morphed into the free-speech and anti-conscription campaigns. Maternity became a more prevailing means of talking about women's contribution to the state; as a result, endowment became a stronger plank in feminist platforms. Utopian thinking gained force, as talk of the post-war reconstruction of society flourished; but it became more pragmatic, and few looked to the individualist utopias of a premodern age.

'Feminism', coined in the five to ten years preceding the war, continued to be malleable in meaning; a 1915 British textbook for Roman Catholic students discussed women's powers of social reform and service under the title *Christian Feminism*.[45] Alice Duer Miller's collection of mostly suffrage rhymes in 1915 included a comment on feminism which suggests that for American audiences it had become a commonplace and unspecific term for women's rebellion. Where feminism had previously been a revolt of daughters against their mothers' ideals, it was now figured as a form of rebellion that mothers could transmit to their daughters:

> 'Mother, what is a Feminist?'
> 'A Feminist, my daughter,
> Is any woman now who cares
> To think about her own affairs
> As men don't think she oughter.'[46]

'Feminism' began to be used to indicate the entire programme of 'the women's movement', including suffragism, or the maternalist politics that avant-garde feminists had found so problematic. Far from connoting the differences amongst women, 'feminism' again came to assert their unity of interests.

END NOTES

1. Sidney Low, 'The Passing of the Superman', *Fortnightly Review* (May 1917), 758, 761; 'Woman, The Peacemaker', *The Vote*, 30 Oct. 1914, 369.
2. Christine Bolt, *Sisterhood Questioned? Race, Class and Internationalism in the American and British Women's Movements, c. 1800s–1970s* (London, Routledge, 2004), pp. 17, 28–9.
3. Jo Vellacott, 'Feminist Consciousness and the First World War', *History Workshop Journal*, 23 (Spring 1987), 90–1; Brock Millman, *Managing Domestic Dissent in First World War Britain, 1914–1918* (London, Routledge, 2000).
4. Kathleen Kennedy, *Disloyal Mothers and Scurrilous Citizens: Women and Subversion During World War One* (Bloomington, Indiana University Press, 1999), pp. 7, 11, 109; Susan R. Grayzel, *Women's Identities at War: Gender, Motherhood and Politics in Britain and France During the First World War* (Chapel Hill, University of North Carolina Press, 1999).
5. Penny Summerfield, 'Gender and War in the Twentieth-Century', *International History Review* 19:1 (1997); Erica A. Kuhlman, *Petticoats and White Feathers: Gender Conformity, Race, the Progressive Peace Movement, and the Debate Over War, 1895–1919* (Westport, Conn., Greenwood Press, 1997), p. 2; Scott, 'Rewriting History', in *Behind the Lines; Gender and the Two World Wars*, ed. Higonnet *et al.* (New Haven, Yale University Press, 1987), p. 27; and M. R. Higonnet and P. L.-R. Higgonet, 'The Double Helix', in *Behind the Lines*, pp. 31–47.
6. Pankhurst, 'Why We are Militant', *The Suffragette*, 21 Nov. 1913, 127.
7. Ennis Richmond, 'What the War Means to Us', *Woman's Dreadnought*, 12 Sept. 1914, 103.
8. Kenney, *Memories of a Militant*, p. 255.
9. Krista Cowman, ' "A Party Between Revolution and Peaceful Persuasion": A Fresh Look at the United Suffragists', in *The Women's Suffrage Movement:*

New Feminist Perspectives, ed. M. Joannou and J. Purvis (Manchester, Manchester University Press, 1998).

10. Haslam, *From Suffrage to Internationalism*; Bolt, *Sisterhood Questioned?* p. 35. J. Liddington, *The Road to Greenham Common: Feminism and Anti-Militarism in Britain since 1820* (Syracuse: Syracuse University Press, 1991).

11. Hubbard, *Woman's Work*, p. 101; Schreiner, *Woman and Labour*; Grayzel, *Women's Identities at War*, pp. 158–9.

12. Schwarz, *Radical Feminists of Heterodoxy*, p. 40.

13. Harriet Hyman Alonso, 'Gender and Peace Politics in the First World War United States: The People's Council of America', *International History Review*, 19:1 (1997).

14. Bourne to Parsons, 15 June [1917?], ECPP.

15. Mary Austin, 'Sex Emancipation Through War', in *American Feminism*, ed. J. Beer *et al.* (New York, Routledge, 2003), p. 453.

16. See for example Vellacott, 'Feminist Consciousness and the First World War'; Susan Kingsley Kent, 'The Politics of Sexual Difference: World War I and the Demise of British Feminism', *Journal of British Studies*, 27 (1988), 232–4.

17. Royden, *The Making of Women*, p. 128.

18. Mayhall, *The Militant Suffrage Movement*, pp. 119–20; Grayzel, *Women's Identities at War*, p. 2; Austin, 'Sex Emancipation Through War', p. 454; Helena Swanwick, *Women and War* (London, Union of Democratic Control, 1915).

19. Blatch, *Mobilizing Woman Power*, April 1918, YWCA Woman's Press, quoted in Ellen Carol DuBois, *Harriot Stanton Blatch*, pp. 206–8; Gail Braybon, *Women Workers in the First World War*, 2nd edn (London, Routledge, 1989), pp. 154–72.

20. Swanwick, *I Have Been Young*, p. 246; Aino Malmberg, 'The Protected Sex in Wartime', *Harper's Weekly*, 8 May 1915, p. 436.

21. Austin, 'Sex Emancipation Through War', p. 455.

22. Lesley A. Hall, ' "Disinterested Enthusiasm for Sexual Misconduct": The British Society for the Study of Sex Psychology, 1913–47', *Journal of Contemporary History*, 30 (1995).

23. Browne, 'A New Psychological Society', *IJE*, 28:2 (1918).

24. Stella Browne, *IJE*, 26:4 (July 1916), 568.

25. Marsden, 'Women's Rights', *Egoist*, 1 Oct. 1914, 361–3.

26. Her analysis mirrored that later developed by *Freewoman* contributor and international jurist Thomas Baty. His equation of women and small nations, in contrast to Marsden, led him to develop a 'feminist' approach to international law in the inter-war period which stressed the need to foster feminine qualities in political culture. See Baty, 'Feminism and Pacifism', *The Contemporary Review* (1939), 95–100; Shinya Murase, 'Thomas Baty in Japan: Seeing Through the Twilight', *British Year Book of International Law* (2002), 315–42, 326–7.

27. Marsden, 'Arms and Disarmament', *Egoist*, 2 Nov. 1914, 402.

28. Meikle, *Towards a Sane Feminism*. Meikle had followed the well-worn path of work with the Charity Organisation Society and the NUWSS in her development as a feminist.

29. Meikle, *Towards a Sane Feminism*, pp. 93–7, 168. Many others have echoed Meikle's division of the thinkers of this period into quite clearly demarcated 'generations', and it is usually assumed that what was distinctive about the experiences of these 'generations' related to their engagement with the war. Mary Gluck's study of avant-garde modernism, for example, contrasts the neo-medievalist pre-war avant-garde, with a younger group, who preferred the idea of art and culture as explosive and violent, and whose social imaginary was dominated by metaphors of machines, the factory, thermodynamics and motion, Gluck, 'Definition of Modernism', p. 870. It was this 'younger generation' of the avant-garde who parted company with feminist politics, and became, as Christine Stansell has argued, highly critical of feminism.

30. Bourne, 'The Later Feminism', *The Dial*, 16 Aug. 1917, 104.

31. Pethick Lawrence to Doty, 23 Jan. 1917, Madeleine Zabriskie Doty Papers, Sophia Smith Collection, Smith College, Northampton, Mass.

32. Alonso, 'Gender and Peace Politics', p. 98.

33. *New York Times*, 10 Oct. 1915, 56–7; 14 Oct. 1917, 35.

34. 'Fear Not', *Little Review*, June 1917, 27. See also W. H. Maine, 'Too British', *Little Review*, Aug. 1917, 24.

35. Kuhlman, *Petticoats and White Feathers*, pp. 17, 47.

36. Bourne, 'Trans-National America'.

37. Grace Bagley, July 1917, quoted in Kennedy, *Disloyal Mothers*, p. 14.

38. Boyle, 1915, quoted in Mayhall, *The Militant Suffrage Movement*, p. 120; Swanwick, *I Have Been Young*, p. 263.

39. *Four Lights*, 27 Jan. 1917, n.p.

40. Kenton, 'North, South, East, West', *Four Lights*, 27 Jan. 1917, n.p.

41. Edna Kenton, *The Provincetown Players*, pp. 14, 16.

42. Duncan, 'The Dance of the Future', in Duncan, *The Art of the Dance*, p. 62; 'Isadora Duncan', *The Little Review*, April 1917, 27; Daly, *Done Into Dance*, pp. 187, 181.

43. Kurth, *Isadora*, p. 330; Andersen, *The Little Review*, April 1917, 5–7; Moore, *New Age*, 21 April 1921.

44. Francis, *Secret Treachery of Words*, p. 29.

45. Margaret Fletcher's *Christian Feminism*, reviewed in the *Times Literary Supplement*, 2 Dec. 1915, 443. Similarly, the *Oxford Essays in Feminism* edited in 1917 by the progressive publisher Victor Gollancz suggests little distinctive avant-garde content to 'feminism', and indeed, Gollancz strongly distanced 'feminism' from the 'extremism' of its 'vanguard' thinkers. Royden, *The Making of Women*.

46. Alice Duer Miller, *Are Women People?* (New York, George H. Doran Company, 1915), p. 64.

CHAPTER 9

'Ephemeral vanguardism': conclusions and post-war developments

The association between feminism and the avant-garde was a volatile one, upset by the changes brought about by war and easily marginalised on both sides. 'Feminism' took on different connotations, and those working at the 'experimental' edge of the women's movement struggled again to find another word. Some of the younger generation of New York radicals who had debated feminism and pacifism in *Four Lights* went on to found a new periodical, *Judy*, in July 1919. They declared:

Judy is a post-feminist. That means that we have left – or are in the process of leaving – that stage where ladies say 'I am a woman. I have standards thus and so. You are a man. You have such-like standards. (Inferior to mine of course.)' We're interested in people now – not in men and women ... I am talking about the woman JUDY represents, young, self-supporting, free ...[1]

Judy's editors associated feminism with a constraining, outworn version of femininity. As Wilma Meikle's work in Britain had also suggested, youth had become a more compelling identity for this younger group. The editorial went on to address 'the feminist': 'Stop considering some desiccated and dried specimen ... and look about for a 1919 model, old dear!' In sharp contrast to its pre-war status as 'ultra-modern', Rebecca West acknowledged that her 'feminism' was by 1924, 'old-fashioned', while another British journalist, Winifred Holtby, wrote, 'I am constantly reprimanded for "flogging the dead horse of Feminism"'. It was not just the term 'feminism', but the overall cultural politics of the experimental 'vanguard' that had become problematic. Millie Price, whose husband was a conscientious objector and who herself had left the women's suffrage movement at the outbreak of war to join the Quakers, recalled that in Britain after the war, there was 'a shuttering down the window of idealism ... Socialism, Woman's Suffrage, craftsmanship, even pacifism had become shadowy.' Her personal response, like many of her peers, was to 'revolt against isms, doctrines and superstitions' and retreat into the private world of family and friendships.[2]

If the vanguardism of feminism was so ephemeral, what can we learn from investigating this brief cultural and intellectual moment? Reading Edwardian feminism as part of the Anglo-American avant-garde adds an important cultural-political dimension to the history of feminism. It highlights the significance of gender within the modern avant-garde movement, and suggests some new readings of avant-garde thought. The avant-garde is frequently read as nihilistic, dehumanising and anti-Enlightenment.[3] Feminists combined something of this with a commitment to humanism, and to the emancipation of women. The Edwardian avant-garde emerges as less 'futurist' and destructive, more open to projects of emancipation (political and sexual), and more complex in its relation to modernity and the past than has previously been allowed. Feminist texts of the 1910s included few eulogies to 'the machine' or 'the skyscraper' that have been taken to be characteristic of the modernist avant-garde. Feminist commitments to originality and personality in artistic labour are easily read as avant-garde, but the backward-looking rural nostalgia is perhaps more surprising and unexpected. 'Back to the land' discourse, however, was used to present a firmly 'modern' view of self-realisation. The conversational and periodical communities of feminism were not anti-provincial, another assumption of avant-gardism; indeed, feminists operated at both provincial and metropolitan levels, and reveal considerable interaction between the two.

This study has explored the idiosyncrasy and diversity amongst feminist avant-garde thinkers. For many, sexual equality was central to feminism, though this did not preclude a politics of advancement for the 'great', or geniuses, of either sex. Equality indicated a belief in ending *arbitrary* forms of discrimination and preferment. But what were perceived as *relevant* factors such as talent, spirit, and personality were still expected to underpin social hierarchies. The gendered nature of these factors remained an open question that feminists compulsively returned to. Such ideas should not be understood as 'high modernist' or proto-fascist, but represent a genuine engagement with the political concerns of the day, shared by a wide range of groups – New Liberal, Fabian, Progressive and feminist.

In broad terms, my reading suggests three distinctive themes of avant-garde feminism: a discourse of introspection, of individualism, and of discontent with femininity.

INTROSPECTION

The first of these themes, the interest in gaining access to 'the inner voice' and understanding the psychological levels of human interaction was not limited to the feminist avant-garde, but can be characterised as a major concern of Edwardians and their successors. For feminists, the intro-spective mode can be traced further back; 'new woman' literature of the 1890s was also concerned with exploring the self, and tracing the spiritual, emotional and psychological trajectory of individuals and their relation-ships. These *fin-de-siècle* writers tended, however, to anchor their psy-chological insights within the explanatory framework provided by biology, and evolutionary discourse. By the twentieth century, feminists moved away from biological explanations through their access to a new language of psychoanalysis (both Freudian and pre-Freudian) and through the growing prominence of psychology and spiritualism.[4] It was perhaps the language of spiritualism that had the widest resonance within the feminist movement. Many who cannot be included within the 'vanguard' were still adamant that feminism, or the women's movement was fundamentally about a spiritual change, located within personality.

There was a conceptual convergence amongst a number of philosophies of social change around the idea that change had to come from within the individual. Social psychologists, pragmatists, anarchists and idealists all stressed in different ways the importance of personality, and the indivi-dual's control over it. The modernist movement, a loose coalition though it was, was also centrally concerned with the interior world, rejecting the stability of self and character and replacing these nineteenth-century narratives with a more malleable, conflictual and uncontrollable account of the psyche. Modernism represented an alienation from bourgeois culture – a culture understood as obsessed with consumption and social status and thus unable to sustain introspection. The inner world was central to modernist innovations in literature, and in expressionist visual arts, and this briefly united them with the concerns of avant-garde feminists.

INDIVIDUALISM

It is perhaps unsurprising that the language of introspection and psyche should also carry with it individualist overtones. Those who directed their attention inwards neglected the social and structural dimensions of social change, and preferred to think in terms of individual self-transformation. In both the United States and United Kingdom, individualism gained importance as part of a renewed interest in liberty and free speech amongst radical and avant-garde thinkers. In this context, the identification by some feminists as individualists represents a distinct version of individualism, and not a harking back to more libertarian or liberal versions influenced by

Spencer or Mill. Feminist individualism was motivated by an egoist desire to look inwards and free the individual self in a self-initiated, self-governed process of freeing one's inner resources of personality.

In general terms, the individualism of avant-garde feminists represented a moral commitment, to the individual being responsible as the author of his or her life. Work, rather than motherhood, was the primary 'moral sphere' for women. Individualist feminism did not mean an absence of collective identities, though it did lay the onus on women to claim or realise such identities. It was not disembodied, as some contemporary feminist theorists have suspected. It did not imply an entirely pre-social individual, but examined the links between individuals and larger, social entities. The social world inevitably crept back in to an individualism that emphasised personal psychological emancipation. As we have seen, initially individualist positions were modified to recognise the power of external constraints, institutions, and structures above the level of the individual.

That these social formations were weakly theorised is evident from the tendency to resort to 'type thinking'. When trying to think about groups, feminists frequently used a 'social type', formulated as an ideal typical individual such as the 'freewoman'. Avant-garde feminists sought to transcend some of the restrictive identities of suffrage-feminism, such as 'woman', 'mother', and 'suffragist'. Yet they tended to base their emancipatory politics on more 'avant-garde' but equally restrictive categories of being such as 'superwomen', 'cold women' or 'bondwomen'. Their lack of interest in shared experiences and focus on *being* was exclusionary and, at times, essentialist. It is no surprise that the utopian thinking of feminists should also be simple. It represented an attempt to compensate for the lack of theorisation of the complexities of social structure by simply removing the social and envisaging a pre-modern barter society inhabited only by individuals.

CONVENTIONAL FEMININITY

The third element – a critical attitude towards femininity – has long-standing appeal to the feminist movement. It characterised the avant-garde feminists on both sides of the Atlantic; Rebecca West had contributed in 1916 a series of articles to the American *New Republic* on the topic of women, the 'World's Worst Failure'. West's main targets were the ideals of elegance and propriety that cursed women of all classes, but the reader was left feeling that there was a much deeper problem with femininity. West felt imprisoned by her experiences of 'a world made by women', and offered instead a paean to an explicitly male world of physical freedom and intellectual rigour.[5]

Like West, others decisively opted for 'masculine' practices; Inez Haynes Gillmore asserted that most women would have preferred to be men. She saw feminists as aliens, hanging in 'a void midway between two spheres – the man's sphere and the woman's sphere'.[6] But this should not be taken as a sign that the feminist avant-garde was not a space of 'sisterhood' and loving support for other women – the evidence from Heterodoxy correspondence shows clearly how important their sense of 'women loving women' was. The life of Dora Marsden, for all her biting criticism of 'bondwomen', was thoroughly women-centred. Living in intimate and intense relationships with her mother, her secretary-companion and her female friends, she did not sustain any significant relationships with men. But these feminists nonetheless made a qualified commitment to sisterhood, retaining a strong sense that women were not alike, and would only come together provisionally and fleetingly in creative or political alliances.

Dislike of women was certainly not restricted to feminists of this historical moment. It has continued to flourish within prominent feminist texts – Simone de Beauvoir's *Second Sex* and Germaine Greer's *The Female Eunuch* both articulate their feminism in these terms. This sentiment can come to resemble misogyny, and has occasionally been read as anti-feminism. The *New Age* journalist Beatrice Hastings, for example, has been kept out of feminist histories by her declared dislike of women and their qualities, and her reservations about feminism. Nonetheless, Hastings closely resembled many of the 'advanced feminists' discussed in this study, and her declaration of 'anti-feminism' can be read as a characteristic 'feminist' dislike of what she called the 'womanly, wifely, motherly, auntly' values of conventional women. Recent work on anti-feminism suggests that no clear line can be drawn around 'feminism' and 'anti-feminism', which in their 'avant-garde' formations frequently inhabited a shared intellectual space.

NETWORKS AND POSITIONS

These three elements are found before and since the Edwardian period in various forms of the 'women's movement', but it was their combination at this *aube-de-siècle* historical moment that created such a distinctive element that it could marshal a neologism, 'feminism'. They can only partially describe what was a rich discursive or intellectual milieu, and not a cohesive group. Suffrage networks to a large extent underpinned the development of the feminist avant-garde, while providing an ideological counterpoint to avant-garde ideas. Some operated outside of these networks, or moved between them. Dora Marsden and Rebecca West, for example, initially inhabited a suffrage network, which formed the basis for the distinct grouping created around *The Freewoman*. While suffrage contacts remained important, from around 1914 both began to look rather to the experimental artists associated with early modernism to provide identities, as, respectively, philosopher and literary commentator.

In situating avant-garde feminism as part of the Edwardian women's movement, it is helpful to characterise a relatively orthodox, or 'mainstream' women's movement, to which the avant-garde was a reaction. What were the characteristic ideas of the 'conventional' women's movement? Some elements of the movement were relatively pragmatic and unreflective. The campaigns for educational and professional reforms, for example, tended to rest their case on a simple assertion of equality, and perhaps wisely, rarely speculated as to the wider meanings of female emancipation. The more reflective intellectual milieu of the women's movement was to be found within some of the suffrage societies and moral reform groups. Sites for reflection included the periodicals of such groups, independent periodicals such as *The Englishwoman's Review* or *Forerunner*, and the penumbra of mostly popular and polemical texts on topics such as 'women's future' or 'modern marriage'.[7] Though these groups and publications display very diverse beliefs and motivations for feminist action, this study has suggested some common features. In general terms, these include a belief in the power and agency of the state in the solution of social problems; a recourse to concepts of duty and self-sacrifice in representing women's social and moral role; an interest in rights and equality balanced by a more fundamental preference for the language of service and its underlying assumptions about sexual difference; a romantic belief in self-development and in the power of a few individuals to compel change; an interest in personal (moral) character as a fundamental justification for the granting of rights and citizenship.

Avant-garde feminism was clearly reactive to this intellectual context, though there were some strong commonalities; there was no straightforward 'centre–periphery' relationship between 'the women's movement' and 'feminism'. Marsden described *The Freewoman* as 'a retort' to the confining intellectual atmosphere of the suffrage movement.[8] This suggests a continuing dialogue or exchange; avant-garde feminism was not, as it has sometimes been portrayed, an isolated, aberrant development. It was rather an expression of the always ambiguous, contested nature of feminism. Amongst 'advanced' thinkers, feminism was given a variety of meanings, but with a widely shared aim of unhitching feminism from the 'women's rights movement' in its suffragist form. It was variously argued that the feminist focus should be women's economic independence, their creative expression, or destroying the institution of possessive marriage. However, these were in a sense secondary effects, while the underlying aim of avant-garde feminism was introspective – to transform women's psyche, and convince some women that they had the power and moral right to make their own choices and exercise their will. Feminism was understood less as a movement, and rather as a personal and individual transformation.

Despite the opposition of 'advanced' feminists to the alleged sentimentality and self-sacrifice of suffrage feminism, there were overlaps between these concepts of women's emancipation. The moral tone of much late Victorian and Edwardian suffrage-feminist writing was also introspective and individualistic, concerned with individual character and agency. This at times came very near to the stress on personality within avant-garde feminism. There was a shared interest in women's 'self-overcoming' (or in Stirnean terms, 'self-mastery' or 'owndom'). Feminist insistence that women had to achieve *personality*, for example, was very close to the more conventional claim that women's freedom was tied up with her *character*.

The vanguard also shared with many suffrage texts a political elitism – an interest in the reform of society by 'leading from the front' and the influence of the 'great'. The idea of the genius or superwoman which grew out of this elitism was not an isolated concern of Dora Marsden's, but was discussed throughout the literature of the women's movement. The 'cultural' politics of the feminist avant-garde – fascination with the pre-modern, dislike of machinery, idealisation of craft work – were also represented in other feminist texts. Even the apparently obvious divides – for example the widespread statism among suffragists versus the anti-statism of the avant-garde – were not unambiguous. Anti-statism amongst feminists was compatible with fairly extensive state action, in an enabling role guided by the principle of individual self-development. The adoption of an *explicitly* individualist and even egoist 'feminism', however, was perhaps the most distinctive and oppositional move within feminism, and the nature of feminist individualism has been a motivating question for much of this study.

For the historian, challenging questions are raised by what are on the face of it, less 'progressive' features of Edwardian feminist political argument – neo-medievalism, anti-democracy, and anti-Semitism, for example. It is important to bear in mind that these positions had equal claim to being 'progressive' at the time as did some more familiar, liberal commitments. The identification of these as major concerns for Edwardian feminists indicates an intellectual and political context for the shaping of modern feminism that was richer and more complex than the simple 'liberal' concern of equal rights. This study enlarges the scope of the historiography of the British and American feminist movements. The focus of feminist histories of this period has moved from an initial concern with great personalities and militant strategies, to a welcome interest in the broader social base of feminism – the links between feminists and trade unions, the inclusion of working women, and diversity at the grass-roots level. While this is clearly necessary, it has skirted those elements of 'progressivism' that have lost resonance in the course of the twentieth century. In other words, those elements of Edwardian feminism that some formative experiences of the twentieth century – two world wars, fascism, desegregation, end of empire and so on – have made unacceptable or of little interest. Nonetheless, these equivocal aspects of the intellectual milieu of feminism are key to understanding its origins, and its trajectory in the following decades of the twentieth century.

POST-WAR DEVELOPMENTS

'Feminism', unlike the myriad Edwardian neologisms that did not survive, may have found a lasting place in English common usage because it quickly became a much more generalised term. The connotations of 'feminism' as an iconoclastic, ultra-modern face of the women's movement faded. It began to emerge as an innocuous synonym of 'women's movement'. Historians have cemented this tendency to over-generalise the meaning of 'feminist' by using it in a blanket way to describe women's suffrage and social activism. The fate of avant-garde feminism was perhaps embedded in its own success – as a generalised term, 'feminism' became less useful to those trying to indicate a distinctive position. Anne Herendeen, an editor of *Judy* as well as a Heterodite, explained the ephemeral nature of the identity:

Well do I remember the day Henrietta Rodman started going round taking Binet tests to ascertain whether her conscious women friends were feminists or humanists. Henrietta asked the question the way my French teacher, who liked us to have good marks, used to say, 'Comment dites-vous 'door' – la fenêtre ou la porte?' I took the hint and tried hard to be a Humanist.[9]

In the new atmosphere, it seems that introspection, individualism and criticism of femininity came to hold less promise for feminists. In Britain, Victor Gollancz's attempt to 'restate the fundamentals of feminism' in 1917 still felt required to distinguish feminism from the 'futile attitude of people who arrogated to themselves the absurdly misleading name of Free-woman'. Gollancz, Schreiner and later commentators have judged the avant-garde formulation of feminism to be 'vicious and antagonistic to basic feminist principles', and it has proved too politically ambiguous to feature large in the historical narrative of the 'origins' of feminism.[10] When, in the later 1920s, an American journalist Dorothy Dunbar Bromley wrote in *Harper's* of a 'Feminist – New Style', she evoked (in somewhat vague and ephemeral terms) a feminism at the 'vanguard of change', symbolised by the skyscraper, abstract art, the modernist novel.[11] The association between the avant-garde and feminism in the 1910s had largely faded from the American cultural memory, and was being introduced as a *novelty* of the late 1920s.

A book titled *Women Have Told: Studies in the Feminist Tradition* published in Boston in 1930 did however include a chapter on 'Rebecca West and the *Freewoman*'. The author, Amy Wellington, a friend and literary collaborator of Charlotte Perkins Gilman, summarised in glowing terms the aristocratic, introspective beliefs of pre-war feminists. Well-ington acknowledged that the feminist identity was no longer used, but stressed that it was the 'feminist tradition' that had allowed women such as Virginia Woolf or Rose Macaulay to abandon 'feminism' and yet develop their creativity and careers. However, when reviewed by the *New York Times*, the reviewer rejected the 'feminist' identity of West and the other women discussed in *Women Have Told*, arguing that they were 'artists first'. Feminism was understood as the arid pursuit of causes. The avant-garde vision of feminism as central to the creative impulse was no longer visible. Feminism represented 'a rebellious past which is over ... [*Women Have Told*] is outworn and old-fashioned, written in a language that strikes no spark of fire today'.[12]

Crystal Eastman, whose involvement with *The Masses* and Heterodoxy had placed her firmly within the feminist avant-garde, came by 1920 to abandon the talk of inner soul that had dominated Edwardian feminism for a practical concern with economic freedom and birth control:

'Oh! don't begin with economics', my friends often protest, 'Woman does not live by bread alone. What she needs first of all is a free soul.' And I can agree that women will never be great until they achieve a certain emotional freedom, a strong healthy egotism, and some un-personal sources of joy – that in this inner sense we cannot make woman free by changing her economic status. What we can do, however, is to *create conditions of outward freedom* in which a free woman's soul can be born and grow. It is these outward conditions with which an organized feminist movement must concern itself.[13]

Despite this renewed focus on economic independence, some feminists continued to be fascinated by the Middle Ages, and by the simple life. In the early 1920s, *The Vote* continued to report on contemporary 'simple life' exhibitions, and to look back with nostalgia to the 'sex equality' of the 'English Gilds'. But there was something rather joyless about the resolution taken at the 1920 International Council of Women, which voted for 'a return to a simpler mode of dress and against luxury in the home or society, and later on against extravagance in dress and dancing, the former as increasing class animosity and discontent and the latter as encouraging immorality'.[14] The focus on passionate self-development through the simple life of the feminist avant-garde seems to have been swept away by a concern for the preservation of social stability and morality.

Those who continued to identify as feminists tended to use the term to indicate a political campaign for equal rights. Those who hoped to organise feminism on a wider basis found little resonance for their ideas. Teresa Billington-Greig, who had left the confining suffrage organisations and sought an independent feminist identity from 1910, simply could not publish her articles in the later 1910s and 1920s. Her correspondence with editors reveals their lack of interest in her articles on domestic organisation, women's work or consumer topics. She aimed some of these articles specifically at an American audience, but did not find the Anglo-American connection of pre-war years. She continued to be associated with feminist campaigns in the Six Point Group, but the scope of her feminist vision found little reflection in the politics of what had become 'equality feminism'.

Time and Tide, the weekly periodical most closely associated with this strand of feminism in Britain, claimed in 1926 that core concerns of pre-war feminists such as birth control had 'properly speaking ... nothing whatever to do with feminism'. Equality, the editor declared, could be the only concern of feminists.[15] Most of her contemporaries even used 'feminism' with reluctance. Wilma Meikle declared that feminists were working towards 'the disappearance of feminism, its ultimate absorption in the common cause of humanity'. This ambivalence about the term can help to explain Virginia Woolf's emphatic rejection of 'feminism' two decades later, in her 1938 polemic, *Three Guineas*. Though the Bloomsbury avant-garde formed a distinct and inward-looking circle in comparison to the more diffuse, politically engaged milieu of 'advanced feminism', Woolf shared many of the aims and concerns of the feminist avant-garde. She floundered, however, to find a language to describe what she vaguely termed

a force which had become so strong in its turn that it is much to be hoped that the psychologists will find some name for it. The old names as we have seen are futile and false. 'Feminism', we have had to destroy. 'The emancipation of women' is equally inexpressive and corrupt.[16]

Woolf concluded that no one word could express the 'force' which her forebears might have identified as 'feminism'. She saw 'Feminist' as a word which had become used as abuse, creating resentment in those at whom it was aimed. Woolf preferred to

destroy an old word, a vicious and corrupt word that has done much harm in its day and is now obsolete ... [Feminist], according to the dictionary, means 'one who champions the rights of women'. Since the only right, the right to earn a living, has been won, the word no longer has a meaning. And a word without a meaning is a dead word, a corrupt word. Let us therefore celebrate this occasion by cremating the corpse. Let us write that word in large black letters on a sheet of foolscap; then solemnly apply a match to the paper.

Feminism had in her reading been reduced to one aim only, that of economic independence. Lacking the avant-garde connotations of experimentation and critical cultural analysis, it had become a deadening influence.[17]

In the United States, Christine Stansell has suggested that there was a distinct disaffiliation of the literary modernist elite from the radical politics that had previously been integral to their project. As the political horizon narrowed in the climate of war and its aftermath, the avant-garde retreated from politics, and political thinkers became repelled by the remoteness of cultural elites from quotidian concerns. Where feminism had, as Stansell argues, been a pre-eminent source of 'cultural and political vitality' for the pre-war intellectual vanguard, after 1920 it became narrowed to a concern with equality. The arid polarisation between the supporters of the Equal Rights Amendment (the new 'ultra-feminists') versus those supporting protective legislation did not make for an atmosphere amenable to the introspective and iconoclastic interventions of the feminist avant-garde. When Suzanne LaFollette (a cousin of Fola LaFollette) brought out her

1926 book, *Concerning Women*, it dealt with many of the same themes that fascinated the pre-war feminist avant-garde – individual autonomy, a desire to live life at first hand, anti-statism, economic freedom. But the author recalled that it was received in silence, with barely a review, and little impact on the historical record of feminism.[18] The experience of publishing 'advanced' feminist views in the absence of the intellectual milieu of the pre-war years brought home just how significant and stimulating that space for discussion and publishing had been.

Some feminists who had been part of the avant-garde feminist circles seemed to be speaking very different languages in the 1920s and 1930s. Floyd Dell, settled into an orthodox marriage and no longer living in Greenwich Village, became a much more conservative commentator. A journalist in 1923 revealed the confused political identification for these former iconoclasts, describing him as 'some kind of Socialist, and might perhaps be called a conservative Bolshevik', who was 'enjoying an old-fashioned happy domesticity'. Dell was still fascinated with gender, but his 1930 book, *Love in the Machine Age: A Psychological Study of the Transition from Patriarchal Society*, insistently referred to 'pre-war feminists' as 'extremists'.[19]

Some Heterodoxy members began to support the view that, as Leta Hollingworth thought, the 'perfect feminist' should be 'a woman happily married and with children'. Hollingworth, a pioneering educational psychologist, argued in *Current History* in October 1927: 'The woman question is and always has been simply this: how to reproduce the species and at the same time to win satisfaction of the human appetite for food, security, self-assertion, mastery, adventure, play, and so forth'. Women were caged, not by men but by their 'cumbersome reproductive system'. Not feminists but 'men of science' were to advance the woman question; Hollingworth felt that feminists could only *publicise* the underlying biological and technological factors that really determined women's lives.[20] Others who had seen themselves as 'avant-garde' seemed to lose this focus. Edna Kenton contributed an article to *Harper's Magazine* in 1926, 'The Ladies' Next Step', making a case for the equal rights amendment. Kenton's pre-war eulogies to egoist women were replaced by talk of 'ladies', and a focus on the injustices to the women under the common law. There is no hint of her former unconventionality in this article, and the focus for change was legislative, not introspective.

Did this retreat from feminism signify an end to the transatlantic conversations that had been so central to its formation? Individuals continued to contribute to periodicals on each side of the Atlantic, and figures

such as the British journalists Rebecca West and Vera Brittain succeeded in
establishing themselves as Anglo-American feminist commentators.
Crystal Eastman married the British poet Walter Fuller and moved
between the United Kingdom and the United States, linking these realms
through her feminist and pacifist activism until her early death in 1928.
Elizabeth Robins, an American writer living in Britain, published *Ancilla's
Share: An Indictment of Sex Antagonism* in 1924, calling for transatlantic
co-operation between women, and looking to American women to shape
the British women's and peace movements. Vera Brittain was sceptical
about feminism, though she still looked to its transnational expression: 'the
present is stagnant and dark, and the future must see a great reawakening
of international feminism if we do not want the women's movement to
founder'. Brittain had lived in the United States for a year, and felt that
American women were 'far in advance of our own perfectly useless type of
leisured woman', with 'less of a nervous desire to please than their comparatively old-fashioned English sisters'.[21] But there were signs that feminism was no longer an active or attractive channel through which British
women might learn from the Americans. The Rochdale Gilman study
circle founder wrote sadly to Charlotte Perkins Gilman in 1926:

I had hoped to tell you that our 'Circle' had widened out considerably, but, alas:
only two members have come into it. I didn't really think it would be so difficult
to get women together to think for themselves. I am now forced to admit that we
have a lot of prejudice to grow out of . . .[22]

Transatlantic interchange was largely limited to forums such as the
American-led International Woman Suffrage Alliance, which continued to
hold European congresses, and (the newly renamed Woman's Peace Party)
the Women's International League for Peace and Freedom (WILPF).
Christine Bolt has however stressed the growing strength of separate
identities for British and American activists. Vera Brittain perceived little
scope for work in these realms of 'international sisterhood' – feminists
were, she felt, 'hopelessly entangled' in 'the complicated machinery of
conferences, conventions, resolutions and recommendations'. The key
issues discussed at international conventions – peace, the protection of
women in the labour market, the welfare of mothers and children – were
far from the avant-garde understandings of feminism. Crystal Eastman
recorded the factionalisation of feminists in these forums, and concluded
in 1926 that 'there is at present no Feminist international with a purpose
and plan of action'.[23] The direct links of friendship and shared intellectual

endeavour that had existed amongst avant-garde feminists were not matched in the decades after World War One.

The programme of the WILPF committed them to 'cooperation with women of other countries in constructive activities which will secure for all women the power to free themselves and protect society from destructive forces'. Its leaders spoke of its aim 'to further carry out the international idea and establish contact between the women of England and America'. While many feminists of avant-garde circles were involved (including Crystal Eastman, Fola LaFollette, Marie Jenney Howe, Florence Tuttle), there was no mention of feminism in their manifesto. Instead, there was a resurrection of the suffrage idea of united womanhood, to the exclusion of men.[24] The feminist man even became mocked by the younger radicals; Anne Herendeen saw the 'Strictly-modern men' with feminist principles as figures of fun. In a playful tone of elaboration of sex-differences, she concluded in *Judy*: 'Men are creatures of brawn and brain with an infinite capacity for learning their lessons. Artists and women understand that lessons are learned only to be forgotten.' Hutchins Hapgood, who had been so confident of male involvement in feminism, wrote that *Judy* should try to convey 'the deeper meaning of women's conversation with one another, when no men were present'. While men were invited as readers and contributors, *Judy*'s overall tone was that of a light-hearted woman's magazine conducting a conversation that could only occur between women.

TRANSNATIONAL HISTORIES

In conclusion, the writing of a transnational history of feminism in the early twentieth century indicates that it, like so many other discourses and identities of the time, cannot be understood without an awareness of how the idea of feminism travelled across borders. In general, we can perceive a common intellectual milieu, and a broadly shared set of periodical communities, operating transatlantically. Ideas do not, of course, travel in a disembodied sense; discourses require the allegiance of human agents, and via this agency, develop and sometimes diverge.[25] Writing transnational history entails showing how periodicals and other texts functioned within international spaces, how friendships, correspondences and speaking tours worked to allow the transnational circulation of ideas and people.

The identification of such circulation is not in itself very significant or surprising; what is important about it is the highly formative role it played in the development of Edwardian feminism and its related discourses. The

Anglo-American frame of reference made a deep impact upon the shifting meanings feminism took on over the first three decades of the twentieth century. Historians have not, in general, acknowledged that much feminist debate took place as a direct exchange between individuals in Britain and the United States (as well as between other countries), or as a commentary upon each other. The transnational element to the debates has rarely registered as historically significant, or has been understood in an etiolated sense; the narrative of British suffrage militancy and its 'transfer' to the 'younger sisters' in the United States has been simply too dominant. But another story has been told in this study – that of the profound influence American feminists had upon their British counterparts. America, commonly 'trailing' Europe in progressive tendencies, was seen as a place in which feminism was initiated, and where ultra-modern women and men could thrive.

The historical exploration of the transnational exchanges within feminism does not imply that an undifferentiated 'conversation' took place, unbounded by space and locality. This study has emphasised that different 'registers' still existed amongst feminists. Discourses may travel, but since they work through the agency of individuals, they can still be situated within a nation, a city, a moment, a set of laws, a specific movement. The 'conversation' between British and American feminists was sometimes a monologue, or became a conversation at cross purposes, or hardened into a 'script' that would no longer admit of discursive development. The different national 'registers', broadly speaking, were shaped by the greater interest amongst American feminists in the family, and the relationships it entailed. This gave them, for example, more opportunities to talk about men and masculinity, and this was one of the perspectives they brought to the transatlantic 'conversation'. British feminists, however, were more interested in talking about the state. The scepticism of avant-garde feminists concerning the influence of the state made them more amenable to thinking about grass-roots, self-governing utopian alternatives than their American counterparts. It has been one of the aims of this study to indicate shared intellectual spaces, but also to identify where differences arose.

Writing transnational history thus still requires the kind of historical specificity, the focus on the local that has been an essential contribution of recent historiography, particularly of social history. It does not imply the marginalisation of all but the very high-profile, successful cultural and political commentators. Quite the reverse, in fact – some figures can only be seen as influential and significant when placed in the transnational context. Within a national perspective, the contribution of someone like

Dora Marsden, Edna Kenton or Frances Björkman can easily be dismissed as marginal, or eccentric. But within the transnational conversation, they were influential figures, whose role in shaping and developing 'feminism' can otherwise be obscured. The focus on feminism within this study should not eclipse the change of focus enabled by transnational history in a number of significant areas. The Edwardian avant-garde, individualism, utopian thinking, political argument concerning the state and its welfare functions – all of these components of Edwardian intellectual life can be recast through a historical awareness of the transnational conversations going on around them. This study has situated feminism, and the 'modern woman', as central to these conversations, and charts their ebb and flow across the early twentieth century.

END NOTES

1. *Judy* 3 (undated, Sept. 1919), 20–1.
2. West, 'On a Form of Nagging', *Time and Tide*, 31 Oct. 1924, reprinted in Spender, *Time and Tide*, pp. 58–63; Paul Berry and Alan Bishop (eds.), *Testament of a Generation: The Journalism of Vera Brittain and Winifred Holtby* (London, Virago, 1985), p. 90; Price, 'This World's Festival', pp. 203–4, MBP.
3. Renato Poggioli, *The Theory of the Avant-Garde*, pp. 2, 26; John Weightman, *The Concept of the Avant-Garde: Explorations in Modernism* (London, Alcave Press, 1973), p. 18.
4. Richardson, *Love and Eugenics*; Buhle, *Feminism and its Discontents*; Mathew Thomson, 'Psychology and the "Consciousness of Modernity" in Early Twentieth-Century Britain', in *Meanings of Modernity*, ed. Daunton and Rieger.
5. Rebecca West, 'The World's Worst Failure', *New Republic*, 8 and 22 Jan. 5 and 19 Feb. 4 March 1916.
6. Gilmore, 'Confessions of an Alien', *Harper's Bazar*, April 1912, 170.
7. The realms of fiction and drama were of course additional sites of reflection upon feminist issues, but fall beyond the scope of this study. Cf. Ardis, 'Organizing Women'; Pykett, *Engendering Fictions*; Cockin, *Women and Theatre*.
8. Marsden, *NFW*, 15 Dec. 1913.
9. Herendeen, 'De Viris', *Judy*, July 1919, 14–16.
10. Gollancz opposed this 'pole' to its opposite, the separatism associated with the allegedly 'man-hating' Christabel Pankhurst, in Royden, *The Making of Women*, p. 27. Schreiner to Ellis, 7 Aug. 1912, in Schreiner, *The Letters of Olive Schreiner*, pp. 312–13.
11. Bromley, 'Feminist – New Style', *Harper's*, Oct. 1927.
12. Wellington, *Women Have Told*; Rose C. Feld, 'Militant Feminists', *New York Times*, 23 March 1930, 14.

13. Eastman, 'Now We Can Begin', *The Liberator*, Dec. 1920, reprinted in Eastman, *Crystal Eastman*, p. 54, emphasis added.
14. *The Vote*, 6 Aug. 1920, 150; 13 Aug. 1920, 157; 24 Sept. 1920.
15. 'Tendencies in the Woman's Movement', *Time and Tide*, 15 Oct. 1926, reprinted in Spender, *Time and Tide*, pp. 271–5.
16. Virginia Woolf, *A Room of One's Own and Three Guineas* (London, Vintage, 1996), p. 260.
17. *Ibid.*, p. 221. Johanna Alberti, *Beyond Suffrage: Feminists in War and Peace 1914–1928* (London, Macmillan, 1989) offers a useful discussion of the inter-war years, though her account is skewed by her definition of feminism solely as an outgrowth of suffrage.
18. Stansell, *American Moderns*, pp. 326–34; Schwarz, *Radical Feminists of Heterodoxy*; Cott, *The Grounding of Modern Feminism*, p. 66; Rossi, *The Feminist Papers*, p. 540.
19. 'Floyd Dell', *The Bookman*, March 1923, p. 70; Dell, *Love in the Machine Age: A Psychological Study of the Transition from Patriarchal Society* (New York, Farrar & Rinehart, 1930).
20. Kenton, 'The Ladies' Next Step', *Harper's Magazine*, Feb. 1926, 366–74; Hollingsworth, 'The New Woman in the Making', *Current History*, symposium on the New Woman, Oct. 1927, 15–20.
21. Brittain, 'Feminism at Geneva I', *Time and Tide*, 25 Jan. 1929, 92; Brittain, 'The Leisured Woman of America' and 'The American Modern Girl', *Yorkshire Post*, 12 Nov. 1926, 4 and 30 May 1927, 6. Brittain argued that feminism had been largely abandoned by the young in her 'Mrs Pankhurst and the Older Feminists: An Impression by a Younger One', *Manchester Guardian*, 20 June 1928, 8.
22. Clegg to Gilman, 22 Dec. 1926, CPGP.
23. Bolt, *Sisterhood Questioned?* p. 75; Eastman, *Equal Rights*, 3 July 1926, reprinted in Eastman, *Crystal Eastman*, p. 211.
24. WILPF manifesto, 15 Feb. 1919, MWDP.
25. Ava Baron, 'Gender and Labor History: Learning from the Past, Looking to the Future', in *Work Engendered: Toward a New History of American Labor*, ed. Ava Baron (Ithaca, NY, Cornell University Press, 1991).

Archives consulted

- Samuel Alexander Papers, John Rylands Library, University of Manchester
- Autograph Letter Collection: Emancipation of Women, British Commonwealth and United States of America, Women's Library, GB 0106 9/3. Cited as ALC
- Teresa Billington-Greig Papers, 3TBG, The Women's Library, London Metropolitan University. Cited as TBGP
- Margaret Byham Papers, 7MBY, The Women's Library, London Metropolitan University. Cited as MBP
- Sheffield Archives, Carpenter Collection, Carpenter MSS 385/6. Cited as ECP
- Floyd Dell Papers, Midwest Manuscript Collection, Newberry Library, Chicago. Cited as FDP
- Mary Ware Dennett Papers, Schlesinger Library, Radcliffe Institute. Cited as MWDP
- Madeleine Zabriskie Doty Papers, Sophia Smith Collection, Smith College, Northampton, Mass.
- Garrison Family Papers, Sophia Smith Collection, Smith College, Northampton, Mass.
- Mary E. Gawthorpe Papers, Tamiment Library/Robert F. Wagner Labor Archives, New York. Cited as MGP
- Oral evidence on the suffragette and suffragist movements, Brian Harrison, 8SUF, The Women's Library, London Metropolitan University
- Elsie Clews Parsons Papers, American Philosophical Society, Philadelphia, Pa. Cited as ECPP
- Charlotte Perkins Gilman Papers, Schlesinger Library, Radcliffe Institute. Cited as CPGP

- Inez Haynes Gillmore Irwin Papers, Schlesinger Library, Radcliffe Institute
- Papers of Kitty Marion, 7KMA, The Women's Library, London Metropolitan University
- Dora Marsden Collection, Manuscripts Division, Department of Rare Books and Special Collections, Princeton University Library. Cited as DMC, with box (Roman numeral) and folder numbers appended
- Grace Thompson Seton Papers, Schlesinger Library, Radcliffe Institute
- Harriet Shaw Weaver Papers, Add. 57345–57365 British Library, London. Cited as HSWP

Bibliography

Note: All publications are London unless otherwise indicated

PRIMARY SOURCES

Anthony, K. (1916) *Feminism in Germany and Scandinavia*. Constable and Co.

Atkinson, Gore-Booth, Pankhurst *et al.* (1907) *The Case for Women's Suffrage*, ed. B. Villiers. Fisher Unwin

Atkinson, M. (1914) *The Economic Foundations of the Women's Movement*, Fabian Tract No. 175. In *Women's Fabian Tracts (1988)*, ed. S. Alexander. Routledge

Austin, M. (1912) *A Woman of Genius*. Old Westbury, NY: The Feminist Press (1985)

Austin, M. (1918) 'Sex Emancipation Through War'. In *American Feminism*, ed. J. Beer *et al.*, pp. 453–63. New York, Routledge (2003)

Baty, T. (1939) 'Feminism and Pacifism', *The Contemporary Review*, 95–100

Bax, B. (1906) *Essays in Socialism, New and Old*. E. Grant Richards

Belloc, H. (1913) *The Servile State*. Indianapolis, Liberty Fund (1977)

Bentinck, R. C. (1910) 'The Point of Honour: A Correspondence on Aristocracy and Socialism'. In *Women's Fabian Tracts*, ed. Sally Alexander. Routledge (1988)

Billington-Greig, T. (1908) 'The Rebellion of Women', *Contemporary Review*, July

Billington-Greig, T. (1911) *The Militant Suffrage Movement – Emancipation in a Hurry*. F. Palmer

Blatchford, R. (1893) *Merrie England*. The Journeyman Press (1976)

Blease, W. L. (1910) *The Emancipation of English Women*. Constable and Co.

Bosanquet, H. (1902) *The Strength of the People: A Study in Social Economics*. Macmillan & Co.

Bosanquet, H. (1914) *Social Work in London 1869–1912*. Brighton, Harvester Press (1973)

Bourne, R. (1916) 'Trans-national America', *Atlantic Monthly*, 118: 1, July, 86–97

Bourne, R. (1981) *The Letters of Randolph Bourne: A Comprehensive Edition*, ed. Eric J Sandeen. Troy, NY, Whitslon Publishing Co.

Brittain, V. (1933) *Testament of Youth: An Autobiographical Study of the Years 1900–1925.* Victor Gollancz

Browne, F. W. S. (1917) 'Some Problems of Sex,' *International Journal of Ethics,* 27, July

Browne, F. W. S. (1917) 'A New Psychological Society,' *International Journal of Ethics,* 266–9

Browne, S. (1917) 'Woman and Birth Control'. In *Population and Birth Control: A Symposium,* ed. Eden Paul and Ceder Paul. New York, Critic and Guide Co.

Bruce, H. A. (1913) 'Genius – A World-old Problem Viewed in the Light of Modern Psychology,' *Harper's Weekly,* 9 Aug., 8–9, 25

Butler, J. E. (1880) *Government by Police.* Dyer Brothers

Butler, S. (1872) *Erewhon.* New York, Airmont Publishing Co. (1967)

Butler, V. (1916) *Domestic Service: Inquiry by the Women's Industrial Council*

Carpenter, E. (1894) *Homogenic Love and its Place in a Free Society.* Redundancy Press (1980)

Carpenter, E. (1896) *Love's Coming of Age.* Manchester, Manchester Labour Press

Carpenter, E. (1908) *The Intermediate Sex.* George, Allen & Unwin

Carter, H. (1911) *Women's Suffrage and Militancy: A Symposium.* Frank Palmer

Chesterton, G. K. (1987) *What's Wrong with the World.* San Francisco, Ignatius Press

Chew, A. N. (1982) *The Life and Writings of a Working Woman.* Virago

Croly, H. (1915) *Progressive Democracy.* New York, Macmillan

Croly, H. (1965) *The Promise of American Life.* Cambridge, Mass., Harvard University Press

Cumberland, G. (1919) *Set Down in Malice.* New York, Bretano

Delisle, F. (1946) *Friendship's Odyssey.* Heinemann

Dell, F. (1913) *Women as World Builders: Studies in Modern Feminism.* Chicago, Forbes and Company

Dell, F. (1930) *Love in the Machine Age: A Psychological Study of the Transition from Patriarchal Society.* New York, Farrar & Rinehart

Dell, F. (1961) *Homecoming.* Washington, Kennikat Press

Despard, C. (1913) *Theosophy and the Woman's Movement.* Theosophical Society

Dorr, R. C. (1910) *What Eight Million Women Want.* Boston, Small, Maynard & Co.

Dorr, R. C. (1924) *A Woman of Fifty.* New York, Funk and Wagnalls Co.

Duncan, I. (1928) *The Art of the Dance,* ed. S. Cheney. New York, Theatre Arts

Duncan, I. (1928) *My Life.* Victor Gollancz

Eastman, C. (1978) *Crystal Eastman on Women and Revolution,* ed. Blanche Wiesen Cook. New York, Oxford University Press

Eder, D. (1908) *The Endowment of Motherhood.* New Age Press

Ellis, E. (1910) *Three Modern Seers.* Stanley Paul & Co.

Ellis, H. (1901) *A Study of British Genius.* Hurst and Blackett (1904)

Ellis, H. (1934, 8th edn) *Man and Woman: A Study of Secondary and Tertiary Sexual Characters.* Heinemann (Medical Books)

Emerson, R. W. (1996) *Representative Men.* Cambridge, Mass., Belknap Press

Ethelmer, E. (1898) 'Feminism', *Westminster Review*, January, 50–62

Farr, F. (1910) *Modern Woman: Her Intentions.* Frank Palmer

Galton, F. (1869) *Hereditary Genius: An Inquiry Into its Laws and Consequences.* Watts and Co. (1950)

Gawthorpe, M. (1962) *Up Hill to Holloway.* Penobscot, Maine, Traversity Press

Geddes, P., and Arthur Thomson (1889) *The Evolution of Sex.* W. Scott

George, W. L. (1913) *Women and To-Morrow.* Herbert Jenkins

Genthe, A. (1929) *Isadora Duncan: Twenty-Four Studies.* New York, Mitchell Kennerley

Gillmore, I. H. (1914) *Angel Island.* New York, Holt

Gilman, C. P. (1966) *Women and Economics: A Study of the Economic Relation Between Men and Women as a Factor in Social Evolution.* New York, Harper and Row

Gilman, C. P. (1999) *Herland, The Yellow Wall-Paper, and Selected Writings.* New York, Penguin Books

Glasier, K. (1909) *Socialism and the Home.* Independent Labour Party

Goldman, E. (1910) *Anarchism and Other Essays.* New York, Kennikat Press (1969)

Green, T. H. (1886) *Lectures on the Principles of Political Obligation*, ed. R. L. Nettleship, vol. 2

Hale, B. F.-R. (1914) *What Women Want: An Interpretation of the Feminist Movement.* New York, Frederick A. Stokes

Hall, G. S. (1904) *Adolescence, its Psychology and its Relations to Physiology, Anthropology, Sociology, Sex, Crime, Religion and Education.* New York, D. Appleton & Co.

Hamilton, C. (1909) *Marriage as a Trade.* The Women's Press (1981)

Harben, H. D. (1910) *The Endowment of Motherhood.* Fabian Tract No. 149

Harrison, E. B. (1908) *The Freedom of Women: An Argument Against the Proposed Extension of the Suffrage to Women.* Watts & Co.

Hobhouse, L. T. (1911) *Liberalism.* William & Norgate

Hobson, J. A. (1909) *The Crisis in Liberalism: New Issues in Democracy.* P. S. King

Hubbard, A. (1908) *Woman's Work.* East Aurora, NY, Roycrofters

Hubbard, B. V. (1915) *Socialism, Feminism, and Suffragism, the Terrible Triplets, Connected by the Same Umbilical Cord, and Fed from the Same Nursing Bottle.* Chicago, American Publishing Co.

Huneker, J. (1909) *The Egoists: A Book of Supermen.* T. Wener Laurie

Hutchins, B. L. (1913) *Conflicting Ideals: Two Sides of the Woman's Question.* Thomas Murby & Co.

James, W. (1987) *Writings, 1902–1910.* New York, The Library of America

Jones, M. C. (1993) *Heretics and Hellraisers: Women Contributors to The Masses, 1911–1917.* Austin, University of Texas Press

Kenney, A. (1924) *Memories of a Militant.* Edward Arnold & Co.

Kenton, E. (2004) *The Provincetown Players and the Playwright's Theatre*, ed. Travis Bogard and Jackson R. Bryer. Jefferson, NC, McFarland & Co.

Key, E. (1909) *The Century of the Child*. New York, G. P. Putnam

Key, E. (1912) *The Woman Movement*, trans. M. B. Borthwick. G. P. Putnam

Key, E. (1914) *The Younger Generation*. G. P. Putnam

Kirchwey, F. (1925) *Our Changing Morality: A Symposium*. Kegan, Paul, Trench and Tubner & Co.

Knight, M. (1909) 'Woman v. The State,' *The Westminster Review*, July, 36–41

Kropotkin, P. (1911) *The State: Its Historic Role*. Freedom Press

Kropotkin, P. (1974) *Fields, Factories and Workshops Tomorrow*, ed. Colin Ward. George Allen & Unwin

Le Bon, G. (1896) *The Crowd: A Study of the Popular Mind*. Fisher Unwin

Lee, V. (1908) *Gospels of Anarchy and Other Contemporary Studies*. Fisher Unwin

Leo XIII. (1891) *Five Great Encyclicals*. New York, Paulist Press (1939)

Llewelyn Davies, M. (1915) *Maternity: Letters from Working-Women Collected by the Women's Co-Operative Guild*. G. Bell

Llewelyn Davies, M. (1977) *Life As We Have Known It, by Co-Operative Working Women*. Virago

Lombroso, C. (1863) *The Man of Genius*. Scott (1891)

Loy, M. (1998) 'Feminist Manifesto'. In *Modernism: An Anthology of Sources and Documents*, ed. V. Kolocotroni *et al*. Edinburgh, Edinburgh University Press

Mallock, W. H. (1898) *Aristocracy and Evolution*. Adam & Charles Black

Marcus, J. (1982) *The Young Rebecca: Writings of Rebecca West 1911–1917*. Macmillan

Martin, A. (1911) *The Married Working Woman*. The National Union of Women's Suffrage Societies

Martin, A. (1913) *The Mother and Social Reform*. The National Union of Women's Suffrage Societies

Masterman, C. F. G. (1960) *The Condition of England*. Methuen

Mayreder, R. (1913) *A Survey of the Woman Problem*, trans. Herman Scheffauer. William Heinemann

Meikle, W. (1916) *Towards a Sane Feminism*. Grant Richards

Mill, J. S. (1911) *The Subjection of Women*. New York, Frederick A. Stokes

Mill, J. S. and H. (1970) *Essays on Sex Equality*, ed. A. Rossi. Chicago, University of Chicago Press

Miller, A. D. (1915) *Are Women People?* New York, George H. Doran

Morris, W. (1993) *News from Nowhere: Or An Epoch of Rest*. Penguin

Murby, M. (1908) *The Common Sense of the Woman Question*. New Age Press

NAWSA. (1971) *Woman Suffrage: Arguments and Results, 1910–11*. New York, Kraus Reprint Co.

Orage, A. R. (1907) *Nietzsche in Outline and Aphorism*. Edinburgh, Foulis

Parsons, E. C. (1914) 'Feminism and Conventionality', *Annals of the American Academy of Political and Social Science*, 56:145, Nov., 47–53

Parsons, E. C. (1913) *The Old-Fashioned Woman*. New York, Arno Press (1972)

Parsons, E. C. (1994) *The Journal of a Feminist*, ed. Margaret C. Jones. Bristol, Thoemmes Press

Parsons, E. C. (1997) *Fear and Conventionality*. Chicago, University of Chicago Press

Penty, A. J. (1906) *The Restoration of the Gild System*. The New Age Book Dept

Rathbone, E. (1924) *The Disinherited Family*. E. Arnold

Ritchie, D. G. (1891) *The Principles of State Interference*. Swan Sonnenschein & Co.

Robins, E. (1913) *Way Stations*. New York, Dodd, Mead and Co.

Royce, J. (1964) *Lectures on Modern Idealism*. New Haven, Yale University Press

Royden, M. *et al.* (1917) *The Making of Women: Oxford Essays in Feminism*, ed. V. Gollancz. George Allen and Unwin

Ruskin, J. (1905) *The Works of John Ruskin*, ed. E. T. Cook and A. Wedderburn. George Allen

Saleeby, C. (1912) *Woman and Womanhood*. William Heinemann

Scheman, N. (1983) 'Individualism and the Objects of Psychology'. In *Discovering Reality*, ed. S. G. Harding and M. B. Hintikka. Boston, Reidel

Schirmacher, K. (1912) *The Modern Woman's Rights Movement: A Historical Survey*, trans. Carl C. Eckhardt. New York, Macmillan

Schreiner, O. (1911) *Woman and Labour*. Virago (1978)

Schreiner, O. (1924) *The Letters of Olive Schreiner 1876–1920*, ed. Cronwright-Schreiner. Unwin

Shaw, G. B. (1903) *Man and Superman*. Westminster, Archibald Constable and Co.

Shaw, G. B. (1921) *Ruskin's Politics*. Ruskin Centenary Council

Sinclair, M. (1922) *The New Idealism*. Macmillan

Smith, P. J. (1916) *The Soul of Woman: An Interpretation of the Philosophy of Feminism*. San Francisco, Paul Elder and Co.

Snowden, E. (1908) 'Women and the State'. In *Woman: A Few Shrieks!* ed. Constance Smedley. Letchworth, Garden City Press

Snowden, E. (1913) *The Feminist Movement*. Collins

Spargo, J. (1914) *Socialism and Motherhood*. New York, B. W. Huebsch

Spargo, J. (1968) *The Bitter Cry of the Children*. Chicago, Quadrangle

Spencer, A. G. (1913) *Woman's Share in Social Culture*. New York, M. Kennerley

Spencer, H. (1994) *Political Writings*, ed. John Offer. Cambridge, Cambridge University Press

Spender, D. (1984) *Time and Tide Wait for No Man*. Pandora Press

Stanton, T. (1884) *The Woman Question in Europe*. New York, G. P. Putnam's Sons

Stirner, M. (1912) *The Ego and His Own*, trans. Steven T. Byington. A. C. Fifield

Stirner, M. (1995) *The Ego and its Own*, ed. D. Leopold. Cambridge, Cambridge University Press

Strachey, R. (1928) *The Cause: A Short History of the Women's Movement in Great Britain*. Virago

Strachey, R. (ed.). (1936) *Our Freedom and its Results*. Hogarth Press

Stubbs, C. W. (1885) *The Land and the Labourers*. W. Swan Sonnenschein & Co.

Swanwick, H. (1913) *The Future of the Women's Movement*. G. Bell
Swanwick, H. (1915) *Women and War*. Union of Democratic Control
Swanwick, H. (1935) *I Have Been Young*. Gollancz
Swiney, F. (1908) *The Awakening of Women, or Woman's Part in Evolution*. William Reeves
Taft, J. (1915) 'The Woman Movement and the Larger Social Situation', *International Journal of Ethics*, 25:3, 328–45
Thoreau, H. D. (1999) *Walden*. Oxford, Oxford University Press
Tocqueville, A. de (2004) *Democracy in America*. New York, Library of America
Trotter, W. (1916) *Instincts of the Herd in Peace and War*. T. Fisher Unwin
Tuttle, F. G. (1915) *The Awakening of Woman: Suggestions from the Psychic Side of Feminism*. New York, The Abingdon Press
Walker, J. L. (1905) *The Philosophy of Egoism*. Denver, Katherine Walker
Webb, S. (1906) *The Difficulties of Individualism*. Fabian Tract No. 69
Weekley, E. (1921) *An Etymological Dictionary of Modern English*. John Murray
Weininger, O. (1906) *Sex and Character*. Heinemann
Wellington, A. (1930) *Women Have Told: Studies in the Feminist Tradition*. Boston, Little, Brown and Co.
Wells, H. G. (1905) *A Modern Utopia*. Chapman and Hall
Wells, H. G. (1906) *Socialism and the Family*. A. C. Fifield
Wells, H. G. *et al.* (1912) *Socialism and The Great State: Essays in Construction*. New York, Harper and Brothers
Wells, H. G. (1914) *An Englishman Looks at the World*. Cassell and Co.
Wilde, O. (1904) *The Soul of Man Under Socialism*. Arthur L. Humphreys
Wilkinson, L. G. (1914) *Woman's Freedom*. Freedom Press
Woolf, V. (1984) *Virginia Woolf Reader*, ed. Mitchell A. Leaska. New York, Harcourt
Woolf, V. (1996) *A Room of One's Own and Three Guineas*. Vintage
Young, R. (1914) 'What is Feminism?' *Good Housekeeping*, May, 679–84

SECONDARY SOURCES

Abrams, M. H. (1953) *The Mirror and the Lamp: Romantic Theory and the Critical Tradition*. Oxford, Oxford University Press
Adickes, S. (1997) *To Be Young Was Very Heaven: Women in New York Before the First World War*. New York, St. Martin's Press
Adickes, S. (2002) 'Sisters, Not Demons: The Influence of British Suffragists on the American Suffrage Movement', *Women's History Review*, 11(4), 675–90
Alaya, F. (1977) 'Victorian Science and the Genius of Women', *Journal of the History of Ideas*, 38:2, 261–80
Alberti, J. (1989) *Beyond Suffrage: Feminists in War and Peace 1914–1928*. Macmillan
Albinski, N. B. (1988) *Women's Utopias in British and American Fiction*. Routledge

Allen, J. (1990) 'Does Feminism Need a Theory of the State?' In *Playing the State*, ed. Sophie Watson, pp. 21–37. Verso

Alonso, H. H. (1997) 'Gender and Peace Politics in the First World War United States: The People's Council of America', *International History Review*, 19:1, 83–102

Anderson, B. (1982) *Imagined Communities: Reflections on the Origins and Rise of Nationalism*. Verso

Anderson, M. (1969) *My Thirty Years' War: An Autobiography*. New York, Horizon Press

Anderson, O. (1991) 'The Feminism of T. H. Green: A Late-Victorian Success Story?' *History of Political Thought*, 12:(4), Winter, 670–93

Anthony, S. B., and Ida Husted Harper. (1902) *History of Woman Suffrage*. Rochester, NY, Fowler and Wells

Ardis, A. (1990) *New Women, New Novels: Feminism and Early Modernism*. New Brunswick, Rutgers University Press

Ardis, A. (1999) 'Organizing Women: New Woman Writers, New Woman Readers, and Suffrage Feminism'. In *Victorian Women Writers and the Woman Question*, ed. Nicola D. Thompson, pp. 189–203. Cambridge, Cambridge University Press

Armytage, W. H. G. (1961) *Heavens Below: Utopian Experiments in England 1560–1960*. Routledge

Auxier, R. E. (2000) *Critical Responses to Royce*. Bristol, Thoemmes Press

Avrich, P. (1980) 'Kropotkin in America', *International Review of Social History*, 25:1, 1–34

Baker, P. (1994) 'The Domestication of Politics: Women in American Political Society 1780–1920', *American Historical Review*, 89 June, 620–47

Banks, O. (1981) *Faces of Feminism*. Oxford, Martin Robertson

Barker, E. (1915) *Political Thought in England from Herbert Spencer to the Present Day*. Williams and Norgate

Barker, R. (1978) *Political Ideas in Modern Britain*. Methuen and Co.

Baron, A. (1991) 'Gender and Labor History: Learning from the Past, Looking to the Future'. In *Work Engendered: Toward a New History of American Labor*, ed. Ava Baron. Ithaca, NY, Cornell University Press

Battersby, C. (1989) *Gender and Genius: Towards a Feminist Aesthetics*. The Women's Press

Bederman, G. (1995) *Manliness & Civilization: A Cultural History of Gender and Race in the United States, 1880–1917*. Chicago, University of Chicago Press

Beer, J., A. Ford and K. Joslin (eds.). (2003) *American Feminism: Key Source Documents 1848–1920*. Routledge

Beetham, M. (1996) *A Magazine of Her Own? Domesticity and Desire in the Woman's Magazine 1800–1914*. Routledge

Beetham, M., and K. Boardman. (2001) *Victorian Women's Magazines*. Manchester, Manchester University Press

Beilharz, P. (1992) *Labour's Utopias: Bolshevism, Fabianism and Social Democracy*. Routledge

Bellamy, E. (1888) *Looking Backwards, 2000–1887.* Constable

Bennett, D. (1989) 'Periodical Fragments and Organic Culture: Modernism, the Avant-Garde, and the Little Magazine', *Contemporary Literature*, 30:4, 480–502

Berg, A. (2002) *Mothering the Race, Women's Narratives of Reproduction, 1890–1930.* Chicago, University of Illinois Press

Berman, M. (1971) *The Politics of Authenticity: Radical Individualism and the Emergence of Modern Society.* George Allen and Unwin

Berry, P. and A. Bishop (eds.). (1985) *Testament of a Generation: The Journalism of Vera Brittain and Winifred Holtby.* Virago

Bishop, E. (1996) 'Re:Covering Modernism – Format and Function in the Little Magazines'. In *Modernist Writers and the Marketplace*, ed. W. L. Chernaik *et al.* Basingstoke, Macmillan

Bjorkman, E. (1913) *Is There Anything New Under the Sun?* Stephen Swift and Co.

Bland, L. (1995) *Banishing the Beast: English Feminism and Sexual Morality 1885–1914.* Penguin

Bock, G., and P. Thane. (1991) *Maternity and Gender Policies: Women and the Rise of the European Welfare States, 1880s–1950s.* Routledge

Bolt, C. (1993) *The Women's Movements in the United States and Britain from the 1790s to the 1920s.* New York, Harvester Wheatsheaf

Bolt, C. (2004) *Sisterhood Questioned? Race, Class and Internationalism in the American and British Women's Movements, c. 1800s–1970s.* Routledge

Boris, E. (1986) *Art and Labor: Ruskin, Morris, and the Craftsman Ideal in America.* Temple

Boucher, D. and A. Vincent. (2000) *British Idealism and Political Theory.* Edinburgh, Edinburgh University Press

Bourdieu, P. (1993) *The Field of Cultural Production*, ed. Randell Johnson. Cambridge, Polity Press

Bourke, J. (1994) *Working-Class Cultures in Britain, 1890–1960: Gender, Class and Ethnicity.* Routledge

Boyes, G. (1993) *The Imagined Village: Culture, Ideology and the English Folk Revival.* Manchester, Manchester University Press

Brandon, R. (1990) *The New Women and the Old Men: Love, Sex and the Woman Question.* Secker and Warburg

Braybon, G. (1989) *Women Workers in the First World War.* Routledge

Bridgwater, P. (1972) *Nietzsche in Anglosaxony: A Study of Nietzsche's Impact on English and American Literature.* Leicester, Leicester University Press

Brooks, D. (1993) *Age of Upheaval: Edwardian Politics, 1899–1914.* Manchester, Manchester University Press

Brown, L. S. (1993) *The Politics of Individualism: Liberalism, Liberal Feminism and Anarchism.* Montreal, Black Rose Books

Buenker, B. *et al.* (1977) *Progressivism.* Cambridge, Mass., Schenkman Publishers

Buhle, M., and P. Buhle (1978) *The Concise History of Woman Suffrage.* Urbana, Ill., University of Illinois Press

Buhle, M. (1981) *Women and American Socialism, 1870–1920*. Urbana, Ill., University of Illinois Press

Buhle, M. (1998) *Feminism and its Discontents: A Century of Struggle with Psychoanalysis*. Cambridge, Mass., Harvard University Press

Bulbeck, C. (1998) *Re-Orienting Western Feminisms*. Cambridge, Cambridge University Press

Burke, C. (1996) *Becoming Modern: The Life of Mina Loy*. New York, Farra, Straus & Giroux

Burton, A. (1994) *Burdens of History: British Feminists, Indian Women and Imperial Culture, 1865–1915*. Chapel Hill, University of North Carolina Press

Bush, J. (2002) 'British Women's Anti-Suffragism and the Forward Policy, 1908–1914', *Women's History Review*, 11:3, 431–54

Caine, B. (1997) *English Feminism 1780–1980*. Oxford, Oxford University Press

Caraway, N. (1991) *Segregated Sisterhood: Racism and the Politics of American Feminism*. Knoxville, University of Tennessee Press

Carswell, J. (1978) *Lives and Letters: A. R. Orage, Katherine Mansfield, Beatrice Hastings, John Middleton Murray, S.S. Koteliansky, 1906–1957*. New York, New Directions

Cass, B. (1983) 'Redistribution to Children and Mothers: A History of Child Endowment and Family Allowances'. In *Women, Social Welfare and The State*, ed. C. V. Baldock and B. Cass. Allen and Unwin

Mitchell, C. E. (1997) *Individualism and its Discontents: Appropriations of Emerson, 1880–1950*. Amherst, University of Massachusetts Press

Chen, C. (1996) *The Sex Side of Life: Mary Ware Dennett's Pioneering Battle for Birth Control*. New York, The New Press

Cheyette, B., and L. Marcus. (1998) *Modernity, Culture and 'the Jew'*. Cambridge, Polity Press

Clarke, B. (1996) *Dora Marsden and Early Modernism*. Ann Arbor, University of Michigan Press

Clarke, P. (1979) *Liberals and Social Democrats*. Cambridge, Cambridge University Press

Cockin, K. (2001) *Women and Theatre in the Age of Suffrage: The Pioneer Players 1911–25*. Basingstoke, Palgrave Macmillan

Collini, S. (1978) 'Hobhouse, Bosanquet and the State: Philosophical Idealism and Political Argument in England 1880–1918', *Past and Present*, 72 Aug., 86–111

Collini, S. (1979) *Liberalism and Sociology: Liberalism and Political Argument in England, 1880–1914*. Cambridge, Cambridge University Press

Collini, S. (1991) *Public Moralists: Political Thought and Intellectual Life in Britain 1850–1930*. Oxford, Clarendon Press

Conn, P. (1983) *The Divided Mind*. Cambridge, University of Cambridge

Copelman, D. M. (1996) *London's Women Teachers: Gender, Class, and Feminism, 1870–1930*. Routledge

Cott, N. F. (1989) 'What's in a Name? The Limits of "Social Feminism;" or, Expanding the Vocabulary of Women's History', *The Journal of American History*, 76:3, Dec., 809–29

Cott, N. (1987) *The Grounding of Modern Feminism*. New Haven, Yale University Press

Cowman, K. (1998) "'A Party Between Revolution and Peaceful Persuasion': A Fresh Look at the United Suffragists'. In *The Women's Suffrage Movement: New Feminist Perspectives*, ed. M. Joannou and J. Purvis, pp. 77–88. Manchester, Manchester University Press

Crawford, E. (1999) *The Women's Suffrage Movement: A Reference Guide 1866–1928*. UCL Press

Curtis, P. and D. Furlong (eds.). (1994) *The Church Faces the Modern World*. Earlsgate Press

Daly, A. (1995) *Done Into Dance: Isadora Duncan in America*. Bloomington, Indiana University Press

Daley, C., and M. Nolan. (1994) 'Between Old Worlds and New: International Feminist Perspectives'. In *Suffrage and Beyond, International Feminist Perspectives*. Auckland, Auckland University Press

Davis, L. (1996) 'Morris, Wilde, and Marx on the Social Preconditions of Individual Development', *Political Studies*, 44, 719–32

Deacon, D. (1997) *Elsie Clews Parsons: Inventing the Modern Life*. Chicago, University of Chicago Press

Delap, L. (2000) 'The Freewoman, Periodical Communities and the Feminist Reading Public', *Princeton University Library Chronicle*, 61:2, Winter

Delap, L. (2005) 'Feminist and Anti-feminist Encounters in Edwardian Britain' *Historical Research*, 78:201, Aug.

Den Otter, S. (1996) *British Idealism and Social Explanation: A Study in Late Victorian Thought*. Oxford, Clarendon Press

Derksen, L. D. (1996) *Dialogues on Women: Images of Women in the History of Philosophy*. Amsterdam, VU University Press

Detwiler, B. (1990) *Nietzsche and the Politics of Aristocratic Radicalism*. Chicago, University of Chicago Press

DiBattista, M., and Lucy McDiarmid. (1996) *High and Low Moderns: Literature and Culture, 1889–1939*. Oxford University Press, New York

Dixon, J. (2001) *Divine Feminine: Theosophy and Feminism in England*. Baltimore, Johns Hopkins University Press

Doughan, D., and D. Sanchez. (1987) *Feminist Periodicals 1855–1984*. Brighton, The Harvester Press

DuBois, E. C. (1991) 'Harriet Stanton Blatch and the Transformation of Class Relations Among Woman Suffragists'. In *Gender, Class, Race and Reform in the Progressive Era*, ed. N. Frankel and N. S. Dye, pp. 162–79. Lexington, University Press of Kentucky

DuBois, E. C. (1997) *Harriot Stanton Blatch and the Winning of Woman Suffrage*. New Haven, Yale University Press

Dyhouse, C. (1989) *Feminism and the Family in England, 1880–1939*. Oxford, Blackwell

Eisenstein, Z. (1981) *The Radical Future of Liberal Feminism*. Longman

Elfenbein, A. (1999) *Romantic Genius: The Prehistory of a Homosexual Role*. New York, Columbia University Press

Endres, K., and T. Luck (eds.). (1996) *Women's Periodicals in the United States: Social and Political Issues*. Westport, Conn., Greenwood Press

Epstein, B. (1981) *The Politics of Domesticity: Women, Evangelism, and Temperance in Nineteenth-Century America*. New York, Columbia University Press

Eustance, C., and A. John (eds.). (1997) *The Men's Share? Masculinities, Male Support and Women's Suffrage in Britain, 1890–1920*. Routledge

Evans, R. J. (1977) *The Feminists: Women's Emancipation Movements in Europe, America and Australasia 1840–1920*. Croom Helm

Ewing, S. E. (2003) 'Ralph Waldo Emerson and the New Aristocracy: Greatness and the Great Man in Democratic Society'. Ph.D. diss. Harvard University

Feldman, D. (1994) *Jews and Englishmen: Social Relations and Political Culture, 1840–1914*. New Haven, Yale University Press

Fernihough, A. (2000) '"Go in Fear of Abstractions": Modernism and the Spectre of Democracy', *Textual Practice*, 14:3, 479–97

Finnegan, M. (1999) *Selling Suffrage: Consumer Culture and Votes for Women*. New York, Columbia University Press

Flanagan, M. A. (1990) 'Gender and Urban Political Reform: The City Club and the Woman's City Club of Chicago in the Progressive Era', *American Historical Review*, 95:4, 1032–50

Flanagan, M. A. (2002) *Seeing With Their Hearts: Chicago Women and the Vision of the Good City, 1871–1933*. Princeton, Princeton University Press

Flint, K. (1993) *The Woman Reader: 1837–1914*. Oxford, Clarendon Press

Forcey, C. (1961) *The Crossroads of Liberalism; Croly, Weyl, Lippmann, and the Progressive Era, 1900–1925*. New York, Oxford University Press

Fowler, R. B. (1986) *Carrie Catt, Feminist Politician*. Boston, Northeastern University Press

Francis, E. (2002) *The Secret Treachery of Words; Feminism and Modernism in America*. Minneapolis, University of Minnesota Press

Frankel, N., and N. S. Dye (eds.). (1991) *Gender, Class, Race and Reform in the Progressive Era*, Lexington, University Press of Kentucky

Freeden, M. (1973) 'J. A. Hobson as a New Liberal Theorist: Some Aspects of his Social Thought Until 1914', *Journal of the History of Ideas*, 34:3, July–Sept., 421–43

Freeden, M. (1978) *The New Liberalism: An Ideology of Social Reform*. Oxford, Clarendon Press

Friedman, M. (1987) 'Care and Context in Moral Reasoning'. In *Women and Moral Theory*, ed. Eva Kittay and Diana Meyers. Totowa, NJ, Rowman and Littlefield

Gaffin, J. (1977) 'Women and Co-operation'. In *Women in the Labour Movement*, ed. L. Middleton. Croom Helm

Gagnier, R. (1991) *Subjectivities: A History of Self-Representation in Britain, 1832–1920*. Oxford, Oxford University Press

Garner, L. (1990) *A Brave and Beautiful Spirit. Dora Marsden 1882–1960.* Aldershot, Avebury

Garvey, E. G. (1996) *The Adman in the Parlour: Magazines and the Gendering of Consumer Culture, 1880s to 1910s.* Oxford, Oxford University Press

Gilbert, S., and S. Gubar. (1988) *No Man's Land: The Place of the Woman Writer in the Twentieth Century.* New Haven, Yale University Press

Gilligan, C. (1982) *In a Different Voice: Psychological Theory and Women's Development.* Cambridge, Mass. Harvard University Press

Gluck, M. (1986) 'Toward a Historical Definition of Modernism: Georg Lukacs and the Avant-Garde', *The Journal of Modern History,* 58:4, 845–82

Goodwin, J. L. (1997) *Gender and the Politics of Welfare Reform: Mothers' Pensions in Chicago.* Chicago, University of Chicago Press

Gordon, A. D. (ed.). (1997) *African American Women and the Vote, 1837–1965.* Amherst, University of Massachusetts Press

Gordon, L. (1994) *Pitied But Not Entitled, Single Mothers and the History of Welfare.* Cambridge, Mass., Harvard University Press

Gordon, L. (1995) 'Putting Children First: Women, Maternalism and Welfare in the Early Twentieth Century'. In *U.S. History as Women's History: New Feminist Essays,* ed. L. K. Kerber *et al.,* pp. 63–86. Chapel Hill, University of North Carolina Press

Gould, P. (1988) *Early Green Politics: Back to Nature, Back to the Land, and Socialism in Britain, 1880–1900.* Brighton, Harvester Press

Grayzel, S. R. (1999) *Women's Identities at War: Gender, Motherhood and Politics in Britain and France During the First World War.* Chapel Hill, University of North Carolina Press

Greenleaf, W. (1983) *The British Political Tradition: The Rise of Collectivism.* Methuen

Gross, J. (1991) *The Rise and Fall of the Man of Letters: English Literary Life Since 1800.* Penguin

Hall, L. A. (2001) 'Stella Browne, the New Woman as Freewoman'. In *The New Woman in Fiction and in Fact: Fin-de-siècle Feminisms,* ed. Angelique Richardson and Chris Willis, pp. 224–38. Basingstoke, Palgrave

Hall, L. A. (1995) '"Disinterested Enthusiasm for Sexual Misconduct": The British Society for the Study of Sex Psychology, 1913–47', *Journal of Contemporary History,* 30, 665–86

Hall, L. A. (1997) '"I Have Never Met the Normal Woman": Stella Browne and the Politics of Womanhood', *Women's History Review,* 6:2, 157–82

Hall, L. A. (2000) 'Malthusian Mutations: The Changing Politics and Moral Meanings of Birth Control in Britain'. In *Malthus, Medicine and Morality,* ed. B. Dolan, pp. 141–63. Amsterdam, Rodopi

Hall, R. (1977) *Marie Stopes: A Biography.* Andre Deutsch

Harris, J. (1993) *Private Lives, Public Spirit: Britain 1870–1914.* Penguin

Harrison, B. (1978) *Separate Spheres: The Opposition to Women's Suffrage in Britain.* Croom Helm

Harrison, B. (1982) 'The Act of Militancy: Violence and the Suffragettes, 1904–1914'. In *Peaceable Kingdom: Stability and Change in Modern Britain*, ed. Michael Bentley and John Stevenson, pp. 80–122. Oxford, Oxford University Press

Harrison, P. G. (2000) *Connecting Links: The British and American Woman Suffrage Movements, 1900–1914*. Westport, Conn., Greenwood Press

Hartman, K. (2003) '"What Made Me a Suffragette": The New Woman and the New (?) Conversion Narrative'. *Women's History Review*, 12:1, 35–50

Harvey, D. (1989) *The Condition of Postmodernity*. Oxford, Basil Blackwell

Haslam, B. (1999) *From Suffrage to Internationalism: The Political Evolution of Three British Feminists*. New York, Peter Lang

Hatheway, J. (2003) *The Gilded Age Construction of Modern American Homophobia*. New York, Palgrave

Heilmann, A. (2000) *New Woman Fiction: Women Writing First-Wave Feminism*. Basingstoke, Macmillan/Palgrave

Higonnet, M. R. *et al.* (eds.). (1987) *Behind the Lines; Gender and the Two World Wars*. New Haven, Yale University Press

Hobman, J. B. (1945) *David Eder: Memoirs of a Modern Pioneer*. Victor Gollancz

Hollis, P. (1987) *Ladies Elect: Women in English Local Government 1865–1914*. Oxford, Clarendon Press

Holton, B. (1976) *British Syndicalism, 1900–1914: Myths and Realities*. Pluto Press

Holton, S. S. (1986) *Feminism and Democracy: Women's Suffrage and Reform Politics in Britain 1900–1918*. Cambridge, Cambridge University Press

Holton, S. S. (1994) '"To Educate Women into Rebellion". Elizabeth Cady Stanton and the Creation of a Transatlantic Network of Radical Suffragists', *American Historical Review*, 99, 1113–36

Holton, S. S. (1996) *Suffrage Days: Stories from the Women's Suffrage Movement*. Routledge

Hunt, K. (1996) *Equivocal Feminists: The Social Democratic Federation and the Woman Question 1884–1911*. Cambridge, Cambridge University Press

Huyssen, A. (1986) *After the Great Divide: Modernism, Mass Culture and Postmodernism*. Bloomington, Indiana University Press

Hyde, W. (1956) 'The Socialism of H. G. Wells in the Early Twentieth Century', *Journal of the History of Ideas*, 17:2, 217–34

Jaffe, K. (1980) 'The Concept of Genius: Its Changing Role in Eighteenth-Century French Aesthetics', *Journal of the History of Ideas*, 41:4, 579–99

Jeffreys, S. (1985) *The Spinster and Her Enemies: Feminism and Sexuality 1880–1930*. Pandora Press

Keller, M. (1980) 'Anglo-American Politics, 1900–1930, in Anglo-American Perspective: A Case Study in Comparative History', *Comparative Studies in Society and History*, 22:3, July, 458–77

Kennedy, K. (1999) *Disloyal Mothers and Scurrilous Citizens: Women and Subversion During World War One*. Bloomington, Indiana University Press

Kent, S. K. (1987) *Sex and Suffrage, 1860–1914.* Princeton, Princeton University Press

Kent, S. K. (1988) 'The Politics of Sexual Difference: World War I and the Demise of British Feminism', *Journal of British Studies*, 27, 232–53

Kerber, L. (1997) *Toward an Intellectual History of Women.* Chapel Hill, University of North Carolina Press

Kerber, L. K., A. Kessler-Harris and K. Sklar (eds.). (1995) *U.S. History as Women's History: New Feminist Essays.* Chapel Hill, University of North Carolina Press

Kerr, H., and C. L. Crow (eds). (1983) *The Occult in America: New Historical Perspectives.* Urbana, University of Illinois Press

Kessler, C. F. (1995) *Charlotte Perkins Gilman: Her Progress Towards Utopia.* New York, Syracuse University Press

Kessler, C. F. (1995) *Daring to Dream: Utopian Fiction by United States Women Before 1950.* New York, Syracuse University Press

Kinna, R. (1995) 'Kropotkin's Theory of Mutual Aid in Historical Context', *International Review of Social History*, 40, 259–83

Kloppenberg, J. T. (1986) *Uncertain Victory: Social Democracy and Progressivism in European and American Thought, 1870–1920.* Oxford, Oxford University Press

Koss, S. (1984) *The Rise and Fall of the Political Press in Britain: The Twentieth Century.* Hamish Hamilton

Koven, S., and S. Michel (eds.). (1993) *Mothers of a New World.* Routledge

Kraditor, A. S. (1965) *The Ideas of the Woman Suffrage Movement, 1890–1920.* New York, Columbia University Press

Kuhlman, E. A. (1997) *Petticoats and White Feathers: Gender Conformity, Race, the Progressive Peace Movement, and the Debate Over War, 1895–1919.* Westport, Conn., Greenwood Press

Kurth, P. (2001) *Isadora: A Sensational Life.* Boston, Little, Brown & Co.

Ladd-Taylor, M. (1994) *Mother-Work: Women, Child Welfare, and the State, 1890–1930.* Urbana, University of Illinois Press

Lake, M. (1994) 'Between Old Worlds and New'. In *Suffrage and Beyond, International Feminist Perspectives*, ed. C. Daley and M. Nolan. Auckland, Auckland University Press

Levine, P. (1990) '"The Humanising Influences of Five O'Clock Tea": Victorian Feminist Periodicals', *Victorian Studies*, 33, Winter, 293–306

Levitas, R. (1990) *The Concept of Utopia.* Philip Allen

Lewis, J. (1987) *Before the Vote was Won: Arguments For and Against Women's Suffrage.* Routledge

Lewis, J. (1991) *Women and Social Action in Victorian and Edwardian England.* Aldershot, Edward Elgar

Lidderdale, J., and M. Nicholson (1970) *Dear Miss Weaver: Harriet Shaw Weaver 1876–1961.* New York, The Viking Press

Liddington, J., and J. Norris, (1978) *One Hand Tied Behind Us: The Rise of the Women's Suffrage Movement.* Virago

Liddington, J. (1991) *The Road to Greenham Common: Feminism and Anti-Militarism in Britain Since 1820*. Syracuse, NY, Syracuse University Press

Malik, K. (1996) *The Meaning of Race: Race, History and Culture in Western Society*. Macmillan

Mandler, P. (2001) 'The Consciousness of Modernity? Liberalism and the English National Character, 1870–1914'. In *Meanings of Modernity: Britain from the Late-Victorian Era to World War II*, ed. M. J. Daunton and B. Rieger. Oxford, Berg

Mann, A. (1956) 'British Social Thought and American Reformers of the Progressive Era', *Mississippi Valley Historical Review*, 42, 672–92

Manton, K. (2003) 'The Fellowship of the New Life: English Ethical Socialism Reconsidered', *History of Political Thought*, 24:2, 282–304

Marsh, J. (1982) *Back to the Land: The Pastoral Impulse in England, from 1880 to 1914*. Quartet Books

Marsh, M. (1978) 'The Anarchist-Feminist Response to the "Woman Question" in Late Nineteenth-Century America', *American Quarterly*, 30:4, Autumn, 533–47

Martin, W. (1967) *The New Age Under Orage: Chapters in English Cultural History*. Manchester, Manchester University Press

Mayhall, L. E. N., P. Levine and I. C. Fletcher (eds.). (2000) *Women's Suffrage in the British Empire: Citizenship, Nation and Race*. Routledge

Mayhall, L. E. N. (2003) *The Militant Suffrage Movement: Citizenship and Resistance in Britain, 1860–1930*. Oxford, Oxford University Press

Mayhall, L. E. N. (2001) 'The Rhetorics of Slavery and Citizenship: Suffragist Discourse and Canonical Texts in Britain, 1880–1914', *Gender and History*, 13:3, 481–97

McCarthy, J. (1978) *Hilaire Belloc: Edwardian Radical*. Indianapolis, Liberty Press

McElroy, W. (2001) *Individualist Feminism of the Nineteenth Century: Collected Writings and Biographical Profile*. Jefferson, NC, McFarland and Co

McFadden, M. H. (1999) *Golden Cables of Sympathy: The Transatlantic Sources of Nineteenth-Century Feminism*. Lexington, The University Press of Kentucky

Mclloyd, J. (1995) 'Raising Lilies: Ruskin and Women'. *Journal of British Studies*, 34, 325–50

Michel, S. (1999) *Children's Interests/Mother's Rights: The Shaping of America's Childcare Policy*. New Haven, Yale University Press

Millman, B. (2000) *Managing Domestic Dissent in First World War Britain, 1914–1918*. Routledge

Morgan, K. O. (1976) 'The Future at Work: Anglo-American Progressivism, 1890–1917'. In *Contrast and Connection: Bicentennial Essays in Anglo-American History*, ed. H. C. Allen and Roger Thompson, pp. 245–71. G. Bell and Sons

Morris, A. J. A. (1974) *Edwardian Radicalism 1900–1914*. Routledge & Kegan Paul

Morrison, M. S. (2001) *The Public Face of Modernism: Little Magazines, Audiences, and Reception, 1905–1920*. Madison, University of Wisconsin Press

Mort, F. (1987) *Dangerous Sexualities: Medico-Moral Politics in England Since 1830*. Routledge

Mumford Jones, H. (1974) *Revolution and Romanticism*. Cambridge Mass., Harvard University Press

Murase, S. (2002) 'Thomas Baty in Japan: Seeing Through the Twilight', *British Year Book of International Law*, 315–42

O'Neill, W. L. (1969) *The Woman Movement: Feminism in the United States and England*. George Allen and Unwin

O'Neill, W. L. (1978) *The Last Romantic: A Life of Max Eastman*. New York, Oxford University Press

O'Neill, W. L. (1989) *Feminism in America: A History*. New Brunswick, Transaction Publishers

Offen, K. (1992) 'Defining Feminism: A Comparative Historical Approach'. In *Beyond Equality and Difference: Citizenship, Feminist Politics and Female Subjectivity*, ed. Gisela Bock and Susan James, pp. 17–31. Routledge

Olwell, V. (2005) '"It Spoke Itself": Women's Genius and Eccentric Politics', *American Literature*, 77:1, March, 33–64

Owen, A. (2001) 'Occultism and the "Modern" Self in Fin-de-siècle Britain'. In *Meanings of Modernity: Britain from the Late-Victorian Era to World War II*, ed. M. Daunton and B. Rieger, pp. 71–96. Oxford, Berg

Palmegiano, E. M. (1976) *Women and British Periodicals 1832–1867*. New York, Garland Publishers

Pateman, C. (1988) *The Sexual Contract*. Cambridge, Polity Press

Pateman, C. (1992) 'Equality, Difference and Subordination: The Politics of Motherhood and Women's Citizenship'. In *Beyond Equality and Difference: Citizenship, Feminist Politics and Female Subjectivity*, ed. Gisela Bock and Susan James. Routledge

Hill, Patricia. (1985) *The World Their Household: The American Woman's Foreign Mission Movement and Cultural Transformation, 1870–1920*. Ann Arbor, University of Michigan Press

Pedersen, S. (1990) 'Gender, Welfare and Citizenship in Britain during the Great War', *The American Historical Review*, 95:4, 983–1006

Pedersen, S. (2004) *Eleanor Rathbone and the Politics of Conscience*. New Haven, Yale University Press

Peppis, P. (2000) *Literature, Politics and the English Avant-Garde: Nation and Empire 1901–1918*. Cambridge, Cambridge University Press

Pick, D. (1989) *Faces of Degeneration: A European Disorder, c. 1848–1918*. Cambridge, Cambridge University Press

Plant, R., and A. W. Vincent. (1984) *Philosophy, Politics and Citizenship: The Life and Thought of the British Idealists*. Oxford, Blackwell

Poggioli, R. (1968) *The Theory of the Avant-Garde*. Cambridge, Mass., Belknap Press

Porter, R., and L. A. Hall. (1995) *The Facts of Life: The Creation of Sexual Knowledge in Britain 1650–1950*. New Haven, Yale University Press

Pugh, M. (1996) 'Liberals and Women's Suffrage: 1867–1914'. In *Citizenship and Community*, ed. E. Biagini. Cambridge, Cambridge University Press

Pulham, P. (2003) 'A Transatlantic Alliance: Charlotte Perkins Gilman and Vernon Lee'. In *Feminist Forerunners: New Womanism and Feminism in the Early Twentieth Century*, ed. Ann Heilmann, pp. 34–43. Pandora Press

Pykett, L. (1995) *Engendering Fictions: The English Novel in the Early Twentieth Century*. Edward Arnold

Radice, L. (1984) *Beatrice and Sidney Webb*. Macmillan

Read, D. (1972) *Edwardian England 1901–1915*. Harrap

Reed, D. (1997) *The Popular Magazine in Britain and the United States, 1880–1960*. The British Library

Rendall, J. (1985) *The Origins of Modern Feminism: Women in Britain, France and the United State 1780–1860*. Basingstoke, Macmillan

Richardson, A. (2003) *Love and Eugenics in the Late Nineteenth Century: Rational Reproduction and the New Woman*. Oxford, Oxford University Press

Riley, D. (1988) *Am I That Name? Feminism and the Category of 'Women' in History*. Basingstoke, Macmillan

Robb, G. (1997) 'Race Motherhood: Moral Eugenics versus Progressive Eugenics, 1880–1920'. In *Maternal Instincts, Visions of Motherhood and Sexuality in Britain, 1875–1925*, ed. A. S. Holmes and C. Nelon. Basingstoke, Macmillan

Roberts, M. L. (2002) *Disruptive Acts: The New Woman in Fin-de-siècle France*. Chicago, University of Chicago Press

Rodgers, D. T. (1982) 'In Search of Progressivism', *Reviews in American History*, 10:4, 113–32

Rodgers. D. T. (1998) *Atlantic Crossings: Social Politics in a Progressive Age*. Cambridge, Mass., Belknap Press

Rose, J. (1986) *The Edwardian Temperament, 1895–1919*. Athens, OH, Ohio University Press

Rose, N. (1985) *The Psychological Complex: Psychology, Politics and Society in England 1869–1939*. Routledge

Ross, E. (1993) *Love and Toil: Motherhood in Outcast London, 1870–1918*. Oxford, Oxford University Press

Rossi, A. (1973) *The Feminist Papers*. New York, Columbia University Press

Rowbotham, S. (1977) *A New World for Women. Stella Browne: Socialist Feminist*. Pluto Press

Rowbotham, S. (1994) 'Interpretations of Welfare and Approaches to the State, 1870–1920'. In *The Politics of the Welfare State*, ed. Ann Oakley and Susan Williams, pp. 18–36. University College London Press

Schneider, Dorothy, and Carl J. Schneider. (1993) *American Women in the Progressive Era, 1900–1920*. New York, Facts on File

Schwarz, J. (1986) *Radical Feminists of Heterodoxy, Greenwich Village 1912–1940*. Norwich, Vt., New Victoria Publishers

Scott, B. K. (1990) *The Gender of Modernism*. Bloomington, Indiana University Press

Scott, G. (1998) *Feminism and the Politics of Working Women: The Women's Co-Operative Guild, 1880s to the Second World War*. University College London Press

Scott, J. W. (1996) *Only Paradoxes to Offer: French Feminists and the Rights of Man*. Cambridge, Mass., Harvard University Press

Scott, J. W. (1999) *The Conundrum of Equality*. Princeton, Institute for Advanced Study, School of Social Science

Shaw, C., and M. Chase. (1989) *The Imagined Past: History and Nostalgia*. Manchester, Manchester University Press

Singal, D. J. (1987) 'Toward a Definition of American Modernism'. *American Quarterly*, 39, Spring

Skocpol, T. *et al.* (1993) 'Women's Associations and the Enactment of Mothers' Pensions in the United States'. *American Political Science Review*, 87:3, Sept., 686–701

Sloan, K. (1981) 'Sexual Warfare in the Silent Cinema: Comedies and Melodramas of Woman Suffragism', *American Quarterly*, 33 Fall, 412–36

Smith, L. P. (1925) *Words and Idioms: Studies in the English Language*. Constable and Co. (1957)

Sochen, J. (1972) *The New Woman, Feminism in Greenwich Village, 1910–20*. New York, Quadrangle Books

Soffer, R. (1978) *Ethics and Society in England: The Revolution in the Social Sciences 1870–1914*. Berkeley, University of California Press

Soloway, R. A. (1982) *Birth Control and the Population Question in England, 1877–1930*. Chapel Hill, University of North Carolina Press

Soloway, R. A. (1982) 'Feminism, Fertility and Eugenics in Victorian and Edwardian England'. In *Political Symbolism in Modern Europe*, ed. S. Drescher *et al.*, pp. 121–45. New Brunswick, Transaction Books

Stansell, C. (2000) *American Moderns: Bohemian New York and the Creation of a New Century*. New York, Henry Holt and Co.

Stears, M. (2002) *Progressives, Pluralists and the Problems of the State: Ideologies of Reform in the United States and Britain, 1909–1926*. Oxford, Oxford University Press

Stedman Jones, G. (1991) *Outcast London: A Study in the Relationship Between Classes in Victorian Society*. Oxford, Clarendon Press

Steedman, C. (1990) *Childhood, Culture and Class in Britain: Margaret McMillan 1860–1931*. Virago

Steele, T. (1989) 'From Gentleman to Superman: Alfred Orage and Aristocratic Socialism'. In *The Imagined Past: History and Nostalgia*, ed. C. Shaw and M. Chase, pp. 112–27. Manchester, Manchester University Press

Steele, T. (1990) *Alfred Orage and the Leeds Arts Club, 1893–1923*. Scolar Press

Stone, D. (2002) *Breeding Superman: Nietzsche, Race and Eugenics in Edwardian and Interwar Britain*. Liverpool, Liverpool University Press

Summerfield, P. (1997) 'Gender and War in the Twentieth Century', *International History Review*, 19:1, 3–15

Susman, W. (1996) *Culture as History: The Transformation of American Society in the Twentieth Century*. New York, Pantheon Books

Sutton–Ramspeck, B. (1999) 'Shot Out of the Canon: Mary Ward and the Claims of Conflicting Feminism'. In *Victorian Women Writers and the Woman Question*, ed. Nicola D. Thompson, pp. 204–22. Cambridge, Cambridge University Press

Terborg-Penn, R. (1978) 'Discrimination against Afro-American Women in the Woman's Movement, 1830–1920'. In *The Afro-American Woman: Struggles and Images*, ed. S. Harley and R. Terborg-Penn, pp. 17–27. Port Washington, NY, Kennikat Press

Thane, P. (1982) *The Foundations of the Welfare State*. Longman

Thane, P. (1993) 'Women in the British Labour Party and the Construction of State Welfare, 1906–1939'. In *Mothers of a New World*, ed. Seth Koven and Sonya Michel, pp. 343–77. New York, Routledge

Thatcher, D. (1970) *Nietzsche in England 1890–1914*. Toronto, University of Toronto Press

Thomas, M. (2002) 'Anarcho-feminism in Late Victorian and Edwardian Britain, 1880–1914', *International Review of Social History*, 47:1, 1–31

Thompson, T. (1987) *Dear Girl: The Diaries and Letters of Two Working Women, 1897–1917*. The Woman's Press

Thomson, M. (1999) '"Savage Civilisation" Race, Culture and Mind in Britain, 1898–1939'. In *Race, Science and Medicine 1700–1969*, ed. W. Ernst and B. Harris, pp. 235–58. Routledge

Thomson, M. (2001) 'Psychology and the "Consciousness of Modernity" in Early Twentieth-century Britain'. In *Meanings of Modernity: Britain from the Late-Victorian Era to World War II*, ed. M. J. Daunton and B. Rieger, pp. 97–115. Oxford, Berg

Tusan, M. (1998) 'Inventing the New Woman: Print Culture and Identity Politics during the Fin-de-siècle', *Victorian Periodicals Review*, 31:2, 169–82

Vaughan, L. J. (1997) *Randolph Bourne and the Politics of Cultural Radicalism*. Lawrence, Kan., University of Kansas Press

Vellacott, J. (1987) 'Feminist Consciousness and the First World War', *History Workshop Journal*, 23, Spring, 81–101

Villis, T. (2002) 'Early Modernism and Exclusion: The Cultural Politics of Two Edwardian Periodicals', *The New Age and the New Witness. University of Sussex Journal of Contemporary History*, 5

Walkowitz, J. R. (1992) *City of Dreadful Delight: Narratives of Sexual Danger in Late-Victorian London*. Virago

Wallas, G. (1908) *Human Nature in Politics*. Archibald Constable & Co.

Ware, V. (1992) *Beyond the Pale: White Women, Racism and History*. Verso

Waylen, G. (1998) 'Gender, Feminism and the State'. In *Gender, Politics and the State*, ed. Georgina Waylen and Vicky Randall. Routledge

Weeks, J. (1989) *Sex, Politics and Society: The Regulation of Sexuality Since 1800.* Longman

Weightman, J. (1973) *The Concept of the Avant-Garde: Explorations in Modernism.* Alcave Press

Will, B. (2000) *Gertrude Stein, Modernism and the Problem of 'Genius'.* Edinburgh, Edinburgh University Press

Williams, R. (1958) *Culture and Society, 1780–1950.* Chatto and Windus

Wilson, B. (2002) 'Charles Fourier (1772–1837) and Questions of Women'. Ph.D. diss., University of Cambridge

Yeo, E. J. (1998) *Radical Femininity: Women's Self-Representation in the Public Sphere.* Manchester, Manchester University Press

Zurier, R. (1988) *Art for the Masses: A Radical Magazine and its Graphics.* Philadelphia, Temple University Press

Index

IDEAS IN CONTEXT

Edited by

QUENTIN SKINNER AND JAMES TULLY

Lightning Source UK Ltd.
Milton Keynes UK
UKOW01f0344030217

293430UK00001B/168/P